Country Boy

Country Boy

A Biography of Albert Lee

DEREK WATTS

Foreword by Eric Clapton

McFarland & Company, Inc., Publishers
Jefferson, North Carolina, and London

LIBRARY OF CONGRESS CATALOGUING-IN-PUBLICATION DATA

Watts, Derek, 1943–
Country boy : a biography of Albert Lee /
Derek Watts ; foreword by Eric Clapton.
p.   cm.
Includes bibliographical references and index.

ISBN 978-0-7864-3658-3
illustrated case binding : 50# alkaline paper ∞

1. Lee, Albert.   2. Guitarists—England—Biography.
I. Title.
ML419.L415W38   2008   787.87'164092—dc22   2008008022
[B]

British Library cataloguing data are available

On the cover: Albert Lee, Red Rocks, Colorado, 1976
(Photograph courtesy of the Lee family)
Background ©2008 Shutterstock

Manufactured in the United States of America

McFarland & Company, Inc., Publishers
Box 611, Jefferson, North Carolina 28640
www.mcfarlandpub.com

To Gerry,
for all her love, support and encouragement.

Acknowledgments

I am indebted to Albert for his unstinting support and patient availability, the cups of tea and the chocolate digestives! To Pete Baron, for allowing me into his home to talk to Albert and to all those people who gave me of their time. To Albert's family—Abigail, Karen, Lucy, Rebecca, Vanessa, Vikki, Wayne—and Mary Evans. To his musical colleagues—Jerry Allison, Joan Armatrading, Peter Baron, Mike Bell, Mike Berry, Gary Brooker, Tony Brown, John Carter, Ricky Charman, Eric Clapton, B.J. Cole, Tony Colton, Gerry Conway, Rodney Crowell, Sonny Curtis, Hank De Vito, Jonathan Edwards, Buddy Emmons, Phil Everly, Chris Farlowe, Steve Fishell, Bob Harris, Emmylou Harris, Harvey Hinsley, Chas Hodges, Brian Hodgson, Gerry Hogan, Mike Hurst, Barrie Jenkins, Buddy Miller, Keith Nelson, Mike O'Neill, Dolly Parton, Arlen Roth, Ray Smith, Ray Russell, Pete Solley, "Big Jim" Sullivan, Steve Trovato, Sylvia Tyson, Tom Tyson, Bruce Waddell, Les Walker, Jesse Winchester, Pete Wingfield and Bill Wyman. To all his old Blackheath friends—Joan and John Baines, Brian Bath, Ron Bell, Noelle Brown, Mo Clifton, Roger Collins, Johnnie Haylock, Malcolm Hutton, Mick Kemp, Carol Lovell, Max Middleton, Terry Scanlon, Colin and Terry Stead, Tony Walter and Susan Waters. To Sam Birkett and Phil Hadler in Herne Bay and all the others—Graham Barker, Geoff Barsby, John Beecher, Simon Evans, Pete Gage, Sue Hargreaves, Clive Jones, Jeffrey Kruger, Robin Melville, Jackie Nelson and Steve York.

I am grateful to Eric Clapton for the Foreword and to the following people for allowing me to use the photographs which appear: the Lee family, Graham Barker, Georg Grimm, Johnnie Haylock, Jerry Allison, Barrie Jenkins, Jackie Nelson and Keith Nelson. Thanks are also due to Graham Barker, David Kemp and Roger Ordish for technical assistance with the photographs.

Finally, to my partner, Gerry, my copy editor and chief critic, for her constant love and support.

Contents

Foreword
by Eric Clapton

When I last saw Albert, about two weeks ago, he was playing in a little club in Chiddingfold, on the Surrey/Sussex border, about eight miles away from where I live. When I first saw him, about forty years ago, he was playing in a little club on Wardour Street, in London, called the Flamingo. Some things never change: Albert is one of them. As I stood and watched and listened at the Chiddingfold gig, marvelling at his wondrous skills, my entire life replayed itself, for we have been a good long way down the road together, and only in the last ten years have we really been separated. He was playing with Chris Farlowe when we met and was already a legend. I had just joined John Mayall and was in complete awe of Albert and Chris. For a young lad like me, up from the sticks, these were men to be reckoned with.

The Gunnell brothers were our agents, and Albert and I would meet on the stairs of their office now and then, usually when we were picking up our wage packets. Albert told me he loved the Everly Brothers, that they were his favorite band, and in that, I don't think he has changed either. He also told me later, after we had got to know one another, that he loved the playing of Jimmy Bryant, so I went out and bought an album of him playing with Speedy West. It took the top of my head off—it was beyond anything I'd ever heard before—and I got a glimpse of what Albert was really aspiring to.

Our paths and influences were very different, but our passion was the same, and it was the differences that made working with Albert so much fun. I was lucky enough to have him in my band for a few years towards the end of the '70s, and we had some outrageous times, playing and laughing together. We dreamed up a "sub band" that we called the Duck Brothers, so-called because we became quite adept at playing popular standards on duck callers. Our repertoire was boundless, we would play anything as long as it was silly, and we kept ourselves amused and entertained for hours, sometimes days on end. Another "sub band" of the day was called Rubbish and Landrover and consisted of Albert and Chris Stainton doing the same sort of thing, but on pianos (louder, but not as portable).

Albert's silliness is as pronounced as his genius and could be easily diagnosed by the kind of thing you would normally hear emanating from his hotel room (should you be lucky enough to be on tour with him). I don't want to rake over old grievances, but how many times can anyone listen to "The Laughing Policeman" before it begins to affect his sanity? Not enough, I suppose is the answer for dear Albert.

1

Strangely enough, he is one of the few people from the old days who has kept his head and stayed true to his dreams, and he is always a joy to see and listen to. There really aren't that many of us left that can actually do the "real thing," and when we're talking about musicians of Albert's stature, you can count them on one hand.

He is a great, great player, fluid, lyrical and free, like a jazz musician but with country scales, like Django, but with a bluegrass past. Above all, he is a truly wonderful singer, soulful and strong, and this for me, is where it all lives, where it all begins.

Albert will almost certainly live until he is 105, probably more, hopefully still playing the clubs, and I for one, want to be there at the edge of the stage, listening to him in wonder, as I always do.

Thank you, Albert.

Introduction

"Heartbreak Hotel" changed my life. Until May 1956, while the wind-up gramophone, a graceful piece of furniture with Queen Anne legs, made beautiful noises (Father was a fan of operatic tenors and Paul Robeson), growing up and listening to music on radio meant an unalloyed diet of cloying pap purveyed by big bands, Brylcreemed crooners and girl singers in cocktail frocks, music which seemed mothballed in time, a throwback to the 1930s. Elvis's impassioned outburst of raw emotion shattered that complacent air of nostalgia forever. Music was now an ever-changing panoply, a kaleidoscope of sound which became the aural backdrop for a young lad trying to make sense of the second half of the twentieth century. A vital component of this brash, loud upstart was that your parents were unable to comprehend it. Yet for me the lyrics of rock seemed to express in stark simplicity the quintessential truths about life—"I Want to Hold Your Hand," "Why Do Fools Fall in Love?" or "Crying in the Rain." The music, through an increasing range of genres, voices, instruments and performers, grew to be a touchstone for the human condition and the songs a comment on the complexity of one's emotional responses to an increasingly confusing world.

In truth, some of the words made no sense at all. What for instance does "Awopbop-a-loobop-awop-bam-boom" actually mean? It mattered little: In 1893, before any of these words appeared in print, anthropologist Richard Wallaschek wrote in his book *Primitive Music* that "the most striking feature of all the savage songs is the frequent occurrence of words with no meaning whatever"[1] and anyway, unless you were Bob Dylan, the essence of rock was the beat, not the lyrics. Unlike the "up-and-down" syncopation of New Orleans jazz, rock had a driving energy, with the distinctive emphasis on the backbeat. And so the beating heart, the engine-room of rock were the players, especially the keyboard men and the guitar pickers. I could have been a player. I should have been a player. My mum, a pianist in a dance band, tried to teach me the piano but I was a reluctant pupil. As the old joke has it, I would give my right arm to play the piano now. So while the great vocal performers like Elvis Presley, Little Richard and Jerry Lee Lewis tore at the heartstrings and pummelled the soul, it was their pounding pianos and the powerful electric guitars of Chuck Berry and Eddie Cochran that thrilled and excited the most.

For Albert Lee it was the same. He, too, had found a new place to dwell. Three weeks younger than me, he grew up in southeast London hearing the same music as I did—the exquisite Appalachian harmonies of the Everlys, the raw power of Gene Vincent and his Bluecaps and that strange hybrid, skiffle, which made Lonnie Donegan the first British pop star. We trod very different paths but we inhabited the same cultural territory. Our landmarks were the same. His talent as a player, of course, marked him out very early, and the story of his career mirrors the changes in almost every musical genre of the late twentieth century. His work in rockabilly with The Crickets, his excursions into soul and blues with Chris Farlowe and the Thunderbirds, his foray into progressive country-rock with the influential outfit Heads, Hands and Feet, his adventures in rock with Eric Clapton and in country music with Emmylou Harris, not to mention his long involvement with The Everly Brothers, mark him out as an icon who has crossed genres and generations. He is now a player respected by his contemporaries on both sides of the Atlantic and by almost every aspiring young guitarist on the American country scene.

Albert's music is flavored with the technical freedom and ethnic élan of his Romany roots and for a man whose story is firmly anchored in the Gypsy culture of southeast London to become a prominent figure in what is essentially American music is an astonishing saga. Yet is it? Should we really be so surprised? As Nick Tosches asserts, "Street balladry, the roots of traditional American music, was pop. The purest mountain airs ... were once the pop junk of urban Britain."[2] In the same essay, Tosches points out that it was the Gypsies who peddled street ballads in Britain from 1550 till the close of the nineteenth century, the first of the breed later to be known as Tin Pan Alley hacks, their single folio sheets sold on the streets or hawked door-to-door. Thus much of the music which became folk, or bluegrass, or country, grew out of the part-songs and ballads which accompanied the Scottish and Irish immigrants to the Appalachians and the East Coast throughout the eighteenth and early nineteenth centuries. They brought with them their instruments, too, the mandolins, the banjos and the pipes, and many were traveling people escaping persecution and the harshness of life on the road in Europe, with the hope of a better life in a New World. "In almost every state," writes Tosches, "the ballad flourished into the present century."[3] In a very real sense, therefore, Albert's transatlantic musical bridge has formed a cultural connection between his own roots and the genre he has embraced with such distinction.

Yet to the wider musical public he remains largely unsung and unheralded. He is essentially a musician's musician, a player's player. The book celebrates a great guitarist and a man whose life and work tells the story of popular music throughout my lifetime and whose roots in Britain and profile in America link the musical strands of our common heritage.

Prologue: A Stopping Place

1924. Late summer. Canvey Island On Sea, as it used to be called, was a very different place from what it is today. On the north side of the Thames estuary, a paradise for wild-fowl shooters and weekend shrimpers, Canvey Island had a rustic feel: the open fields, the tiny wooden bungalows with corrugated tin roofs, the unmade roads—muddy cart tracks under water in winter months—the vast number of dykes and hedges, and the marsh and its rivulets whose grassy banks were covered in pretty blue sea lavender. Kids clambered over rocks at low tide in search of mussels and winkles for Sunday tea and when the tide came in it was another world. The place exuded genuine solitude and a salty air. All of it lay below sea level with only the sea walls for protection. Behind the wall, whose impotence against the full force of a Thames flood was exposed when 58 people drowned in January 1953, at the end of Seaview Road near the jetty, lay Sutherlands fair-ground, with a roundabout, boat swings, mountain slide and the usual coconut shies, shooting gallery and pinball machines. It is August Bank Holiday, late evening, the sun dipping over the estuary and Albert Lee and his son Dave have done another fair, lugging their coconut shy all the way up from Greenwich. Some of the nuts, called "nobblers," would be filled with lead—"You didn't want the punters winning too many!"[1] Before the building of the bridge in 1931, the only means of crossing to or from the mainland was by ferry, or by stepping-stones at low tide. Two punts and two row-boats served as the ferry and were on duty all hours of the day and night.

Albert is a swarthy, stoutly built, moustachioed fellow, a man to be reckoned with. His son is shorter, with the open, ruddy-cheeked countenance of a man accustomed to the open-air life. Both wear the classic waistcoat, collarless shirt and neckerchief of the Romany, and their heritage is part of the mobile cultural population into whose mix down the centuries have been stirred people like the charcoal-burners in Kent, who spent their lives going from one wood to another with their families, the drovers and the canal-people, the water-gyp-sies, the musicians, the entertainers, and later the modern showmen and fairground folk. Indeed, Albert's mother would tell fortunes during the Derby meeting on Epsom Downs, including, on one celebrated occasion, "dookering"[2] the Aga Khan!

Travelers have traditionally been economic nomads, moving in search of work oppor-tunities. In the past they served local communities by providing labor on farms at harvest time. Gypsy travelers tended to be identified with an area, one which afforded seasonal work: thus Kent had one of the highest gypsy populations in the country, together with

Essex, parts of Surrey and Norfolk, and Herefordshire. The traveling people provided an essential pool of labor upon which Kentish farming—market gardening, fruit and vegetables—depended. It would scarcely be an exaggeration to say that without this mobile labor force there would have been no Kentish agriculture. From April to November there was a regular cycle of work in the rural areas, with established stopping places—soft fruit in May and June, hop-picking in September, then apples, pears, and potato-digging in places like Romney Marsh and Essex.

Wintertime and the gypsies would head for the edges of the towns, places on the south London fringes like St. Paul Cray, St. Mary Cray and the Thamesside marshes, in Dartford, Erith, Belvedere and Greenwich. Although there are more cultural allegiances between different nomadic groups than there are between them and the settled population, travelers would go into London, forming cultural, commercial and personal connections with the vibrant, close-knit communities of the East End. The stereotypical East-ender, the "Del-boy," the rag-and-bone man with his horse and cart, the market trader, the bloke with a wad of cash in his top pocket and a healthy contempt for the law—that kind of wheeler-dealer had much in common with the traveling people, accustomed to existing on the fringes of society. During the winter, gypsies would stop off in the yards in the East End of London used by the rag-and-bone men, and perhaps some travelers even had yards themselves.

The Romany input has thus long been an essential component of the working-class culture in north Kent and the East End—and the Lee family was an integral part of it. Albert senior, a wheelwright by trade, was born in Plumstead, just east of Charlton and Woolwich, in 1864. The 1901 census records the Lee family's address as "Caravan, North Street." David, born to Albert and Harriett in 1892, was the second eldest of six, born variously in well-established stopping places such as Epsom, Hadlow and Farnborough, David's birthplace. However, the two youngest were born in Charlton, which, the caravan notwithstanding, seems to have become some kind of permanent home. Young Albert, the wheelwright's great-grandson, is aware of his Romany origins: "Of course Lee is one of the main Romany families and the family's roots were certainly acknowledged on my father's side." His great-grandfather's cultural origin was never something which the young Albert would try to conceal, as Chas Hodges, a friend and musical colleague for forty years, remarks: "I knew Albert had Romany roots. He acknowledged it, but it wasn't a great heritage thing with him. I knew his Dad pretty well. He was a great bloke and he'd often joke, 'Yeah, that was old Grand-dad Albert, the other pikey[3] in the family.'" That would have been Albert, the fairground huckster on Canvey Island. His great-grandson has two sepia photographs of him. "In one of them he's posing with a Purdey shotgun and my grandfather used to say 'You know, a few times he went shooting with Edward VII.' I don't know how that happened but he had this Purdey gun, which someone ended up with in the family. I hope someone has still got it, it would be worth a bit of money now."

Great-grand-dad Albert was a real character, as was his son. They both possessed in abundance the uninhibited joie de vivre, the extrovert freedom of the spirit of the Romany race. When the Great War broke out in August 1914, the Lees had, to all intents and purposes, settled—at 35 Selcroft Road in Greenwich. Albert had become what many Romanies became, a general dealer,[4] and Dave was laboring in Woolwich Dockyard, where he later lost several fingers when a chain fell and crushed his hand. In June 1915, he married Maud

Wager, a 21-year-old, born in Welling and the second youngest of eight children. Maud's father, Samuel, was a driller by trade and was also working on the docks. The couple set up home over the road from his parents, Albert and Harriett, at number 32, and there, in February 1916, David Arthur, young Albert's father, was born. Simon Evans, an authority on Romany history and culture,[5] points out that "Gypsy people have always intermarried with the *Gorgers*, or non–Gypsy. Hence there are very few 'pure' Romanies in this country. The Roma in mainland Europe, in Hungary, the Czech Republic or indeed in Romania are very, very dark, very Asian-looking. In England that's not the case because the contemporary Gypsy-traveler culture is a mixture. The Gypsies are as much of a mongrel breed as the English are." Thus Albert the wheelwright and his son David were not unusual in intermarrying. He was also absolutely typical, too, in living many years of his adult life in a caravan, leading a seminomadic existence on the roads and marshes around the peripheries of

Great-grand-dad Albert and grand-dad Dave at Canvey Island fair, ca. 1920 (courtesy the Lee family).

the towns of north Kent. But then this had been the pattern for the Gypsies down the ages.

For centuries the Romany people have been driven from place to place, vilified as beggars, thieves and vagabonds. According to Simon Evans, "the gypsy stereotype has two main strands—the dirty, thieving pikey who is not a 'proper' gypsy somehow, and the true Romany, with a crystal ball who plays a fiddle round the campfire at night and lives in a horse-drawn caravan. The truth lies somewhere between the two." The Gypsy community is made up of many extended family groups, who took on local names to appear less conspicuous—Boswell, Buckley, Cooper, Lee, Price, Smith, Stanley and many more. In adversity the Romany people developed a strong will to survive and became adept at subterfuge. Wary of letting the *gorgio*[6] know about their race, they insulated themselves and protected their traditional beliefs and customs beneath a veil of conformity, observing Christian rites and accepting indigenous beliefs. Above all, the Romany people developed an astute self-defense against officialdom, which they saw as irksome and threatening. In assimilating the mores of mainstream society, the Romany faced a degree of cultural tension: sedentarizing the culture was

Four generations of Lees: Dad, Wayne, Albert, Abigail and Grand-Dad, Kidbrooke Park Road, mid–1970s (courtesy the Lee family).

not a step which people took lightly or easily. Those Gypsies who settled down escaped the privations of life on the road and some consciously abandoned their culture; they became "Gorgerfied," like the "Gorgers" or non–Gypsies. Nonetheless, as Simon Evans points out, "If you go into people's houses you can tell it's a gypsy house. There are always frilly lace things, Crown Derby in the cupboard. There are a lot of chintzy, plush, some would say slightly naff, ornaments." Eric Clapton recalls going to the Lees' home in Blackheath: "Albert showed me the front room with the cut glass and everything and it's pure Romany."

There have always been sedentary gypsies who were not entirely nomadic and moved in and out of houses at different times of their lives. "Where a culture has evolved, developed and been sustained by nomadism, where the extended family is the prime social unit, as opposed to the hierarchical structure of sedentary society, the family is the cradle of the culture—and it is an oral culture. So the music, dance, song, language—all these would be sustained round the fireside of an evening. Young gypsies growing up, certainly till the 1940s, '50s and early '60s, would be mixing only with other gypsy children: as a result the amount of language the older people have got is much greater. One of the consequences of sedentarization is that through going to school, living on housing estates and in streets and mixing a lot more with non–Gypsies, among the young the Romany word-count per sentence is diminishing all the time. The language has been the subject of much recent study, some of which has noted a close affinity between Romany, Sanskrit and modern Hindi. The vocabulary is still current even though there are probably very few if any English Gypsies who today speak pure Romany, which has traditionally been a secret language—rather like Cockney rhyming slang, which to the Gorger would remain unintelligible."[7] Albert recalls: "I do remember my Dad and Granddad using Romany words which I didn't understand. I don't know that my father knew a lot of Romany. Granddad knew more."

The Lees, David and Maud, were living close by Blackwall Tunnel, on Greenwich Marsh, a traditional stopping place. It was a far from salubrious area, and several factories, like the Blakey Ordnance Company which made "great guns" in the 1860s, had their own, adjacent, workers' housing. The tunnel was built in the 1880s as a free crossing for East Londoners because they did not benefit from the abolition of tolls on upriver bridges. The most salient features of Greenwich Marsh today are the A102 (M), the two Blackwall Tunnels and of course the Millennium Dome. At the end of Tunnel Avenue by Draw Dock Road where once stood the largest gas works in Europe, the huge white Dome looms as a great white elephant—a monument to fin-de-siècle folly. The area's semi-detached houses are undistinguished and somewhat drab—the sole reminder of what was once a large community. The London School Board School remains, tall, red-brick and forbidding. Tunnel Avenue was once Ship and Billet Lane and ironically enough a community of fairground operators now lives on the site of the Blakey workers' homes.[8]

In 1858, the London Bridge to Deptford railway line was extended to Greenwich, and Londoners began to visit the area, especially at Easter and Pentecost for the Greenwich Fair. In the latter half of the nineteenth century the fairs attracted vast crowds and the Fair gained a certain notoriety. The crowds and the revels began to get out of hand and in 1870 the Fairs were suppressed as a nuisance to local residents. Greenwich was one of the original twenty-eight metropolitan boroughs formed under the Local Government Act of 1888. In that decade the present railway station was built and the arrival of the enhanced railway service launched a new era of prosperity for the town. The borough has the longest river embankment (eight miles) of all London boroughs and many new industries were attracted to Greenwich because of its proximity to the Port of London. Widespread development followed and the town's economy flourished well into the 1950s when with the advent of containerization and the hemorrhaging of dockside jobs[9] the late twentieth-century decline began. Charles Jennings writes: "There *is* an enigmatic quality to the part of the world (the timeless presence of the river helps)...In this part of London you're off the beaten track....on the way to nowhere special—and yet it has enough history, architecture, heritage, sense of place and natural environmental resources,....to make it a place worth living in. You're in London, but not necessarily *of* London; you're not trapped by it. It's a place for artistic individualists."[10]

By the 1930s the Lees may have settled but they also had in their bones the gypsy's love of entertaining and a fondness for music and dancing. The young Albert, one of Jennings's "artistic individualists," stands in that proud tradition: "I guess music is a big strand in Romany culture." Simon Evans agrees: "It makes sense that Albert's Dad was a pub pianist and accordionist. Wherever you go in the world there is a tradition of music-making amongst gypsies and one of the romantic theories, going back to the original Diaspora, was that they were a band of musicians and performers who were ejected from India. Certainly in Europe, whether it's the flamenco in Spain or the fiddlers in Hungary, they are musicians and singers and dancers, assimilating and adapting the culture wherever they are. In the same way that language tells us about the various cultural components in a society, then a repertoire of song does the same. People hang on to songs that are relevant to them, with whose meaning they can identify. Ambrose Cooper, a traditional Romany folk singer, has adapted songs from the yodeling Jimmy Rodgers tradition, talking about traveling the Oregon Trail, hitching rides on boxcars. All of these songs remain in his repertoire today and the fact that Albert's dad was a performer is interesting, because people try to find their own bit of music in a repertoire. When people like Cecil Sharp went out and researched the folk genre, they were interested in recording only what they perceived as traditional folk songs and disregarded the rest, like music-hall songs, as being not of any interest. In fact those music-hall songs sprang from the community and were very important: It is the same with the Gypsy repertoire."

Evans warms to his theme: "Country music is still big among traveling people—there's a kind of identification. They look at the bow-top wagons rolling down the Oregon Trail and see people on the move: Many gypsies went to America anyway to escape persecution here. In America—peach-picking time in Georgia, following the fruit harvest—that's exactly what people did here in Kent. So there are all kinds of cultural affinities. I recently got involved with a community radio station in St. Mary Cray, which has one of the highest traveling populations in the country. When we did a survey amongst teenagers there we were astonished to find that the favorite vocalist was Elvis Presley—that's because it is a gypsy area. Look at Presley's features—they say he came from a Scots traveling family,[11] and the 1950s acoustic country music—and rockabilly—is still very big among Gypsies today."

Although they were now to all intents and purposes sedentary, the Lees still toured the fairs in the summer. "My great-grandfather lived in caravans for quite a while," says Albert. "I remember my Grand-dad saying that in the winter, his Dad, the journeyman wheelwright, actually built caravans. There's a pub called the Sun in the Sands on a roundabout in Blackheath and just down the side of it is Sun Lane, with a yard there where my great-grandfather used to work. Nowadays there are small garages—I got my Mini fixed down there once."

It is a "very old cobbled lane and late at night if you choose to take this shortcut, you could well imagine yourself back in Dickensian times, in the sort of place where you might be attacked by Jack the Ripper!"[12]

The gypsy caravan came into being in the mid– to late nineteenth century—before that the gypsies were tent-dwellers. "The belief is," according to Evans, "that the caravan was evolved by circus and fairground people who initially put cages on wheels to move their menagerie about. Then they thought 'Hey, perhaps we should live like this as well instead of putting the tent up!' Thus the traditional tent, or 'bender,' was rigged on a horse and cart, transmuted later into the more substantial 'gypsy caravan.' There were people who were still using the horse-drawn caravans in Kent until the 1960s—a lifespan of about a century. There were of course very grand versions of caravans but there were also the Morris Minor versions to go with the Bentleys and Rolls-Royces!"

As a nomadic culture, it was essentially nonmaterialistic as "you couldn't own a lot when you were horse-drawn. Your emotional allegiances were with people and not material possessions."[13] For the Romany people, the whole notion of transience is fundamental, as is the relationship with the land, which they regard as all theirs, or everybody's. "This idea that people should fence it off is foreign. It is the same attitude as hunter-gatherers like the Inuit, the Aboriginal peoples in Australia and the Native Americans—'This land is your land, this land is my land.' The relationship with place is transient as is our stop on this Earth. The Gypsy outlook on life is very much 'here today and gone tomorrow,' always moving on and looking towards the future."[14]

For young Albert, however his future began, not in Greenwich, but on the Welsh borders, in a rented cottage on a wooded hillside.

One

The Blackheath Years

From the fields and meadows around Leominster, the land of Ryelands sheep and Hereford cattle, the rolling country of the Old Red Sandstone, rises westwards to the Welsh Marches. At Presteigne, once the smallest county and assize town in England and Wales, the River Lugg marks the English border. It is an ancient, attractive town with distinctive black-and-white half-timbered houses and numerous inns; the seventeenth-century Radnorshire Arms has a priest's hole and secret passages. North of Presteigne steep, narrow valleys run between rounded hills a thousand feet high. Less rugged and dramatic than much of Wales, the area has a tranquil beauty all its own.

Tourism—pony-trekking, rambling and fishing—and forestry are the chief economic lifeblood today, but as the Second World War drew to a close this border country of central Powys was exclusively a sheep-farming landscape. Hill farms, stone walls, and tiny remote cottages dotted the sweeping hillsides. The hamlet of Willey, three miles north of Presteigne, lies between Norton and Stapleton and does not appear on most maps. Willey Lodge, the "big house" on the estate, has Globe Hill to the south, Harley's Mountain and Brierley Hill to the east, while a mile to the west lies the huge, mysterious rock "dome" of the Radnor Forest. Field Cottage, two shepherds' dwellings on a hill above a wood, was rented by Bill Galliers from the Willey Lodge estate. It was the home of his sister, Elizabeth, and her husband, David Lee.

Late in 1943 the tide of the war was beginning to turn and Churchill, Roosevelt and Stalin met in Teheran amid an atmosphere of growing confidence. There was even talk of a Second Front. On December 21, 650 aircraft of Bomber Command raided Frankfurt and in the Pacific heavy bombers of the U.S. Seventh Army Air Force attacked enemy installations on Maloelap Atoll. In Italy, troops from Canada's Loyal Edmonton Regiment fought a savage battle to oust German soldiers from the Adriatic port of Ortona, while the U.S. 5th Army was heavily engaged at Monte Sammucro. On the Eastern Front, the Red Army destroyed the German bridgehead over the Dnieper River at Kherson.

On that day, December 21, at Field Cottage in the deep midwinter, Albert William was born to David Arthur, a driver (L/171008) in the Royal Armoured Service Corps, and Elizabeth Phyllis Lee. The couple had married in Greenwich a year earlier, when on her marriage certificate Elizabeth was described as a "capstan operator," working on a lathe in a factory. Back in Tunnel Avenue, the older Dave, now grandfather to Albert William, might have slept soundly in his bed on that day, too. Though the *Times* reported an Alert in London, the raiders coming up the Thames estuary, there were probably one million fewer rats in London's sewers than there were a fortnight before. The Ministry of Food and the L.C.C. had attacked them with 60 tons of sausage rusk baited with two tons of zinc phosphide. David, the pianist, accordionist and dockside laborer, could have celebrated with Haig Gold Label at 25/9 a bottle. Had he bought the *Times* (for three-pence) he would have read of a new product ideal for his baby, National Milk Cocoa, "a new food drink evolved by the Ministry of Food's scientific advisers. One-third of a pint taken daily will provide that first-class protein so beneficial and necessary during the critical 'growing-up' period. The Ministry," the report continued, "is taking special steps to safeguard the health of the under-eighteens during this fifth war winter"[1]: even to the extent, as the *Daily Telegraph* told its readers, of "endeavoring to secure the luxury of a shell egg for each consumer on Christmas morning."[2]

Ordinary life in the Welsh borders in that week before Christmas, however, went on. The *Radnor Express* carried appeals for the return of two black and white sheep-dogs, valuable assets in this pastoral country, with a reward of £5 offered for one of them. The *Leominster News* reported that a laborer was sentenced to 12 months hard labor for stealing three cabbages from an allotment. It is surprising he was not transported to Australia. Amid the advertisements for Weetabix, Rowntree's cocoa, Ovaltine and Aspro, the Ministry of Agriculture and Fisheries mysteriously appealed for "Better Bulls for More Milk." David, if he had purchased the paper, might have spotted amid the Small Ads "For sale, folding pram, £4/10-" and if he'd fancied a night out at the Clifton Cinema in Leominster he could have seen Betty Grable and Victor Mature in *Hot Spot*, a moody thriller, and appropriately enough, Roy Rogers in *Romance on the Range*.

David had joined up in the '30s on the death of his first wife, Violet, from tuberculosis, and was posted with the R.A.S.C. to Herefordshire, where he met Elizabeth, the daughter of a small tenant farmer, Charles Galliers. She came from a local family of farm laborers in Adforton, living in tied, or rented, cottages like the one in which young Albert was born. Vanessa, his younger sister, remembers it as "a lovely old cottage—no electricity, no water, no toilet. You had to carry buckets of water from the stream at the bottom of the track." The spot was so remote "you could virtually strip off and have a bath. You cooked with coal or wood on a range in the kitchen and when my Mum's brothers had been out hunting, they cooked the meat and you baked bread in the oven on the side. There were oil lamps and candles and when you opened the windows you could hear owls in the trees down in the forest. My Mum also remembered her brothers tickling trout in the stream at the bottom of the field." For some years after Bill died, Vanessa continued to rent the cottage— "for 10/- a week!"—and although Albert has no recollection of Herefordshire, "my wife Karen and I drove down there in the '70s and stayed the night—slept in the bed I was born in. The woman next door had electricity so we ran a line in. They were a spartan couple of days but we did it."

It may have been coincidence but this Army driver, a dockside worker with Romany in his blood, found himself posted to Herefordshire, another center of Gypsy population. A message on BBC Kent's Romany Roots website points this out: "I see from the site that the Lee family hail from the Kent area. I believe from some of my research that there was a settlement in the Shropshire/Wales border (Lee family). I have traced my great-grand-

Albert and Karen outside Field Cottage, Willey, Albert's birthplace, in the late 1970s (courtesy the Lee family).

mother Lizzie Lee through the 1891 census, registered to the Gypsy Tents in Llansullin Broughton, Denbighshire." Certainly David, still only 27 when his son was born, had seen hard times. Albert recalls that "he and his brother joined the Army but his brother died in a unfortunate accident. He was a keen swimmer and he dived into a stream that wasn't deep enough and broke his neck. That really did upset my father because they were really tight, the two of them. They'd come from a broken home and for a while had been farmed out to various families. He also lost his first wife to TB, which was rampant at that time. Not long after I was born Mum came back to Greenwich, to a maisonette my grandfather had found in Tunnel Avenue. So she lived there with me and my grandfather while my Dad was in the Army."

By spring 1944 the war was going badly for Germany. Roger Mercer[3] writes, "By 1943 my sister and I were back in London. The Blitz was over and things had calmed down apart from the odd night raid." In September, Roger became a pupil at the Roan School for Boys, Greenwich, whose portals Albert would later grace. "That winter," Roger recalls, "a stick of three bombs straddled the school bringing down the plaster from the ceiling of the school hall, and killing people living in the house opposite." On the night of 13 June 1944, East Enders heard a strange new sound in the sky, variously described as "like a motorbike without a silencer" or "a badly maintained steam train going uphill." People saw what they assumed was a burning enemy aircraft crossing the sky with flame coming from its tail. The reality was far worse. There were no warning sirens for the V1: while you could hear that buzz you knew that you were safe, but when the engine ran out of fuel the buzz-bomb went quiet, banked to one side, and glided down to deliver its deadly cargo on southeast London.

London was experiencing its first night of the flying bombs, the V1 "doodlebugs." For two weeks the attack continued at the rate of about 100 V1 flying bombs a day, each with a ton of high explosive, inflicting a considerable amount of damage in southeast London. In all, almost 9,250 V1s were fired against the capital, but fewer than 2,500 reached their target. Nonetheless, over 6,000 people were killed and more than 42,000 injured by V1s, mainly in London, Kent and Surrey.

It was debilitating—and for a mother with a young child, not good for the nerves. On 3 August 1944, the buzz stopped and the largest fire to be caused anywhere by a V1 broke out at Ordnance Wharf in Tunnel Avenue. Falling among large creosote and tar storage tanks at the South Metropolitan Tar Works, the bomb sent "a river of flowing burning tar down the street like lava from a volcano."[4] The V1 had exploded "in the allotments out the back, blowing all the windows out so Mum said 'I'm going back to Wales, to the cottage' and we stayed there until the bombing stopped." After the advent of peace in 1945, David was demobbed and the family moved back to Greenwich, where in October Elizabeth had young Albert committed to celluloid for posterity at Williams Pioneer Studios in the High Street. The family moved into a maisonette in 134 Tunnel Avenue—"I lived there with my parents and my grand-dad."

Soon after the war Albert's father received sizeable compensation for an industrial accident at the gas works, bought himself a Renault station wagon and entered the building

Albert's dad at work in Seething Lane, London, in the early 1950s (courtesy the Lee family).

trade in the City as a general laborer. It was a grim time. "The initial mood of postwar optimism was finally dissolving in the harshest winter of the century"[5] and while there may have been "optimism in post–1945 Britain there was also a certain Calvinistic greyness."[6] The mood of English life during the post-war decade was molded predominantly by the memory and aftermath of the war. Through the years of austerity and the long struggle to economic recovery Britain remained, despite the brief burst of radical fervor following the Labor election victory of 1945, fundamentally a conservative country. Many farms were still plowed by horses, and in the towns, where for most people the bicycle was still the most complicated form of personal transport, the English way of life was still, in its outward forms and customs, unlike that of any other country. "At all levels, with the exception of the American influence which had already broken in through the cinema and dance music, the Englishman's culture was still more or less home-grown and unique—whether centered on the heroes of the last days of music hall, Gracie Fields or George Formby or Vera Lynn, or on the BBC. Yet, despite her position in the world and her comparative cultural self-sufficiency, England's mood could scarcely have been bleaker."[7]

Against this depressing background, Albert started primary school: "For a couple of weeks I went to Dreadnought Primary School in Dreadnought Street at the end of Tunnel Avenue. It was pretty close to where we lived—you had to walk down towards Blackwall Tunnel. One day I came home swearing so they put me into Annandale, which was across the Woolwich Road." Albert's parents were determined to bring him up "properly." "My mother, being from farm stock in Wales, was kind of ashamed of my Romany roots. She used to tell me, 'Don't you ever mention that to the neighbours!'" Simon Evans is not surprised: "The self-esteem of the Gypsy community was very low in the immediate post-war years. If it were known that he was from a Romany family, that might have brought trouble down upon their heads. He might be bullied at school and teachers might pick on him."

There were happy times, too. "We went back to Wales a couple of times when I was about 5 or 6. Dad rented a car and we stayed at the cottage. My uncle was still there." And Albert got his first introduction to music. "The first country record I heard—and one of these days I'll track down a copy—was called "Yodelling Bill" by Bill Carlisle, if I remember correctly; I was five or six years old. It was a 78, and one day I found it and ran off to play it. But I dropped it and it broke, so that was the end of that. Dad was furious— so if anybody knows about that record, I'm looking for it." Dad, too, was something of a musician. While his customary demeanor was dour and taciturn, he would come to life on

Albert at Annandale Primary School (ca. 1950) (courtesy the Lee family).

high days and holidays, and given a little alcoholic stimulus, would blossom into musical life. "I remember my father picking up a guitar at a friend's house, putting it across his lap and playing Hawaiian-style with a cigarette lighter. Dad always liked music: I don't know where he learned to play because my grandmother had bought a piano for his younger brother. She told me, 'This was for Albert.' I was named after him. Anyway Dad played it and accordion, too, which I think he picked up in the Army. He also had a fiddle which would appear every Christmas: I now have it." Vanessa remembers the fiddle with affection: "When Dad played it, it was unbelievable, because it's not the sort of thing you'd think a normal chap, a bricklayer or builder, would play."

A delightful cameo of Albert's musical roots is featured on the cover of the Hogan's Heroes CD *Tear It Up*. Dad and Grand-dad Dave are laughing, dancing and no doubt singing along at a Lee family gathering—"I took that picture in Blackheath on New Year's Eve around 1980." Grand-dad Dave "didn't play an instrument but he was the head of the fam-

ily and there was a strong bond between us all. He'd burst into song now and then when he'd had a drop to drink—on special occasions and impromptu parties. He had a banjo for a while which he kept under his bed. We'd all be round the piano, which Dad played, and of course I did, too, later on. Dad thought it was important for me to carry the musical thing on. I'd started bashing on the piano[8] as soon as we had it, making up tunes, so they decided I should take lessons."

Albert was seven or eight and studied formally for the next two years. While he was still going to Annandale Primary, Albert had a teacher across the road from the school gate. "I went to her just for a few months and I got on quite well: then I just lost interest and my parents didn't push me." Perhaps the lady failed to stimulate her gifted pupil, for "after that I had another teacher for maybe a year who used to come to the

Albert's dad and grand-dad, Kidbrooke Park Road, New Year's Eve, 1980 (courtesy the Lee family).

house. They were both pretty good, but the second teacher was maybe more qualified. I learned to play 'Für Elise' by Beethoven—I can barely still remember it—but then I never used to practice so I dropped it." But the piano had "triggered [*his*] initial quest into musicality"[9]: soon he was delving into the classics and dabbling in popular songs, songs he would have heard on the radio, for relatively few people had the money or the inclination to buy records. There was no chart of record sales until 1952 but there were lists of best selling sheet music. The BBC broadcast very little popular music, much to the delight of its rival, Radio Luxembourg.

Levy captures the *Zeitgeist*: "Grey. The air, the buildings, the clothing, the faces, the mood. Britain in the mid–50s was everything it had been for decades, even centuries ... But somehow, in sum, it was less. In 1953—fully eight years after the war had ended—Britons were still eating rationed food, answering nature's call in backyard privies, and making their daily way through cities that bore the deep scars of Luftwaffe bombing.... For many Britons, the mid–1950s were materially and psychologically a lot like the mid–1930s."[10] It was, in the words of critic Kenneth Tynan, "a perpetual Dunkirk of the spirit, made more bitter, perhaps, with the false glimpse of spring that was a young queen's coronation."[11]

In a summer made utterly memorable by Gordon Richards's Derby, the conquest of Everest, Matthews's Cup Final and the winning of the Ashes, on the damp, monochrome morning of June 2, 1953, Albert watched Queen Elizabeth's Coronation "on one of the neighbors' TVs. Or it might have been a relation. We had a lot of relations living about two minutes' walk from us"—after all, Great-grand-dad Albert and Harriett had had six children. Soon after that, when young Albert's sister Vanessa was born in August, the family had outgrown the maisonette and in the autumn decamped to the upper end of Kidbrooke Park Road, only a quick stroll south of Shooter's Hill. The Lees had arrived in Blackheath.

Blackheath, whose name derives from the dark color of the soil, and not, as was popularly believed for many years, from the burial of victims of the Black Death on the heath in the fourteenth century, grew up in the 1820s to cater for the middle classes moving into the area, a development which increased with the coming of the railway in 1849. It is a place which touches the history of England at prominent points. Settled by the Romans as a stopping point on Watling Street, Blackheath was also a rallying point for Wat Tyler's Peasants' Revolt of 1381 and for Jack Cade's Kentish rebellion in 1450. With Watling Street crossing the heath carrying stagecoaches en route to north Kent and the Channel ports, it was also a notorious haunt of highwaymen during the seventeenth century.

Kidbrooke, to the east of Blackheath Park, takes its name from the Kyd Brook, a stream otherwise known as the River Quaggy, watercourses still marked on today's London street maps. Throughout 1954 Albert was still "the whining schoolboy with his satchel and shining morning face, creeping like snail unwillingly to school,"[12] across Shooter's Hill, past Greenwich Park down Vanburgh Hill, to Annandale. In early July, in Memphis, Elvis Presley, Scotty Moore, and Bill Black recorded four songs[13] for Sam Phillips, including an up-tempo romp through Arthur Crudup's 1949 hit "That's All Right, Mama." Scotty Moore, later one of the major influences on the fledgling guitarist Albert, suggested that the strange hybrid of (black) blues and (white) country would offend the southern radio and musical community. Be that as it may, rock 'n' roll, which had been evolving in embryo for a year or two, was ready to fly.

It could be said that 1955 was the year that rock took off—not that you would have known it in Britain. In the mid–1950s, rock 'n' roll fans had to make do with Radio Luxembourg and its poor reception. British popular music during 1955 pretended to be aloof from the shame of rock 'n' roll. The BBC adopted a censorious stance towards this strange hybrid of country and blues which was spreading such widespread societal fear across the Atlantic. "The BBC played skiffle, which was acceptable and banned rock 'n' roll records, which it deemed 'unsuitable for broadcasting.'" One clergyman expressed it: "Rock 'n' roll is a revival of devil dancing....the same sort of thing that is done in black magic ritual.'"[14] The overwhelming tenor of the Top Twenty was much the same as the music that had been around since the end of the war, dominated by vocalists backed by big bands churning out heart-rending ballads, enlivened by novelty songs and the occasional up-tempo, probably Latin-flavored, dance tune. Dickie Valentine, Ruby Murray, trumpeter Eddie Calvert and the Stargazers topped the polls, Ronnie Hilton, Lita Roza, and Anne Shelton were as popular as ever and for a lad in Blackheath, learning the piano and hearing tantalizing snatches of Hank Williams and Bill Haley on "Two-Way Family Favourites," this was stultifying fare. Where was the help, where was the hope? Who would be the savior to lead him to the promised land of rock 'n' roll? However, the bugles were calling across the airwaves—and across the sea. Help was at hand: the cavalry were coming over the ridge...

Earlier that year, Albert had taken the 11 plus exam. "I had the flu at the time and I didn't do very well. I remember the teachers writing a letter to whoever explaining that I was a little sick when I took the exam—so they gave me a pass." Max Middleton was one of Albert's earliest schoolmates and still lives in Kidbrooke Park Road: "When Albert said he'd been ill at the time of the 11 plus it's possible that he had been really quite ill. People didn't admit things like that then. He wasn't tough at all. We lived a few doors up the road and knew the Lees well. They had a piano and they used to come and play our piano too. When Albert sat his 11 plus and didn't quite make it, my Mum was involved because she would have been Chairman of Education at the time. His parents were keen on his having a grammar school education because it was a step to success." In September 1955 Albert, who had acquired another sister that month with the birth of Rebecca,[15] began at the Roan School for Boys, Maze Hill, where the first year was called the Third Form and the second year was Shell. As Max said, "It was a very traditional school."

That same month, disturbances were reported among teddy boys at a number of South London cinemas which had been showing a violent new American film, *The Blackboard Jungle*, featuring behind the opening credits a track by Bill Haley and His Comets.[16] It was Britain's first fleeting introduction to rock 'n' roll. In late November "Rock Around The Clock" topped the chart and was prevented from becoming a Christmas No. 1 only by Dickie Valentine's saccharine "Christmas Alphabet" but returned to the top spot for two weeks in early January.

Anyone who looks at the course of English social history following the Second World War will be struck by the profound change that took place around the start of 1956. Out of the relative calm of the previous decade, Britain suddenly entered a period of upheaval, "marked by a trail of signs, storms and sensations: the coming of commercial television, the rise of the Angry Young Men, the Suez crisis, the coming of the rock 'n' roll craze, and even after a period of comparative quiescence, the beginnings of a crime wave."[17] Variations on the "teddy boy look" had begun to spread outwards from the slums, as a kind of general working class teenage uniform, into many areas of London and even out into the provinces. In the West End the first coffee bars appeared, giving the young their own contemporary meeting place. Not only, apparently, in the West End, according to a friend of Albert's: "Down in Blackheath village there was the Rendezvous Coffee Bar and he—and the rest of us—used to go in there to socialise."[18] The arrival of commercial television, in the London area, brought with it a breed of brashness and Americanization that to English viewers (still well under half the population) was startlingly new. One or two of the traditional jazz bands were also winning a wide following through the skiffle groups which they had formed, singing a crude form of urban blues to the monotonous accompaniment of guitars and washboards. For Albert, this was the time "when I discovered Lonnie Donegan." In January 1956 "Rock Island Line" was released, reaching number 8 in the charts, but it was his trio of hits in the first half of 1957 which set the seal on the skiffle craze. Despite rumours of its early demise, reports of the death of rock 'n' roll had been greatly exaggerated. In May HMV released two records by Elvis Presley which were to change the lives of many: the powerfully atmospheric "Heartbreak Hotel" and the joyfully impudent "Blue Suede Shoes." When Tommy Steele hit number 1 just after Christmas with "Singing the Blues," the Brits had a rock star all their own. Jack Payne might have been right when he said of skiffle in *Melody Maker*: "this huge appeal lies in the fact that a large proportion of these audiences are Rock 'n' Roll fans... For does not skiffle music share three distinctive traits with Rock 'n' Roll—an exaggerated use of guitars, a heavy exaggerated off-beat, and an exaggerated style of mouthing the words?"[19] But then he was a prewar band leader who looked like a bank manager: what did he know?

Against this heady backdrop, the largely academic focus of the Roan School for Boys was passing Albert by. It seemed to him to bear little relevance to what was happening in the real world. Even the music at school was locked in the past. "The music teacher's name was Elliott and we used to call him 'Jelly' as his initials were G.E. He wore glasses and looked like Peter Ustinov. He was a nice guy but it was like a choir thing. It wasn't really a music class." Terry Scanlon, a school contemporary, concurs: "The music at Roan was dreadful—Elliott didn't like modern music at all." Though Albert was by no means a fool, the glittering prizes did not beckon the kid from Kidbrooke Park. "I've always been pretty bright but I've never really applied myself." As Max said, "I was in the same year as him but neither of us did very much at school. We had a deputy head called Mr. Berry who used to walk around in a cap and gown smoking his pipe at a certain angle because it was so burnt-out. He'd walk into a classroom and say 'Put your hand out' and he'd whack it several times. When you said 'Why?,' holding back the tears, it was just to let you know he could.[20] This was probably one of the reasons we were always playing truant—we were frightened of going to school. I'd say Albert was quite frail at school." Albert concedes the accuracy of the image, but insists he enjoyed playing cricket, football and "running about." He would have loved to have played more cricket and "I'd love to give it a try now. You hear Bill Wyman talking about cricket. The guy walks so slowly, you can't imagine him playing, yet he's mad about it."

John Roan was well-known throughout the south of London for cross-country running. Max remembers having to "run through the park and we used to hide behind trees. I smoked but I don't think he did. He was a really quiet, shy, very charming kid—not aggressive at all. I don't think he was religious though. We used to go to the church youth club and if we wanted to go to the club we had to go to church. We would sit at the back getting bored." Albert began to express his individuality in this new age of essentially youthful rebellion against conventional authority, not overtly as a tearaway at school, nor even at home, but in his own single-minded dedication to the medium which became exclusively the territory of the young: "The only thing I've applied myself to is playing the guitar."

One weekend at the beginning of 1957 Albert got Max to lend him a guitar to practice on. "My brother was in the navy and he had come home from Hong Kong with two guitars—one lovely cello guitar, probably a Spanish one, and one that Albert used, a cello-type with metal strings." It was "a very cheap arch-top with an horrendous action. I played for the next 18 months or so on borrowed guitars, and my friends' parents would understandably get quite irate!" Ronnie Bell, a friend for nearly half a century, understood why: "Pretty quickly Albert had tuned it correctly and was strumming along to the Lonnie Donegan songs. He became a bit of a hero to his friends at the youth club—but not to Max's Mum, who immediately asked Albert to return the guitar! He had surpassed Max, who was his mother's pride and joy, and she didn't like it!" Max, described by another schoolmate as "a real Bohemian whose Mum was mayor of Greenwich once," decided they needed a guitar tutor book. "There was a music shop in Blackheath village which sold records and we used to listen to music there. One of us bought that 'How To Play The Guitar' book. Albert still says 'I've always borrowed other people's guitars and the first one I half-inched was Max's cello guitar!'"

But nobody taught Albert. "I really learned by ear and it all began to take shape. I admit I did get the Bert Weedon book and I did learn a couple from the Eric Kershaw chord book. When I picture harmonies and so on I see a piano keyboard. It seems much more logical to me." That was the year of "Don't You Rock Me, Daddy-O," "Cumberland Gap" and "Puttin' On The Style," and as Albert told *Guitar Magazine* in 1984, "Lonnie Donegan started me playing guitar, I suppose. To be able to play skiffle all you needed was a flat-top guitar and three chords, and you were off. It seemed easier in those days than I imagine it would be for a kid who wants to start playing guitar today."

Max and Albert were not only schoolmates. "We used to go to the same church youth club—St. Mary's Youth Club halfway down Kidbrooke Park Road," Max recalls. "The girls would all sit down one side and we'd all sit down the other. My sister used to come with us as well and lots of people from the council estate. That was when we first began listening to music—'Rock Around The Clock' and that. We used to hang about the chip shop after and chat up the girls. The club's been knocked down and it's a garage now."

"Then the skiffle era began and we wanted to play skiffle." Skiffle became a popular craze in Britain between 1956 and 1958. Its accessibility offered to a wide range of young people the possibility of approaching some of the excitement and novelty associated with rock 'n' roll. An acoustic guitar, broom-stick bass, and improvised percussion, and you were away. "My sister played the tea-chest bass," said Max. "Somebody else played the washboard and Albert and I bashed out three chords on the guitar. And we did things like 'Don't You Rock Me, Daddy-O' at the church youth club."

Lonnie Donegan, a member of Chris Barber's traditional jazz band and according to many leading artists and commentators the most influential performer in British pop music, thought "Skiffle was originally associated with rent-house parties. If one of the guys was short of rent, he'd hold a party and people would come round with bottles and guitars for a bit a whoop-up. He'd pass the hat round during the proceedings, just like in the Irish song 'Phil the Fluter's Ball' 400 years earlier. The kind of music they would play was very improvised, very folky and a bit jazzy."[21] Chris Barber made Donegan's skiffle a feature of the band's performances. "The word 'skiffle' was just coined. We took it from an old Dan Burley record. He was an American Negro who edited a black newspaper in Chicago and was a very good rent party pianist. It was back-room music, rent party music, casual and not self-conscious."[22]

Skiffle swept the country, "extending the popularity of semi-amateur music-making over a much wider and predominantly younger section of the population than had even been covered by the traditional jazz cult."[23] Whatever its origin, skiffle launched a thousand careers, from Lennon and McCartney to Eric Clapton and Hank Marvin. "It was the first American-devised music to be brought home and spread on a large scale, from inner-city jazz clubs out to bedrooms in suburbia. There were skiffle groups everywhere, in schools, housing estates and coffee bars"[24]—and in Kidbrooke Park.

Ronnie Bell knew Albert from the club, too. "I was passing the youth club one night and I could hear these guitars twanging away. I went in and there was this geeky guy with glasses and curly hair, unlike everybody else at that time, because they had their hair slicked back, full of Brylcreem and stuff. This was Albert, strumming away on one of Max's guitars, and he was the only one who knew what he was doing. We got chatting straight away and became friends, so one Saturday night, we decided to form a proper skiffle group, with a regular lineup, not the ad hoc affair it had been until then. The big problem was that Albert didn't have a guitar! We had the best guitarist and no guitar for him to play, so he used to borrow Max's. Max Middleton had formed a group with some other kids so we couldn't borrow his guitar any more. I overcame this handicap by trying to borrow guitars off people for Albert to play—like David Payne, a kid who lived in Lee Green. I used all sorts of underhand methods to get hold of David's guitar. I would tell his sister that David had said I could borrow the guitar when in fact he hadn't! So our group was Albert [guitar], me [washboard], and Brian McNeil, who lived near me, played a tea-chest bass. We hadn't yet got a name."

In July, Albert and his family went on their annual summer holiday to Allhallows-on-Sea. Ronnie remembers it well. It was quite an expedition. "They all piled into their old Renault shooting brake and away they went. It was enormous and the whole family used to go in it—it was like going on hop-picking. If he still had it now it would be worth an absolute mint."

It was just after the First World War that Kent County Council and London County Council proposed the transformation of the remote and inhospitable marshland hamlet of Allhallows, on the northern edge of the Hoo Peninsula, into a major seaside resort, after the fashion of Victorian Herne Bay. By the 1930s the riverfront at Avery Farm, about a mile north of the village, on the River Thames was planned as the best holiday resort in Europe. A special railway line was constructed with these proposals in mind and Allhallows-on-Sea railway station was opened in 1932, built to serve the new holiday complex. But Allhallows failed to attract enough visitors and has since been demolished and the site sold off as a holiday caravan park—the Lee family's annual destination.[25]

Albert, his grandparents and the Renault, Canvey Island, early 1950s (courtesy the Lee family).

While Albert was away, events were moving quickly back in Kidbrooke Park. In Brian McNeil's shed Colin Stead, a schoolmate of Ronnie's, told him about "this guy in the prefabs where I live who's a really good guitar player." So Ronnie went to St. German's Place in Blackheath one evening "to hit a cricket ball about and that's how I met a mean off-spin bowler and guitar player called Bruce 'Bugs' Waddell. After the knockabout we went to Bugs' prefab and he got out his very old battered guitar. He could tune and play it and I was impressed. We spent the evening singing Lonnie Donegan songs. Over the next couple of evenings I invited Bugs to practice with us. When Albert got back from his holidays I said to him, 'I've met his other fellow who plays guitar. He's very good.' We all met in Brian McNeil's garden shed and Albert and Bugs got on well straight away. Apart from the music, they had the same sense of humor: they both loved the Goons. We had a problem, though. We had only the one guitar. It was great to have two people who could play major chords, but Albert was the better of the two. So we had to persuade Bugs to lend Albert his guitar, but what was Bugs going to play? By a bit of luck Brian had an old banjo. So I said to Bugs, 'Lend Albert your guitar and play the banjo.' Very reluctantly he tuned the banjo up as for a guitar and made a noise on it. Now we had the skiffle group everyone dreamed of—guitar, banjo and I was on a tea-chest bass but I soon went on to a washboard and Bugs played bass. The main practices were in my front room in Delme Crescent. The skiffle group that emerged was the Dewdrops, the first group actually to play pubs, youth clubs, on the street, stations, anywhere. So I was instrumental in bringing Albert and Bugs together."

"He was borrowing everybody's guitars—including mine," says Bugs. "After we'd met and had our little challenge, we realised that we could at least play whereas some of the others couldn't. We saw that we would be better off combined than if we stayed apart. After all, there was only one guitar in town and only one lead guitarist." As with many of the Blackheath crowd, Bruce—or Bugs, as he was always called—has remained Albert's lifelong friend. Phil Hadler, a friend and technical colleague in Herne Bay, remarks: "He really loves his roots and likes to stay in touch."

During the first half of 1958, Albert would practice and practice at home, using Bugs' guitar—"a small Victorian ladies model. I was heavily influenced by Scotty Moore on all of the early Presley records, like the stuff on 'The Sun Sessions.' I spent hours figuring out those solos; it was a good place to start. Lonnie had a great guitar player called Denny Wright, who still plays. He's very much in the Django Reinhardt vein. But the first really good guitarist I heard—I thought I'd give anything to play like him—was Cliff Gallup, my favourite guitar player in the late '50s. He was with Gene Vincent's Blue Caps. Their first records just blew me away; songs like 'Blue Jean Bop,' 'Jumps, Giggles, And Shouts,' 'Pink Thunderbird'—really intelligent themes! One single that wasn't on an album then, 'Race With The Devil' [now available on 'The Bop That Just Won't Stop'], had an absolute killer solo where Cliff jumps from E to F. That is a real tough solo; it's so clean. I got as close to it as I could. It really helped me a lot, trying to work out his solos, because they really got me to develop more of a jazz technique, using all my fingers and playing scales as opposed to two-fingered walk-ups across the strings. He was the one guy that really made me sit down and work on solos. I really liked Buddy Holly's playing as well, of course. His solos were a lot simpler, but I suppose everybody was knocked out with the *sound* of his guitar—that great bell-like tone. I particularly liked his solos on 'That'll Be The Day' and 'Looking for Someone to Love.' They were a lot easier to work out than the Cliff Gallup things."

The skiffle boom died, of course. For one thing, according to Marty Wilde, "a lot of the skiffle songs were silly songs, just like folk songs tarted up. Not that the early rock 'n' roll songs were a lot better but there was a certain amount of honesty in rock 'n' roll."[26] Skiffle's limited instrumentation and home-grown acoustic sound could not compete with the power and excitement of rock 'n' roll. Larry Portis has written that the "strong element of black intonation in Donegan's 'skiffle' productions surely influenced the growing taste for rock 'n' roll among British youth,"[27] and Chambers feels that skiffle "provided an access to the interior of American popular music, to a part of its hidden attraction, a route into the mysterious chemistry of rock 'n' roll."[28]

That "mysterious chemistry" was exerting its powerful alchemy on the hearts and minds of Britain's youth. In those two years, 1956–7, the parameters were formed of that "independent teenage sub-culture which was to play an increasingly prominent part in English life—centered round its three basic pillars of dress, beat music and an aggressive nonconformity to everything except its own values. For the avant-garde of the teenagers it was as if they had been caught up in an iridescent bubble, bringing for all those inside it a vision of eternal youth, freedom and excitement."[29] The Crickets topped the chart in September 1957 with "That'll Be the Day," Jerry Lee Lewis followed with his pounding epic "Whole Lotta Shakin' Goin' On" to which the Crickets responded with "Oh Boy!," a simple yet profound expression of what passes for teenage romance.

What was the Establishment response to this outpouring of trans–Atlantic youthful vitality? The *Melody Maker* reported that at Doug Dobell's shop in Brighton, Her Majesty's Customs had seized American discs.[30] Some problem with import duty, no doubt, for there was a government embargo on American luxury goods which was not lifted until the summer of 1959—hence the reliance on European guitars such as Hofners and Graziosos.

Not that these ramifications of international trade sanctions dampened the enthusiasm of youngsters like Ronnie, Albert, Bugs and their mates. "Looking back now, what our parents put up with was incredible. We are indebted to all of them," says Ronnie. "My Mum just thought 'Let these kids enjoy themselves.'" Bugs's Mum was happy to let them practice in the prefab. As a single woman, she was out a lot of the time. Ronnie got to know Albert's parents "because we started to go there to practice, and Albert's Dad, who was a very musical guy as well, an old Gypsy fiddler and piano player, took us to a couple of pubs where they let us play. I don't know if he was really an extrovert performer. It was just that music was in their culture."

Grand-dad was living there too, of course. Vanessa describes her Mum having "to put up with a little scullery to cook and do everything in. We cobbled together a sink and whatnot and what was Mum's kitchen became like a bed-sitting room for Grand-dad downstairs. He did all his own cooking in there and was quite independent. We used to eat in the other rooms and then my sister and I and Albert would pop in and see him." Ronnie remembers him with real warmth: "Grand-dad was great—very, very down-to-earth. They were all earthy people and very working-class and in many ways didn't move on with the times. Sometimes he'd come in moaning and groaning, saying, 'It's too loud—all get out!' He was a cantankerous, lovable old sod."

The Dewdrops did not always practice in Kidbrooke Park Road. "We was [sic] in my front room practicing one day," Ronnie remembers, "when my cousin came in and said, 'Play something for me—come on.'" They played a couple of skiffle tunes and being "so surprised at how good we were he pulled out a fiver for us—one of the lovely big white ones. So we got straight on the bus and went up to Well Hall Road in Eltham and bought a pick-up for Bugs's guitar for £3 10/- and a set of brushes. We put the pick-up on the guitar and plugged it into the back of my parents' valve radio. That was our first electric guitar and we did 'Tutti Frutti.' Of course Albert knew it and I thought 'We've arrived.'" Albert recalls that pick-up with affection: "We plugged Bugs' guitar into the back of Bugs' Elizabethan tape-recorder, too, and thought 'Wow, this is electric!' There were no amps about—it was a luxury to have an amplifier. During this period a relation had given me a mandolin/banjo which I never did learn to play. Then my folks got me a cheap Spanish guitar for about a fiver which I immediately put steel strings on. Nobody had any money nor were there many quality instruments around so it was all done on a shoestring."

Meanwhile, throughout 1958, the year of Jerry Lee Lewis's classic "Great Balls of Fire," Presley's electrifying "Jailhouse Rock," and the ethereal Appalachian harmonies of the Everlys' "All I Have to Do Is Dream," Albert's progress up the ladder of academic success had ground to a halt, foundering on the rock 'n' roll of Buddy Holly, Gene Vincent, and a new British rock sensation. Max remembers: "I can tell you exactly when I knew Albert had a spark—we were at the church youth club and Cliff's 'Move It' had just come out. The guitar sound on it was so amazing that we all listened to it non-stop. We came back the next week for a skiffle session and Albert played it. It was quite astounding and everybody thought

'Fucking hell, we can't keep up with that!' By then we could play about six chords and he was doing about 600!"

John Roan School was "just like Greyfriars. It was Third, Shell, Fourth, Remove, Fifth and Sixth. Each one was divided into Alpha, Form and B. I think Albert started in Alpha and soon got demoted into B, where I was," says Mo Clifton, now a well-established guitar-builder in Shooter's Hill. "We weren't overenamored with school. I wasn't aware of Albert until about the third year when I went down to the bike sheds for my lunchtime smoke. Albert and Max were sitting there learning the chords for 'Oh Boy.' I was into rock 'n' roll myself so I was quite impressed and started making a friend of Albert and hanging around with him. The only things Albert and I were interested in were music, bicycles and girls. Albert needed a bike for his paper round from which he earned 7/6 a week which used to go to pay off his bicycle, so he couldn't afford a guitar. We used to cycle everywhere—nobody had any money so the only guitars I saw Albert using were ones he borrowed. I don't know how often he took a guitar into school but we must have been about 14 and I remember the deputy head walking round the bike sheds one day, trying to catch people smoking so he could beat their butts. When he saw Albert he said, 'What's that, boy?'

"'It's a guitar, sir.'

"'You're wasting your time,' Berry replied, scornfully. 'Get on with your studies! You'll never make a living out of that!'"

It was clear that Albert's days at John Roan were numbered.

Two

The Times They Are A-Changin'

On Friday, December 19, 1958, two days before his 15th birthday, Albert was summoned to the headmaster's study. He stood in front of the Head, Gus Gilbert, an austere academic figure with the erect bearing of a military man,[1] who told the shy teenager with the curly black hair, "You're not making much progress here, are you? I think you'd better leave at the end of this term." After all, as Mo Clifton recalls, "John Roan School wasn't keen on people failing."

Albert had mixed feelings: "I was kind of disheartened, but I thought, 'I'm not doing any good here so I guess I'd better leave.' I wasn't coming in every day and in the last couple of weeks I didn't show up at all. I didn't even clear out my desk—I can't remember what I left in it. Most of the time I was hanging round home, or with my friends or whatever." Max Middleton was a willing accomplice: "Towards the end of our school career we were hardly ever going to school, or we were turning up, then leaving at break-time. Albert and I used to bunk off because John Baines, who lived in a prefab overlooking the Heath, had two gorgeous sisters. I got thrown out because I was round there all the time—but also what was even more important was that they had a reel-to-reel tape recorder, which was almost unheard-of."

Albert's parents "got pretty upset. I used to put my mother through it, saying I didn't feel well and she'd tell my Dad and he'd give me a whack. He wasn't a violent man but it was the done thing then. I guess they were sad about it." After all, strings had been pulled to get Albert into Roan, but as Mo points out, "They doted on him and he couldn't really do any wrong. He wasn't a naughty boy." His dad and grand-dad may have complained occasionally about the noise but Albert's parents "were so encouraging. A week after I left school my folks spent nearly all of their Christmas club money on my first good guitar, a Hofner President acoustic arch-top which they'd found in *Exchange and Mart*. It cost over £20. You could add on a pickup at the end of the fingerboard but it was so easy to pull the wire out by treading on it! It's in the photo in Mo Foster's book. I have a number of shots from that session. Although the standard of guitars was pretty poor in those days, I found I could play things on the Hofner I couldn't play on anything else. Suddenly all these solos I was trying to work out became a lot easier—it had a pretty good neck on it." After two years of begging and borrowing other kids' instruments, Albert finally had a guitar of his own.

Albert's Hofner was his passport into the changing world of Britain in the late '50s, though the country had scarcely undergone an overnight conversion. A month before Albert

The back garden at Kidbrooke Park Road, June 1959. Albert with his Hofner, Tony Walter, Bugs Waddell on Elsie, the upright bass, and Johnny Haylock (courtesy the Lee family).

left school, the influential music weekly, the *Melody Maker*, fulminated in an editorial headed "Pop Rot! Call a Halt Now" and thundered out a clarion call for an end to the promotion of rock 'n' roll.[2] The worthy journal, which had been for three decades the bastion of the jazz establishment, was suspicious of this brash new musical upstart. Though it was fundamentally swimming against the tide, two days after Christmas it could chalk up a minor success for the forces of reaction. *6.5 Special*, the first youth program on British television, went off the air. First broadcast in February 1957, it went out in the dead time on Saturday between children's TV and adult programs. Albert had watched it from the start. "Saturday was a great evening—*6.5. Special* and then *Bilko*—I loved both of them." Another great favorite with Albert and his dad was *Wells Fargo*, starring Dale Robertson.[3]

Like British rock itself, the show was all rather hand-to-mouth. Producer Jack Good explained: "They only gave us a budget of £1,000 for the whole program—that's the set, the costumes, the artists, everything. I had to find British rockers"[4]—the American stars were too expensive. Nevertheless, the show had been a breakthrough of a kind but as George Melly observed, "In those days if anything became successful, the adults took over ... so it was a patronising show, but not without excitement. It didn't have the looseness or the pro-youth feel of what came later like *Ready, Steady, Go!* The atmosphere was like that of a rather oppressive youth club."[5] For the *Melody Maker*, it was a hollow victory—the BBC's "youth club" was superseded by ITV's louder, more iconoclastic *Oh Boy!*

On the day that Albert walked out of the gates of John Roan for the last time, the inexorable march of rock 'n' roll was marked when Conway Twitty's "It's Only Make Believe" reached no. 1—and stayed there for 5 weeks. Twitty's style—a sonorous baritone—was closely modelled on Elvis: his desperate panting built to a dramatic climax. Albert's life was anything but make-believe as "straight after Christmas my Dad marched me down to the Youth Employment Office and I got a job at the Plan Reproduction Company in Brockley. They used to reproduce blueprints in a process involving a big table with a rubber belt. You'd pour all this jelly on the table, then it would set. They'd put a blueprint on it and roll it, leaving an impression which you would ink. Then you would roll some paper or plastic carefully across it and get a perfect reproduction."

The job in Brockley, mundane and repetitive, was merely a stepping-stone, a holding operation. To paraphrase John Lennon, life was happening to Albert while he was busy making other plans[6]—and practicing. "I found James Burton's sound very appealing, but it seemed totally alien to me, because I couldn't figure out how he was doing it. I'd started to learn how to play like Cliff Gallup, with a wound third string. Burton's was a different approach altogether—all that string bending with an unwound G. My favourite record of his was 'My Babe' by Ricky Nelson, and all the early Ricky Nelson albums were great, although some of the songs were pretty schmaltzy. 'Just A Little Too Much' is another classic example of the way Burton played then, and 'It's Late' has such a simple solo—he plays so few notes—but it has an incredible feel which is really hard to get."

Albert had secured his first job, humdrum as it was, in the employment boom of the late 1950s. The British economy "had finally relaunched itself: key industries were denationalised by a conservative government; American multinationals were choosing Britain as the home base for their expansion into Europe; unemployment dipped, spiking the housing, automobile and durable goods markets; credit restrictions were eased, encouraging a boom in consumerism.... Inevitably, as in America, prosperity led to complacency and nostalgia for a prewar era that only in retrospect seemed golden.... The Prime Minister, Harold Macmillan, patting himself on the back in 1957, declared 'You've never had it so good.' And in many respects he was right—if you were of certain tastes and strains of breeding."[7]

If you were not, if you came from the outer fringes of society which the new prosperity had passed by, if you were in a dead-end job, practicing your guitar day in and day out, you were beginning to feel a wind of change, engendered by "the rhythmic urgency of rock music."[8] This powerful hybrid, a fusion of black rhythm and blues and white country music, spoke in a language which became the argot of certain very clearly defined groups, such as the young and the urban working class which, as English society lost its prewar cohesion, would be most attracted by the collective fantasy, the fantasy that wealth and fame lay just around the corner. "For each age is a dream that is dying or one that coming to birth."[9]

The Britain in which Albert began his working life, listening to Scotty Moore, Cliff Gallup and James Burton, practicing and practicing until he had the solos to perfection, was one in which rock 'n' roll and "the extraordinary infectiousness of the imagery of America"[10] became part of the lifeblood of almost every teenager. This imagery—material prosperity, a brash mass culture, expressed in the increasing influence of television and advertising, electrifying popular music which was uniquely the preserve of the new commercial demographic, the "teenager"—represented the American Dream, a particular idea of freedom and affluence which the young found overwhelmingly seductive.

Although Albert had been asked to leave school, he was never a teenage rebel, never a nascent Jimmy Dean. For many teenagers, "rock 'n' roll was not a revolutionary force.... It was merely their popular music.... Most teenagers' adherence to rock 'n' roll music signifies their acceptance not rejection of society and culture during the 1950s and early 1960s."[11] Seen in its historical context rock grew out of the indigenous musical heritage of the society which spawned it. While it was blatantly commercial, while its star performers adopted styles of dress, speech and appearance which were overtly rebellious, rock 'n' roll had respectable roots. Q magazine puts it vividly: "Electric guitars and wild women? Boozing, narcotics, sweaty sex? Yeah, it's rock 'n' roll, but you don't really think the cool cats invented all that? Rock just tore the fringe off the buckskin, rode a motorcycle instead of a horse, traded the fiddle for a ... well, hell, let's just smash the fiddle.... 'If Chuck Berry had been a white man,' Buck Owens has stated, 'he'd 'a been a country singer.'"

Ian Cawood[12] has attributed the rise in rock 'n' roll in the 1950s, apart from the growing impact of American culture on British life and "discovery" of the teenager, to the introduction of new electronic recording and amplification techniques—a development in which Albert and his group were becoming increasingly interested. Whatever the wider sociological forces which were driving the advance of rock 'n' roll, at heart the new music was exciting, visceral and sexy. Above all else, it offered the possibility of escape: it held within its hypnotic four-to-a-bar beat the chance to stand on the threshold of a dream.

Booker has written about the social groups who would come to be seduced by American culture, the groups for whom the imperceptible shift in political power away from the Establishment had not yet become a reality and those groups for whom life—especially the new, exciting, prosperous life—seemed to be a party to which they had not been invited. The first of these groups was the one in which Albert and his friends moved and grew up— the young urban lower class.

"It was this group," Booker points out, "which would provide the stage armies of the future, the 'teenage market,' the pop fans in their anonymous millions, the Mods and Rockers—just as it had already provided their first foretaste in the Teddy Boys of South London. It was this group too which would provide the individual heroes of the New England, symbols of a class revolution—the working-class writers, the pop singers and actors, idols who would eventually command the attention of the whole nation ... such diverse figures as John Stephen (Glasgow) and Mary Quant (South London), John Osborne (South London) and Colin Wilson[13] (Leicester), Tommy Steele and Marty Wilde (both from South London)."[14] In fact, Marty Wilde grew up in Greenwich and when he had his first hit moved to Eastbrook Road, only a stone's throw from Kidbrooke Park. One day Albert and Bugs knocked on his door.

"Good morning, Mr. Wilde. We've got a band. Can you give us any tips?"

Though he did not invite the youngsters in, he made encouraging noises. Wilde was clearly something of a local celebrity and Colin Stead remembers him "rocking his baby daughter Kim in his Ford Fairlane!"

Marty Wilde was one of the new breed of gold-lamé-clad rock 'n' roll idols whose antics and rags-to-riches success fascinated the popular press. Looking for the most part like gilded teddy boys, with names such as Dickie Pride, Terry Dene and Wee Willie Harris, almost all of them were managed by impresario Larry Parnes and many were products of the Soho coffee bar the Two I's. Teenagers at the end of the fifties, "personified perfectly in Colin Macinnes's stylised *Absolute Beginners*, were sharp and self-confident, although unsophisticated and gauche compared to their American equivalents.... They drifted into the world of Espresso bars and were drawn musically to rhythm and blues, particularly small groups."[15] The Blackheath crowd was no different: there was the Rendezvous Coffee Bar in Blackheath village where Albert and the rest used to socialize, although Albert was not the focus of the group. Despite being blessed with a dry wit and a self-belief in his developing talent, he lacked confidence in a crowd, as Joan Baines observed: "He was sort of shy—an introvert in personality who became an extrovert with his music."

A potent combination was brewing. While Parnes' pretty boys dominated the scene, skiffle—that strange blend of American folk, blues, country-and-western and crude home-made British musicianship—had, by 1959, given rise to a heady mix: easy-to-play music, quick fame, a ready audience and the new coffee bars to play. This formula suited almost any lad, as Albert and his mates had found in Blackheath.

A new character entered the scene. Noel Bronley, known as Bron, was married to Gordon Williams, whose professional name was Glen Gordon. Both were ballet dancers with the International Ballet and Ballet Russe who lived in the basement of a large house in Shooter's Hill Road, with a spacious, sparsely furnished living room. Bron taught ballet at a dancing school in Blackheath and one of her pupils asked if she could have a birthday party in the flat. "Thereafter," says Bron, "Jenny brought her friends round on Sundays and it became a sort of informal club for teenagers, where they could meet and talk and play records. The eclectic group expanded as the youngsters brought other friends and some of the boys formed a band with various primitive instruments."

"One lad had a real guitar and played with talent and flair. This was Albert. He had a wide mouth, usually smiling, big, very dark brown eyes and a lot of unruly, curly black hair. The whole crowd was impressed with his virtuosity. The band practiced in our bedroom, which adjoined the living room. This was also sparsely furnished and uncarpeted and made an ideal studio." Carol, Bron's daughter, has vivid memories of those sessions: "The flat was full of colourful characters, dancers practicing or teenagers dancing. We had an old wind-up gramophone and not a lot of furniture so the boys sat on my rocking-horse and broke its head off. Albert's hair had a life of its own and stood out from the rest so I decided that he would be my champion against all those insulting teenagers. I was only 5 and would climb on his knee and to his intense embarrassment reach up to kiss his spotty face, announcing to anyone within earshot that he was MY boyfriend."

The landlady was not impressed by Albert's virtuosity or anybody else's. "She often complained bitterly about the noise," Bron recalls, "but my husband and I were unsympathetic. We remembered what it was like to be young and noisy and not have a place where we could escape in order to have fun. We saw ourselves as benefactors to these teenagers and felt even more justified when a friend who worked for the BBC came to one of the Sunday sessions and featured some of the boys and girls in a brief session demonstrating the virtue of a suitable meeting place with harmless pursuits to keep the youngsters off the streets." As the journalist Peter Evans remembered, "London was a kind of grown-up town, an old man's town. Nightclubs were where you went if you wanted to hear people playing the violin. There was nowhere to go. Even Soho closed early. There were drinking clubs, but they were private." Mary Quant, a South Londoner herself, concurred: "There was nothing for young people, and no place to go and no sort of excitement."[16]

Bron's place caught a whiff of the essence of the time. "At a pace that seemed wholly un–British, various strains of unofficial culture—defiant, anti-authoritarian, and hostile to such commonplaces of tradition as modesty, reserve, civility and politesse—were coalescing, not so much in unison as in parallel. Bohemians in Chelsea and Soho; radical leftists from the universities and in the media; teens with spending money, freedom and tastes of their own."[17] It was also fun, according to Max: "Ah, yes, the ballet people in Shooter's Hill Road. We used to stay late at night drinking and things. Strange things used to go on there and I remember being there very drunk at the age of 14. It was a bit wicked." Bugs has fond memories, too, of Bron: "They were a very odd couple—very Bohemian for the late '50s and avant-gardish. I remember the evening of the ouija board or Bron doing a bit of a ballet. Then we'd play some music on other occasions—and record it. The trad music people were there too." Whatever else went on at Bron's—and many of his friends believe strongly that Albert's relationship with Bron went beyond purely artistic admiration—there can be little doubt that there was, at weekends, "a most extraordinary ongoing house-party."[18]

Albert was especially interested in the wire recorder. "The guy was really into electronics and he'd built himself this big old radiogram out of bits and pieces. It had a wire recorder—pretape—like a bit of fuse wire on a spool. We recorded our skiffle group on it. God, I wish I still had those recordings. He went off to Jamaica to teach ballet for a couple of years and I ended up buying this unit from his wife for £15. I couldn't believe my luck that she was letting me have it. It was made out of chipboard and it looked amazing. You lifted the lid up and it had all these knobs and things. I had a music machine!"

"A drop-in for the arty." That was Ronnie Bell's pithy epithet for the Shooter's Hill Sunday afternoons. One night in January 1959 "we were playing at the Catholic youth club in Blackheath. I'd got this old set of drums—ex–Salvation Army and very rough. One guy who was already there on stage had a snare drum and a high-hat. He said, 'Can I play as well with you?' I was a bit reluctant but he did and he was much better than me—this turned out to be Tony Middleton, who introduced everybody to Bron's." By then Brian McNeil had departed and Albert and Bugs met John Haylock, Dave Wombwell and a jazz singer nicknamed Lonnie in Bron's. The three of them wanted to sing with the band, so an audition was held in Bugs' prefab. Dave was eliminated straight away as he couldn't sing, so the choice was between John and Lonnie. Albert went round to Ronnie's:

"Ron, We've got a real dilemma. There's Lonnie, who's with the trad jazz lot and has a great skiffle voice, and a rock 'n' roller, John, who looks the part. What do you think?"

"Well, I think rock 'n' roll's in and skiffle's fading, so I'd go for John."

Albert agreed, "Yeah, that's what I thought."

Albert now had the core of his first proper rock 'n' roll band "but we still hadn't got a proper name. Dave Wombwell didn't want to be left out. So, with the help of his parents he got himself a guitar. I helped him a bit, Dave became the rhythm guitarist and was a quick learner." So the new lineup was Johnnie Haylock, singer; Albert, guitar; Dave Wombwell, guitar; Bugs Waddell, bass; and Tony Middleton, drums. "We didn't do much in the way of gigs—mostly we'd play at Bron's," recalls Bugs. In February Buddy Holly, Ritchie Valens and The Big Bopper died in a plane crash and at Bron's the following Sunday, Johnny Haylock recalls "a bit of a wake, sitting round with guitars playing Buddy's songs."

One night at Bron's, Ronnie remembers, "this very camp fella turned up and said, 'Hallo, darling! I'm Lord Anton' and asked if he could sit in on drums. Everyone said, 'Fine,' except Tony Middleton who wasn't too keen on a stranger using his kit—especially when he sat down and blew Middleton away. This was Tony Walter, and he was really excellent—much better than Tony, who found himself out of the group." He took it badly. "Poor Tony Middleton, bless his heart, he was a bit of a lonely soul," recalls Albert. "We called him the 'Moaner' because sometimes you'd be in the middle of a rehearsal and he'd just pack his drums up and walk off. The first time I went to Hamburg in '62, I think, I recommended him for the gig. He did OK but that was the last time we ever played together."

Everyone liked Tony Middleton, shy, shabby and unkempt. Tony Walter, with his D.A. quiff and his confidence was not the most popular of the group: "He was so in your face," says Ronnie. "He wanted to be front of stage with the band behind him. He had girls flocking round him." The British have never taken to big heads. Lord Anton was "a year or two older than us," Albert recalls. "He'd come from Brighton where he'd sat in with Syd Lawrence and Ray McVay and he was a pretty good jazz drummer," and he knew it. "I was quite excellent on the drums even at that age and was something of a child prodigy," Walter says. In fairness, Walter recognized Albert's talent, too: "Albert was so very very good. It was obvious that he was far beyond that group in capacity."

The new outfit used to play at the Rivoli in Crofton Park just outside Catford every Sunday. The lads used to hump all their gear on the train. Roger Collins[19] remembers "we used to get three half-crowns each for the whole evening. We would always talk about whether we'd agree to do it for that amount but we had to pay our train fares home so we did. Before we went onstage we used the men's toilet for tuning the instruments, which was difficult owing to the frequent flushing sounds in the background. We never did see the irony of emerging from the toilet and proceeding to the stage." The Rivoli has not changed down the years, says Terry Stead: "The velvet wallpaper's the same. It's where McCartney filmed that bit where Gilmour plays that solo in *Give My Regards To Broad Street*."

So the band was becoming known but Albert "wasn't the leader," according to John Baines. "It was either Bruce or Johnnie Haylock who took that role. He left other people to make decisions and he just got on with what he wanted to do. Then, as now, he was always very laid-back and quiet. He wasn't there to get the limelight but to play his guitar as only he knew how. He's a musician's musician."

A real musician needs a proper instrument and the lads used to look in the music shops in the West End, and Albert's dog went, too. He had a stud collie named Kim on loan from the Steads, who on occasion were somewhat overrun with show dogs. One Saturday Colin was with Albert when he saw a solid Grazioso guitar in the Jennings store in Charing Cross Road. "It looked just like the guitar on the cover of the *Chirping Crickets* album and if you remember," Albert told *Vintage Guitar* magazine in 1999, "the headstock was cut off in that photo, so you couldn't tell that the tuners were just on one side of it. It had three pickups and a whammy, but the tuners were three-on-a-side. It looked like the guitar that Buddy

At the Rivoli, Crofton Park, 1960: Collin, Albert, Bill and Allan (courtesy the Lee family).

Holly was playing so that was good enough for me—I thought it was so cool. I'd missed seeing Buddy Holly when he toured England in '58 and I'll regret that the rest of my life. The guitar cost £85—an outrageous price but my Dad signed the HP [hire purchase] papers. He never refused me and I always made a point of paying him back. I'd had the Hofner for only a few months but I got £20 for it as part exchange. I thought the Grazioso was a Fender Stratocaster, but I didn't know what one was at the time because you couldn't buy them. I soon realized I didn't have the real thing, but I had an electric guitar, which was exciting because there weren't any American guitars to speak of. You couldn't walk into a British music store and buy a new American guitar at the time, because there were still import restrictions which were lifted in '60 or '61." Terry Stead remembers Albert arriving home: "He played 'Teddy Bears Picnic' and then 'Guitar Boogie Shuffle' in about 40 seconds flat, reading the newspaper out loud at the same time."

As 1959 sweated through a scorching summer when Elvis's "A Fool Such As I" topped the charts for five weeks, *Jukebox Jury* premiered on BBC and Blackheath's own Marty Wilde reached no. 2 in June with the poignant "A Teenager in Love," capturing the painful angst of adolescent romance, Albert's fledgling band, as yet unnamed, started playing small gigs. By then both Albert and Bugs were working, earning all of about £2/18/-a week, so they pooled their resources and bought a Selmer amp with one 12-inch speaker—a Truvoice 19T. Albert was very proud of it: "It was 18 or 19 watts and it had a tremolo on it with a big 12-inch Goodman speaker. It didn't sound too bad really for the time. Though three of us were going into that amp, we were now a electric band."

They played at the Rochester Way Social Club a few times, a local pub, the Dover Patrol and a church youth club in Bellingham, where Harvey Hinsley, later of Hot Chocolate, first saw Albert: "He was in a young band and I remember thinking that the skinny little guy

Buggs Waddell, Tony Walter, Albert and Grandma, approximately 1959 (courtesy the Lee family).

with a shock of black curly hair was pretty good. They were doing Buddy Holly, Gene Vincent—stuff like that." According to the Baines sisters, however, "the first live gig they did was at the Granada, Woolwich, before the film. We went with them sometimes on Saturday mornings—we were 12 or 13, sort of little groupies."

Saturday morning cinema was an important social phenomenon in the 1950s. "A WEA survey of the leisure activities of 3,036 Ilford schoolchildren found that ... the most popular were cinema clubs which put on Saturday morning performances.... Saturday was the best day of the week. No school and Saturday Morning Pictures. Apart from the films, there was other good stuff. Local artists would try to entertain above the din of two hundred screaming children."[20] Kids saw it as their treat of the week. "Ah! Sweet memories! We proudly wore our ABC Minors badges, and sucked on our half-penny, boiled gobstoppers that lasted for the whole performance."[21] Barry Gibb of the Bee Gees reminisces, "We were joking about kids miming to Elvis Presley records with plastic guitars at the local theatre before the matinee started on Saturday morning."[22] Gibb recalls dropping his sister's Christmas present in 1957, the Everlys' "Wake Up, Little Susie," which smashed on the steps of the Manchester Gaumont. "We had to sing for real and it was awful!" At least Albert and the lads played live. The routine was that the Saturday morning kids' film started at 10:00, then at about 11:00 there was an interval, "during which the manager of the cinema encouraged anyone to get up on the stage and perform while the audience tucked in to ice-cream and refreshments."[23]

Johnny Vincent and the Delroys, live at Woolwich Granada, early 1960. Albert is far right, Bugs is on bass (courtesy Johnnie Haylock).

It was not only Saturdays at the Granada—on Sunday evenings the band did 15 minutes before the movie came on, Albert says. "There were a couple of other bands we'd run into on that circuit and they'd make fun of us—'See you at the Palladium' and all that." Such banter went with the territory but Bugs loved it all: "I can't remember whether we got paid but we would have played for nothing because we really thought we were rock 'n' roll stars in bright lights on a huge stage with young girls screaming at us." Both Albert and Bruce were always chatting up the Baines girls, though Carol fancied Bruce. "They played a lot of Buddy Holly and Lonnie Donegan," she remembers. "Albert used to cycle over from Kidbrooke Park with Joyce Campbell on the handlebars. She was always out late and she used to pretend to her mother that she was with us when she wasn't" and although they used to practice in each other's homes, the Baines garden was always a favorite and according to Terry Stead, at one time they would practice in the middle of the heath.

Albert had always been surrounded by women and "it was great growing up with them. I've got two sisters and I just had these little girls running round. I'd go up the road with my mates and they'd come running after me and I'd have to shoo them home. They'd want to go everywhere with me." For a young girl, only six or seven, it was natural to want to be with her big brother. "I had my red Triang three-wheeler tricycle with a little box at the back," Vanessa recalls. "Albert had a drop-handlebar racing bike and whenever I saw them about to go off I'd get my tricycle out. I used to plead with them to let me go, too, but they used to say 'No, you can't come. You won't keep up.' Albert would play tricks on me, too: he would rig up a speaker in the wardrobe at the top of the stairs and he was in his room with a mike. As I walked past this voice said, 'Hallo. Help me. I'm locked in the cupboard.'"

Becky, the younger sister, was good friends later with Jools Holland. "I remember a party over at her place and Jools came in—a teenager—and he played my piano. Mum always used to provide cups of tea. People always used to show up—nowadays you wouldn't dream of just showing up at somebody's house. We'd be having a quiet Sunday and Uncle Tom would knock on the door and he'd come in with his wife and kids and expect tea and sandwiches and cake. We didn't have telephones."

Friends like Mo Clifton would drop in. "About 10 or 20 of us would go round Albert's house. The upstairs was the living room which became the sort of music room. There was the piano, of course, and I remember him picking up a saxophone or it might have been a flute and he just started playing it. Whatever he picked up he could do, musically. I could tell pretty well straightaway that he was gifted. He would just hear something and play it. The guitars they used to borrow—I couldn't hold the bloody strings down. The action on those old guitars was half an inch high and they weren't thin strings. They weren't 9s or 10s—they were 12s, 13s and 14s on the top E and the strength you needed to hold those chords down as you started going up the neck was phenomenal. Those guys who learnt at that time on those guitars—one of the reasons they're so good now is that they gritted their teeth and as soon as that when they got on a Fender or a Gibson, then 'Whoosh!' I'm sure that is one of the reasons that Albert is such a phenomenal speed player today is that it is easy for him after all that apprenticeship. He practiced a lot and we certainly didn't know of any guitar teachers."

Every time Johnnie Haylock went round to Kidbrooke Park Albert would be playing the guitar in his bedroom. He used to drive his mom and dad mad sometimes and "although Dad was very supportive of Albert and his music," says Vanessa, "there were limits to his tolerance. One day Dad was having his tea downstairs and Bugs was playing the drums upstairs. Suddenly the knife and fork went down by the side of his plate and Dad marched upstairs. He said, 'Just go downstairs.' So Bugs reluctantly went down and there was Dad on the drum kit, showing them how loud it was. Once, when Dad told Albert to turn it down a bit, he just carried on, so to get some peace Dad went down and turned the power off in the house! Albert just carried on on the piano!"

In general though his parents were very supportive. "When we got electric instruments they turned their living room in to a music room for me. They moved up to a smaller room so I'd have a room to rehearse in. We put blankets and egg-boxes on the walls as insulation and the neighbors only complained a couple of times."

It was more or less open house, says Johnny. "We'd go there any time and just walk in and start playing. He'd play 'Badpenny Blues' and Jerry Lee Lewis—he'd just rattle it off. There were lots and lots of groups around at that time but he really did stand out." Tony Walter—Lord Anton, as he became known—concurs: "He played wicked piano, too—he was a born genius, that boy. We were listening to some Elvis and Gene Vincent one day and Albert said, 'I don't want to be big-headed but I can play the things those guys are playing—now.' And he could. At 15 he could play all those licks."

Johnnie recalls: "His Mum and Dad were lovely people. They put no pressure on him—

where most of us got kicked out to work at 16 or 17, they just let him get on with what he wanted to do. Mum was quiet and used to do us tea and biscuits." Albert's Dad still had his old Renault station wagon and sometimes the boys would rush in while Dad was having his tea. "Someone's let us down. We need to get to this gig"—and in such emergencies they put a blanket on the top of the shooting brake [the car], on would go Bugs's double bass and off they'd go. Albert had talked him into buying the double bass that summer— still unamplified. "We called the bass 'Elsie' after a girl we knew who was a little overweight." Another fellow, George Reid, became the band's unofficial road manager: he had a "Black Maria," an old Morris police van, which was used for gigs.

Despite driving the Renault, a somewhat exotic vehicle for a general builder's laborer, Dave Lee remained at the heart of a down-to-earth south London family. "When we all used to go from the Dover Patrol up to Canvey Island in a coach for the day," Vanessa remembers, "Dad used to get on the piano in the pub and there'd be a huge sing-song and nobody would leave all afternoon. This was in the days when you normally got chucked out at half past two or three. It was unbelievable." Bugs would see Albert's Dad "on the joanna [piano] doing a couple of numbers in his own inimitable way. He'd play with a darting left-hand and vamp a lot. He'd play either the main chords or melody with his right hand and the equivalent of strumming the chords with his left, keeping the rhythm going. He was bloody good at it as I remember. Even though Albert would say 'I can't play it like he plays it,' he could play a mean boogie and taught me some, but what would take him an hour to work out would take me a week."

At the beginning of August, after six consecutive months with higher than average temperatures, Cliff Richard began a six-week reign at the top with Lionel Bart's exquisite pop ballad "Living Doll." At the end of the month, Paul Addinsell, who ran a portable studio from Pond Road, Blackheath, to record weddings, bar mitzvahs and the like, recorded four tracks in the church hall in Kidbrooke Park Road. On the record label Johnny, Tony, Albert and Bruce, calling themselves Johnny Vincent and the Delroys,[24] cut "Livin' Doll" and "Whole Lotta Shakin' Goin' On." Two of the original 78s still exist. Johnny Haylock admits "we didn't bother to rehearse and it sounds really rough but we thought we were the bees' knees. When we came to record 'Livin' Doll' I said to Albert, 'It's too low. It's in A!' Albert said 'I only know it in E!' so we had to do it in E! I'm also screaming on 'Whole Lotta Shakin' to be heard above Albert who's trying to get as much volume as he can to drown out Tony Walter." At another session, the teenage trio backed vocalist Micky Teely on two self-penned numbers—"Give Me A Chance" and "Rock A Little While." The session was recorded at the Maze Hill Working Men's Club, which Micky's Dad ran: the label shows the pressing as credited to Rocky Ford and the Zodiacs.

Sometime, too, in that blazing summer, John Shakespeare and Ken Hawker had travelled down from Birmingham on the freight train to Denmark Street with their guitars and knocked on publishers' doors. At Noel Gay Music Terry Kennedy said he would "think about it and asked what we were doing that evening. We said, 'We're going to Ken Colyer's Jazz Club.' He came and found us and offered us a deal." Soon John and Ken were busy demoing songs for other writers, doing backing vocals and performing for the BBC (*Easy Beat* and *Saturday Club*) as Carter-Lewis and The Southerners.

Tony by then had landed a job, oddly enough, in Noel Gay Music: "I've always had the gift of the gab and been able to fix things." As Terry Stead put it, "He had plenty of bunny and was always up-front." Lord Anton secured the band an audition with the BBC "and although they didn't have anything for us at the time, Terry Rowe, who was also working at Noel Gay's, was at the audition and was very impressed. He was Terry Dene's guitarist in the Dene-aces, known professionally as Terry Kennedy, and as a result we got some session work for John Carter. They were new and interesting writers so we did a few demo recordings." Albert, Bugs and Tony cut two sides in Berwick Street for Saga Records. The songs— "Can't Forget?" and "Sunset Story"—were written by Hawker and Shakespeare, who also did the vocals. Albert is not certain if the record was ever issued.

Terry Kennedy then got a gig playing for Tommy Steele and Tony Walter "secured an introduction to Mark Foster, who was Larry Parnes' right hand man." Ronnie takes up the story: "Anton, because of his sexuality, got on very well with Larry Parnes who fancied him like mad. One evening when we were niggling him about getting more gigs, he said, 'Why do you think we get all these gigs? It's only because Parnes is trying to sleep with me all the time!' We'd turned professional but all that meant was that we didn't have a job—or any money. Bugs had slung in his apprenticeship as a compositor. I had been an apprentice electrician, Albert was doing various jobs and Tony Walter was at Noel Gay Publishers. We'd been professional for about a month and Tony came to us one day when we were sitting on the Heath and said the only thing that was going was in Saudi or somewhere. I was willing to do anything and said, 'Let's do it! It's rock 'n' roll!' But they wouldn't do this Middle East thing. They were afraid they'd never get back as they had no ideas where they were going."

Just before Christmas, Albert bumped into Ronnie in Kidbrooke Park Road. Albert said, "Ron, we've got to talk. We've been offered this tour—but it's only for a trio. What do we do?" "Just go," replied Ronnie. "Best of luck." He and Johnnie were upset at missing the chance of touring, but Ronnie was not prepared to sling in his job. Tony, well-spoken and an extrovert, had had the chutzpah to march into Larry Parnes' office and say, "We've got a band. We're really good—have you got any work for us?" Albert cannot remember if there was an audition. In any event, the trio were booked for a tour of Scotland, starting in January, with Dickie Pride.

A year after leaving school, barely sixteen years old, Albert was now a professional musician.

Three

Parnes, Shillings and Pence

On Tuesday, January 26, 1960, the Blackheath Three[1] set off from Euston. Before then however there were commitments of a more local nature. One Sunday the band played the Woolwich Granada and Johnnie Haylock recalls, "We got £3/10/- each! That was good money." Then one night at a club in Bellingham, where Harvey Hinsley had seen them, there was a mass brawl and the lads beat a hasty retreat—life in the south London clubs could be rough. Johnny still has his pocket diary, which records that on Saturday, January 23, the band played the Shepherd's Bush Gaumont, and a nostalgic photograph shows the band and friends outside the Gaumont, Holloway.

Elvis was now a GI in Germany, and the initial energy of Jerry Lee Lewis, Gene Vincent and Little Richard was somewhat spent. A report in *Melody Maker* in early January claimed that rock 'n' roll was now respectable: "The wild stuff has given way to beat ballads, and this is what our audiences want to hear."[2] Carlo Little, Screaming Lord Sutch's drummer, has claimed that 1959 "sounded the death knell for the golden age of rock 'n' roll." Nevertheless, in Britain Cliff Richard and the Shadows were the new rock sensations and Albert talked Bugs into going electric: "He traded Elsie in for a Hofner violin bass. We weren't very good. Three of us were going into the Selmer Truvoice 19T amp with one 12-inch speaker, which probably sounded pretty grim as nothing was miked up, but we were only young lads and so excited it didn't seem to matter. We were professional musicians and we were on the road," steaming north through Birmingham and Crewe bound for a musical outpost on the shore of the Solway Firth.

Maryport on the Cumbrian coast seems an unlikely setting for the start of anyone's career, but in those days, the Palace Ballroom was a premier venue for touring rock stars and at the end of January 1960, Albert Lee made his first professional stage appearance, backing Dickie Pride, who topped the bill. Pride (né Richard Knellar) was a dynamic performer but made very few records and was part of Larry Parnes' stable of stars that included Billy Fury and Marty Wilde. Parnes, the first true pop impresario, gave his singers names which they found hard to live up to. Billy Fury was seldom furious; Dickie Pride was charmingly modest; and Marty Wilde did his menacing best but was hampered by a hairpiece (he went bald agonizingly early) and a kind-hearted nature. Parnes also managed a number of other young hopefuls with varying degrees of success. These included Duffy Power (Ray Howard), Johnny Gentle (John Askew), Sally Kelly, Terry Dene and Georgie Fame (Clive Powell). The press gave him the nickname "Mr. Parnes, Shillings and Pence"—but he missed

Outside the Holloway Gaumont, late 1959. From left, Ronnie Bell, Albert, Roger Collins, Lord Anton, Bugs Waddell, Johnnie Haylock, unknown, and Mike McQueen (courtesy Johnnie Haylock).

two opportunities to manage the Beatles. (At a time when they were called the Silver Beetles, he used them to back his singer Johnny Gentle later in 1960 and was also given the opportunity to sign them up as their sole promoter in 1962 but declined.)

Although he let the world's greatest band slip through his fingers, Parnes knew how to run a tour, as Lance Fortune remembers: "If you were doing one of Larry Parnes' package shows ... Joe Brown would probably be on the show and definitely Dickie Pride—he seemed to be on everything and he had a fantastic act. They were great shows: the girls would scream from the word 'go.'"[3] The tours were organized like a military campaign, though there was no vast stage crew. Parnes "used a coach for the artists who didn't want to travel under their own steam and another for the equipment, which was not a lot by today's standards." There can be no doubt that Parnes worked the young bands hard but there were few 20,000-seat arenas so the bands had to work six or seven days a week, for five or six weeks, often with two shows each evening. With no national pop radio network, it was the surest way to maximize exposure.

All the musicians who did the Scottish tour stayed in Broughton Place, an elegant Georgian Terrace in the heart of New Town, Edinburgh. Albert was paid £20 for 12 days but "we had to pay our own hotel bills out of that," he recalls, "so I came back with about £10." (This was par for the course, according to Jet Harris: "In 1959 Larry Parnes stopped me in Old Compton Street and asked me to back a new boy who was going to be big. I said, 'What's the wages?' and he said '£11/10/- a week' and I said 'You must be joking.' I would have had to pay for my digs out of that.") Duncan McKennan was the master of ceremonies and tour manager. "An amazing man," according to Tony Walter. "Absolutely legless when he went on stage every night and presented the bands saying, 'You bunch of heathen bastards, calm down now. I'm bringing you some beautiful music and you're going to appreciate it.' Dickie Pride had a broken ankle and on one or two occasions got booed as the Scots got a bit rough—so he used to swing his crutches at them."

Those twelve days were Albert's first taste of the road but he soon had to rejoin the real world. "I went back to work for a company called National Enamels down in Greenwich. I was spraying Ascot water heaters. I was pretty good at it: we had masks and you had to be artistic to get it right. You'd spray it evenly, it would dry off and then you'd run it into this furnace, which was at about 500 degrees. When we opened it twenty minutes later it was amazing—they'd come out coated in baked enamel. I left there to go on the road again." He did another Scottish tour, this time with Sally Kelly, who in 1958 had recorded "Little Cutie" for Decca, after which he "jacked it in. I didn't want to go back to Scotland again. I don't know why. I think my Dad may have persuaded me to go and get another proper job because what I was doing at that time was a bit hit and miss. Even so, I still saved enough money to put a deposit on an amp when I got back! They'd just started to import American equipment and the whole world opened up to us then. Selmer's in the West End stocked a tremendous range of Gibsons, and that's where I bought my first amp. They didn't even have them in the store. I just pointed at this catalogue and said, 'I want that one' and put a deposit on a Supro with a 15-inch Jensen. It turned out to be a really great amp. At that time, *everybody* had to have a tape echo unit. There were a number of units around, and I had a KlemptEcholette, which was German."

The three lads returned from Scotland with Dickie Pride on Monday, February 8. Two days later Johnnie turned up at Kidbrooke Park Road with Roger Collins and Colin Stead, announcing that plans were afoot for a party from Bron's to see Gene Vincent and Eddie Cochran that Saturday at the Woolwich Granada. While Albert was in Scotland, Cochran and Gene Vincent had opened a 10-week Larry Parnes tour in Ipswich, backed by Billy Fury, Joe Brown and Georgie Fame. Soon after the gig, the legendary rocker's path crossed with the young guitarist from Blackheath. The lads had left their old Selmer Truevoice in Larry Parnes' office and apparently Eddie had taken it back to his hotel for some reason. Although Cochran was only 21 himself, to Albert, Bugs and Tony he was everything they aspired to be—supremely gifted, the object of massive adulation, a huge star, and if possible, American. So with some trepidation they went to the hotel to pick up the amp and the rock legend "was real nice. We were dying to talk to him but we just had a quick discussion on those English amps and how bad they were and he said, 'Oh yeah, no sound, man, no sound.'"

Cochran, arguably the foremost exponent of teenage rockabilly, was touring a Britain where change was affecting the music establishment. In the middle of March, EMI issued its last 78, Russ Conway's "Rule Britannia" and "Royal Event," and *Melody Maker* stoutly maintained that rock music had to be kept under control, otherwise members of youth clubs would want just to jive and play. They found in talking to British young people that music was far more important to them than to adults. In the words of a fifteen-year-old boy, "In our crowd you have to like rock or you're dead.'"[4] His words were sadly prophetic, for at 4:10 P.M. on Easter Sunday, April 17, near Chippenham in Wiltshire, traveling from Bristol to Heathrow at the end of their U.K. tour to catch a night flight back to America, Eddie

Cochran was killed and Gene Vincent injured when their car skidded into a lamppost. Cochran's death robbed the music world of an important guitar stylist and a wonderful rock songwriter, whose potential was sadly unfulfilled. Vincent, his left leg already shattered by a motorcycle accident in 1955, broke his collarbone and, psychologically affected by the loss of his closest professional friend, was never quite the same performer again.

Albert thinks he had more Gene Vincent records than anything else at the time. Cliff Gallup did two albums with Gene Vincent, to be succeeded by Johnny Meeks. "I liked Johnny a lot, but not as much as I liked Cliff. It was Cliff who hooked me, and I really worked at copying his solos, which had kind of a swing feel; they were different from what someone like Chuck Berry was doing."[5] Equally important was a record which "totally blew me away—still does to this day: *Johnny Burnette and the Rock 'n' Roll Trio*. I could put that record on now and get really enthusiastic over it and play along with it. There's just so much energy and a real rawness about the guitar. 'Honey Hush' has a great solo, and 'Lonesome Train,' where he[6] does pull-offs on the first and second strings. I've got about four copies of that album—reissues from various countries—because I'm in danger of wearing my original one out."

Albert was also becoming interested in country music, buying a series of RCA EPs called "Country Guitar." "There'd be a track with Chet Atkins on it, ones with Don Gibson and Hank Snow. It was like a mini-introduction to country music. I bought four or five of them, but I wasn't playing that style of music." He also bought a Capitol album, *Country's Best*; his favourite track at the time was "I Don't Believe You've Met My Baby" by the Louvin Brothers. Another major influence continued to be Lonnie Donegan, whose live version of "My Old Man's A Dustman," with advance orders of 250,000 in April, was the first single by a British act to go straight to number 1 in the British charts.

After the excitement of Scottish tours and the meeting with Cochran, Albert got a job in a rag factory in Hither Green, cleaning industrial engineering rags. "The laundry—yes, I did that for a week and it was horrendous. I was outside in the freezing cold envying Bugs who worked in the warm drying unit. It was really dusty, not very good for your chest. Trucks used to come in with bales of rags all bound together with wire, which you'd have to cut, then pull the rags off and throw them into this big boiler. I probably got about £4 a week for that. After work I'd to take my guitar up to London." Colin Stead recalls: "He'd often put cardboard in his shoes when they had holes in them."

Around April 1960 the Cruisers changed their lineup yet again. Johnnie Haylock, Albert and Bugs were joined by Ronnie Bell on rhythm guitar and Tony Middleton on drums: this band was together for some months. Then in the summer Lord Anton re-emerged with an offer for Albert and Bugs to join him a couple of nights a week in the Melody Bar in Lee Green, which had a basement club only large enough for a trio! For a time the Cruisers stayed as a five-piece doing gigs and the trio played the Melody Bar twice a week. They soon became very popular, as Malcolm Hutton recalls: "When I was 11 or 12 they wouldn't let me in to see Albert. All I could do was stand outside and listen. I'd just started playing guitar and I heard about this guy [Albert] playing my cousin Trevor Brown's Stratocaster. Trevor was the only bloke in the area who had one and he'd told me about this fantastic guy playing all these Scotty Moore things. The Browns were quite well off and Albert used to go round there in Southbrook Road and play it as he couldn't afford one himself."

Then Buzz, who owned the Melody, asked the trio to play six days a week. This was a permanent gig, which suited Albert: "I'd been through various jobs and I still hankered after being able to earn enough playing in a group. We used to play in there every night and the guy used to give us a pound each a night. At that time I was only earning about £3 a week. Under the age of 18 you were paid peanuts, so getting a pound a night for playing the guitar was fantastic." Albert, Bugs and Lord Anton could quit the day jobs but the Melody Bar gig lasted until problems with fire doors caused the place to fold.

A friend of Albert's, Dave Trevelyan, who sometimes sat in with the trio in Lee Green, had expressed a desire to buy a guitar. Nicknamed Buddy, because he had glasses, he was planning to buy a Burns but Albert persuaded him to buy an American guitar. "So we went uptown and Buddy bought this Les Paul Junior. When I plugged it into my Echolette tape-echo with the Supro amp I'd bought after the Scottish tour I was able to recapture the sound of the Scotty Moore solos and Cliff Gallup. They were my heroes"—and immediately Albert decided that he had to have an American guitar. Fortunately for him, Fenders had started arriving and when in August The Shadows' "Apache" reached number 1 every young lad wanted a Stratocaster. Two other classic hits of that otherwise damp summer were the Everly Brothers' all-time biggest seller, "Cathy's Clown," which stayed at the top for eight weeks, and Johnny Kidd and the Pirates' spine-chilling smash, "Shakin' All Over," written in six minutes in the basement of Chas McDevitt's Freight Train club.

Albert used to go up to Selmer's every Saturday. In 1960 there were three great music stores in Charing Cross Road and Albert, Bugs, Colin, and Ronnie "used to ogle the guitars and think 'Which one could I afford the payments on?' Albert decided he had to have a Gibson and was just about to buy an ES-175: "I was going to have a Bigsby on it." One Saturday, like any other Saturday that winter, he was in Selmers playing the Gibsons.

Unknown to him, someone was listening.

"Do you want to join a band?"

"Well, I'm not really doing anything."

"You won't need a guitar. We've got one already. Come over to my house."

It was Bob Xavier, who ran a band called the Jury. Xavier was a black saxophone player from St. Lucia, and modelled his band on Emile Ford and the Checkmates. While most of the other groups around London were still wedded to rock 'n' roll, Xavier played the Drifters and Brook Benton repertoire.

"When we got to his place he opened up this guitar case and there was a brand new 1960 Gibson Les Paul Custom[7] with three gold pickups and a Bigsby [vibrate]. I said, 'Sure, I'll join your band!'" Albert still chuckles at the memory: "I couldn't believe that he let me take this guitar home that night with a promise that I'd be at this rehearsal next day. He didn't know who I was or where I lived. I showed up the next morning and met up with Pat Donaldson[8] outside a cinema in Charing Cross Road. He became a lifelong friend. He had a Gibson bass and from that moment on we really hit it off."

So, in March 1961, Albert joined Bob Xavier and for the rest of the year wore a variety of open-necked silky shirts and worked American airbases and London clubs. Ray Smith[9] recalls seeing Albert that month at the Putney Ballroom, where according to him, "Albert didn't have much to do. They did a sort of ska-flavored 'Wooden Heart,' Elvis' hit of the month." Albert was also busy doing sessions for John Carter, who was gaining a reputation as a writer and producer and a member of Carter-Lewis and the Southerners, regulars on BBC's *Saturday Club*. Carter reckons the sessions must have taken place early in 1961: "Three tracks were recorded at Joe Meek's studio in Holloway Road with our manager Terry Kennedy[10] producing [so Joe only engineered these sessions]." The lineup at the sessions was Albert on acoustic guitar, Geoff Goddard, Bobby Graham and Chas Hodges (subsequently a member of Heads, Hands and Feet and of course Chas and Dave).

While Albert was plying his trade as a session man in London and working occasionally with the Jury out of town, much was happening in the wider world of popular music. In April, nineteen-year-old Bob Dylan started a two-week residency at Gerde's Folk City in Greenwich Village, and a week later pianist Floyd Cramer's "On the Rebound" reached number 1 in Britain. Fundamentally a Nashville session man, Cramer had evolved a spare yet ornate style whose central motif was a characteristic right-hand "slip-note" technique. His two great hits, "Last Date" and "On The Rebound," continued as features of Albert's shows in the competent hands of keyboard maestro Pete Wingfield, until he left the band in the summer of 2006. In May Billy Fury, for many fans the greatest British rock star, had his most evocative and enduring hit, when "Halfway to Paradise" reached number 3. Then Del Shannon attained number 1 in July with "Runaway." With its galloping beat, Max Crook's proto-synthesizer Musitron solo, and Shannon's faltering falsetto, this truly original record has matured into a '60s pop classic.

Then, to darken the scene, England lost the Ashes cricket series at Old Trafford when it seemed easier to win; then in August the Berlin Wall went up and the Cold War became a physical reality. On the other hand, walls came down in London when in November, new regulations allowed clubs in London offering music and dance to serve alcohol until 3 A.M. seven nights per week. This opened the door for such legendary venues as the Flamingo in Wardour Street to expand operations and to launch the all-nighters, which became in the mid-sixties the breeding-ground for so many British rock, soul and blues giants. One of the best-known venues for British R&B and soul music outside London was the California Ballroom in Dunstable, which in December featured Bob Xavier and the Jury, with Jackie Lynton and Dean Brenland and the original Strollers.

The Jury was a sort of a workers' cooperative band: "we never got paid. The few gigs that we did were paying the HP installments on the van, the PA, the guitars, etc. That went on for four or five months, until my dad said it didn't sound like a very good idea, so I took over the payments on the guitar and ended up owning it, which was great, because at that time I couldn't have afforded to buy one new. The ES-175 would have cost me about £140, but a new Les Paul Custom with a Bigsby was over £200, so it would have been out of my price range."[11]

Barrie Jenkins, a friend from Charlton and later a colleague in Germany, recalls those days: "I remember Albert with his Les Paul Custom, getting the train up to town, saying he had to do a session and working with the Jury at the Two I's." The Jury, formerly the backing band for Jimmy Justice,[12] were based in London's West End and often played in the Two I's, as Bob Xavier had a connection with Tom Littlewood, who ran the little coffee bar in Old Compton Street. For Albert, the dingy basement became a focus where he met a wide range of interesting players. "It was a good step forward for me, because loads of people would get up on stage and play. There was Big Jim Sullivan, then the only real British rock 'n' roll guitarist, and I met Jimmy Page, who was playing with Neil Christian at the time. We became good friends: he was listening to James Burton, Scotty Moore, and Cliff Gallup, as I was. We'd go to each other's houses and listen to records and marvel at all these great solos. He really liked the sound I was getting so he bought the same rig. I believe he used that Supro on some of the early Led Zeppelin records." Later that summer, Tom Cleghorn, a singer and a friend of Albert's from Blackheath, booked three hours for £12 at Regent Sound in Denmark Street, where the Stones' early records were cut. Albert recalls cutting "about ten songs. I had my Les Paul Custom, Buddy Trevelyan was playing his Les Paul Junior, Roy Mills played drums and Pat Donaldson was on bass. There were three acetates—Tom had one, I had one which I've since lost and Jimmy Page wanted one because he really liked the way I played."

The way he played had a new influence: "I stumbled across Jimmy Bryant and Speedy West, the great steel guitarist. I heard a track called 'Arkansas Traveler' on *Saturday Club* and I thought, 'God, this guy is absolutely the best!' It wasn't until '68 or '69 that I eventually tracked down the album: a 10-inch version of 'Two Guitars, Country Style' on Capitol T-520—I'll never forget it. Jimmy Bryant and Cliff Gallup's playing were closely related. It's not what the jazzers would call bebop though Gene Vincent called it bop; I suppose it was just swing guitar. I was never really dedicated enough to sit down and figure everything out note-for-note, except for Cliff Gallup, whose solos are still logged in the back of the brain. I never figured out the Jimmy Bryant solos. I just kind of took it all in by osmosis—

James Burton, Albert and Jimmy Bryant at the Palamino Club, North Hollywood, ca. 1975 (courtesy Keith Nelson).

just the general feel of it, his approach. I recently found another great album by him called *Country Cabin Jazz*, which has a lot of swing tunes."

Chet Atkins remained a hero although his albums were unavailable in Britain, which was frustrating. The first to be released "was probably *Teensville*, a pop record, and then one that was all gut-string flamenco, which was ... nice but we didn't have all those breakdowns— the essential stuff he was famous for. The album that really knocked me out was *Mister Guitar*. I tried to figure out Chet's style, and persevered with a thumbpick, but I didn't get very far." To Albert, using a thumbpick seemed incompatible with other styles which he wanted to play, as it lacked freedom and the opportunity for self-expression. He evolved therefore a way of playing with a flatpick and fingers together. There were players around London who could emulate Atkins but to him they seemed stuck in a groove, unable to adapt or to play along with anybody. They played only what they had absorbed from Atkins's records— mistakes and all.

There were newer influences around as well: Albert bought a few Duane Eddy records, which he still has: *Especially For You*, with "Peter Gunn," was one of his favorites. "I loved the sound of it. They just got such great sounds on records back then, and they don't seem to get them now—and they certainly weren't getting those sounds in England in the early '60s. I also liked the Everly Brothers' singing, but I was very much influenced by Don Everly's rhythm playing. He's very much neglected as a guitar player."

Chet Atkins and Albert backstage at the Ryman Auditorium, Nashville, 1998 (courtesy the Lee family).

The gigs with Bob Xavier and the Jury were intermittent and as Albert was not getting paid, for a while early in 1962 he returned to National Enamels, leaving once the gigs picked up. John Stead, Colin's uncle and one of his workmates there, was a music fan and had a tape-recorder. He also had a daughter, Yvonne, who went to school at Bluecoats.[13] One day one of Yvonne's school friends had dropped round for tea when Albert turned up after work and sat quietly, playing his Les Paul. Albert had taken a job for a week at Monk and Glass's custard factory in Tunnel Avenue slicing open hundredweight sacks of corn flour "and I left work completely white." The friend was Lucille [Lucy] McKenzie, according to Max, "an exquisitely beautiful Anglo-Indian." Lucy remembers "the first time I saw Albert he was covered in custard powder. It wasn't at all show biz."

Lucy, only sixteen, worked in London as a copy typist and before she met Albert used to go to the Flamingo to listen to modern jazz. She knew nothing about guitars but after meeting Albert took herself off down Charing Cross Road, not far from her job in Drury Lane, and studied all the instruments. After only a few weeks she was madly in love: "Albert was very gentle and totally different to the guys I'd met before. His parents were wonderful." However Lucy's mother was horrified, not only that she had taken up with a musician, but that "he'd got a Cockney accent." On one occasion Lucy, naturally curious to see where her new boyfriend worked, ventured to the Two I's on a Friday night, a real adventure for a sixteen-year-old girl. She had to ask a policeman where it was. "He said, 'You don't want to go there, love,' and then walked me to the Two I's from Charing Cross Road. Bob Xavier and the Jury, with Albert, of course, were playing but it wasn't my scene."

Still needing to earn some money between the sessions and the Two I's, Albert landed a job via the Youth Employment Office which turned out to be perfect as it was in a small wholesalers of hairdressers' supplies in Denmark Street, Soho. "I had to fill up cardboard boxes with combs, shampoos and razors for the salesmen." That job was a bonus for Lucy, as Albert supplied her with all the hair care products she needed. Then in the evening he would play at the Two I's or at the weekend "we'd drive up to Oxford for a gig." It was a bustling, frenetic time in the burgeoning London music scene: "by the early 60s, the city positively overflowed with out-of-nowhere high energy."[14] Lucy recalls the hopeful extrovert Smoky Dean[15] "buttonholing us on the corner of Berwick Market nearly every day." He must have cut a striking if bizarre figure: Albert recalls "a good-looking guy with blond hair and a slight lisp, saying, 'I've written a song' and then performing it in the middle of the street." Ray Smith remembers Albert packing supplies for the hairdressing company just around the corner from Selmer's: "He'd pop in and try out the latest guitars. Tommy Cleghorn came in one day and said he had recorded an album with Albert. I thought I was a pretty good guitar player but when I heard Albert on Tommy's record I was blown away."

In those days Selmer's was a mecca for all the session musicians. In addition to the famous Charing Cross Road premises, Selmer's also owned the Lew Davis shop near the corner of Denmark Street, purely for retailing guitars. Colin Falconer, who worked there with Ray, recalls that "it was staffed by Geoff Livingstone, myself, and Ray Smith, who was the funniest guy you could ever meet. He had us in stitches doing one-man impressions of whole movies. He was also a pretty good guitarist and prolific music writer—he formed a small music publishing business called Jaymarnie Music with a friend called Tony Colton,[16] whose claim to fame was he could chat up women like no one else. He even tried chatting up Princess Margaret at a party on one occasion! It was a great bludge.[17] Most days we'd be jamming with people like John McLaughlin, Jimmy Page, Big Jim Sullivan, Albert Lee, Eric Clapton, Jeff Beck, Steve Howe. It really was the 'in' shop for guitarists."

Albert was now becoming known both as a session player and for his work with Jackie Lynton. The Jury was doing more gigs, playing at the Two I's almost every night. He stuck with the hairdresser suppliers for a few weeks but in the end he gave up the day job. He had begun to do what he had always wanted and no longer felt like getting up early to do a mundane job all day and then play in the evening. "It was great—we just spent time around the West End, hanging out round Soho, running into different musicians and doing the odd gigs and sessions." Living where he did he escaped many of the pitfalls for the young and unwary in the capital. "Trying to make it as a rock musician was a very haphazard business in the early sixties—and it was pretty dangerous too ... you could get caught up in all manner of things, living in dodgy old flats with a bunch of other guys.[18] I was really lucky— I had a 20-minute tube journey back down to Blackheath. I often wonder if I'd ever have become a professional musician if I'd been living somewhere like Cornwall, because I wasn't the sort to move into some sleazy digs and endure all that stuff. I had a stable home life yet I was just able to jump on a train and be right in the thick of it." Also in the thick of it at that time were four lads from Merseyside, for on June 6, 1962, at the EMI Studios in Abbey Road, the Beatles auditioned for George Martin. He had thought their demos were "pretty awful," but when "I met them I liked them"[19]—especially after they had performed three original songs.

That same month Bob Xavier[20] left and the Jury became the house band at the Two I's coffee bar. The trio—Albert, Pat Donaldson and Roy Mills—were paid £1 a night each, less Tom Littlewood's ten percent commission, "so you'd get 18 shillings and you could probably get a glass of Coca-Cola." Littlewood, a Runyonesque entrepreneur, ran a small agency out of the place, where the larger-than-life Jackie Lynton, a rocker from Shepperton, sang Elvis covers with a band called the Teenbeats. Lynton had had a bad car accident, and Keith Kelly, another Teenbeat, was on crutches, so Tom asked the Jury to back Jackie on a few gigs, which Albert still remembers. "Jackie's quite a character—a wild one. Great performer and probably still is. He used to be quite foul on stage. Lucy and my father went to see him play, without me, and they were pretty disgusted with some of the language but musically he was great. He was a huge Elvis fan. I was in Memphis with Emmylou Harris the day Elvis died. I bought up several newspapers that morning and sent one to Jackie."

Apart from his penchant for Presley, Lynton had a bent for customised oldies and in August released a truly outstanding single, "All of Me."[21] It was a landmark in that it represented Albert's commercial recording debut. The single was well reviewed, achieved considerable radio airplay that summer and autumn, sold steadily and although it missed the charts it made people sit up and take notice—including Lynton, who thought Albert was "a great bloke, fantastic guitarist ... even back then no one could touch him except perhaps Big Jim Sullivan."

By the late summer Albert was a full-time working musician, playing in the coffee bar five or six nights a week and backing whoever wandered onto the stage. At weekends the Jury would go out of town doing one-nighters backing Vince Eager, Keith Kelly and Jackie Lynton.

The Two I's, at 59 Old Compton Street, had become the nerve center of Albert's work‐ing life. Now a branch of the bistro chain Dome, it was opened in 1956, deriving its name from its two original owners, the Irani brothers, who went on to own the Tropicana Club, which in turn became the famous Establishment Club.[22]

The coffee bar as a cultural phenomenon was full of significance and symbolism in postwar Britain. By 1957, there were a thousand of them throughout Britain, with two new ones opening in London every week. The 1950s espresso bar was seen as a foreign invasion, a mix of American kitsch and Continental pretension, while the ubiquitous jukebox was thought to encourage delinquency and moral decay. The cappuccino expressed in shorthand the older generation's confusion. "Once our beer was frothy but now it's frothy coffee," sang Max Bygraves on his 1960 hit "Fings Ain't What They Used T' Be." Despite the suspicion of the older generation, coffee bars became the haunts of the young, and in 2005, the *New Statesman* summed up their contribution to the social and urban fabric:

"Unlike today's coffee chains, however, the 1950s espresso bars filled a cultural void. An early chronicler of the café society, Tosco Fyvel, wrote about the 'pall of boredom,' the 'dead and shuttered look' that descended on the average English town after dark. For an emerging teenage culture starved of other entertainments, the coffee bar was convivial and classless, bringing together Teddy boys, beatniks, mods, and a growing clientele of art-col‐lege and university students." [23]

The Two I's was no exception, its patrons the general flotsam and jetsam of Soho's demi‐monde—rock 'n' roll hopefuls, jazz buffs, students, poets, agents and characters of dubious employ. Rock's history in London was one of the most vibrant in the world, with some of its most colorful performers, like Screaming Lord Sutch, who saw the Two I's as Britain's first real rock 'n' roll venue. "It was electric to play there: at the most, you could only get in 150 people but there was a tremendous atmosphere."[24] Dave Sampson, who sang there with the Hunters, recalls that "the Two I's had steaming walls and people used to pass out down there."[25] Perhaps its most illustrious graduate was Cliff Richard, who points out "Tommy Steele and Terry Dene had been discovered at the Two I's so I thought, 'I'll go down there'.... It was jam-packed. If you wanted a Coke, it had to be passed over people's heads. It was hot, sweaty and very exciting. It was the birth of European rock 'n' roll."[26]

Yet the Two I's was just a coffee bar, with room for about 20 people to stand comfort‐ably. From the main coffee bar area some narrow stairs led to a gloomy basement about the size of a large bedroom, lit by a couple of weak bulbs. At one end were a few milk crates with planks on top of them, which passed for the stage. There may even have been some sort of microphone system, left over from the Boer War. The nearest toilets were probably at Piccadilly Circus Station. A door at the back led to the kitchen, which was also Tom Lit‐tlewood's office. Tom was a "Mad Frankie" Fraser type, with a slight Northern accent, unin‐terested in rock 'n' roll, except for the amount of extra cash he could wring out of it. He had even appeared in the film *The Tommy Steele Story* as the judo instructor he really was.

What made it so special? What was so different about this sweaty cellar where for a year or more Albert had spent much of his working life? How did this poky basement which sold nothing stronger than Coke and coffee become the mecca of British rock 'n' roll? Sim‐ply perhaps that it had launched the careers of two of the biggest British stars of the time, Terry Dene and Tommy Steele. After all, Tom Littlewood had once let Thomas Hicks[27] sing there, and Anglo-Amalgamated made much of the place in the 1957 *Tommy Steele Story*. Then in April 1958 Cliff Richard and the Drifters played there before they were anybody. "Only Tom Littlewood could have thought of putting on 'entertainment' in that basement, and charging people to go In. Free enterprise works!" [28]

In September, the Jury folded and for a while Albert once again spent his time around the West End running into different musicians and doing the odd gig. One day he was sitting in a recording studio while Joe Meek was producing Screaming Lord Sutch. Joe needed someone to provide a high-pitched backing vocal, so Albert was paid £5 and can just be heard on the Decca single "Jack The Ripper." Then Albert was involved in the Dean Shannon cover of Warren Smith's "Ubangi Stomp." Shannon used to sit in at the Two I's and would peddle his songs in Berwick Street Market. One morning, Albert was having a coffee when "Dean came in and said he'd got a deal with EMI. So, after doing a demo at Regent Sound in Denmark Street, we went into the EMI studio at Abbey Road and cut it with Pat Donaldson on bass and Roger Cable on drums. I played piano and Chris Farlowe's old guitarist Bobby Taylor played guitar. I think John Puddy of the Flintstones played baritone sax."

Over the previous couple of years it had become de rigeur for any self-respecting British beat group to have paid its dues in the bars and clubs of Germany, especially Hamburg. The trail had been blazed by bands like Tony Sheridan and the Jets, Derry and the Seniors, Rory Storm and the Hurricanes and of course the Beatles. John Puddy had arranged a few gigs in Germany so in the Gardenia, an all-night club in an alley off Wardour Street, he and Albert put together a band called the Nightsounds. "Cass from Cass and the Casanovas was the vocalist—he was one of the first Liverpool singers to come down to London. His real name was Brian Casser, who had worked with a variety of Liverpool groups and ran Casey Jones and the Engineers." At that time, the metropolitan bias was beginning to break down and if musicians could claim genuine Merseyside ancestry, the London scene would at least take them seriously. Albert recruited Pat Donaldson on bass but the band needed a drummer. "I couldn't find anybody else so we gave Tony Middleton another chance. He was OK but it didn't seem like he was really into it at the time. Ricky Barnes, the tenor sax player whom I'd met in Scotland, ended up in London and he came to Hamburg with us."

Thus it was in October 1962, against the somber background of international crisis, with Kennedy and Kruschev in a potentially lethal face-off in Cuba, "we went to Hamburg for three weeks playing the Top Ten Club. It was my first trip abroad."

Four

Learning the Game

In late October 1962, the Nightsounds arrived in Hamburg. This ancient trading city at the mouth of the Elbe, Germany's major seaport, was enjoying the commercial prosperity of the country's postwar economic miracle. Musically, however, it was a much less exciting, vibrant city than Liverpool, where thousands of youngsters were pouring into venues to listen to hundreds of bands. Rock 'n' roll hardly existed in Germany at the time: the Hamburg scene comprised only two major clubs, within walking distance of each other, the Star Club and the Top Ten. The Kaiserkeller, where the Beatles took up residency in 1960, had closed the year before. The Beatles, along with other British bands, largely but not exclusively from Liverpool, were spearheading a major boom in rock music in a city which till then had been at the heart of German jazz. That era was on it last legs, but it would have been prohibitive for German promoters to bring American stars across the Atlantic to play in an uncertain market. Just across the North Sea, however, English bands were copying the Americans reasonably well. Dave Dee explains: "There were very, very few places for young bands to play in Britain. So it was easy to bring them in for twenty quid a week and work them to death."[1] It was an apt coincidence that Albert's arrival in Germany coincided with the arrival of the Beatles in the British charts, with their insistent, harmonica-based plea, "Love Me Do." Suddenly all things seemed possible: somehow British pop music would never be quite the same again.

Just before he left for Hamburg, Albert was playing in a club when two Americans in the audience came up to him during the break. They told him they had enjoyed the set and that they were in the Everly Brothers' band. Albert fell out of the clouds, as of course he had been for years a huge Everly Brothers fan. One of the two American musicians was guitarist Don Peak, who told Albert about B.B. King and Howard Roberts. "I'd never heard all this vibrato stuff that B.B. was doing. There was one Howard Roberts album in particular called 'Color Him Funky.' I suppose I was influenced by that from a jazz point of view. I've never really been a jazz player, but I did like to listen to those records. Les Paul, of course, was a big influence, but there was only one record that you could find in England then, *Hits By Les And Mary*."

Albert then met Phil himself, who was having a hard time of it. The Everlys' tour had opened in East Ham with Phil doing the show alone. Don had collapsed on stage in rehearsal at the Prince of Wales Theatre and was suffering from a nervous breakdown. With guitarist Joey Page on harmony vocals, Phil continued the tour solo, to a warm and sympathetic response: as Albert says, "The Everlys were so big at the time and everybody wanted Phil to do well and that probably made it easier for him."[2]

Albert was not to know at the time that the chance meeting with Don Peak was the start of a personal and professional association with the Everly Brothers which was to stretch over twenty-five years. The Everly Brothers brought into rock 'n' roll a tradition of close harmony singing which stretched back through Appalachian country duos like the Louvin Brothers to centuries of Scottish and Irish folk music. It was essentially from this that their sharply observed—though sometimes mawkish—vignettes of girl or parent trouble gained their emotional intensity. "Bye Bye Love," their first British hit, had been written by Felice and Boudleaux Bryant, a middle-aged husband and wife songwriting team who had an uncanny ability to catch the angst and self-absorption of the average teen. The Everlys retained their achingly pure harmonies, but backed them with robust acoustic guitars and a rock 'n' roll beat, recording it at RCA's renowned Studio B in Nashville, with their musical mentor, Chet Atkins, producing. More than any other major rock 'n' roll act, the Everly Brothers were responsible for taking country songs into the pop charts.

The Top Ten Club at 136 Reeperbahn was a rectangular space which once housed a subterranean circus, with the bandstand in the middle of one of the long sides. The Beatles played there between April and July 1961 and lived upstairs. The Star Club was Hamburg's most famous venue, but the Top Ten was where The Beatles really found their feet. In this Reeperbahn basement, they became the backing band for the English singer Tony Sheridan, with whom they cut their first record at the Friedrich Ebert Halle, over the river in Harburg, Hamburg's Birkenhead. Today, the Top Ten is a disco, but in Hamburg the Beatles legend lives on.

The Nightsounds played at the Top Ten Club for nearly three weeks. For Albert, still only 18, traveling to Germany and playing at this legendary venue was exciting. "You'd stay in digs, where the bands always stayed, above a club with maybe three or four in a room." In those days, every musician had to pay his dues in Hamburg—nightly, dusk to dawn. In this cavernous basement in Hamburg's red-light district, Albert began to learn his trade. "It was great experience, playing six hours a night, seven days a week—slave labor really, making us play all those hours, but we really got our chops[3] together. It's very sad that those opportunities aren't there any more." Working through the long nights, the band honed their act in arduous sets in front of raucous, demanding audiences, providing an invaluable musical education for the adventurous lads.

Pete Best, the Beatles' original drummer, in an interview with triumphpc.com/merseybeat, recalls, "While most gigs lasted an hour or two a night, the Hamburg clubs wanted us to play from early evening until the bars closed in the wee hours of the morning. It was something we weren't expecting until we went out there, but you didn't complain. We just loved playing and working those long hours consistently made the band so tight and so prolific. It was like practicing every night for three months solid." Horst Fascher, the founder and co-manager of Hamburg's famous Star Club, told the same website that the Beatles and many other British and U.S. bands who came to Hamburg learned from each other. "The bands would sit together in the mornings, exchange tips, show each other different chords. It was a melting pot and everyone got something out of it. In the whole world, there wasn't anything like it before and there hasn't been anything like it since."

Germany with the Nightsounds had been a steep learning curve for Albert but "it was too crazy and we came back." Albert's return from Hamburg only just preceded the arrival on the big-time music scene of a later luminous colleague of his. In early December, former RAF Aircraftman First Class William Perks auditioned for the Rolling Stones at the Wetherby Arms in Chelsea and made his debut on electric bass at the Ricky Tick in Windsor the following week.[4]

It was a harsh winter, with an average temperature of only about 35 degrees Fahrenheit, the coldest since 1795. Economic activity dropped by about 7 percent and unemployment increased with 160,000 workers being laid off. At least 49 people were killed by the direct effects of the severe weather. On his first visit to London, Bob Dylan stayed with British folk singer Martin Carthy at his flat in Hampstead. It was such freezing weather that Dylan, a native Minnesotan accustomed to bitter winters, helped Carthy chop up an old wardrobe to fuel the fire. Bruce Waddell had a typically idiosyncratic reaction, according to Lucy: "Bugs brought his MG round on Christmas Day and we went down Eynsford Lane with the top down!"

In late December 1962 Albert bumped into Scottish vocalist Don Adams in the West End. Adams was trying to put a band together as he knew a German agent able to set up gigs. Albert set to work. Through his ex-Melody Bar mate, Buddy Trevelyan, he knew a drummer, Barrie Jenkins, whom he found sitting in his bedroom in Charlton listening to Radio Luxembourg. When Albert asked, "Do you want to come to Germany?" it was a no-brainer—Barrie was in. Albert now needed a bass player and the choice was obvious. Bugs said: "When I went to Germany with Albert I think the gig came to me for once. I bought a little A35 ex–Post Office van at the last minute—probably for about a tenner—off a bloke I'd worked for who owned a pet shop in Blackheath village." The van was repainted yellow and as Albert had just discovered Johnny Burnette and the Rock 'n' Roll Trio, the legend was emblazoned on the side—"Don Adams and the Original Rock 'n' Roll Trio." So, just after Christmas Albert was back in Germany: at the same time The Beatles were playing The Star Club for the fifth and last time, supporting Johnny and the Hurricanes.

Don Adams was already in Hamburg doing cabaret, so with Bugs at the wheel the trio headed off down the A2 for the Ostend ferry. "Bloody hell! We almost froze to death," says Albert. "It was that really cruel winter, and there was no heater in the van." They arrived in Belgium at six in the morning and in the subzero temperatures the band almost wrote themselves off on the Hamburg road. Bugs takes up the story: "On the solid black ice I lost control and we skidded down the dual carriageway the wrong way, getting nearer and nearer to the central reservation. I could see the tall poplars looming; fortunately they slowed us down and we ground to a halt in the trees." With a large bass cabinet strapped to the roof the van was top-heavy and slowly tilted over on to its side. The back wheels buckled under the van and the cabinet flew off across the road. Bruised but otherwise unharmed the lads crawled out of the van. Eventually, a German AA patrolman came along who Barrie thought "looked like one of the Gestapo. He helped us right the van, change the wheel and get the roof-rack and bass cabinet back on." Bugs kicked out the dent in the roof from the inside: "it pinged out and you could hardly see any damage. I took it a lot easier for the next 330 miles to Hamburg." Nevertheless, Barrie recalls, "When we arrived Bugs decided the ice was thick enough to drive the van on to the Elbe." It was nearly midnight when the Original

In Germany in 1963, with Don Adams and the Original Rock 'n' Roll Trio. From left, "Bugs" Waddell, Don Adams and Albert. The drummer is Tony Middleton (courtesy the Lee family).

Rock 'n' Roll Trio checked into a guest house, Albert nursing a nasty bruise and a nervous rash.

Lucy had never been abroad—in fact it was Albert's grandmother who paid for her passport and gave her £8 for the fare. It was an exciting prospect for her—the opportunity to be with her boyfriend living it up in the rock clubs of Germany, but it was a long and cramped journey in a train crowded with the winter sports enthusiasts heading for the slopes. Hence it was a tired and bedraggled Lucy who stumbled off the local train in Kitzingen-am-Main, a few miles east of Wurtzburg, early on New Year's Day. The boys had had a good night: Lucy has a vivid image of "rather pretty champagne icicles festooning this yellow post office van."

The trio were working hard in Kitzingen, playing for six hours a night at a German club, patronized largely by GIs from the nearby base. Lucy, a keen dancer, went to all the gigs where she became a kind of agony aunt for the young Americans. The GIs would read all their "Dear John" letters to her, much to the annoyance of the club's owner: "He had all these hostesses at the bar and I always had a circle of American servicemen round me." Occasionally some of the GIs would get drunk and fights would break out. Albert recalls that Don Adams, a diminutive Glaswegian no stranger to a spot of alcoholic fisticuffs, "diving off the stage amongst them picking on guys who were two feet taller than him."

There were positive vibes, too. Some of the Americans used to get up and sing with the band; one in particular, called Jay, was from Lubbock, Texas, and claimed to know the Crickets. He would say "I remember being over this guy's house when Joe B. first played the double bass." This was no vainglorious boast fuelled by strong German lager. In later years Albert mentioned the man to the Crickets, who remembered him as someone whose uncle or parents owned a bowling alley in Lubbock. Jay was only young but told Albert that he made his money "by loan-sharking to all the servicemen." He wanted to take the band back to Lubbock with him and even gave them a small PA system. When he got home, however, he decided that it was probably not the best commercial idea, so Albert had to wait another eight years for his transatlantic debut.

Nevertheless the band enjoyed themselves: the Americans would supply them with brands of coffee unavailable in England, in catering-size cans pilfered from the PX. Once Albert asked a GI to get him a bottle of Southern Comfort: "I'd never seen a bottle in England but I remember my Dad telling me that during the War he'd drunk this Southern Comfort that the Americans had given him." Time went by and Albert thought little more about it. Then at the end of a particularly good night the club's owner asked Don and the band to play another hour—a bit cheeky, thought Albert, "as we'd been playing six hours already. He went behind the bar and brought out a bottle of Southern Comfort, saying 'I'll give you this bottle.' So we did, but I'm pretty sure that it was the bottle the guy had left for me. Typical club owner!"

All the band were learning the game and for Albert, playing in the club six to eight hours a night and on Sunday afternoons marked another significant stage in his apprenticeship. After a fortnight, the club owner booked Don and the trio to play in another club he ran in Wiesbaden, 30 miles east of Frankfurt. On the morning the band left Kitzingen Bugs woke to find the van covered in snow. "We couldn't get it started. This GI said he'd get us a jump lead and a blue Cadillac drove up—what a knockout!" The band stayed just outside Wiesbaden in a tiny old boardinghouse, which the lads soon found to be the local brothel. Barrie remembers these spartan digs. "It was so cold and all the old tarts were upstairs in a sort of dormitory. We had this tiny one-bar electric fire and we all sat round it trying to make our toast. There was ice on the inside of the windows and to see out we had to hold the heater up to the inside to melt it."

Then one night, someone had given the band a bottle of champagne which they left in the van overnight. That evening, recalls Bugs, "was the last time we used the van before things thawed out. The next day we went back and it wouldn't start. The plugs were standing out on icicles and the champagne had frozen. After that we walked to the gig looking like Scott of the Antarctic. When the thaw did come we put the plugs back into the A35. It started first time."

If the Original Rock 'n' Roll Trio's outward trip had been eventful, the return journey matched it for sheer drama. Barrie was in the front passenger's seat and Lucy was sitting in the back with Albert, who emphasizes the lack of heating in the van: "It was so cold we were wrapped up in blankets, huddled round a tiny Primus stove to keep ourselves warm." It was almost inevitable. The Primus stove between Barrie's knees fell over and set fire to clothes and blankets. They all leapt out, throwing snow into the van in an ultimately successful attempt to douse the flames. To cap it all, the van's lights failed and Lucy recalls "driving behind articulated lorries using their headlights to go a bit further. When they took off we had to pull in again to wait for the next lorry."

When Albert, Lucy and the boys arrived back at Dover it was no warmer than when they had left. On February 6 a blizzard started and snow fell continuously for 36 hours. While Albert was away the industry had received a major boost when the purchase tax on records was cut from 45 percent to 25 percent[5] and there had been a couple of significant hits. Mike Berry and the Outlaws reached number 6 with "Don't You Think It's Time?" The Outlaws contained Chas Hodges, later of Chas and Dave and a friend of Albert's for over forty years; in recent years Berry has toured with and produced albums for Albert and Hogan's Heroes. Then the Rooftop Singers, one of the one-hit wonders of the Sixties folk revival in America, strolled to number 10 in the British charts with "Walk Right In," a song written and originally recorded by Gus Cannon and his Jug Stompers in 1929. With its driving guitar introduction, the record saw the arrival in pop music of the twelve-string guitar, played by Big Jim Sullivan for the first time on ABC-TV's "Thank Your Lucky Stars" when the Kestrels mimed to their cover recording of the tune.

Albert had been abroad for six weeks or so and was glad to come home again—but flew straight back to play with German band Mike Warner and the Echolettes—"that was a weird thing." Albert was still doing the odd local gigs with Barrie Jenkins, whose father, Ernie, was a film extra. In late February Warner, who needed a drummer and guitar player immediately, had advertised in *Melody Maker* and an agent Ernie knew got a call from Germany. Warner paid the agent's commission, bought the air tickets and 48 hours later, Barrie and Albert jumped on a BEA Viscount to Dusseldorf: "neither of us had flown before." When Albert produced his Gibson at the first gig Warner and the band were less than impressed. They were sold on Fenders; furthermore, Barrie wasn't playing a Ludwig drum kit. However they soon agreed on a song—"Johnny B. Goode" was always a good choice—and they got under way. When Albert started to play, Warner's jaw fell open; he almost forgot the opening lines.

The Echolettes worked in the club for about a month, which was a standard booking. Albert would have liked to have gone home at the end of it. "Mike and his band were just crazy and he was a real bullshitter," but he didn't have the money and Mike "made excuses that he didn't have enough to give us." Barrie remembers Warner having dyed his hair blonde and "strutting his stuff with the Elvis gold coat and his Fender Jaguar guitar, which he'd plugged into the radiator at the back of the stage while Albert did all the licks." It was a chaotic time. The band was a five piece—two guitars, vocal, bass and drums—all German except Barrie and Albert, who confesses "we were all a bit crazy but the little bass player was crazier than most. His name was Gert Komm and he had this great old Mercedes we drove around in, one of the old 190s which in the end ran out of oil and blew its big-ends." Komm fell foul of Barrie on one occasion. "I beat him up in the club. We were rehearsing and he kept laughing and winding me up, mucking it up deliberately. I just pushed him down the stairs, falling over chairs and all, laying into him and calling him 'a fucking wally.'"

The band moved on to a club on the outskirts of Dortmund, where Albert had a disconcerting experience. "We'd played there only two or three nights when the German military police burst in and hauled Billy, the other guitar player, off the stage. Billy really looked the business. His hair was greased back: he used to dye it with boot polish." It turned out

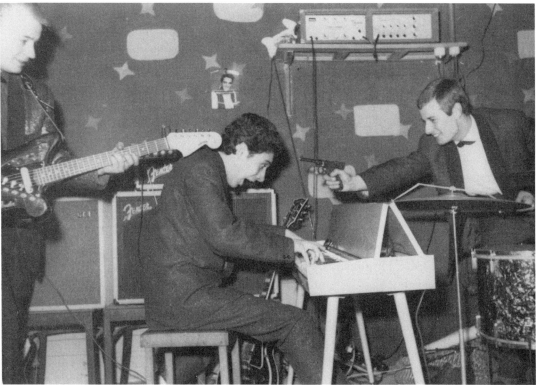

Top—Albert, fourth from left, with Mike Warner and the Echolettes in Germany in the summer of 1963. Bassist Gert Komm is third from left. *Bottom*—Don't shoot the piano player! Barrie Jenkins with gun, Albert at the keyboard, and guitarist Mike Warner in Germany (photographs courtesy the Lee family).

that Billy had deserted the Bundeswehr.[6] There was compulsory military service in Germany at the time and he was on the run.

So now the Echolettes were a four-piece, playing to dwindling audiences. The inevitable happened—"we got fired. I don't know if being a four-piece was their excuse," says Albert. "The music wasn't bad but Mike decided that we'd better go on to the next gig two or three weeks early. What else could we do? We were stuck. We'd no money so we went on to Wuppertal, to a club called the Wilhelmstubschen." Fortunately the club's owner gave the band some digs for a couple of weeks. Albert and the lads used to get a free beer and a cheese roll at the club every night, where they would watch the other band, and "maybe get up and play a song or two."

Albert had taken his old Supro amp with him to Germany. As it was a half-hour walk back to the digs and the band were usually the last to leave the club, he often left it backstage. One morning the amp wouldn't work: Someone had spilled beer over it. Albert was devastated. He even used to leave his precious Gibson Les Paul hidden behind the stage— "God, when I think about it today..." The club is still there, a disco now, though Wuppertal is almost unrecognizable. In 1963 the impetus of new building was only slowly repairing the ravages of wartime destruction.

Albert had worked with Warner for about three months and he had had enough. He and Barrie were homeward bound at the end of May. "Mike gave us just enough money for the fare. I heard afterwards that he was saying to the German guys 'Oh, I fooled them all right. Look, I've got all this money left over,' but we actually left with some instruments which I managed to get through British customs." Poor Barrie had had a hard time: "After three months I had the flu really bad and Albert helped me through it. He told me to lay in bed and sweat it out for three days—but at least I ended up with a Ludwig snare drum and a big Wieder cymbal."

The year 1963 would be a remarkable year, representing "the central hinge between one kind of Britain and another ... a continuing climax to all that process of change which had been gathering force over the previous seven years."[7] The Profumo scandal, the controversy over the Bishop of Woolwich's *Honest To God* paperback, the largest-ever Campaign for Nuclear Disarmament march from Aldermaston at Easter, the collapse of the age of Macmillan, the Great Train Robbery in August and the simultaneous emergence of Harold Wilson and the Beatles marked the peak of the fever of change which had been rising since the mid–'50s. In early June, when Profumo resigned over the Keeler affair, the *Daily Mirror* bellowed in a banner headline: "What the Hell is going on in this country?" It was a year of political, social and religious ferment and for Albert, too, it was a fluid year, one in which he admits, he "was jumping from one thing to another," trying to find a new direction.

Aptly enough, soon after he arrived back from Germany, Albert came across a copy of Hank Garland's *Jazz Winds From A New Direction*. This was a landmark, an influential LP featuring the Nashville studio legend playing progressive jazz backed by vibraphonist Gary Burton, drummer Joe Morello, and bassist Joe Benjamin. This was the first of two significant developments that summer in Albert's maturing as a guitarist. The album was "a tremendous influence" and Albert derived a good deal of enjoyment from it, more for its innovative styling and dazzling virtuosity than as a work to be analyzed and copied, like the Gallup and Burton singles of the late '50s.

The second milestone was when he bought his first Fender Telecaster. "I'd really become a big fan of James Burton, who played with Ricky Nelson." Albert was in Selmer's one day when Ray Smith picked out an old Telecaster, just in, which he told Albert was a "James Burton guitar." "It must have been about a '59," thought Albert, "because it had a rosewood fingerboard.[8] It was a bit worn, and it cost £53, whereas a new Tele would have been around £120. In England at that time there weren't many Telecasters around. They had an image of being a cheap Fender for rhythm guitar players, because the biggest band at that time was Cliff Richard and the Shadows." (The Shadows' lead guitarist, Hank Marvin, played a Stratocaster, and rhythm guitarist Bruce Welch played a Tele.) However, Albert believed that "Telecasters gave a great sound, so alive and bright and wiry." So he bought the one in Selmer's "and it *totally* turned my head around…. I loved my Gibson, but this guitar was completely different; I'd never heard anything like it. From then on, it was my number one guitar, though I continued to play the Gibson Les Paul until about '65. Around that time, I'd also heard some of Jimmy Bryant's playing, and I thought it sounded like he was playing a Fender. In the late '60s I finally got a copy of *Country Style*, the album by Speedy West and Jimmy Bryant, and there he was on the cover, playing a Telecaster. I ran home and put it on, and it was every bit as good as the song I'd heard on the radio. All of the great sounds that James Burton and Jimmy Bryant were getting came out of Telecasters."[9]

Scarcely had Albert got off the train at Victoria when he was back at work. In early June, he worked on a session for '50s skiffle star Johnny Duncan's single "The Ballad of Jed Clampett" and at the end of the month found himself backing a rock legend. Albert had not played with Gene Vincent in Hamburg, but when the Star Club Combo came over to Britain to back Vincent their guitarist contracted the flu and Albert was called in. The combo rehearsed in an old music hall on the Edgware Road then went to Haverfordwest for a one-off gig, where "Gene was pretty drunk," Albert recalls, "and threw up all over the audience." Despite this unfortunate calamity for the front row, it had been a great experience for Albert to work with the singer, who coveted his role as the keeper of the rock 'n' roll flame. "He was a strange one," says Albert, "but undoubtedly Gene Vincent's legacy remains as potent as ever. The roadie who drove the van was a big friend of the Beatles and I remember driving back from the gig listening to *Saturday Club* and The Beatles were on. I'd heard about them from these guys from Hamburg, but I never met them there." Albert thought they were a pretty good rock 'n' roll band at that time though George Harrison's solos were nothing very special.

Many British rock, blues and country bands made a decent living churning out for the GIs serving on American bases in Britain the kind of music which reminded them of home. Albert of course had played U.S. bases in Germany and that summer he played with R&B outfit the XL5 for two or three months. "We had sax, organ, bass drums and guitar, playing R&B instrumentals. I'd just bought the Telecaster and this XL5 gig at Chicksands was one of the first ones I did with it. Geno Washington[10] told me recently that I had had a big influence on him when he had seen me with the XL5." A former twelfth century priory, Chicksands, near Sandy in Bedfordshire, is architecturally one of the most striking military bases in the U.K. It was where the secret German codes were intercepted before being passed to Station X at Bletchley Park for decryption. In the crowd at Chicksands that summer was a man who would become a significant figure in Albert's later career. Gerry Hogan was in a country band called Johnny and the Hayriders, which became Country Fever. "We drove up there," says Gerry, "and found XL5 set up on stage. We rang the agent who said we should have been at Greenham! So we stayed for the gig and I first heard Albert—but I didn't speak to him. I was too intimidated; he was so good."

Neil Christian, born Christopher Tidmarsh in London's East End in 1940, started fronting his backing group the Crusaders in the early '60s. Jimmy Page was the guitarist at the outset, joining the band more or less straight from school, but left in mid–1963 after contracting glandular fever as a result of almost constant touring. Page originally suggested Jeff Beck as his replacement. Christian tried him out in a West End club: "I didn't like him so I gave him a fiver to go home!" In July he recruited Albert and replaced bassist Jumbo Spicer with Andy Anderson. "He was all right, was Neil," says Albert. "Like all singers at that time, he looked good and was a bit of a jack-the-lad, but he had the front to get up there and do it, which I certainly didn't. When you look back at it, I could have sung as well as any of those guys, but I didn't have the confidence to do it."

Christian was one of the pioneering acts of Britain's pre–Beatles era who made a major contribution to the evolution of British rock. Apart from Albert, other fine musicians such as Nicky Hopkins, Ritchie Blackmore and Mick Abrahams would pass through the Crusaders on their way to bigger and better things. As a singer and recording artist, though, Christian was distinctly lacking, with a tremulously tentative voice. He tried his hand at bobby-sox style tunes, Merseybeat-type numbers, British R&B, and overproduced pretentious pop, but could not overcome his fundamental lack of strong material. He fell into that peculiar contingent of male solo singers who had a stronger visual image than vocal prowess, like P.J. Proby and Dave Berry. Christian, however, did not enjoy the chart success of either Proby or Berry, landing just one U.K. hit, the jauntily commercial "That's Nice," which made number 14 in April 1966.

Nevertheless, despite Christian's shortcomings as a recording artist, the Crusaders were a consistently big club draw. They played established venues like the California Ballroom in Dunstable, where in September, for the sum of 6/6d., you could have seen them with the Eagles[11] and the Allegros. "We earned good bread on the road," says Christian, "even though we didn't have any major records out." In such an uncertain year, "Neil Christian was good," recalls Albert, "because he paid me £15 a week whether I worked or not. He had this old ambulance we used to go around in."

The ambulance may have been an unfortunate choice—though it may have been so uncool that it was actually trendy—but Christian and the Crusaders were a smooth-looking bunch. "Fashion?" says Albert. "Sure, if we were a regular band then we wore matching things"—which was just as well, for in 1963, as Levy points out, "a cool-looking person could only be from London."[12] Barbara Hulanicki, who kitted out so many of London's beauties at her Biba boutique, concurred: "The postwar babies had been deprived of nourishing protein in childhood and grew up into beautiful skinny people. A designer's dream. It didn't take much for them to look outstanding."[13]

Andy Anderson, the bass player with the Crusaders, had a Beatle haircut, Albert recalls, "a grey shirt with a rounded collar, leather waistcoat, and a knitted cotton tie. I thought that was pretty cool. I didn't comb my hair forward until ... well—I never did. It just kind of fell forward but I didn't make a point of having a Beatle haircut." Never a dedicated follower of fashion, Albert avoided the opprobrium heaped on the controversial style, much-derided by the generation which had fought the war, who believed that men with long hair was just not proper. There were vain attempts to stamp out The Beatles' mop tops but nothing was going to stop the trend going into fashion history. Though the style was tame by today's standards, the hair dared to reach shoulder-length in days when men were expected to have it neatly cut above the ears. Some schools attempted to ban the fashion and there were calls in the columns of the *Times* and the *Daily Telegraph* for the government to reinstate National Service to "stop the rot."

The forces of reaction were not yet in full retreat. In November, the BBC banned Joe Brown from performing the George Formby song "With My Little Ukelele in My Hand"[14] on the *Billy Cotton Band Show*. Later that month, the cataclysmic event of 1963—indeed, one of the major events of the twentieth century—occurred in Dallas. Like most people, Albert recalls where he was when John F. Kennedy was assassinated. "I was with Neil Christian playing a gig in Southend and the buzz was going around, 'Kennedy's been shot. The shit will hit the fan now.'"

The assassination had an impact on Mike Warner, too. Warner and his band had been making a good living appearing at American bases in Germany, but after Kennedy was killed bookings dried up: the GIs were in no mood for rock music for two or three weeks. Just before Christmas Warner turned up with his 21-year-old second wife, knocking on Albert's door in Kidbrooke. He sang at some gigs with the Crusaders and went down well, which ruffled Neil Christian's feathers. Warner had split up his old band, kept the drummer and bass player and said to Albert: "Things are going to be different this time. I've got some really good gigs and I'm putting this band together. I've got this new wife and she's got lots of money." She certainly had. When Warner had married her in October, her wedding present to him was a voucher for a music shop, which enabled him to buy amplifiers, microphones and several Fender guitars. Warner had a kosher contract, so Albert bade farewell to the Crusaders and drove back to Germany with him. He told Albert, "Don't bother bringing your Gibson, I'll get you a guitar"—and picked up at the music shop a brand-new red 1962 Fender Stratocaster. "I wish I still had it because it would be worth a fortune."

Mike had also acquired with his gift voucher a Fender piggyback Bassman with two 12's,[15] which Albert loved. A year or two later a bass player approached Albert at a gig. "He told me he had a 4X10 Fender Bassman,[16] which wasn't really suitable for bass." It is generally agreed that Fender had never produced a really satisfactory amplifier for the bass guitar and "he wanted to get a piggyback model. I'd heard through the grapevine that all of the cool guys in America were using 4X10 Bassman amps, and you couldn't get those in England. So I did a swap with the bass player, and within 18 months I'd acquired another, and I still have them. The guy who sold me the second one told me he thought it had belonged to Eddie Cochran."

Pleased as he was with the new Strat, Albert wrote to Lucy asking her to bring out his Gibson "because I missed it." A few days later, on New Year's Eve, she set off for Germany. Albert's girlfriend had an uncomfortable journey, carrying her bags and the precious guitar. The train was packed with skiers who had reserved seats so Lucy stood on the train all the way to Dover. It was the same story on the ferry and on the train to Darmstadt, where she sat on her suitcase in the corridor. Eventually a couple of GIs took pity on her. "I hadn't had anything to eat as I couldn't leave my luggage and the guitar so they bought me a pretzel."

Warner had a booking at the U.S. base in Darmstadt and for a month, the band stayed at a beautiful guesthouse out in the woods. Warner's contract was for a five-piece band so "we persuaded Lucy to get up and sing," Albert recalls. "She couldn't sing but I'd sing with her. She looked quite exotic, you know, a half-Indian girl up on stage and she could dance as well." According to the club's owner, however, she did not constitute a fifth band member. As a result he cut the band's money and Mike was unable to pay them their full wages.

The band moved on to Worms, where they also played at a U.S. base. Warner booked himself into a hotel in Wiesbaden, about 30 miles down the Rhine, and his wife drove him to the gig each night. The rest of the band stayed at a smaller hotel in Worms. One night, his wife was ill and with the drummer at the wheel, the car was written off in a serious accident, prompting Warner to break up the band and disappear. "In fact," Albert says, "Mike had lost interest and split. However, Georg Grimm continued to play bass and luckily, we'd met this English guy called Pete who played rhythm guitar." Pete had a big station wagon so "we had some transport and stayed in Worms till the end of the month. The guy who ran the club at the base was a black sergeant, a cool guy called Al Portiss with a '59 Cadillac. He liked a drink so he employed this German guy to drive him about. We got on really well and had a lot of fun."

Left to their own devices, the band drove on to the next club, which was in Friedberg, 20 miles north of Frankfurt, for another month's work. The reformed band went down well and at the end of that month had enough money to go home. "So we drove back in this American station wagon," recalls Albert. "Georg Grimm desperately wanted to come to England with us and was interviewed on the boat by an English guy who spoke excellent German. He asked Georg what he was going to do in England. Sadly, they wouldn't let him in so he had to turn round and go home—on the same boat."

At last, Albert was home—"Thank God!" Barely twenty, he had experienced the rock business on the road, warts and all: the best—the rehearsals, the teamwork and the buzz of the gigs—and the worst—at the mercy of people, places and things: equipment problems, unreliable transport, substandard accommodation, broken promises and if not shattered dreams, a measure of real disillusion. The pop explosion of 1963–4 marked the zenith of the cultural and social upheaval which had begun back in the jazz clubs and art schools and among the south London Teddy Boys of the early '50s. Most of the new wave of actors, playwrights and novelists came from the same cities and seaports and had primarily the same working- or lower-middle class origins as Albert and emerging pop stars like the Merseyside groups, the Rolling Stones, the Yardbirds, or Cilla Black. Beatlemania was about to sweep the nation and would soon become a global phenomenon. For Albert it was a time for reflection; he did not know it, but early in 1964 he stood on the threshold of a major career move.

Five

Thunderbirds Are Go!

One lunchtime in early February 1964 Albert sat nursing a Guinness at the bar of the Crown in Brewer Street when Ray Stiles wandered in. Ray's father, Len, owned a music shop in Lewisham High Street which had become something of a mecca for the youngsters from Blackheath.

"Hi, Ray. How's things?"

"Pretty good, you know, mustn't grumble."

"Oh, what are you up to these days?"

"Well, I've been with Mike Hurst for a few weeks—you know, used to be in the Springfields with Dusty. Well, they split in October."

Albert had heard. Ray went on to tell him that Hurst had formed a band, recruiting Ray Smith and Jimmy Page, along with Nigel Menday on drums and Tony Ashton on keyboards. Page had then left as he wanted to play rock. Ray Smith decided to stay at Lew Davis's. So, Ray said, "We need a guitarist." He knew that Albert was at loose ends—news travels fast in the Soho village—and Ray saw the tour as an excuse to play with an old friend, a guitarist he'd long admired.

"Listen, mate, do you fancy doing a tour with us, on a bill with Gene Pitney and Billy J. Kramer?"

Was the Pope a Catholic?

"I was unemployed and I thought it might be interesting."

Hurst auditioned Albert in the basement of Douggie Millings' shop in Soho. Millings was a tailor whose premises in Great Pulteney Street adjoined a coffee bar frequented by Britain's first generation of rock stars, including Cliff Richard, Tommy Steele and Adam Faith. Millings' suits soon became fashionable with musicians, and the Beatles' manager Brian Epstein asked Millings if he could create "something different" for the Liverpool foursome: the result was the famous collarless suit. The audition was a formality. "As soon as he came in," recalls Hurst, "and started doing all the James Burton licks I knew it. He was a great player even then, and a lovely bloke." Albert was now part of the Method: "So that was two gigs now that I'd replaced Jimmy Page!" Tony Ashton was on keyboards, Albert and Mike Hurst on guitar, Ray Stiles on bass and the drummer was Nigel Menday. "What a great band we actually were," says Hurst, "but unfortunately five years or so before our time. Nobody was listening to country-rock in 1964."

On February 29, Gene Pitney's first tour, a 20-date, twice-nightly package, opened at the Odeon, Nottingham. Albert found it "kind of interesting working with Gene Pitney, Cilla Black, the Swinging Blue Jeans and Billy J. Kramer and the Dakotas. I remember Billy J. and Pitney wrestling in the aisle of the bus," which Ray Stiles remembers, too. "Gene was very business-like," says Ray. "When you got to know him, he was OK but he would start off by telling you he'd studied electronics at university and had written one or two hit songs." Mike Hurst found Billy J. "a lovely lad and a good singer, well-built and fancied himself." Kramer, an underrated performer responsible for some classic '60s hits,[1] suffered from appalling stage fright: "It was quite amazing to see Billy J. in the wings waiting to go on," says Ray. "He would be almost physically sick but the minute he walked on stage he was right on the button."

The Method were third on the bill, playing a mix of basic rock 'n' roll and some country-based material. Marooned in the theatre from late afternoon until almost midnight, the lads were left with a lot of time on their hands and grew increasingly bored. As a consequence, mischief and mayhem were never far away. Mike recalls that one night the drummer Nigel Menday "crept on behind Pitney's curtain to where our gear was already set up and began playing along to Pitney's set, lightly on his kit. The next night, we all went on and did the same. Next day, Pitney came up to me. 'Hey, Mike, there's a funny thing. I can't help feeling there's a kind of echo, like my backing is coming from somewhere else.

Maybe it's my ears. What do you think?'

The Methods, spring 1964: Mike Hurst and Ray Stiles on the roof, Albert and drummer Nigel Menday inside (courtesy the Lee family).

"'Dunno,' I said. 'It must be the acoustics in here.'

"We did it on all the other shows and Pitney never discovered it was us. He just thought there was something up with the sound!" Nonetheless, forty years later, talking to Bob Solly, who played organ with the Manish Boys on the tour, Pitney remembered he had enjoyed the experience: "I loved those days," he said. "The comradeship, the fact that everyone travelled together was one of the pleasures of going on tour at that time."[2]

The tour ended at the Odeon, Guildford, and as so often happened in those days, the band never got paid for the gig. As the offers of work dried up Mike Hurst could not hold the band together and began to produce emerging artists, most notably Cat Stevens. He was unable to let go completely, though. He took Ray Stiles on his honeymoon: "He had his new wife but he wanted me to muck about with and go fishing with!"

Albert was now "resting," but could at least survey a Top Ten in which for the first time in chart history not a single American record was featured. The British pop music industry was beginning to undergo that sea change which over the next two years launched "the British invasion" and swamped the American scene.

That change was marked a week after the Pitney tour ended when on March 28, Simon Dee uttered the immortal words, "This is Radio Caroline on 199, your all-day radio station." Ronan O'Rahilly, the station's founder and manager of Georgie Fame, had anchored the ex–Danish ferry *Fredericia* off Harwich and named the ship after Caroline Kennedy. The early programs from Radio Caroline now sound mild and somewhat gauche, but for the British people, all-day pop music radio was a revelation. No lectures, gardening tips or cookery suggestions. No *Woman's Hour* or *Listen with Mother*. No shows where massed banjo bands emasculated current pop hits. No *Mrs. Dale's Diary* or *Housewives Choice*. No programs of dance bands with featured vocalists introduced by middle-aged men in jackets and ties reading beautifully modulated but oh-so stilted scripts. Radio Caroline spoke the language of 1964—and what is more, it played the music the young wanted to hear. By the autumn of 1964 Caroline had more listeners than the three BBC networks combined.

The proliferation of pirate radio in 1964 which Caroline sparked was the expression in the broadcast media of the explosion in popular music, which owed much to the fact that so many British bands had worked their apprenticeship in Hamburg and had returned as seasoned professional performers. Of the five bands who supported Chuck Berry and Carl Perkins when they began their tour in May at the Finsbury Park Astoria, three—King Size Taylor and the Dominoes, the Swinging Blue Jeans and the Nashville Teens—had done their time in Hamburg, while a fourth, the Animals, had sweated through all-nighters in a dockside club above a warehouse in Newcastle. Yet the bastions of conservatism were still fighting a rearguard action. The day after Berry and Perkins opened in north London, the Rolling Stones were refused lunch at the Grand Hotel in Bristol, where they were staying, because they were not wearing jackets and ties.

In late May Albert bumped into Ricky Charman in London. Albert had known him since 1961 when Charman was playing with R&B bands and had met Albert and Lucy in a club in Camberwell. "We started talking," says Ricky, "and we realized we both loved country music." Since late 1962 Charman, or Mousey, as he was always known in the West End, had been playing bass in Chris Farlowe's backing band, the Thunderbirds. He was the only professional in what Charman thought "was an incredibly good band—Johnny Wise on drums, one of the best rock drummers I'd ever heard, and Bobby Taylor—what a guitar player. He always wanted to be an actor—he was a good-looking guy and had a great stage persona." Early in 1964 Taylor announced he was leaving and going to drama school. Albert had been aware of Farlowe as a name around the Two I's while playing with Bob Xavier and the Jury.

Farlowe was already an established performer on the London club scene, notably at the Flamingo, where his manager, Rik Gunnell, was manager and promoter of the All-nighter Club. The Blue Beat craze was sweeping London after West Indian immigrants turned nightclub owners on to their native ska. Chris Blackwell of the Island label had brought 17-year-old Millie Small over to record her Jamaican-style single "My Boy Lollipop." It was a smash, reaching number 2 in May. Decca persuaded Farlowe and the Thunderbirds to record two songs in the ska vein. Farlowe's single, "The Blue Beat," credited to the Beaz-ers, was an outstanding record and won rave reviews in the clubs but it was a non-event chart-wise. The follow-up, "Girl Trouble," released in March, also attracted little interest. Farlowe was a hard taskmaster and knew what he wanted. The lack of chart success was a major disappointment, and the Thunderbirds' ever-fluid line-up underwent a major reshuffle. With Taylor on the point of leaving, Ricky Charman asked Albert if he wanted the job. "After the old boys stood down," says Farlowe, "we had guitar players up to audition.

"I'd say, 'We're doing "Stormy Monday Blues in E"—it's a 12-bar blues.'

"'What goes after E?' some hopeful would ask.

"'Don't call us, we'll call you,' I'd reply—and that was even before he hit the stage."

"Albert Lee walked in, got up there, plugged in and did his thing.

"'Don't get down!' I shouted up to him. 'You might as well stay there.'

"He was phenomenal."

On June 13 *Melody Maker* reported, "Organist Dave Greenslade and lead guitarist Albert Lee have joined Chris Farlow [sic][3] and the Thunderbirds." Albert had made a major break-through: he had been offered a permanent place in a band that seemed as if they might have a future.

Bobby Taylor and Albert played together a couple of times at the Flamingo but, as Char-man recalls, "Bob played atrociously—he wasn't interested. Johnny Wise thought Albert had the wrong sound, as we played hard-driving R&B, like Micky Green was doing with the Pirates. In a way he was right." Dave Greenslade, who had been with fellow Flamingo-reg-ulars The Wes Minster Five, gave the band an extra dimension with his Hammond organ, and as customers grew to appreciate Albert's intricate solos, the sound of the Thunderbirds changed markedly, from straight down-the-middle R&B to a swinging, riff-based, soul reper-toire. Charman had, however, worked closely with Wise for several years and eventually managed to convince the drummer of Albert's worth. In the summer, however, the band underwent a major reshuffle. Ian Hague, formerly with the Mike Cotton Sound and the Attack, replaced Wise and shortly thereafter, the group added saxophonist Bernie Green-wood, who left for Greece seeking stardom with Eric Clapton in August 1965, to be replaced by Dave Quincy.

At the time Farlowe had claims to be the outstanding R&B and soul vocalist in the country and his record contract with EMI's Columbia label meant that for the foreseeable future Albert could look forward to the certainty of regular work. His first recording ses-sion with the new band was at Advision studios in Bond Street, where the Thunderbirds cut "What You Gonna Do," a Farlowe original, and "Just A Dream," a cover of teen idol Jimmy Clanton's 1959 U.S. hit. Although a softer number than usual, Farlowe nevertheless gave it the full blues treatment and the song soon became a huge hit live in the clubs. It was the first number he performed on *Ready Steady Go!*, where it went down a storm. The record was released in July, and its tremendous live popularity suggested he might at last score some chart success. However, Farlowe was again disappointed, for "although the birds loved it—they were always coming up and asking me to do that slow, romantic one again at the end of each gig—it just didn't convert to record sales." Ricky Charman thought he knew why: "Record producers wouldn't let us do the stuff we did on stage. We had to do rubbish like 'Itty Bitty Pieces.'"

As Albert began his career as a Thunderbird, the summer of 1964 saw other significant happenings in music and the media. In July, Jim Reeves, whose silky-voiced baritone had made the smooth transition from country to pop, joined Buddy Holly, Patsy Cline and later Ricky Nelson on the sadly long list of performers killed in airplane crashes. In August, Manfred Mann's "Do Wah Diddy Diddy" and the Kinks' "You Really Got Me" reached number 1 in the *NME* charts. Both singles would become classic tracks of their times, and another band destined to become icons of the '60s, the Zombies, made their debut at number 12 with the consummately ethereal "She's Not There." Most notable of all perhaps, certainly for the young men of Britain whose attention span stretched only as far as Page 3, September 15 saw the first issue of *The Sun*.

Back from Germany, the band recorded a cover of "Hound Dog," closer in feeling and dynamics to Big Mama Thornton's raucously ferocious 1953 original than Elvis's hit, and "Hey Hey Hey," a calmer version of the Billy Boy Arnold blues standard "I Wish You Would." Released in November, the record failed to find a commercial market, although the Thunderbirds were one of the hardest-working bands on the road in 1964—and had been for two years.

In the autumn of 1962, Farlowe and the Thunderbirds, so-named after Chris's favorite car, arrived back in London after a residency in Hamburg. The line-up was Bobby Taylor (guitar), Johnny Wise (drums), Vic Cooper (Hammond organ) and Ricky Charman, late of Duffy Power's band, on electric bass. Farlowe used to frequent the Flamingo in Wardour Street ("where I saw Howlin' Wolf and John Lee Hooker") and met Rik Gunnell, then manager and promoter of The Allnighter Club, which operated in tandem with the Flamingo. Rik also ran the Ram Jam Club (among others) with his brother Johnny, who doubled as master of ceremonies. One night Johnny Gunnell asked Farlowe,

"You've got a band, haven't you?"

"I've got a great little band."

"Come along and play."

And they did. At once the Gunnells loved Chris's voice and the band became almost the resident attraction.

The pop charts that autumn were at an all-time low—but the sound that made London the most exciting city in the world was being born in the sweaty, smoky clubs of Soho. The Scene featured Guy Stevens, the man with the best R&B collection in the country, and across the road was the Flamingo, a long-established jazz club that had become a fixture since Jeffrey Kruger first opened its doors in September 1952. In its early days the club ran

The Thunderbirds in London, circa 1965: drummer Ian Hague, keyboardist Dave Greenslade, Albert, Chris Farlowe and Arthur Sharp (vocalist with the Nashville Teens at the time) (courtesy Barrie Jenkins).

a once-a-week jazz night and eventually secured permanent premises in a basement on Wardour Street below the Whisky-A-Go-Go. Kruger, later the hugely successful founder of Ember Records, established a reputation for high-quality modern jazz, blues, and the soulful sound of artists like Ray Charles. The Flamingo became *the* night spot for discerning music fans, including legions of GIs from the bases around London. On weekend leave they needed a bolt-hole, a refuge from the prostitutes and police of Piccadilly. They approached Kruger: "If we brought our kind of records along and someone to play them, would you reopen from midnight to dawn?" Kruger was none too keen. However, manager Tony Harris was prepared to give it a trial run. After all, reasoned Kruger, ever the shrewd entrepreneur, the GIs would pay in dollars. The price for 1962 was high—at least £10—ensuring a self-selecting clientele. The bar sales tripled. The staff were happy because they were earning good money. There was no trouble: two MPs built like the Hoover Dam saw to that. Thus began the legendary Flamingo all-nighters.

The all-night sessions, on Friday and Saturday nights, mushroomed, and the club began to open on Sunday afternoons, when Count Sickle played some reggae and ska. Of course, American GIs flocked to the all-nighters, their tastes influencing those of the local audience. Harris took care of everything, though Kruger was always on the scene. Eventually, Kruger said to him, "I can't run an agency during the day and be here all night"—and Rik Gunnell was taken on to book the acts and set up the gear.

For a few months there were no problems. Then one night Kruger found Gunnell "doing the announcing and walking about like he owned the place, big cigar, flash suit. I smelt trouble. Rik was getting too big for his boots." A few weeks later Gunnell told Kruger he wanted to start an agency. "It was OK by me because I couldn't take any more work on. If he wanted to handle Georgie Fame and Long John Baldry, fine." Gunnell set up his agency in Gerrard Street and soon had on his books most of the big R&B and soul bands of the '60s. Naturally, they all played the Flamingo—Georgie Fame, the leading light in the Gunnells' stable, Ronnie Jones and the Midnighters, Herbie Goins and the Night-timers, Zoot Money, Brian Auger and the Trinity, John Mayall's Bluesbreakers, Bluesology, and the Animals.

The Thunderbirds were regulars, having built their reputation on professionalism and sheer hard work, playing a minimum of a gig each night, at colleges, universities and the American bases. Albert recalls, "When we did the all-nighter, we'd often do a gig somewhere like Windsor, leaving at three in the afternoon. You'd get there around six, set your gear up—there were no roadies in those days—and you played till midnight. Then you drove back to London, unpacked all the gear again, humped it down into the Flamingo to play the second set for the all-nighter." Some days, they would even squeeze in an afternoon gig as well, as Chris later recalled: "The next day, you might do an afternoon in the Flamingo, an evening gig somewhere, and then have to get back to do the all-nighter again." On one occasion, Ricky Charman remembers, the band did thirteen gigs in three days! No wonder, he says, that many musicians were on uppers—"they needed them to keep awake."

Albert began to attract aficionados to the Flamingo. He was getting a name among London's session guitarists. Kruger remembers him "with black curly hair and a permanent grin." One night Ray Smith made a tape of Albert's solos for Jimmy Page. "Jimmy wasn't interested in Chris's vocals," Ray asserts, "just Albert. When the story got out Albert was embarrassed, Jimmy was angry so I gave my tape to Albert." Some contemporary recordings exist of the Thunderbirds in performance. When he was with Neil Christian, earning regular money, Albert had spent £160 on a Vortexion stereo tape machine. Always a lover of gadgets, Albert was fascinated with the unit's two independent stereo channels "on which you can record separately and then bounce to the other while adding another instrument—a bit like Les Paul."

In Mike Figgis' documentary *Red, White and Blue*,[4] Fame, Farlowe and Clapton describe the busy club scene of the mid–1960s, focusing on the Flamingo. "It was the best place," Clapton says, "the place I was scared to go until I was actually in a band. If you could hold your own in that kind of crowd you'd made it as a player. It was a school of hard knocks playing the Flamingo all-nighters." Clapton first saw Albert playing with the Thunderbirds in the Flamingo. "That's where we met up and made our bones as players." The GIs were enthusiastic, says Kruger, "but always well-behaved and deferential to the white girls." They had more to fear from the wildlife in the Soho basement, as Lucy recalls: "Once I went into the ladies room and there was a rat behind the door." One of the Gunnells gave a ten shilling note and a broom to Albert, who went in and killed it. The place was lively and heaving, and the music was on the edge, but the police never raided it. There were probably drugs going round, mainly amongst the musicians, Kruger concedes, "but that wasn't my business. If there was trouble, the two big MPs would show up and squash it."

Albert, Lucy, Kim the collie and Eden Kane's Jaguar, Kidbrooke Park Road, 1964 (courtesy the Lee family).

On Monday, March 15, 1965, Lucille McKenzie did something which later she advised her daughter never to do—she married a musician. At the Registry Office in Greenwich, she became Mrs. Albert Lee. On a Monday, for of course Saturdays were out—Albert and the Thunderbirds always had a gig. Lucy knew what she was getting, however. Albert had been an only child for a decade, and she saw him as "very protected by his parents. Even when he went out to work his Mum did almost everything for him." The couple had also lived together before they were married, albeit very discreetly: It was still only 1965. At Kidbrooke Park Road there was a room with a balcony at the back of the house, and after the wedding, Lucy remembers, "his Mum and Dad gave us that for a little while." The newlyweds' first home was a basement flat near the Three Tuns[5] at 4 Southvale Road, Blackheath, which had just two rooms and a tiny kitchen. "You shared the toilet with the landlady," recalls Lucy, "and had to go home for a bath once a week."

At the time Albert was still playing his Gibson Les Paul as well as the Tele but then sold it and acquired a Super 400, the top of the Gibson jazz guitars. He thought it was a good deal because it was a "Scotty Moore guitar, but that was a mistake because it wasn't suited to the way that my style was developing. So I sold the Super 400 back to the guy I'd bought it from and in part payment he gave me a white SG Custom. It wasn't nearly as cool as my original Les Paul." In June Eric Clapton bought a Gibson Les Paul from Lew Davis's in Charing Cross Road and set off for Greece in a large American car. Little did Albert know that the same Gibson Les Paul would enter his story fifteen years later (see Chapter 10).

The Thunderbirds had been one of the busiest bands on the road in 1964, in a summer when the majority of British youth was split into two factions called Mods and Rockers, who each dressed in their own distinctive style. Mods were the sharper dressers and wore lightweight suits or smart jackets over polo necks or Fred Perry shirts, and donned U.S. Army parkas to ride their Vespa and Lambretta scooters to a club to dance to black soul music. Rockers wore winklepicker shoes, tight jeans and leather jackets. They rode large motorcycles such as Triumphs, BSA's and Nortons. Every Saturday night the Mods and the Rockers would dress with precision, groom their hair with extreme care, go out on the town and beat the hell out of each other. On bank holidays throughout that summer seaside resorts such as Margate, Clacton, Hastings and Brighton became battlefields for the warring clans. Levin argues that the violence "had its roots in the dissatisfaction with society felt ... by those who were now demanding society's total overthrow and replacement by something that would give meaning to their lives and to the lives of the masses. No Mod or Rocker would have put it so eloquently, but the plea was, at bottom, the same."[6]

Farlowe's next single, "Buzz with the Fuzz," was "the ideal soundtrack for the mass media's moral panic over Mods, Rockers and troublesome youth."[7] Released in June 1965, the song, a mélange of modish idiom and hip talk, was original, danceable and interesting. Featuring a cool jazzy solo from Albert and some mature Hammond work from Greenslade, it immediately became a Mod anthem in the clubs and looked as if it would be the long-awaited hit. However, once EMI discovered what "rolling up a joint" meant—something to do with the ingestion of illegal substances, apparently—the record was withdrawn and EMI soon cut the band adrift, just as they were beginning to gain critical attention.

Is "Stormy Monday Blues, Parts 1 and 2" by Little Joe Cook *really* the greatest British blues record ever made? Chris Farlowe has heard that claim often over the last forty years and he repeats it today with a ruefully ironic grin. For one thing, while Chris poured everything he had into his rendition, the band did it as a demo—"we didn't know it was being recorded as a take." One day in June, he and the Thunderbirds were merely warming up for a recording session by running through a laid-back version of a classic 12-bar blues by T-Bone Walker, described by B.B. King as "one of the greatest guitarists we've ever had."

The other irony was that for contractual reasons Farlowe was called Little Joe Cook. The next thing he knew, the record was in the shops but to his surprise, the name Little Joe Cook was on the label—on Sue Records. Farlowe rang Guy Stevens at Sue and asked what was going on. Stevens said, "Well, you're under contact to EMI so we couldn't let them know who you were." Stevens, the former DJ at the Scene who had often dug out obscure R&B material for Farlowe, made a desultory effort to claim it was actually a little known American blues disc he'd licensed. Britain's blues fans were taking it for the real thing and only gradually did it get around that Little Joe Cook was not a sharecropper's son from the Mississippi Delta but the former John Deighton from Islington. "I can't grumble. It was never a chart hit but has become a cult record"—and they were clearly Farlowe's melodic tones, EMI contract or not.

Apart from the powerful vocal, Albert's solo is one of the most memorable of his career. It has a greater impact today for being markedly out of character: Albert is not known as a major exponent of the blues. "When other players like Jeff Beck and Jimmy Page heard it," says Farlowe, "they realized that he was the guv'nor. He played slightly country-rocky with us but when we'd play a blues, all of sudden he would transport his guitar into another medium." Eric Clapton didn't like it, telling Albert "Your tone's too jazzy," but then Albert had learned about blues guitar through meeting Don Peak, the guitarist with the Everly Brothers. "I played the same kind of licks as B.B. King but with a different kind of feeling and attack. I had also been listening to Howard Roberts, a good funky jazz player in L.A., and people like James Burton and Don Rich, the Telecaster country guys." Richard Williams sums up the solo: "The first notes from Albert Lee's mellow guitar define a mood of after-hours relaxation with a confidence that was thought to be beyond the reach of British musicians at the time."[8] Clapton has now modified his view of Albert's interpretation: "It became a famous guitar solo at a time when guitar solos in this country were few and far between, apart from Jim Sullivan and Jimmy Page. I was intrigued by his take on 'Stormy Monday' because I was coming from a Chicago-blues angle. I thought it was a bit light, but when I talked to him later about his tastes and influences I saw that he was coming from another place. It was the Everly Brothers—so he came from rockabilly and I'm coming from Robert Johnson and Muddy Waters."

Later in his career, Chris had an argument with Dionne Warwick: "She wrote to *Melody Maker* saying that black people are the only ones who could sing the blues. I wrote back and said she didn't know what she was talking about. I was born in London in the early part of the war, and we had bits of bread with dripping on it, went through the bombing, moved out of our house—we suffered. You're born with a voice and just because you're black doesn't make you a great singer. I was one of those very fortunate white persons who was given a voice and it's regarded one of the greatest blues voices."

Whatever the rights and wrongs of the debate, the performance remains Farlowe's tour de force.[9] His vocal performance, with its absence of blues clichés, coupled with Albert's sublimely lyrical solo, attains a profound authenticity and represents the peak of British blues.

Albert remains a great admirer of Farlowe today—"he had a similar sort of voice to Eric Burdon but to our ears he was a far superior singer. I didn't think the Animals and others were musically as accomplished as we were. They really loved Farlowe. Old Chris never really learned any song from start to finish. He'd be making it up, ad-libbing and scatting, as he went along and he still does that, but he's an exciting singer." Farlowe was a larger-than-life character even then, with all the warm hospitality of the native Londoner. Lucy recalls that she and Bugs Waddell would go to Farlowe's flat before they went on to somewhere else, "but Tubby, as he was always known, would be nattering all the time and would say, 'Don't go yet. Have another drink.'" Later his mother would bake cakes for Lucy's children.

At about this time Chas Hodges, another great London character, went with Dave Peacock to the Cooks Ferry Inn in Edmonton to see Chris Farlowe. "Albert was with him. We were knocked out with his guitar playing and we went up and spoke to him after the gig. It turned out that Albert loved good C&W music like George Jones and Earl Scruggs and Jimmy Bryant. It was unusual at the time." In that month, July 1965, the Ivy League's evocative "Tossing and Turning" reached number 3 in the chart, featuring an unmistakable introduction played by another future Heads, Hands and Feet colleague, Mike O'Neill. In August, Andrew Loog Oldham, formerly a waiter at the Flamingo, opened Immediate Records for business under the buttock-clenching slogan "Happy to Be a Part of the Industry of Human Happiness." Farlowe's long-standing friendship with Mick Jagger led to his being one of the first artists to be signed to Oldham's new label.

Farlowe's Immediate debut, backed by the Thunderbirds, was a compelling revival of Sanford Clark's 1956 hit "The Fool," backed with Chris's own "Treat Her Good," a rewrite of Roy Head's R&B classic "Treat Her Right." Released in October, it failed to make the charts, despite a robust production by Eric Burdon and some heartening reviews.

In November Farlowe was summoned to Harley House, a mansion block near Regents Park which housed Andrew Loog Oldham's office. A "very business-like"[10] Jagger suggested "Out of Time" and "Think" as suitable singles. Although Jagger and Richard had written "Out of Time" with him in mind, Farlowe was unimpressed, "mainly because Jagger was singing it to me and playing a guitar." Jagger and Richards had already recorded the song as a track on the Stones' "Aftermath" album, due out in the spring, "more or less as a demo for Chris to hear," thought Bugs Waddell. The discussion also presaged the demise of the Thunderbirds as a recording entity.

Farlowe's close relationship with Jagger resulted in the Stones' front man jointly[11] producing the EP *Farlowe In The Midnight Hour*. For the first time Oldham employed Arthur Greenslade as musical director: otherwise the line-up was the standard Thunderbird unit, a practice which would become a rarity. Featuring powerful revivals of soul standards "In the Midnight Hour" and "Mr. Pitiful," together with the Stones' anthem "Satisfaction" and an unlikely reading of Anthony Newley's "Who Can I Turn To?," it charted within a week of release in January 1966, eventually reaching no. 6 on the EP listings. It was also the last recording which Ricky Charman made as a Thunderbird.

After the German escapade with Don Adams, Bugs Waddell had landed in Eden Kane's band, but early in the new year he bumped into Albert in Blackheath. Albert had a proposition. "Look, we're trying to row out Ricky Charman, our bass player. He's causing bad vibes in the band. I'll put you up." "I don't want any confrontation," said Bugs. A week later Waddell played a gig with the band: "It was out west somewhere. We had a great night. I knew most of the songs and it was happy days from there on." The band had reached a point where they just could not tolerate Ricky the Mouse any longer. He had been with Farlowe since "we'd been doing one gig a night, for £4 each a night, plus the all-nighters. Then when we were getting big, the management took Farlowe aside, resigned him on his own, and told us, 'We'll give you £50 a week.'"

That permanent flat rate was little good to Charman: "most weeks we were earning £90." Charman had always been outspoken and said what he felt. "The truth was that I was an obnoxious little fucker. They got rid of me in the end and in retrospect they were right, but I didn't think so at the time."

There was no personal animosity between Albert and Ricky, who perceived Albert's single-minded dedication to his craft. "Chas once said to me, 'Albert's got his own agenda. He'll smile and he'll do things, but he'll go his own way.' Albert was very ambitious about where he wanted to go," says Charman, "but he didn't always tell *you*. I loved playing with him—and with Johnny Wise. He instinctively knew what I was going to do next. He knew that we would keep a rock-steady platform. When he played ten feet off the floor he would always come back to us." Now, with a very clean, almost faultless technique, Albert was looking to new horizons. He wanted a ten-pedal steel guitar and had talked to Farlowe about adding one to the group. According to Albert, Farlowe liked the sound: "Most people think they are strictly for country stuff, but in America they're used for jazz and pop." In a contemporary interview Albert confessed that while it might take him a while to learn how to play it he would "soon get into the swing of it."[12]

In early 1966 when Gerry Ford, an American steel player from High Wycombe, was drafted to Vietnam, Gerry Hogan bought his steel guitar. Hogan had already started to play with the Flintlocks on the Fullers' country music circuit in west London, in clubs and pubs like the Clarendon, the Red Cow, Hammersmith, and the Red Lion in Brentford.

Chas Hodges often dropped in to see the Flintlocks and one night invited Albert, who had heard about this band, to join him. Albert and Chas were kindred souls who loved the Buck Owens music the Flintlocks offered.[13] "I went down to the Red Cow with Chas and Dave. I could have picked any night, but the Flintlocks were playing and I sat in. It was great fun." Albert began to sit in regularly with the Flintlocks, when "it was unfashionable to confess to liking George Jones and Buck Owens." Chas was and remains an unrepentant lover of country. "Most people took the piss out of C&W music. There was, and still is, and always will be a lot of duff C&W records, but the good ones amongst 'em are gems. It's a fact that they are few and far between, but the musicians who think for themselves, and don't go by what they read, will find 'em if they look for 'em. Me and Dave had found 'em and so had Albert."[14]

At the end of January Farlowe registered his first-ever Top 40 entry with "Think." By far his finest single yet, it received substantial airplay on the pirate stations for several weeks. Albert played on very few of the records Mick Jagger produced: in fact, the Thunderbirds did not play on many of Farlowe's releases. Jagger had decided that Farlowe would benefit from a big band sound, appointing Arthur Greenslade as arranger, who insisted on using regular session musicians—men like Jimmy Page, Big Jim Sullivan, John Paul Jones, Nicky Hopkins and Ronnie Verrell on drums. John Carter[15] ascribes this to the time element. "Musicians who didn't read took a lot more time in the studio, which was more expensive. Companies wouldn't stand for that—they wanted sessions done in three hours." Bugs Waddell concurs: "It was partly about cost and partly getting their mates in to do it. It wasn't a bias against the band but it was the thing to do—like Dusty Springfield, who had a big orchestra on the early hits and toured with only a backing band."

The exception which proves the rule was the album which the band recorded in March at IBC in Portland Place. Albert and Bugs played on about half of the tracks, which were engineered by Glyn Johns. "It was the first time I'd met him and he's been a friend for a long time now," says Albert. "We worked a lot years later with Eric Clapton." The album, entitled *Fourteen Things to Think About*, was an accomplished debut which also sold reasonably well, reaching number 19 in the LP charts. As well as "Think," hence the title, it contained excellent revivals of Tommy Hunt/Dusty Springfield's "I Just Don't Know What to

Do With Myself," Benny Spellman's "Lipstick Traces," Ben E. King's "Don't Play That Song," Huey Piano Smith's "Rockin' Pneumonia and the Boogie Woogie Flu," Bob Dylan's "It's All Over Now, Baby Blue" and for some reason known only to Farlowe and Johns, an exceptionally hideous cover of "Yesterday." The latter was apparently Paul McCartney's idea. He turned up at Farlowe's home at 4 A.M.: "I called my Mum and asked her to make a cup of tea. 'Oh, no, you haven't brought someone home! I've got to go to work in the morning.' When I told her it was Paul you never saw anybody get dressed so quick in all your life—lipstick and all. She kept his empty cigarette packet as a souvenir."

The Thunderbirds were still on the road—in March fans of Farlowe could have caught the band at Dunstable's California Ballroom with Fleur De Lys and the Essex Five for 7/6d (37½p).[16] The California was the southeast's top soul venue outside London, attracting major American artists such as James Brown, Al Green and the Commodores. In 1979 it was demolished to make way for a housing estate. The Cavern Club in Liverpool, which had become globally famous, did not last so long. In February 1966, barely five years after its heyday, the Cavern was declared bankrupt and had to close.[17]

While Jagger admired Farlowe for the R&B and soul he preferred singing, he felt that "Out of Time" could be given a commercial edge. By the time they arrived at Pye Recording Studios early in May, Farlowe still doubted that it was any better than other album tracks but Jagger convinced him.

"'Wait till we get into the studio. With just that little bit of what you could offer, Chris, you'll like it.'

"'And I did,' says Farlowe today. 'When I got down there they'd already done the intro with the strings.' His clearest memory is of 'Jagger working diligently in the studio while Oldham ... blinked distractedly behind his octagonal lenses.'"[18]

One of the backing vocalists was John Carter, who remembers it as a great session. "We did a couple of takes and it sounded good." Then Jagger, whom Farlowe describes as "a true professional," came down from the box. "Throw it away," he said. "I don't like it at all" and started again. He went round all the musicians saying things like "Give us some more," wanting more attack. "Everyone got more and more excited," recalls Carter. "Then he joined us in the backing group and that was something!"

"Yeah," says Farlowe. "Mick, Keith and some others were on backing vocals. I just sang it. Albert isn't on it—the unions were involved in the studios and when you use a big orchestra like on the 'Out of Time' session, you had to have all their players. You couldn't have your band too. Albert didn't mind—never said nothing to me." As Albert says, "We earned pretty good money, especially after he had his hit. Though I would have loved to have played on the session, I played it a million times at gigs. It's still a good record."

It was more than good; it was majestic. Farlowe's performance, infinitely superior to Jagger's demo, was boosted by a powerful Greenslade arrangement. Released in June, backed by "Baby Make It Soon," the song was heavily plugged. In the week after release, the band appeared on ITV Granada's *Scene at 6:30*, *A Whole Scene Going* on BBC TV, *Ready Steady Go!*, and at the Radio London Trophy meeting at Brands Hatch Racing Circuit with the Small Faces and David Bowie, followed by *Parade of the Pops* on BBC at the end of the month. Heavy pirate radio airplay drove it up the charts and the bandwagon was rolling. "Out of Time" entered the charts at number 23 in the first week of July and climbed steadily.

When the Thunderbirds played the Mayfair in Newcastle with Alan Price on July 14, the single stood at 13. Farlowe recorded a session for BBC radio on July 22 and the next day, the Thunderbirds were at number 1, knocking another '60s classic, the Kinks' "Sunny Afternoon," off the top spot.

It was an exhilarating time. The first supergroup, Cream, were formed and the Beatles released their groundbreaking LP *Revolver*, subtly original and exquisitely recorded. Lucy recalls that heady summer as she was pregnant: "There was so much happening then." There certainly was. Saturday, July 30, 1966, is arguably the most memorable day in English sporting history. At Wembley, in black and white and after extra-time England beat West Germany 4–2 to win the World Cup. While Moore, Hurst, Peters, the Charltons, et al., made football history the Thunderbirds were at the Sixth National Jazz and Blues Festival at Windsor Racecourse, playing the evening set with the Who, the Yardbirds and the Move.

Farlowe's "Out of Time" held the number 1 spot for two weeks and stayed in the charts for three months. Though his version was a huge hit in England, most genuine Stones fans express scorn for Greenslade's extravagant string-and-horn arrangement, which made "Out of Time" seem much more of a pop song than it actually was. The hit single begins as a dialogue but quickly turns into a liberation, an outpouring of jubilant venom. It is a performance both cynically funny and achingly cruel and when Farlowe attacks the chorus with that huge "Well!," it is an invitation to join in the exuberant singalong and as the triumphant track fades, he can hardly form the words anymore—nothing new there, then.[19]

In an interview with *Record Mirror* that week Farlowe looked back on his career and talked about his songwriting. He had just signed a publishing deal with Chappell and had had material accepted by Percy Sledge, Ernestine Anderson and Billy Walker. "My songwriting partner is ... Albert Lee," he told the *Mirror*. "I started writing with him after I did 'I Remember.' He's a brilliant guitarist, and I find it very easy to work with him. I do the words and music and he fits in the chords and arranges it all. It's amazing how we sort of gelled."

During this intoxicating summer Farlowe and the Thunderbirds were hot property, much admired by their peers and attracting huge crowds at their gigs. Farlowe loves to tell the story of how highly regarded they were: "I was singing at the Flamingo one night and one of the musicians sidled up to me and said,

'Ol Otis Redding's standing on the side of the stage listening to you.'

Sure enough, there he was.... He stayed there for the whole gig and never moved. We went offstage and he came into the dressing room, introduced himself and then said, 'I really dig you, man, really *dig* you—hey, I'm doing *Ready, Steady, Go!* next week. How would you like to be my guest?' That's a very special memory." So, on September 16, ITV's flagship pop show featured soul legend Otis Redding—and Chris Farlowe—on stage with Otis and Eric Burdon.

There were dark shadows, too. As the nights drew in, the British pop scene was dimmed by the tragic death in a car accident of Johnny Kidd, one of the greatest home-grown rockers, responsible for "Shakin' All Over" and "I'll Never Get Over You," two of the most enduring recordings on the soundtrack of British rock 'n' roll. At the Flamingo Kruger had begun to receive complaints from musicians about Gunnell's behavior. He had not realized that Rik Gunnell "would lean on bands, saying that if they complained about him again, they'd get no more work." A year later, the police and underworld figures were looking for him and his attitude to business had upset Robert Stigwood and other promoters.

Kruger thinks Gunnell "did a runner to Australia, or was it New York? [20] I never liked him: except for Rik I never had any trouble at the all-nighters." It was a frustrating autumn for the Thunderbirds as Farlowe found "Out of Time" almost impossible to follow. In October "Ride on Baby," good as it was, struggled to break into the Top 30.

Nevertheless, the band was still gigging. There was a brief tour with the Butterfield Blues Band, Georgie Fame, Geno Washington and Eric Burdon and visits to Sweden and Germany, which triggered an abiding passion in Albert. He had always been fascinated by Breitling watches and in Bremen, he bought a Navitimer. "In England they were £43 and they were a bit less in Germany. I got a sub [advance] off Chris and I still have that watch. It's still running, never had anything done to it. Since then I've bought about five of these watches in twenty-odd years."

After another German trip Albert brought back an Iron Cross and introduced Farlowe to the artifacts of the Third Reich, "which held a certain morbid fascination for us. I was no Nazi but there was a market for that stuff." Bugs recalls that while the other band members were out on the town "Chris would be visiting the local junk shops seeing if there was any Nazi gear to be had—but not because of the Nazi connection. It was much more because it grabbed him as a collector. It could have been Royal Doulton china or Dresden pottery. Other militaria also attracted him but there was more money in the German stuff. Life goes on and collectors are collectors, despite what the Nazis did which was unforgivable and awful."

Back in London, Farlowe started looking for more stock and every Saturday "Chris and I went to a little basement near the Elephant and Castle, an Aladdin's cave of Nazi stuff. Chris would spend £40 or £50 a week there and he began to trade it, building up quite a business." It was kitsch memorabilia and there was a market. Albert had a sergeant's jacket from the Transport Corps. "There's a picture of me wearing it on the sleeve of *Old Soldiers Never Die*. I sold that jacket back to Chris and though I wish I still had it, I'd never get into it now. I've put on a bit of weight since then." He also had a huge Kriegslag about 12 feet across, the war flag which used to fly from battleships. "I'd lay it out in the back garden and look at it but then I got to thinking 'What can I do with it?' So I sold that back to Farlowe. I'm still looking for one of those long leather coats. I have a long coat which I wear in California in the winter which I paid about £60 for in Holland but I'm after the long green double-breasted one, not the black Gestapo coat."

On that European tour, the Thunderbirds worked in Pisa as the backing band for Doris Troy, who in 1963 had a Top Ten hit in the U.S.A. with "Just One Look"[21] and a year later took "Watcha Gonna Do About It?" into the British Top 40. With Albert in Italy, Lucy gave birth to Abigail on November 18 at the flat in Southvale Road. She had become resigned to his absence. "He had to go. That was his lifestyle and it didn't bother me at all. By this time I had done a lot of traveling, been to a lot of gigs and seen an awful lot of dressing rooms." She was not able to join him as much on the road now she had a baby, "though Albert's Mum would often say 'Leave her with me'—she loved it." Abigail now recalls spending a good deal of time with her grandparents. She remembers Albert's Grandfather—"fat Grand-dad, we called him"—giving her snuff when she was a toddler. She recalls, too, her Grandfather taking Oscar, his ferret, for walks in a special harness and her Grandmother trying to bathe the animal in the sink.

A second album, *The Art of Chris Farlowe*, was cobbled together and rushed out in time for the Christmas market, charting briefly in December. Pre-eminent tracks in this more R&B and soul-oriented set were Jimmy Ruffin's "What Becomes of the Broken-Hearted?," a dramatically rococo version of "Paint It Black," "I've Been Lovin' You Too Long" and the melancholic "Life Is Nothing." The Thunderbirds themselves played on Johnny Watson's bluesy "Cuttin' In," "Rockin' Pneumonia" and Farlowe's own, somewhat imitative "North South East West," which perhaps explains why these tracks sound more laid-back and spontaneous. They also played on Farlowe's next single, "My Way of Giving," written by Steve Marriott and Ronnie Lane of the Small Faces, which reached 48 in February 1967. But Farlowe's purple patch had passed and he never registered another hit single.

The Thunderbirds were still a huge live draw nonetheless. "Out of Time" secured them an appearance at Wembley's Empire Pool in the *Daily Express* Record Star Show just before Christmas, with the Troggs, the Tremoloes, Cream, the Move, Dave Berry, Geno Washington, Lulu and Freddie and the Dreamers. Change was imminent, however, both in the business at large and in the band itself. At the turn of the year the government announced that the BBC would open a new radio channel devoted entirely to pop music, signaling the end for the pirates. In August 1967 the Marine Offences Act banned pirate radio stations and in September Radio 1 went on the air.

The other change was in the drummer's seat. When the Thunderbirds played a gig in Birmingham, it was opened by local outfit the King Bees, whose drummer was 16-year-old Carl Palmer. Albert recalls Farlowe "raving about how great he was." The singer gave the youngster his London address and asked him to get in touch when he left school. Ian Hague was "a perfectly good drummer," says Albert, "not flashy at all but a great groove player. But poor old Ian got the sack and Carl Palmer joined the band. He was a great kid but he was more suited to rock stuff." Farlowe was impressed with Palmer's dynamism and during his spell as a Thunderbird Palmer began to develop the scintillating, energetic style which later came to fruition in Emerson, Lake and Palmer. Hague went off to join the Nice, possibly driving off in Albert's 1948 Rover, for Albert had sold him the first car he had ever owned. So, for the best part of 1967, the Thunderbirds' line-up was Farlowe, Albert, Bugs Waddell on bass, Dave Greenslade on Hammond organ and Carl Palmer on drums.

Albert had little opportunity to spend time with his baby daughter over the next two or three months. Farlowe and the Thunderbirds were sell-out attractions on the college circuit, playing Liverpool University with Manfred Mann and the Norwich Rag Barbecue at Earlham Park. Other interesting gigs were the Starlight Room in Boston, the inevitable visit to the California Ballroom, the Fifth Dimension in Leicester, followed by a memorable evening in Melton Mowbray. Clive Jones takes up the story: "My group, Pesky Gee!, were booked to play Melton Mowbray Corn Exchange as support to Chris Farlowe and the Thunderbirds. The place was heaving. We finished our set and for some reason Chris turned up with only Albert Lee and Carl Palmer. Chris asked if we would back him as I think there would have been a riot if he had not gone on. He went down a storm but of course he had to 'Out of Time,' a song we had never played before. Carl and Albert joined us and somehow we got through it but I remember us all laughing on the stage. It must have been the worst version poor Chris ever sang but it went down a bomb."

Amidst the incessant gigging, Farlowe was still pursuing that elusive follow-up to "Out of Time." In May Jagger produced "Yesterday's Papers," another Jagger-Richard product, followed by the old jazz standard "Moanin," an inspired choice from Mike Hurst, which restored Farlowe to the Top 50 in June. All other singles released in that summer of love were, however, dwarfed by the monumental impact of one of the greatest pop tracks of all time. In June Procol Harum reached number 1 with "A Whiter Shade of Pale" and stayed there for five weeks.

In the meantime Albert and Lucy were on the move. Yvonne Stead, Lucy's school friend, had married and was living opposite Albert's parents. In July, when the flat below hers became available at £4 a week, Albert, Lucy and baby Abigail moved in. On the ground floor, with two bedrooms, a bathroom, a living room and a kitchen, 10a Kidbrooke Park Road was much bigger than Southvale Road, and they needed the space.

In October EMI reissued a compilation of his old Columbia material as *Stormy Monday*, [22] and Farlowe returned to the Top 50 in December with his last U.K. chart entry, Mike D'Abo's magnificent "Handbags and Gladrags." It is ironic that despite soi-disant Sixties liberation, songs extolling traditional values are some of the decade's most enduring features. [23] "The moral of the song," says D'Abo, "is saying to a teenage girl that the way to happiness is not being trendy. There are deeper values."[24] When Albert had joined the band, it had at times been a six-piece—guitar, bass, drums, keyboard, sax—plus Gerry Temple, a good mate of Farlowe's, singing and playing conga drums. Temple returned to play harmonica on the single, together with Albert and Bugs, who has fond memories of his time as a Thunderbird. "Chris was all right to work with and it was such a shame that he never had the hit with 'Handbags.' It was so much better and more soulful than [Rod] Stewart's version"— or the Stereophonics' twenty-first-century cover.

But soon, by the end of 1967 Bugs had left and Farlowe had cut the band down to a trio, recruiting Pete Solley on keyboards. "It worked quite well for a while," recalls Albert. "We were knocking out quite a good sound. I did an album with Gerry Temple around that time." Produced by Alan A. Freeman and engineered by Glyn Johns, it was recorded for the Spark label at Olympic Studios. Called *No Introduction Necessary*,[25] it featured such stellar session players as Jimmy Page, Nicky Hopkins, John Paul Jones, Jim Sullivan and Clem Cattini. The best-known track is probably "Everything I Do Is Wrong," credited to Jimmy Page and Albert only, but Chris Welch, in his review in *Melody Maker*, was dismissive: "Don't get too excited ... in fact, don't get excited at all. It's just a bit of clever packaging for some old tapes that would have been better erased, or thrown in the studio bin." While that critique may be somewhat harsh, Keith David De Groot, aka Gerry Temple, was a mediocre rock 'n' roll singer, who was lucky enough to have some good session musicians working for him. The album was reissued under Temple's name in the early 1970s and again in 2001. It can be found now called *Albert Lee and Jimmy Page* or *Jimmy & Friends 2*. Albert has his own typically wry take on it today: "It's another one of these albums that I'll probably end up bootlegging myself. Why shouldn't I make some money?"

In the first few months of 1968 Albert felt "it was all slowly moving towards a dead end." His chart popularity in decline, Farlowe was considering getting off the road to concentrate on his burgeoning antique business. The slimmed-down band were gelling smoothly enough. Solley recalls, "There were no egos involved. First of all, Albert Lee is the most modest man in the world. He always was a country music picker hiding inside a pop guitarist."

The band was still working, playing the Queen's Hall in Leeds with the Move, the Herd, Brian Auger, Julie Driscoll & The Trinity, Edwin Starr and Chuck Berry! Then down to earth a week later at the Cat Balou Club in Grantham and the California in Dunstable. The touring could take its toll, though. On the pier in Hastings, Andy Fairweather Low, later a colleague of Albert's in Bill Wyman's Rhythm Kings, collapsed for the third time in two months, and a week later at the same venue, Syd Barrett, the creative intellect behind the early Pink Floyd, made his last appearance with the group.

In February, rather too late in Albert's career as a Thunderbird, the Musicians' Union announced a code of conduct under which "session musicians will no longer be permitted to 'ghost' for beat groups on pop records."[26] A month later, Joe Cocker's album *With a Little Help from My Friends*, which included his first hit single, "Marjorine," was released. Produced by Denny Cordell at Olympic and Trident Studios, it featured Albert along with other first-rate session men Jimmy Page, Henry McCullough, Chris Stainton, Matthew Fisher, Steve Winwood and Clem Cattini. Cocker's debut coincided with a Farlowe single, appropriately titled "The Last Goodbye."

By May it was all over. Albert still ponders on leaving Farlowe. "He was on a soul kick and I wasn't really too knocked out by that. I was also dissatisfied with the way we were being handled so I decided to cut out. I was getting a bit bored with R&B and the way the rock scene was going. People were getting louder, with huge Marshall stacks and maximum power, and that sort of thing held no appeal for me." Farlowe and the Thunderbirds were undoubtedly a major live act, yet fundamentally failed to move beyond the club and college circuit. The band had never received recognition in the singles market. They had never concentrated on it and "we certainly didn't have the right image. We were wearing suits most of the time and by then most of the bands were looking rougher, with an individual look like the Stones, which I would have preferred."

Throughout the halcyon years of British R&B, Albert had been absorbing the styles and licks of RCA's *Country Guitar* EPs, and he wanted to express that absorption in his own music. He began to play gigs on the U.S. bases with Jamie, Jon and Gerry, the successor to the Flintlocks. Gerry Hogan was going to university, and it seemed sensible that Albert took his place. When Pat Donaldson joined up because the bass player was reluctant to abandon his day job, the embryo of a country band was conceived. Not that Farlowe was aware of it. "Albert told me he was leaving to join a country band. I didn't know he was doing stuff around Hammersmith on the country circuit but I guess he wanted a change of direction." As Albert told Willie Moseley of *Vintage Guitar* magazine in 1999, "I did a complete about-turn. I'd been buying Buck Owens and George Jones records through the sixties: at the same time I was playing Stax-type stuff with Chris Farlowe, which I loved. But I really wanted to play Country."

That February, Alan Lomax, the distinguished American musicologist and observer of the British music scene, wrote: "Before skiffle, relatively few people in London made their own music. Pub singers mulled over and over the dry bones of the cockney music-hall songs which had little meaning for the younger generation.... Nowadays the young people of this country have songs they like to sing. They have the confidence to sing them. They are not ashamed of making music but enjoy it."[27] Albert, seeking the most suitable vehicle to express his talent, was about to play the music that *he* enjoyed.

Six

A Country Boy at Heart

Albert had always wanted to play country music: with Romany blood in his veins it could scarcely have been otherwise. "It goes back to skiffle, really. I'd always liked playing a bit of everything, but when it came down to it, I knew that if I was going to concentrate on one particular kind of music, it would be country rather than soul." Keyboardist Pete Solley recalls Albert saying his ambition was "to go to America and play with Buck Owens"— and that meant California.

The foundations of country music in California were laid even before the singing cowboys arrived in the 1930s. In the years after the Dust Bowl in the Midwest and the Depression, "a large influx of Okies, midwesterners, southerners and all manner of migrant workers … brought with them their love of hillbilly, honky-tonk and Texas-style swing dance music."[1] Owens, who had moved from Texas to California via Arizona in 1951, was just one of those migrants to the Golden State, and in Bakersfield, a hot and dusty blue-collar town about a hundred miles northeast of Los Angeles, players like Ferlin Husky, Owens and later Merle Haggard developed a distinctive sound. Bakersfield was a classic honky-tonk town, where "crowds appreciated things a little more raw and gritty. The music that developed here and in other San Joaquin working-class towns came to be marked by the sharp, loud, high-end sound of the electric guitar (often a Fender Telecaster), a prominence of pedal steel and fiddle, and strong vocals"[2]—vocals powerful enough to be heard in the rowdy atmosphere of the honky-tonks. Owens' style, influenced by rock 'n' roll and rockabilly as well as country, featured a straight-ahead rhythm as opposed to the country shuffle beat. To Albert, Owens "was doing a new type of country music," and he particularly admired the solos of Don Rich, "Buck's right arm," on "Act Naturally" and "Tiger by the Tail"—"really simple, but they had a real good sound."

The Beatles had recorded "Act Naturally"[3] in ironic acknowledgement of Ringo's image as "the deadpan Joe Ordinary of the group."[4] Bill Wyman and Keith Richards of the Rolling Stones had become fans of George Jones since they shared a Texas stage with country's preeminent singer in 1964. Six years earlier Cliff Richard had sung about "real country music that just drives along" in "Move It," and in the mid-'50s the skiffle boom had been nourished by American country and roots music. However, while the Beatles recorded Carl Perkins tunes like "Matchbox" and "Honey Don't" and Gerry and the Pacemakers essayed Hank Williams, most groups preferred their country leavened by the energy of rock 'n' roll. There were exceptions. In 1965, the Downliners Sect, an uncompromising R&B band from west London with a justifiably high reputation on the club and college circuit, cut an entire country LP, which prompted Epic Records' Nashville boss, Bob Morgan, to claim, "this package sounds more authentic than the Grand Ole Opry." Within a few months, the Strawberry Hill Boys were playing the Club Folksville in London, billed as a "famous country music trio": they later achieved wider recognition as The Strawbs.

Albert was therefore not the only British rock musician to respond to the music coming out of Nashville and Bakersfield, which was the focus of the country-rock scene. There, a whole generation of rock 'n' rollers who had grown up under the influence of the Beatles and the Stones had gravitated towards country music. Since 1965, the Byrds had offered America's most progressive response to the British invasion, and in 1968, Gram Parsons joined forces with bassist Chris Hillman to drive this resolutely avant-garde band down what was viewed by critics as a retrogressive highway.

The *real* pioneers of country-rock, however, perhaps belonged to an earlier era, for the Everly Brothers, Johnny Cash and Rick Nelson began to create a similar synthesis of rock 'n' roll and contemporary country in the mid to late '60s. The Everlys and Nelson had something else in common: their strongest country-rock experiments featured James Burton, whose rapid, languid but never ostentatious guitar licks had graced Nelson's records since the late 1950s. Burton became the guitarist of choice in the mid–'60s for anyone in California who was dabbling with even the slightest country influences.

Burton was of course one of Albert's heroes and in the summer of 1968, Albert was striving to carve out a niche in the restricted tradition of British country playing. Sitting in with the Flintlocks in the pubs of Hammersmith gave him an unwitting connection to a 1950s dance band called the Hawaiian Serenaders, a combo led by steel guitarist Gordon Huntley, one of the unsung heroes of British country music. In the late 1950s, Huntley ran into a fellow enthusiast called John Derek, who shared his passion for the western swing sounds of Bob Wills and His Texas Playboys. Together, Huntley and Derek founded the Black Stetson Boys but by 1964, the duo were at the heart of a band entitled Johnny and the Hounders.

When Huntley left the group in the mid–1960s (he would re-emerge at the end of the decade as a key member of Matthews Southern Comfort) the Hounders became the Flintlocks, who recorded some tracks in the Buck Owens style for Decca. Legendary manager Don Arden, the man behind the Small Faces' success, persuaded the Flintlocks to change their name once again—to Jamie, John and Gerry—and encouraged them to record country ballads in the same vein as the Bachelors. Desperate, however, to veer away from the smooth, middle-of-the-road ballads that their manager preferred towards a more authentic country feel, they began to include Albert on gigs around U.S. bases. Gerry Hogan, however, was planning to go to university and in May 1968 he quit the road. Bass player Jamie Gunn checked out as well, and Albert and John Derek decided to put a band together from the remnants of Jamie, John and Gerry. Pat Donaldson left Zoot Money and joined on bass, so "we had John Derek, Jed Kelly on drums and sometimes we'd have Gerry back on steel," recalls Albert. "We called ourselves Country Fever, after the Rick Nelson country-rock album issued a few months earlier. Pat quit after about eight months and Pete Oakman, who had worked with Joe Brown and Lonnie Donegan and wrote 'Picture of You,' took over on bass."

John Derek was the driving force behind the band. He had the gigs and the contacts.

Country Fever played the Fullers' pubs, but were also playing American bases and backing a series of American country artists, who gave the band their seal of approval. "They told us," says Albert, "that we were playing the music right and that gave us the boost we needed." Country Fever backed performers such as Lonzo and Oscar, Jody Miller, Hank Locklin, Rose Maddox, George Hamilton IV, Bobby Bare, Skeeter Davis and Guy Mitchell, who

Country Fever in late 1968. From left, Pat Donaldson, Jed Kelly, John Derek and Albert (courtesy the Lee family).

Albert found "a pretty wild character. He was a nice fellow, though, having a hard time fighting the demons of alcohol—which taught me to stay clear of it."

At this juncture another wild character, an itinerant banjo player from Carmel, California, enters Albert's country story. In March 1968 Keith Nelson landed in England on vacation, eventually "sharing a flat in Crystal Palace with an American folky mate." Following up an ad in *Melody Maker*, Nelson joined an English bluegrass band called the Tumbleweeds, whose guitarist, Ray Flacke, two decades later replaced Albert in the Everlys' backing band. Along with Country Fever, the Tumbleweeds played the Fullers' circuit, which Nelson remembers as "very incestuous. Sometimes Albert used to sit in with us, I sat in with Fever and Chas and Dave came and played as well." At that time, says Nelson, British country music was "a very cult thing and the venues were basically dumps." The Tumbleweeds also appeared about once a month on a BBC radio show called *Country Meets Folk*, hosted by Wally Whyton. Major visiting folk artists like Buffy Saint-Marie or Gordon Lightfoot were guests. There would also be traditional artists like Martin Carthy and an electric country band such as Country Fever. In rehearsal Nelson saw Albert playing: "I thought 'Wow'! We got chatting about country music and discovered we were both huge Everlys fans." At the same time Bob Powel, an influential Canadian journalist on the country scene, ran a show on Radio London called *London Country*: Nelson has a tape of one broadcast, featuring himself, together with Albert, Chas and Dave. Before the broadcast Powel asked Albert for an interview. Nelson found Powel's request hilarious, because "while Chas would talk for Britain, Albert was then a bit reserved and is still rather shy—although he's come out of his shell a lot more."

Keith Nelson became a close friend of the Lee family. "His Mum was very very deaf and an absolute sweetheart." He remembers one party at the flat in Kidbrooke Park Road. "I was living in north London at the time. Farlowe was there and Bugs and I scrounged a lift back home in his Buick Riviera. He used to drive like a lunatic and we got from Blackheath to Camden in about 10 minutes. It scared the shit out of me." Nelson also performed duties of a more personal nature: "I remember changing Wayne's nappies." In late November 1968, Lucy gave birth to Wayne[5] in Kidbrooke Park Road. Albert arrived home from backing American singer Jody Miller in Europe to find his son had been born the night before.

Supporting transatlantic artists like Jody Miller, best-known for "Queen of the House" and "Long Black Limousine," was the icing on the cake for Country Fever. It was regular work but Albert "wasn't earning great money—£20-odd a week. The rent was only £4 a week so I was surviving." The weekly round of the Fuller's pub circuit was a hard grind, often for a fiver a night, because the customers wanted "the same old Johnny Cash and Jim Reeves imitations," says Albert, "and we usually got a pretty hostile reaction. If you did something slightly away from the norm, you were a rock 'n' roll band—there was no compromise. Then I used to sing Roger Miller's 'Dang Me' and people would call it jazz! In America, country rock was only just beginning and it was unheard of here, but we were trying to blend rock 'n' roll and country, much as the Burritos did a few months later."

The Flying Burrito Brothers, "too wild for country boys and too hillbilly for rock Snobs,"[6] together with other free spirits like the Byrds, Jackson Browne and Neil Young, were making ground-breaking music in the canyons, clubs and recording studios of Los Angeles, music at a tangent to mainstream country. The turning point for Albert was *Sounds of Goodbye*, an album by Vern and Rex Gosdin, best known for their 1967 hit, "Hangin' On." "Gib Guilbeau, who I know in L.A., played on it and I'd love to talk to him about those sessions because the sound of this record is exactly how country and bluegrass should mix. Clarence White was the guitarist and Gene Parsons, who was the Byrds drummer. I started to like Glen Campbell, too—it was more orchestral but it was another approach to country music."

Albert was playing the circuit but as the months wore on he came to realize that he was unlikely to make a living playing country music—at least, not the style he wanted to play—and probably not in Britain. Albert was now singing for the first time but "in the end, it was just too frustrating, so I went into session work." Lucy was acting as his unofficial agent. "That became my thing. I'd get him session work or I'd phone up other bands—after all, we had two children. He wouldn't push himself forward, relied on the wrong people and was too trusting. I had worked in offices and had a sense for the other side of people. We had slightly different values."

Albert's values expressed something of his Romany heritage. "I've never been an organizing person—I just drift along with things." As Albert listened more and more to country-rock outfits such as the Burritos, Poco, and the Band, a new style of playing was opening up to him—"Clarence White's bending technique, Jimmy Bryant, of course, and Buck Trent's solid-body electric banjo." This new world of playing was not far removed from what John Beland of the Flying Burritos talked about in 2000. "Blues music is what influenced Hank Williams, Sr. He was learning guitar and singing from an old blues musician he knew. That's how country music evolved, a combination of blues, Irish music and bluegrass.... A lot of country players would tell you that they could trace their early influences to blues. You know the stock blues and country riff are two different things, though, but when they merge you get a wonderful approach to playing guitar. Take Roy Buchanan, Albert Lee—they melt the styles together. My heroes were guys like Lonnie Mack, James Burton on the old Ricky Nelson records, Clarence White from the Byrds."[7] Albert has similar thoughts: "My style tends to be an amalgam of all these guys I've been talking about. I can hear it. I know when I play with different bands—a rock group or a country band or whatever—I always play the same style. It sort of fits in the middle somewhere."[8]

At this point, things become bewildering and not a little chaotic: from the summer of 1968 for the next eighteen months, Albert was doing three or four things at the same time. He was on the road with Country Fever—the "day job"—when Chas Hodges rowed Albert in to play on some impromptu sessions with producer Derek Lawrence. Lawrence had been a junior to the legendary producer Joe Meek and had first met Hodges when he and Ritchie Blackmore were recording with Meek in the Outlaws. Later Lawrence was instrumental in launching Deep Purple on an unsuspecting world, after which, he explained, "I started working with some of my old mates again. I'd always liked the idea of the Muscle Shoals studio set-up, where you had a studio band, and whatever you were doing, that was the band who played it." Hodges was part of Lawrence's studio collective, along with Ritchie Blackmore and Ian Paice (the Deep Purple connection), together with Nicky Hopkins, Big Jim Sullivan and many more. Albert joined the fluctuating team during the sessions for an album (still unreleased) by soul singer Tony Wilson, who later helped form Hot Chocolate and went on to become a major Third World solo artist in the '70s and '80s.

Life around Kingsway Studios was laid-back in the extreme. Lawrence would "decide on a song I wanted to do, then we'd get to the studio at about 12 o'clock, and work on the track 'til around 8 o'clock, when we'd finish it.... Then we'd go down the pub until it closed—and come back and jam old rock 'n' roll stuff for three or four hours." As Albert recalls: "It was a free-for-all really. We'd show up at 10 in the morning and mess around all day. We'd just get in there and decide whose turn it was to make a record that day. We'd be cutting songs for the fun of it. Chas would sing one and Derek would say 'All right—we'll put that out under this name.' So as for remembering tracks, I've no idea. I don't know how he did it and how he paid the bills."[9] Lawrence suggested a few tracks such as "Lay Lady Lay" and "Too Much of Nothing" but Albert was never particularly a Bob Dylan fan, though he liked a few of his songs and of course the country-tinged *Nashville Skyline* album was a favorite. Chas and Albert were, however, enormously influenced by the Band, of whom more later.

"When we'd finished the Wilson LP," Lawrence later recalled, "I thought it would be great to try something with Albert. He was a great talent, and I couldn't understand why he wasn't doing a solo thing and singing." Thus between the end of 1968 and May 1969 Albert, backed by Lawrence's Country Fever—Chas, Harvey Hinsley, B.J. Cole, Ian Paice, Matthew Fisher or Nicky Hopkins—recorded twelve tracks[10] which Lawrence took to the legendary Gold Star studio in Los Angeles, site of most of Phil Spector's '60s sessions, so that engineer Stan Ross could do the final mix. The Bell album remained unreleased for years and Albert frankly began to hope that it would never see the light of day. He was unsure of his prowess as a vocalist and felt that the songs were unrepresentative of his later more mature work. In fact, when the material was released in 1991[11] he managed to view it objectively. "I'm so far removed from it now that I can look at it and say, 'Well, that's not a bad effort really. I'd only just started to sing.'" It is a characteristically modest appraisal. Although the album is over thirty years old it has a contemporary country-rock feel. Albert's fluid, sinuous picking on "Country in Harlem" and "Rocky Top" demonstrates his debt to Bryant and Tal Farlow while his respectable readings of the Dylan tracks and his energetic attack on Merle Haggard's "Mama Tried" indicate a voice of flexible promise.

At the same time Lawrence was preparing a series of singles under the name of Country Fever for the Bell label, in particular two songs from Bob Dylan's "Basement Tapes," "Tears of Rage" and "Too Much of Nothing."[12] The nominal A-side was "Tears of Rage" but Bell featured "Too Much of Nothing," as the better-known Dylan song, in their promotional campaign. Although Albert played and sang on the record, none of the other members of the John Derek personnel were involved. "We didn't differentiate between Country Fever and Black Claw in the studio," Lawrence later recalled. "They were exactly the same band. It was just a question of who took the lead vocals. If it was Albert, they became Country Fever tracks and if it was Chas, then they were Black Claw." Black Claw's name derives as an amalgam of Lawrence's penchant for colors (cf. Purple) and "The Claw" by Jerry Reed, his favorite instrumental record at the time. According to Lawrence, the studio ensemble on these sessions included Albert (on both guitar and occasional piano), Chas Hodges (bass, piano), rhythm guitarist Harvey Hinsley, B.J. Cole (pedal steel), pianist Matthew Fisher, drummer Mickey Burt and various backup singers including Elaine Corlett and Liza Strike.

Lawrence also produced a solo single by Albert aimed at the American market. In late August 1969, between the four-day extravaganza of the Woodstock Music and Art Fair[13] and the Isle of Wight Festival with the Band, Dylan and the Who, Albert recorded "That's All Right, Mama" and his own "Best I Can."[14] Although he had been present at the birth of Black Claw, Albert was never part of everything they did. However he was featured on another single on Bell[15] by the group, a cover of the Band's "Across the Great Divide," backed by "Sally." To confuse things even further, the A-side in America was a revival of the Easybeats' "Good Times," recorded at the same August session and issued on Lawrence's own ephemeral Revolver label.

Chart success and critical recognition may have eluded Lawrence and his session bands but at least for Albert, with his young family, it was a time of relative plenty. Derek Lawrence was paying him a weekly wage, so "I had a bit of pocket money and was even thinking of buying a proper car at that time, a Lotus Seven, which cost about £700." However his fascination with Breitling watches[16] got the better of him. "I saw another model called a Co-Pilot in a little jewelers' on the corner of Piccadilly Circus. It cost £65. I thought 'God, I'd love that watch. It seems silly when I already have one but I really like it.' So anyway I bought this watch but felt kind of guilty and actually gave the first one to my father. For years and years I'd swap back and forth. I'd say 'Dad, wanna swap watches?' and he'd reluctantly say 'Oh, all right,' and we did."

Further sessions with Lawrence and Black Claw over the following autumn and winter included interesting work. In September, Albert recorded a cover of Sanford Clark's "The Fool,"[17] on which he chose to omit the Al Casey guitar lick which was the core of the original record, and "Send Me Back to the Mines," a song written with session singer Elaine Corlett, which sounds as though it could have been cut in Nashville last year in a duet with Rosie Flores or Emmylou Harris. Then in late January the Easybeats' "St. Louis," "Lookout Cleveland" by the Band, Dave Dudley's "Six Days on the Road" and the self-penned "Brother Preacher" completed Albert's involvement with Black Claw. The band, comprising Chas, Dave Peacock, Harvey Hinsley and Mick Burt, recorded an album, *Country Pie*, had a disastrous trip to Berlin and played a few more gigs, but Black Claw was short-lived.

Meanwhile, throughout 1969 Albert continued to gig with John Derek's Country Fever—hence the germ of some of the confusion. The band played on a live circuit which included London's own country-rock showcase, the Nashville Room, with its mix of traditional cowboy décor and psychedelic glitz. Next to West Kensington tube station, the venue is now the Famous 3 Kings sports bar. The previous winter, on December 21, 1968, Country Fever had appeared on Radio 1's *Country Meets Folk* as a featured act. It was Albert's twenty-fifth birthday and Wally Whyton led the assembled company in "Happy Birthday" on the air! Country Fever did a Merle Haggard medley of "You Don't Have Very Far To Go," "Branded Man" and "I'm A Lonesome Fugitive." This was followed by Hank Williams' "My Bucket's Got A Hole In It," "Jambalaya" and "Hey, Good Lookin." Albert performed "Dang Me" and finally John Derek sang a Buck Owens medley, "Love's Gonna Live Here," "Act Naturally" and "Truck Drivin' Man." Albert was touched: "I've got a tape of it somewhere. They all sang 'Happy Birthday' to me on live radio—that was pretty cool."

The band were also in the studio. A short-lived deal with Decca resulted in a couple of tracks, "Fine On My Mind" by Jerry Reed and "How Little Men Care," a Sonny Curtis song, but they were never released. Albert thinks the band may have recorded other material for Decca "that's still just sitting around." Then the Decca deal fell through and in May

1969, John Derek's Country Fever signed a recording deal with what was touted as the first British label exclusively dedicated to country music. Certainly Albert felt the founder of the Lucky label was more in tune with the band's musical approach—after a less than auspicious beginning. Evincing a somewhat ingenuous sense of American history, Gordon Smith called his company Confederate Records, until it was put to him that this would not be well received in the States. So Confederate Records became Lucky Records and Country Fever were proclaimed as one of their initial signings. Smith produced the band in the studios in the basement of the Orange Music shop in London where sessions were augmented by Gerry Hogan on steel and Johnny Van Derrick on fiddle and a single[18] was issued in September. Albert sang the Gordon Lightfoot song "Did She Mention My Name?" backed by Mel Tillis' "Mental Revenge" with John Derek on vocals. Reviewing the record, *Country Music People* commented "Far from being country, in my mind, although I do like the song. John Derek sounds like a woman on this! Good production here—and some BRILLIANT guitar work!"

The main thrust of the band's activities was still however live work on the road, largely as the backing band for visiting American country artists. In late September Country Fever opened the show for Faron Young, "The Singing Sheriff," who, with his backing group the Deputies, was booked to appear at three U.S.A.F. bases. Young's itinerary was hectic. Arriving at Heathrow at noon on Saturday from Naples, by 4 o'clock he was off to Alconbury, where he did two shows. He got back to his hotel at 4 in the morning. On the Sunday there were three more shows, one at South Ruislip and two at Mildenhall, Suffolk.

At the end of October, just before the end of Albert's time with the band, an RCA package toured six countries in eleven days, starting at the Nashville Room with the London band the Kingpins. Bob Powel's review records that Country Fever "had polish, something which the majority lack. First song was a Beatle number,[19] which was as country as you can get and was sung well by Albert Lee. John Derek then sang 'Gentle on My Mind,' 'Your Cheatin' Heart' and 'Make the World Go Away.' Albert Lee then returned with 'Sounds of Goodbye.' ... Two numbers were sung from the upcoming LP on Lucky. They were John Derek's rendition of 'It's My Time' and Albert Lee's 'Did She Mention My Name?' ... A fine spot from a group who must now be challenging for the title of Britain's best band. The final song was 'Mental Revenge,' their latest single. They finished off with 'Twelfth Street Rag,' a guitar instrumental which clearly illustrated why Albert Lee is considered our finest country guitarist."

On the package Country Fever backed Nat Stuckey and Connie Smith, and the Hillsiders backed George Hamilton IV, Skeeter Davis and Bobby Bare. After a couple of weeks in Europe, the tour wound up on November 16 at the Walthamstow Granada and finally at the Royal Albert Hall, Chet Atkins appearing on the two final London dates.

Bob Powel had mentioned in his review an "upcoming LP on Lucky." The band was already contracted to record for Rediffusion so it seemed like a good idea to cut both the Lucky and Rediffusion albums on the same day. In November 1969, Gerry Hogan recalls, "we did the Rediffusion one in the afternoon at the Langham Studios then zoomed off to Denmark Street to do the Lucky album with Gordon Smith producing." Denny Wright played guitar and acted as musical director on the Rediffusion session, Charles Berman producing.

The Rediffusion label had an outlet through supermarkets and although the LP, called *Mountain Music Jamboree*, was a cut-price item, with twelve tracks it was good value. It opens with some novel scat-singing from Albert on Roger Miller's' "Dang Me," followed by John Derek's insipid attempt at "Ring of Fire," which was rescued only by a mature Burtonesque guitar break from Albert. Hank Locklin's hit "Please Help Me, I'm Falling," "Buds Bounce," with a coolly articulate solo from Albert more akin to Wes Montgomery or Tal Farlow, "Country Fever," which Albert had put together in a matter of minutes and John Derek's sympathetic vocal on Tim Hardin's classic "If I Were a Carpenter" complete the first side. Instrumentals on Side Two are "Orange Blossom Special," Hank Garland's "Sugar Foot Rag," Buck Owens' "Tokyo Polka" and Duane Eddy's arrangement of the traditional "Wildwood Flower." The final cut, "Crying Time," comes from Buck Owens, with acoustic guitar backing from Albert and Gerry. The Rediffusion album[20] was one of the few that Albert was ever paid for. "I knocked off 'Country Fever' in about two minutes and I still get checks of £40 or £50 for writing it. Rediffusion sold it to a Muzak company—I've heard it in cafes and bars all over the world!"

In Denmark Street recording started at 8 o'clock and finished in the early hours of the morning. As well as the band, John Van Derrick played fiddle on both albums. The LP, called *Listen to the Country Fever*,[21] was a combination of contemporary country/folk material with Albert's dexterous guitar-playing a highlight. Albert takes the lead vocals on "Listen To The Band," a Mike Nesmith song, Sonny Curtis's "Gypsy Man" with Albert on acoustic guitar, a quite soulful version of Mel Tillis's "Ruby, Don't Take Your Love to Town," Bob Dylan's "You Ain't Goin' Nowhere" and another outing for "Wildwood Flower" featuring Gerry. John Derek sings on the remaining tracks, "With Pen in Hand," which had been a hit for both Johnny Darrell and Sammi Smith, "My World Has Ended," another ballad, the Gosdins' "Sounds of Goodbye," Jackie DeShannon's "Come Stay With Me" and the John D. Loudermilk song "It's My Time," which had been revived by the Everlys in 1968.

Both albums were issued at about the same time, in March 1970, and it is interesting to compare them with the Albert-led Country Fever album, recorded with Derek Lawrence over a year earlier. On the Lawrence album, Albert's picking on "Country in Harlem"—half hoedown, half Booker T and the MG's—owed much to Clarence White, who with James Burton was the other guitar wizard to emerge from country-rock. White's family group, the Kentucky Colonels, were the unrivalled champions of West Coast bluegrass through the mid-'60s, although unlike most exponents of the genre, they refused to be restricted by the stylistic constraints of bluegrass inventor Bill Monroe. As early as 1965, Clarence White was breaking new ground, jamming with jazz musicians, avant-garde folkies, and the Byrds, with whom he first recorded in late 1966. Two years later, he joined the band full-time. Peter Doggett, on the sleeve notes for the 2003 Country Fever/Black Claw album, describes White as "a master of dexterity and taste, but his trademark was a thicker, meatier sound that seemed to encompass Country, R&B and Psychedelia in every phrase."

With these two albums in early 1970, Albert demonstrated that he was now developing an individual style in which his rock roots were beginning to fuse with the essence of country picking. His singing, now more assured, had acquired a wider range and his playing indicated an assimilation of increasingly eclectic influences: in the words of Keith Nelson, "he's like a sponge—anything he likes he absorbs." On these two albums not only can we hear James Burton, Cliff Gallup and Jimmy Bryant, but there are more insistent echoes of Buck Owens, Don Rich, Tal Farlow, Hank Garland and Clarence White.

Soon after the two albums were recorded, Country Fever backed Hank Locklin, Don Gibson, Marvin Rainwater and Wanda Jackson, but by Christmas, Albert had left the band. Country Fever had never really achieved success: Albert had been in the band for about a year before he realized that it was going nowhere and "we were just playing for ourselves. It's funny really because they got Roger Dean in after I left and they were voted the top English country band."

Country Fever may not have been the gateway to success in country music that Albert might have hoped for but it did open up to him the world of country playing and country players. One such player was Jerry Donahue, an American from Manhattan who had arrived in the United Kingdom hoping to further his academic education. A fluent, gifted folk guitarist, he had ended up working with fellow exile Keith Nelson in the Tumbleweeds, where Albert first met him. He was working as a salesman in Selmer's in Charing Cross Road so he knew Ray Smith, an old mate of Albert's, who was at Lew Davis's[22] a hundred yards away. In the autumn of 1968, Smith was writing with Tony Colton, who had a production deal with Polydor under the name Jaymarnie Music. Smith recalls writing songs for Zoot Money, Georgie Fame, Herbie Goins and Cream. Colton, whose real name is Anthony G. Chalk, had worked with Smith in the R&B outfit the Crawdaddies, who played the Flamingo and had once opened for the Stones. "We'd all be hovering around Charing Cross Road and Soho," so Albert had run into them now and again "but they didn't do as many gigs as we did. I didn't know Tony that well—I might have met him doing a demo." Over the next five years he would get to know him *extremely* well.

Tony Colton is imbued with abundant energy and charisma. In his career he clearly also never suffered a moment's selfdoubt. Before working with the Crawdaddies, he had recorded some soulful singles for Pye and Decca in the mid–'60s. According to the *Record Collector Rare Record Price Guide*, Colton recorded two solo singles and three with the Big Boss Band. All of these 45s are highly collectable, and mint copies of "I've Laid Some Down in My Time," which was a minor hit in the spring of 1966, now change hands for around £25. Colton recalls first seeing Albert "at the Two I's, when he was playing with Pat Donaldson and Roy Mills and Paul Raven[23] was singing. They were playing 'Honey Hush' and I had never heard anybody play it like the original record before—he just blew my mind. In '68, Ray was managing Lew Davis's and all the guitar players congregated there. You had Jerry Donahue, Paul Kossoff, John McLaughlin, but when Albert came in everybody stopped because they all knew he was the boy."

Smith and Tony Colton were writing for MGM and had been nagging the musical director, Ian Ralfini, to let them assemble their dream rhythm section so that they could record their own songs themselves instead of flogging them round Tin Pan Alley. To Smith's surprise, "One day he just said, 'Go in the studio. Make an album. It had better be good but just do it.'" Colton was busy producing a new band from Ireland called Taste, featuring Rory Gallagher. Nevertheless he and Ray gathered together Albert, who was in two kinds of Country Fever, Pat Donaldson, who was dividing his time between psychedelic band Dantalion's Chariot and session work, Nicky Hopkins on piano, Barry Morgan of Blue Mink, Jerry Donahue, who was working in the shop with Smith, Mike O'Neill, who had been the organist in The Crawdaddies and Nero and the Gladiators, and was juggling two gigs, one with The John Barry Seven and the other with Ivy League, and drummer Pete Gavin from Jody Grind.

In December a photograph appeared in *Beat Instrumental* of "a session in progress at Advision Studio. 'Tony Colton makes an album with noted session men Albert Lee and Micky [sic] Hopkins.'" Eddie Offord, the engineer at Advision, recalls that the equipment was basic, a hangover from the 1950s: "There was one studio and back in those days it was sixteen tracks. So it was a very outdated, very old antiquated console. Some of the faders weren't even faders—they were these big rotary parts."

Antediluvian or not, Offord's machinery recorded a remarkable album,[24] the eponymous "Poet and the One Man Band," essentially a vehicle for the song-writing talents of Colton and Smith. With the addition of Speedy Acquaye on conga drums, William Davies on cathedral organ and John Bell on clarinet, this ad hoc assemblage of session players cut at least fourteen original tracks, nine of which emerged in the spring, Colton and Smith's MGM connexion having secured a record deal. Albert is featured heavily on "Ride Out on the Morning Train" and "Dirty Heavy Weather Road" and contributes to the outstanding track "The Days I Most Remember," which contains Colton's most telling vocal on the album. The song, whose production values are reminiscent of The Moody Blues at their best, also includes fine Hammond organ from Mike O'Neill. Ray recalls that there were at least three early unissued Poet tracks, "Women's Privilege," "Pedro" and "Geneva." At that time *Poet* was merely a recording enterprise: there was no band as such, about which Albert was professionally realistic. "*Poet* was really their album. We were just session players."

The *Poet* story does not end there. One day Ray, who had become close to Offord, asked him, "Can we slip in after hours and do 'Poet 2'?" He agreed and the sessions took place under extraordinary circumstances between October and December 1968. As Colton remembers, "Midnight would chime on Bond Street outside of the original Advision studios and the guard would change." As soon as Taste left the studio, Eddie Offord, the engineer to whom Colton passed on the gig as the producer of Yes, changed tape reels and off would come Taste and on would go Colton and Smith's "pirate sessions." The personnel was the basic *Poet* line-up, augmented by an ever-growing choir as Jerry Donahue demonstrated his talent for arranging vocal harmony. As Colton graphically describes it, "From the neon shadows of the Bag of Nails, the Speakeasy, the Marquee bar and a dozen others, we dragged them away from the clutches of tequila, cognac and groupies, gave them a part to sing and hit the red light: Some came for the money, some came as a favor, but they all came in the spirit that pervaded the sixties; no time, day or night was too late to sing and play." Among those who were part of what the album called the Bond Street Midnight Choir were John Anderson, Zoot Money, Andy Summers, Madeline Bell, Linda Lewis, B.J. Cole, David Foster, Ray Osborne, Jamba, Leslie Duncan and Tony Ashton.

By April 1969 Colton and Smith had recorded a second album. About six weeks after the first LP came out in March Ralfini told Smith, "Sorry, Ray, I'm taking everybody to WEA. You can have the rights to the second album but don't release it in England for five years." Colton and Smith were understandably peeved. In fact the album was not released until late in 1995 when Ray Smith recalls Colton saying, "We won't call it Poet 2. We'll call it 'Heads, Hands and Feet: The Missing Album.'"[25] This suited Smith because he and Colton owned the master tape—the musicians were paid only session fees. It was a piece of shrewd marketing to put it out under the Heads, Hands and Feet banner. In the intervening decades, Heads, Hands and Feet had become something of a minor cult band, acknowledged as Britain's most influential country/rock band, whereas Poet and the One Man Band were definitely the arcane preserve of the more dedicated rock aficionados.

A decade on from the 1995 release, *Home from Home*[26] feels set in its own time, like an intriguing fossil captured in amber, lacking the creative energy of the later albums from the standard Heads, Hands and Feet line-up. It has been described by Colton as the best album Heads, Hands and Feet ever made. This may be characteristic Colton hyperbole but his view naturally reflects the balance in this early work, which is tilted as it is towards the vocals of Colton and places much less emphasis on Albert's guitar licks. In that sense it is more like a second *Poet* album—not necessarily a criticism: Colton is a creditable vocalist. The arrangements are imaginative and under Donahue's direction the vocal support is impeccable, but tracks like "Friend of a Friend" and "Windy & Warm," for instance, would not feature in any "Best of Heads, Hands and Feet" compilation. On the other hand, "Bringing It All on My Own Head" encapsulates the band's essential harmony and vitality and "Achmed" is a bizarre curio. The lyric-writing in "Home from Home," which has a "Gasoline Alley" feel in its depiction of a bleak "dirty town but I love it" and "Who Turned Off the Dark?," an engaging offering, is evocative and sharp. The title of the latter song, according to Ray Smith, came from Tony's daughter as she woke up one morning.

Early in 1969 the first album, *Poet and the One Man Band*, was released, to enthusiastic reviews. Then, a bombshell—a month after the album was released, the MGM empire was split up. With the collapse of the label, and the lack of subsequent support or promotion, the album went nowhere. It was especially galling as Jerry's father, Sam Donahue, who had been a well-known tenor saxophonist with Artie Shaw during the war, had landed the band an American deal with Paramount but following the collapse of the MGM record division the album was not released across the Atlantic.

In London, however, the hype was in full swing. In February, MGM arranged a promotional show at the Speakeasy, at 48 Margaret Street, just behind Oxford Circus in central London. Well-established as the hipsters' hangout, the venue had already become part of Britain's rock history. Jimi Hendrix performed a 30-minute version of *Auld Lang Syne* on New Year's Eve, 1967, and King Crimson played their first gig there the following July. The Speakeasy, according to Doherty, was "a legendary club which all the known groups frequented.... Drugs, groupies and on odd occasions, violence, were all part of its vibrant scene. One night, during one of my visits, a 'heavy' rushed up to a well-known lead vocalist and smashed him over the head with an iron bar. His crime? He was trying to switch managers."[27]

Melody Maker reported the band's very first live appearance "on a crowded club night when hosts of angels and musicians were jostling around and emptying the bars." The paper also quoted Des Brown of MGM as "enthusiastically predicting a healthy future for a completely unknown act." In March *Beat Instrumental* reported Eddie Offord talking of "an album made by a group called 'Poet And The One Man Band.' This group was put together simply to record in the first place, but it looks as if the line-up may stay together for future work. Among the participating musicians are Nicky Hopkins and Albert Lee, two giants of respective instruments, piano and guitar, so we may be in for some really fine music."

Albert thought so too: "I was playing with Country Fever at the time but Poet could have been commercial as it was an adventurous and forward-looking outfit." So forward-looking that after their spectacular debut at the Speakeasy club Poet and the One Man Band were booked for the Golden Rose of Montreux Festival ten days later, on the strength of the one performance. Albert has mixed feelings about that gig. "We went to Montreux with Poet and I had this brand-new Fender head I'd bought from a friend. When the roadie got back to London it had mysteriously disappeared off the van. We reckoned he'd sold it." That spring, Albert lost not only a new Fender head but an old friend, when in late March Dickie Pride, "the Sheik of Shake," died in Thornton Heath of suspected drug abuse. He was 27.

So, at the same time as he was on the road with Country Fever and recording for Derek Lawrence, Albert did two or three gigs in town with Poet and the One Man Band and they did some without him: Ray recalls Albert saying, "I'm not in the band," "although he did the choice gigs with us." In May 1969 Albert left altogether, deciding to stick with Country Fever. Talking to *Zigzag* in 1970, Albert asserted that "Ray and Tony tried to get a band on the road.... But we only managed a couple of gigs and we had trouble getting an agent, and it all seemed to fold up. So I stayed on with Country Fever because at least I was making a living wage with them.... It's steady money but you have to work 7 nights a week to make enough."[28]

Albert may have left Poet, although of course in a formal sense he was never actually part of the band. He nevertheless continued to work with Poet's rhythm section doing a session for Ray Smith on Des Ryan's "Summer Gold" and "Carlita,"[29] and in October, when Andrew Loog Oldham needed some numbers to fill his Immediate album, "Blues Leftovers, Volume 4,"[30] Ray recalls Odham "bunging us twenty quid and Tony and I knocked out three songs which were credited to Albert—'Crosstown Link,' an instrumental, 'Next Milestone,' with Tony on vocal, and 'Water on My Fire,' with Paul Williams doing the vocals. The album's been re-issued several times, but nobody's been paid royalties. Sally Kelly[31] tried, but Andrew had gone to Antigua!"

By the end of 1969 Albert had moved stylistically in the direction of the new country/rock movement which was gathering momentum in California. His playing was grounded in the skiffle and rockabilly tradition of Lonnie Donegan and Johnny Burnette but it had increasingly absorbed over the last two years the country influences of Buck Owens and Clarence White, overlaid with the sound of contemporary folk artists such as Bob Dylan and Gordon Lightfoot. Thus, when Britain's leading female folk-rock singer Sandy Denny quit Fairport Convention and looked to form a band with Eclection's Trevor Lucas, she asked Richard Thompson's opinion as to the best guitarist around. According to Eclection's drummer Gerry Conway, the band idea had originally come up as a result of "a [long] conversation with Trevor and Sandy ... chatting about musicians and music. She liked to have people around her ... people that she liked and respected."[32]

Thompson immediately recommended Albert for the gig and the line-up of the new band, Fotheringay, lasted long enough to be profiled in the music press. Clinton Heylin, Denny's biographer, writes, "Albert Lee may have been happy enough with the Gordon Lightfoot and Bob Dylan covers but when it came to the Fotheringay originals his way of picking did not gell all that well with those folksy time-signatures. After a fortnight, the others began to observe a certain taciturnity bordering on disinterest."[33] Conway concurs: "Eventually Trevor said, 'I don't know if Albert's happy, we'll have to tackle him.'...So we asked him and he said, 'Well, I've been meaning to say ... '—and he went on ... 'there wasn't enough for me to do—it wasn't heavy enough ... I introduced Pat Donaldson to the band, then I left and Pat brought in Jerry Donahue to replace me.' Donahue, a versatile guitarist, believes Fotheringay 'wasn't enough of a vehicle for Albert.'"

Albert's brief flirtation with folk/rock was over before it had begun. Nearly forty years on, nobody who was there is precisely sure of the order of the events of 1968 and 1969 and the documentary evidence is less than conclusive. Yet in the early weeks of 1970, the U.K. country magazine *Opry* (forerunner of today's *Country Music People*) seemed to know what was going on. It was still picturing and describing Albert as a member of Country Fever and looking forward to the imminent release of their album—which was certainly not the record produced by Derek Lawrence for Bell.

For Albert, the details mattered little. He had a wife and two toddlers and in January 1970, "I was offered a job by Tony Secunda, recording an LP called 'Short Stories' with a guy called Steve Gibbons, so I did that."

And 1970 would be a helluva year.

Seven

Heads, Hands and Feet

Side One

Early in 1970 there were two sad farewells in British music. In the first week of January, at Abbey Road, the Beatles held the last recording session as a group for their final album, *Let It Be.* Six weeks later Immediate Records went into voluntary liquidation after producing some of Britain's most innovative pop music in its brief four-year history. The label, named for the moment, proved aptly ephemeral, leaving its mark with classic singles such as "Out of Time," "Angel of the Morning" and "Itchycoo Park."

Albert, meanwhile, was working with Birmingham-based rocker Steve Gibbons on *Short Stories,* an album of what Albert describes as "nice little rock 'n' roll tunes."[1] Gibbons' manager was Tony Secunda, who never formally managed Albert but paid him £60 a week as a retainer. Albert also worked sporadically with Derek Lawrence, recording "Six Days on the Road" and "Brother Preacher" in early February and he became involved with *Green Bullfrog,* Lawrence's interesting project for Ritchie Blackmore.

The *Green Bullfrog* album,[2] now eminently collectable, is the legacy of two days' intensive jamming. Studio jams are generally too indolent, self-indulgent or shambolic ever to emerge as recorded products but this was an exception. The tracks were recorded at Kingsway Studios and owing to contractual constraints none of the protagonists were identified on the original sleeve, but were given pseudonyms. The line-up was Earl Jordan (aka Jordan), vocals; Ritchie Blackmore (aka Boots), guitar; Big Jim Sullivan (aka Boss), guitar; Rod Alexander (aka Vicar), guitar; Chas Hodges (aka Sleepy), bass; Tony Ashton (aka Bevy), keyboards; Matthew Fisher (aka Sorry), keyboards; Ian Paice (aka Speedy), drums; and Albert (aka Pinta), so-called because his stock reply whenever anybody said, "Great solo, Albert, but you can do better" was "but I'm only here to deliver the milk." Chas was called "Sleepy" because, says Lawrence, "he's the heaviest sleeper in the world.... He's been woken up on buses in depots by policemen who thought he was dead. And 'Bevy'? Well, Tony Ashton's well known as a man who enjoys a beer.... He always seemed to have an empty crate of light ale under his organ."

Lawrence had originally wanted to work with Tony Dangerfield, Lord Sutch's bassist. "Tony was a tremendous singer, and I pulled in Ritchie, Chas and Ian Paice. It never really happened but we did get a buzz going ... so I decided to indulge a whim.... I'd always thought it would be great if we could get Big Jim, Albert and the rest of the old crew to do something together. Amazingly more or less everyone was free and they all wanted to play with each other, many of them having been in bands or doing sessions together for years, long before anyone made the big time. They were all great musicians: Jim was everyone's hero and virtually taught Ritchie how to play. They both admired Albert—everyone did—and Chas was easily the best bassist around."

The album was recorded in two days, starting around 11 o'clock at night, Blackmore and Paice turning up after far-flung Deep Purple gigs. It was cut live on four-track, Lawrence largely selecting the material, apart from "Who Do You Love?" and "Makin' Time." When Lawrence played the demo of his own "Loving You is Good For Me, Baby" to Sullivan, the big man groaned, "Oh, no, not another blues. Let's make it more interesting" and kicked off with a weird timing riff. As Lawrence recalls, "If you'd told Ritchie and Albert the next number was in 17:9 time they'd have looked at you as if you were barmy.... But Jim plays it and they both go 'Oh, right, yeah.' ... at that stage the only flats they knew about were furnished and diminished fifths were empty bottles of scotch."

The extended instrumental track, "Bullfrog," began with Blackmore launching into a lick, says Lawrence, "and as he played it, Jim came in underneath him and Albert came in on top of him, in harmony.... Ritchie just played the lick once, fiddled about for a bit, went off on one, played it again ... and the other two came straight back in, both in perfect harmony again ... unbelievable.... I really like Tony's keyboards on 'Bullfrog,' which considering he was virtually lying under it at the time was remarkable." For Lawrence, however, the star of the album was Albert. "Everything he did on this album is just marvelous ... but Matt Fisher's piano on 'Ain't Nobody Home' is tremendous.... And Big Jim's soloing on 'Who Do You Love?' is out of this world."

The album bridges the gap in Albert's musical journey between Country Fever, Black Claw and Heads, Hands and Feet, combining soul, gospel, R&B with heavy rock and a hint of country. Lawrence's view of Albert's contribution is accurate. He is the most distinctive player on the album, because while Sullivan and Blackmore use distortion and wah-wah, Albert's performance is free from such artifice. His work on "My Baby Left Me" alludes to the Dave Berry/Jimmy Page arrangement and "I'm A Free Man" features a fluent but funky solo running alongside Sullivan's country-style picking.

Alongside this venture into the world of rock guitar, Albert did not neglect his penchant for country music. Although February's *Country Music People* erroneously reported that Albert was forming "a new contemporary group, which will include the Southern Ramblers' banjo player, Keith Nelson," he did appear with Country Fever at the Second International Festival of Country Music at Wembley over the Easter weekend, backing Charlie Walker and Willard Pierce, as well as the headline act, Don Gibson, whom they also supported on Easter Monday at the Nashville Rooms, with Loretta Lynn and her band. Albert, John and Gerry backed Don, with the drummer and bass player from the Thunderbirds. At the same time the Country Fever albums were released.

Albert was also in the studio in the late spring when he worked with Chris Spedding, Gerry Conway, Pat Donaldson and Mo Foster among others on the eponymous *Mike D'Abo* album, released in July, featuring D'Abo's version of his classic "Handbags and Gladrags." Albert was not paid for some of the sessions—"I didn't put in an invoice." For a man in a notoriously precarious business, with a young family to support, when the wolf needed keeping away from the door, this may seem odd, but it emphasizes Albert's focus on the music and not on the paperwork. Albert has always needed an executive assistant.

Soon after the Wembley Festival and the D'Abo album, Colton and Smith appeared on the horizon. They had formed a link with Johnny Harris, the conductor and arranger, who had been associated with Tom Jones, Lulu, Petula Clark, et al. Harris had met Ray Smith while working on the brass arrangements for Zoot Money and had been commissioned to write the music for an ITV documentary, *The World of Georgie Best*. His manager was Danny, the cousin of Tony Secunda, and he insisted that Secunda contract Colton and Smith to write the lyrics. Danny made an instantly vivid impact on Smith. "Secunda," he says, "looked like a gangster, a bit like Rasputin with a great nose—wonderful man. Everything was visionary."

Joining up with Johnny Harris was a breakthrough and allowed Colton and Smith to re-unite the rhythm section from Poet and the One Man Band when, in early April, they went to Milan to record with Shirley Bassey. It was a turning point in her career. After 14 years it was in the doldrums and Harris opted for a radical new musical approach. Instead of Bassey working with a full orchestra, Harris gave the songs fresh arrangements with Albert, Ray, Tony, Pat Donaldson and Pete Gavin to back her. The songwriting duo contributed "The Sea and Sand," the first single to be released from an album[3] which became the most successful in the Welsh diva's recording career and whose title song, "Something," turned out to be one of her biggest hit singles. It was the first time she had recorded with a basic rhythm section and she enjoyed the experience—as did Albert: "Johnny directed it, she sang just to the rock 'n' roll rhythm section then Johnny put all the strings and brass on top. I don't remember her being much of a diva: she was quite polite and friendly. We didn't need too many overdubs—I did a few on 'Spinning Wheel' when we got back to London."

Back in London Danny Secunda had been networking. Johnny Harris was scheduled to provide the orchestral backdrop for a concert by Dionne Warwick at the Royal Albert Hall: Secunda persuaded him to include the Smith and Colton rhythm section on the show, with addition of Jerry Donahue. On April 13, Albert recalls, "we opened for Dionne Warwick as the Johnny Harris Movement, which was Johnny's orchestra plus a 20-strong youth orchestra from the Royal College and the Royal Academy of Music led by Brian Gascoigne [Bamber's brother]. We played 'Something,' 'Wichita Lineman,' 'Light My Fire,' 'Paint It Black' to promote Johnny's album,[4] then, instead of doing a straight instrumental slot, we did a selection of original Colton, Smith, Harris numbers, like 'Windy and Warm,' 'Help,' 'Diane' and 'Phoenix.'"

Colton and Smith flew to Cyprus for a fortnight's break, where Johnny Harris tracked them down. "How would you like to work with Richard Harris when you get back?" Harris, the charismatic and volatile Irish film star, was an unlikely pop hero but had had a huge hit in 1968 with Jimmy Webb's "Macarthur Park." Colton and Smith agreed at once and in late May the team recorded "Ballad of a Man Called Horse."[5] Albert found Richard Harris "quite a character" and remains a huge fan of Jimmy Webb. "He grew up on show tunes and always wanted to write a musical. His music was so open and country-like in a way."

In May Brian Golbey, one of the country players on the Lucky label, released a bluegrass-flavored album,[6] on which Albert played acoustic guitar. He also found time to do yet one more session with Lawrence, cutting "What A Stupid Thing To Do" and "Another Useless Day." Ray and Tony, together with Pete Gavin and occasionally Pat Donaldson, were working regularly, and Albert, after a few insecure months, was having fun. He recalls *Top of the Pops* with Shirley Bassey, "with a picture of a big white buffalo as a backdrop."

In June 1970 Johnny Harris left Danny Secunda to join Paul Anka, after which Secunda took an interest in Harris's favorite rhythm section, put his money where his influential mouth was and became the outfit's manager. Albert remembers that "he was paying us and he'd given the band a flat."[7] As he told *Zigzag*[8]: "Danny had the right ideas about handling the group. Everyone was interested in it before, but no one was actually willing enough to do anything about it." At the time, Colton was getting a lot of production work, "and Danny had got me to the point with United Artists that the next project would have been Sammy Davis and possibly Sinatra. So I had two hats. I was either going to be a rock singer on the road or this huge career in front of me."

Secunda had unbridled energy and chutzpah. His cousin Tony was trying to persuade Albert to join Steve Gibbons. The music press had fun for a while with the family struggle but Danny was clear-sighted enough to see that Albert was integral to his plans for the new band, which had the same line-up as Poet—except that Pat Donaldson adopted the Sam Goldwyn approach—"Include me out." Colton had had a foretaste of future problems when Poet had played the Montreux Jazz Festival a year earlier. Rory Gallagher and Yes, two acts produced by Colton, were also on the bill. "It was weird then," says Colton, "to be an artist and a producer, not so much for me as for the record company. So I decided to pursue my production career." Pat Donaldson told him, "I understand your decision, but don't ever ask me again to go into a band with you." So, a year on, when Colton invited him to join his new outfit, he declined, concerned lest Colton might be tempted to jump ship again. "Brilliant man," says Colton today, "but ballsy—stood by his word."

So in July 1970, Chas Hodges got a phone call—from Albert. "He was joining a new group: they needed a bass player and he recommended me." Chas was reluctant to leave Black Claw but he was broke. "It was a hard decision to make, but all agreed Black Claw's future looked dim without money behind us. And money was nonexistent." So Chas came on board and Pete Gavin chose the name for the new band. He came up with Heads, Hands and Feet, which Albert and the others found "interesting."

Danny Secunda had arranged an audition gig at the Revolution Club near Grosvenor Square in the middle of July and the band decamped to a farm near Staplecross in rural Sussex for a fortnight to get material together and rehearse. It was scarcely five-star accommodation: Ray Smith remembers Albert washing his feet in the sink in the mornings! Albert had always been very conscious of personal hygiene[9]: "In our first flat we used to have to wash in the kitchen sink." Ray also learned of Chas's interest in astronomy, as he'd brought his telescope with him. As Colton points out, "Chas likes to come across a bit of a Cockney geezer but there's a lot going on underneath." He thought Chas's arrival changed the nature of the band. Donaldson was a more sophisticated bass player but Chas had a down-home persona and gave the band broader musical horizons—keyboards, fiddle and writing. With Albert, he would ensure that the band would set off down roads trodden by the Band and the Byrds—a country-rock direction almost unique in London at the turn of the decade.

At the Revolution, the band played a 45-minute set, featuring songs from the Poet repertoire and some original material, including "Country Boy." Ray Smith explains: "With Albert in the band we had to write more country stuff, in particular a vehicle for him. That's how 'Country Boy' came about. Albert was doing 'Twelfth Street Rag,' which Danny felt was a bit corny." The band met up one Saturday afternoon at the office in Edgware Road near Marble Arch. Tony Colton asked Albert to play something as fast as he could in his favorite key of G. Ray remembers "he already had the introduction, that bluegrass sort of thing, which was on a Country Fever album."[10] Albert was trying to recreate on his guitar the sound of a bluegrass banjo; what emerged was eerily reminiscent of "Rocky Top." Then Albert vaguely hummed a melody, Tony Colton chipped in with the first line and "nailed it," says Ray. "Tony was very good at getting the essence of what you wanted melodically but as he's a lyricist we had to bend the notes to fit the words." Albert chuckles, "You do have to explain 'Read *Exchange and Mart*'[11] to the Americans!" The song haunts Colton to this day: "If I'd known what it was to become I'd certainly have taken more time with the lyrics. I did it in five minutes and it's one of the worst I've ever written—but it's his showcase piece on stage."

Ray Smith had a lot to do with the song's structure. Once Albert had the first part of the verse and had "Read *Exchange and Mart*" from Tony, "I came in with the E flat, B flat [for the last two lines of the chorus] and we'd finished. Originally it was just a one-bar break, but because Albert was on his own we thought it would be more exciting to give him an open-ended solo." The creation of chord links was Ray Smith's forte. "He was brilliant at that," says Albert. "He wrote Chad Stuart and Jeremy Clyde's chords for the bridge[12] on 'Yesterday's Gone' in the shop one lunchtime and just handed it to them. He was always doing that."

Notwithstanding Smith's chord changes and Colton's lyrics, "Country Boy" remains Albert's song and Albert's trademark piece. It bears his unmistakable signature, a tour de force which blends the rhythmic attack of the British rock tradition with the dexterous exuberance of Appalachian bluegrass. Its lyrics affirm that at the heart of the mundane existence of a lad from suburban south London beats a yearning for the simple pleasures of a rural life. For Albert, whose soul fused the Romany traditions of the horse and cart, the broad highway, caravans and camp fires under an open sky with the realities of rock 'n' roll in a commercial, metropolitan world, the song has a particular resonance. As Eric Clapton asserts, "He has brought a lot of his heritage with him. He plays with what is in his blood.... He's been influenced by rockabilly and country music's great playing but he brings something else to it that they don't have. It's a mixture of Django Reinhardt and James Burton and a lot of others. He's not simply the greatest country player—he's unique and doesn't fit into a box."

Heads, Hands and Feet, in the anything-goes world of 1970, were seen as the next big thing. "When you looked at the content of the band, musician-wise," thought Mike Berry, "it's not surprising." As Keith Nelson put it, Heads, Hands and Feet were "a seriously blinding band" and Danny Secunda had enticed the major labels along to the Revolution to hear them. Ahmet Ertegun, the founder of Atlantic Records, and Art Mogul of Capitol had traveled from the States to join Island's Chris Blackwell—all cajoled into coming by the band's charismatic promoter. Ertegun particularly liked Albert because he saw dollar signs surrounding the next guitar hero and Ray recalls almost signing to Atlantic: "Ahmet had already got a handshake off Secunda so when we decided to join Capitol he was cheesed off." Tony Colton was concerned that Ertegun wanted only Albert and said "Go with Capitol because they want the band." Legend has it that Heads, Hands and Feet, after just one gig, landed what was at that time the biggest advance ever offered to a band—a quarter of a million dollars.

In the event, the band signed to Capitol for the USA and to Island for the U.K. "Island didn't have as much money to offer but they had a hipper image," says Tony. "Capitol had the money but Island was part of EMI, who had Cliff Richard and all those people who were great in their own way but a bit staid for those days. By signing to both companies we got the best of both worlds."

After the Revolution, so to speak, the band spent six weeks or so on a sheep farm near Tirabad, a tiny village on the edge of the Brecon Beacons, writing material for the first album. Reg Locke, the band's road manager stolen from Richard Harris, had driven his motorbike into mid–Wales and stumbled across Farmer Davis' farm, ten miles north of Llandovery.

"By the time we went to Wales," recalls Albert, "we already had the deal with Capitol and although money started to flow it was less than I had been getting before." Through the whole period with Heads, Hands and Feet Albert was earning only £40 a week: he had been getting £60 with Tony Secunda. After the recording deal, Colton and Smith had deposits for houses. "They wanted to keep me sweet, so they got me a deposit too—about £1,400. With that I bought 15 Canberra Road, Charlton. It cost £7,300 and we'd just moved in when we went to Wales."

In Llandovery the band frequented Masochi's coffee bar near a girls' school, Ysgol Gyfun Pantycelyn. Mary Hemming takes up the story: "My best friend Gwen Rice, also called Muff, said one day, 'I met some people last night. Come up to the caff after school—they're going to be there.'" In Masochi's, Albert, Tony and Ray met three sisters, Misty, Muff and Sparks—and Mary. She had just turned sixteen but seemed older than her years and more worldly: she had lived on the remote South Atlantic island of Tristan da Cunha for two years where her father, Alan, now a farmer, had been a communications officer. She was vivacious and pretty and Albert found her open friendliness beguiling. Soon the girls were at the farm every day listening to music, as Gwen recalls: "We used to go up to the cottage in a huge Mercedes van," but, says Albert, "If we had the girls at the cottage we took them home." Mary presumed they would all go back to London at the end of the summer and that would be the end of it, but Albert and Mary stayed in constant touch and when Mary left school at the end of July 1971 she moved to London and continued the relationship, with cataclysmic consequences for both of them.

Mary was not the only one. Her friend Muff became Tony Colton's girlfriend. "It was kind of innocent," says Colton, "full of youth and nonstop music—just wonderful. It was one of those summers none of us will ever forget. We were all married, of course, but we were pretending to be rock stars." Amazingly enough, nobody ever complained that the girls were a bit young. Mary's parents in particular had always brought their girls up to be their own selves and gave them the freedom to be the people they wanted to be. However, Danny Secunda was so worried about local gossip that he went to the mayor and proposed a free gig at the local community center at the end of the stay, a chance for the band to test the new material live.

And there was a lot of material: a collage of odes to unrequited love, to drinking, quitting drinking and to decadence and self-effacement. Most of the songs on the first album were written in Tirabad, filtered through Colton and Smith's songwriting experience. "We had all these tunes and when you write for someone specific, like a band, you get inside their heads. It's like making a suit for someone—you have to find what fits." Mike O'Neill, who wrote many of the arrangements, like "Devil's Elbow," cannot believe how anything ever got done, because "Chas, Pete and Albert were in the pub every night till 2 o'clock." Many public houses in rural Wales—at least in those days—took a flexible approach to licensing hours. The hostelry in question was the Glanbran Arms at Cynghordy, on the road to Llandovery, where Chas and Albert would lead a sing-song round the piano—"Boiled Beef and Carrots," "Knees Up Mother Brown" and the rock 'n' roll canon. The band also rode a dirt bike and had many escapades with horses. One night Chas and Tony "borrowed" a horse and rode it to the pub, only to come to grief on the way home—a saga immortalized in the song "Tirabad." Indeed, there is much about Wales in the songs. Farmer Davis gets a name-check in "Everybody's Hustling" and reference is made to "Going up the Sugar Loaf," a local hill, in Gavin's virtual drum solo "Pete Might Spook the Horses," a title which speaks for itself. Muff and Mary are referred to in "Devil's Elbow" and "Song for Suzy" mentions Lucy.

Danny Secunda felt that Capitol should release *Home from Home*, in effect the second Poet album, as the Heads, Hands and Feet debut. He tried to convince Colton of this, but by the time the Capitol deal was signed the band was slightly different and in a burst of youthful altruism Colton felt that the first album should reflect the new line up. Accordingly, between November and February, the band recorded the debut LP at Advision, engineered by Eddie Offord, with Tony Colton producing.

The band did not gig while recording, which Ray felt was a pity: "We could have tightened up the songs. The live versions we did for the BBC just after are much better, especially 'Country Boy,'" which was cut three times. Albert recorded it with the Telecaster, with Ray's Les Paul Custom and

Albert rides bareback during the Heads, Hands and Feet sessions, in Wales in 1970 (courtesy the Lee family).

with his Baldwin Electric Classic, plugged into Albert's 4X10 Bassman or a blackface Fender Twin. Albert was "into Jerry Reed at the time and we bought the Baldwin because of that: it cost about £100 with the amp." Although the Telecaster was an integral part of the sound of Heads, Hands and Feet, the track with the Baldwin was the one that was used. Although the Baldwin was a cheap guitar, probably Japanese-made, "it had a really cool pickup that got the best sound for that song. It was reworked in the mid–'70s with Chas and Dave. Chas really brought the song to life—it was his idea to do the solo in the key of E which makes it much more interesting. Ray suggested to Albert that he scatted some of the parts at the end of 'Country Boy,' playing piano at the same time. He did—"it was tremendous," says Smith. "I suggested he did it on stage but Albert's natural reticence kicked in: 'Oh, I don't know. I'd feel a bit stupid.'" When Albert sang "Delaware," a song inspired by Jimmy Webb, Mary was in the studio: She and Muff had skipped school and hitched to London to go and see them recording. He shared lead vocal with Tony on "You Because You Know Me" and with Chas on "Trying To Put Me On." Elton Dean, from the R&B band Bluesology, contributed tasteful sax to the album as well as part of Reg Dwight's stage name.[13]

The music press soon got wind of the sessions. At the end of February, *Melody Maker* ran a piece under the headline "Albert lands on his feet," in which he talked about the album. "It's very hard to define the direction of the music. We play all sorts of different styles. In the band I'm the hands, the drums are the feet and Tony and Ray are the heads! But I like the LP and it's got a bit of melody. There's no raving twenty-minute blows." He also spoke about his guitar style: "It's not out and out country, just pop and country. I've never really been knocked out by hard, heavy stuff, but I prefer things with more melody."

In March 1971 the Laura Nyro/Jackson Browne tour concluded with a performance in London at the Festival Hall. While Browne was in town he cut some tracks[14] with Chris Stainton on piano, Jim Keltner on drums, and Leon Russell, who played piano on "Jamaica Say You Will." Albert met Browne and later that month guested with Jerry Reed at the Nashville Rooms, and Heads, Hands and Feet joined Johnny Harris once again on Carl Wayne's second solo album, cutting "Take It Easy," Leon Russell's "A Song For You" and "If I Go Where You Go," "Respect Yourself" and "Delaware." The album is still unreleased.

As a plug for the planned summer tour, Danny Secunda had secured through Capitol a ten-day gig for the band at the Troubadour in Los Angeles. "All the brilliant moves with Heads, Hands and Feet," says Colton, "came from Danny." The Troubadour, on Santa Monica Boulevard in West Hollywood, is one of Los Angeles' oldest clubs and achieved legendary status in the late '60s and early '70s hosting singer-songwriters like Tom Waits, Jackson Browne and Emmylou Harris and bands such as Poco and the Eagles. Heads, Hands and Feet excited considerable interest. "We were the band of the month, the one that everyone wanted to see," recalls Tony Colton. Mort Lewis, Simon and Garfunkel's manager, was interested in handling the band in the States, talking about getting them into the Hollywood Bowl, but Colton was unimpressed: "He was very pedantic, not a patch on Danny. Lewis was a prop plane but Danny was a jet."

For Ray Smith, the ten days at the Troubadour were a dream come true. He met Nelson Riddle on the plane going over and "he was asking about the arrangement of one of our tunes!" For Albert, too, the trip was a watershed. Throughout the '60s he had felt like an odd man out in England and "couldn't wait to get to America. That was where the music was. I wasn't too enamored with a lot of British bands I was hearing in the late '60s. I wasn't a big Jimi Hendrix fan although I knew him. It wasn't the way I wanted to play. I wanted to go off in a different direction. Then we went to the Troubadour." Exiled Brit Terry Slater worked at a music publishers in the Capitol Tower as well as writing for the Everly Brothers and took the band under his wing. He told Jerry Allison and Sonny Curtis of the Crickets, "You've got to see this band, especially the guitar player." Allison and Curtis remember Heads, Hands and Feet being more of a rock band than a country band. "They were good players and it was enjoyable music, is all," says Allison. Curtis was highly impressed with Albert. "He blew me away. I liked the way he played with all his fingers, even the little pinky." Albert had met the Crickets briefly backstage at a gig in Charing Cross Road "but I was totally in awe of them and just mumbled 'Hallo.'" On this occasion however, Albert met them on an equal footing: there were others, too. "Gordon Lightfoot admired my electric mandolin, which Keith Nelson had made for me," and Tony Colton recalls that "Kris Kristofferson was in one night and still talks to me about that gig today."

While he was in Los Angeles, Albert met Sterling and Ernie Ball, major figures in his later career. "They'd heard 'Country Boy' on the radio, which had blown Ernie away; he was quite surprised to discover it was an English band. They came to see us play a number of times, and we visited the factory in Newport Beach." At that time, Sterling's godfather, Tom Walker, had just started the Music Man company with Leo Fender, and Albert got one of their first amps, and still uses them. Albert also played on Jackson Browne's eponymous debut album, sometimes called "Saturate Before Using"—a legend printed on the sleeve. Albert had met Jackson in London when Jackson was working on the album with Joe Cocker's producer Denny Cordell. After Browne and Cordell fell out, the album was abandoned, only to resurface in Los Angeles on David Geffen's new Asylum label. When Browne recommended work on it he called Albert to play on "A Child In These Hills" and "Under The Falling Sky."

The band was now hot property. Mike O'Neill recalls Dick Clark[15] inviting them on his nationwide TV show. Then, one day near the end of the gig, Secunda announced that he wanted to see the whole band at breakfast next morning, which was odd—they had never had breakfast together before. "We were all there," recalls Ray, "when suddenly Danny laid into Mort Lewis with the most foul abuse. 'You fucking bastard! Here you are, trying to steal my band!'" Ray was shocked: "I don't like rows at the best of times and neither does Albert—and certainly not when I'm not prepared." Secunda told them to pack their bags and fly home. "Back to the 51 Club, Windsor—that's the gig." The band wondered what was going on. They were in Los Angeles, they were going down a bomb, they had their visas— why Windsor? Mike O'Neill thinks Secunda was "in trouble ... and didn't want to hang around." Once back in England, Ray got a call from Chris Blackwell. "Stay by the phone. You'll get a call soon from America." It was Art Mogul from Capitol: "Come over, boys. Let's sort this out. Look, we'll say you've broken up."

Tony, Albert and Ray flew back to Los Angeles and met Mogul in his office in Capitol Tower. Ray was annoyed and upset. "For all his madness Danny had done everything but he'd lost the plot.... What are we doing? The album's out. Frankie Valli[16] was at the reception to launch it. We should be on a tour promoting it." Secunda walked into the meeting and fell off his cloud. He asked the band what they were doing there and very politely, they told him, "Sorry, but we don't want you to manage us any more." Secunda panicked, pulling Albert to one side. "He tried to get me into his camp," remembers Albert, "saying he'd look after my career. I told him I wanted to stay with the band. I knew I was hot property—the band had many facets but my guitar-playing was one of its leading assets." Shortly after that Secunda was hospitalized. However, Secunda's behavior certainly seems curious. For someone with such a sharp eye for the main chance to pass up opportunities for nationwide exposure such as the Dick Clark show and a management deal with Mort Lewis was out of character. The band had a work permit for six months and should have been capitalizing on all the interest but with no tour there was no hit single and the chance was lost to build on the original impetus: it was in the end a wasted trip.

Chas has written perceptively, with deep regret, of the whole scenario. "Danny Secunda, the manager, got aimed out. The man who got the band off the ground. Who had faith when no one else did. The band, instead of being a unit, began to be, once more, just a bunch of talented musicians with no leader and therefore no positive goals. Unrest began to settle in the camp."[17] For Tony Colton, the grisly experience still cuts deep. "Danny's departure has haunted me all my life because he was a genius. I was an idiot to let him go but he was in Malibu giving me some very strange answers. It wasn't the Danny I knew.... Reggie egged me on and I allowed him to talk me into getting rid of Danny. It was the worst day's work I ever did but I was as screwed up as anyone."

Reg Locke took over as manager in May 1971, "when it all went down the toilet," says Ray. "Reg was 6 feet 4 and Tony was 5 feet whatever and he was ordering him about. He could get Reg to do anything." Colton sees that now: "Reggie was like a wrecking ball because he didn't have the experience. It wasn't his fault, it was my fault." Albert felt Colton was very controlling: "He wanted to do everything—write, sing, play piano and produce. I was dreading success because I felt it would all go out of control, with no check over the money. Reg Locke was a lovely guy but he spent money like water. Suddenly we were thinking 'This isn't the same.'"

Despite the backstage shenanigans, however, there was work to do. The band toured Scotland with Deep Purple, then played with Buddy Miles at the Royal Albert Hall. The Zoom in Frankfurt was followed by the Montreux Jazz Festival and at Pentecost the Great Western Express Festival, Bardney, near Lincoln, with the Faces, Ry Cooder, Helen Reddy, Roxy Music and Nazareth.

At the end of May their eponymous debut album[18] was released, with a logo designed by Mike O'Neill. The band had written so much in Wales that they floated the idea of a double album with Capitol, which agreed. Island Records, however, did not consider the British market strong enough for a double album as a first release and issued it only as a single LP. Its music, heavily influenced by the band, had a country flavor and met with some critical acclaim. *Melody Maker* reviewed "Country Boy": "Love that guitar picking, sounds like one of those good old Hofner semi-electrics. Fabulous vibes from this, the kind you find around bars in New Orleans, a great country feeling. Christ, he's too good. It's strange isn't it how an Englishman learns his music from the States, then kicks it right back in their faces?"

Then, another shock in a tumultuous year: Mike O'Neill left the band. Ray recalls "it wasn't his fault he got the sack. On 'Silvermine,' the B-side of 'Warming Up the Band,' the next single, Albert plays solo piano." Chas had also played piano on some German gigs and Pat Donaldson was asked to fill in on bass. "We'd then have three potential keyboard players," says Ray, "so Mike was the sacrificial lamb." Colton thinks that O'Neill was "engineered out. Chas saw an opportunity—Mike was a bit jazzy and didn't fit with him and Albert. I had to fire Mike: it wasn't pleasant for I'd been with him a long time. *Home From Home* is his album—he arranged it. He's a wonderful musician, an insightful player and arranger. Georgie Fame wouldn't have a career if it wasn't for Mike. Don't get me wrong—Georgie is almost my favorite artist." O'Neill had grown increasingly disillusioned with the band: "It was getting too countrified and I leant more towards rock 'n' roll and jazz. I did some sessions for Donovan's 'Open Road' album and then went on tour with his band, also called Open Road."

Side Two

Throughout the summer of 1971, when Charlie George won the Double for Arsenal, Don McLean released "American Pie," Jim Morrison and Louis Armstrong—two iconic performers of vastly different genres and generations—passed away, and George Harrison organized the Concert for Bangladesh, the band, like Mike O'Neill, took to the open road. From the Torrington in north Finchley to the Starlight Club in Crawley via an appearance on Bob Harris's radio show[19] and a gig with Mott the Hoople at the Royal Albert Hall, the band went to Scandinavia, Germany and France between U.K. dates. In July Heads, Hands and Feet played their biggest gig to date in front of about 250,0000 in Hyde Park with Grand Funk Railroad and Humble Pie. Albert recalls the band "nearly running out of petrol driving down from Wales but there were very few gas stations en route. I was in my own car[20] and heard the next day a couple of the guys got arrested for siphoning petrol. I went to court with them where they were let off with a fine. It was not something we would normally do."

It was a summer of festivals and stadia. The Weeley Festival in Clacton was followed by Liverpool Stadium and Hereford United Football Ground with Mott the Hoople and Amazing Blondel and a gig at the Lyceum, interesting for a not entirely uncritical review in the *Melody Maker*: "It is easy to comprehend the reasons for the aura of superlativeness that surrounds Albert Lee. Simply, he is a natural, uncluttered and attractive guitarist who has obviously never heard of the word 'cliché' in relation to the versatility of his instrument. Unfortunately it seems that his full talents are left rather unexploited on a good deal of Heads, Hands and Feet material. Apart from such gems as 'Country Boy' ... a lot of the band's compositions seem too unconvincing and restrictive and tend to deny Lee the support he deserves. He always appears to be struggling to work around stock-type heavy riffs and one tends to wonder how much more adept he would be, given the correct vehicle for his talents." In late September, the band was reunited with Bob Harris when they became the first band to play on *The Old Grey Whistle Test*.[21]

Against this hectic backdrop of touring and gigging, Albert was naturally spending very little time at his new home in Charlton. This lifestyle of the wandering minstrel Lucy accepted with equanimity. What was more serious was that Mary was becoming an important feature of his life. She had been persuaded to return to Wales for long enough to do her O Levels but "I was away a lot of the time with the band on the road. When I finished school at the end of July 1971 I went to live with my elder sister Lindy, a costume designer, in her flat in Bewdley Street, Islington." Mary worked in a clothing store and as a seamstress making costumes—and she and Albert carried on their relationship. Mary was aware, of course, that he was still living with Lucy: "He continued to live with her all the time we were together." Lucy discovered the relationship, Ray Smith believes, because "he got stopped by the police for speeding and when the notice came through she asked him, 'What were you doing in Llandovery when you were playing in Sheffield?' He'd driven from London to pick Mary up."

For Lucy, "the Mary incident was rough." What disturbed her even more was discovering Mary's youth. "If I had found out that my Abigail at 16 was seeing a married man of 28 who had two kids I would have been furious, but her Mum turned round to me and said, 'You can't blame her for getting what she can.' It all came as a bit of a shock. As he came through Highbury where her sister lived he used to stop off and then Mary would phone me at five in the morning to let me know he was coming home." She is philosophical about the affair today: "it could happen to anyone."

Rather less philosophical was Albert's hot-headed younger sister, Vanessa. At a Heads, Hands and Feet gig in Islington she saw Albert looking down at a young girl. "I thought, 'That's Mary standing there. What a bloody cheek!' Lucille had told me that she existed; I think she knew that Mary was a bit more than a 'life-on-the-road' thing and that was why it affected her more. I approached her outside and we had a bit of a fracas. Perhaps I shouldn't have done it but I was upset for Lucille and for my parents." Mary stood her ground. "After all," she says, "I was still only seventeen and at that age you don't see the implications very much of your actions. You just *do*." Albert concedes, "Music was the important thing but I had all this other stuff going on in my life—it was a pretty chaotic period." Mary recognizes his disarming honesty. "He has always had a twinkle in his eye and there have always been ladies. Even when I was the thing in his life there were other women on the road. He'd say, 'I'm very sorry. I've been...' And I'd say, 'Well, that's life. You're a rock 'n' roller. That's what you do.' I thought it was part of the package. What more do you expect?"

In October, a live version of Jon Lord's rock symphony, *Gemini Suite*,[22] initially conceived for Deep Purple, was released. Lord changed his mind and composed it for different players—Albert, Tony Ashton, Yvonne Elliman, Roger Glover and Ian Paice, as well as the London Symphony Orchestra conducted by Malcolm Arnold. The album has three tracks per side, with each track composed for a different instrument. Albert plays "Guitar," the eight-minute opening track, and while the album has other highlights it is weighed down by the London Symphony Orchestra, "the size of the project no doubt matching Lord's ego at that time. The bucolically suggestive gatefold jacket features two naked men gazing at each other and as the gatefold opens, the back features them from the waist down, transformed into monstrous tentacles and clawing at each other. The Albert material is well worth the eyesore though."[23] *Gemini Suite* attracted the critical hostility which such "progressive" musical ambitions engendered: Indeed, the recording of the original studio version was never released on record and had to wait until 1993 for a commercial release. Albert's "Guitar" movement is more measured than Ritchie Blackmore's exciting live version and his languidly lovely cadenza outclasses Blackmore's solo in its musicality, despite the loss of the beautiful closing diminuendo.

In the second half of October and early November the band continued its relentless round of the university and college circuit, playing the University of Warwick at Coventry with Van Der Graaf Generator, Keele University, Aston University, St. Luke's College, Exeter, Lancaster University, Leeds University, Sheffield University, Hatfield Polytechnic, as well as the Kensington Court Club in Newport, Redcar Jazz Club, the Village Roundhouse in Dagenham and the Pop Roots show at the Royal Festival Hall. The band was beginning to make headway with audiences. "When people saw us at first they couldn't quite understand what we were trying to do," says Albert, "but the great thing about audiences, especially colleges, is that they were prepared to listen to what we were doing." *Melody Maker* ran an interesting review of the Aston gig,[24] where, according to Dennis Detheridge, the band had the crowd, "stamping and shouting for more. Tony Colton was at the mike for the first three numbers, 'I'm in Need of Your Help,' 'Warming Up the Band' and the slower 'Dirty Heavy Weather Road,' then he went on to piano while Chas Hodges had a hoe-down on 'Trying to Put Me on.' Albert Lee's 'Country Boy,' featuring his incredible lightning guitar work. They were in happy-go-lucky mood for 'Hang Me, Dang Me,' providing Albert with an opportunity for a bit of honky-tonk piano, before ending with 'Pete Might Spook the Horses,' a workout for Pete Gavin on drums."

The same journal in early November carried a long piece[25] by Chris Charlesworth, in which Albert talks about his '59 Fender Telecaster, bought in 1963 and a Martin 000 28. "I only paid £50 for the Telecaster. I've put a Gibson pick-up on it and had the neck inlaid with mother of pearl. It's a bit battered but it's all right for me. I would like to get another Telecaster, but even if I did I wouldn't part with this one."

The interview was somewhat out of date. "When we came back from America that summer—1971—I gave Ray my Telecaster. On that trip I'd got a maple-neck '53 Telecaster, a B-bender mechanism, an amp and pedals, an Echoplex and Ray didn't come back with anything. I felt sad for him so I gave him my Telecaster. A few years later I found out he was hard up and he'd sold it. I wish he'd told me as I would have bought it off him. I tracked it down to a Scottish bass player who was with Clodagh Rodgers. The only way I recognized it was by the pearl inlays which Keith Nelson had put in the neck. The body had been stripped, it had all different pickups and a rosewood fingerboard. I didn't even ask how much he wanted as I would have had to strip it down totally and put all new pickups on it. What's the point?"

Albert told Charlesworth he had the Martin[26] for two years and was lucky to get it for £130, "which is very cheap for them."

The band's sets at that summer's gigs had been promoting the first album and road-testing songs which would appear on the follow-up, *Tracks*, recorded at Advision between December 1971 and February 1972. Co-produced with Tony Colton and engineered by Eddie Offord, the sessions also included Gerry Hogan on pedal steel, with backing vocals from Jerry Donahue. Mary also occasionally dropped in: "When they were recording the album I used to go into the studios after work and sit in on the sessions."

The album, perhaps the most satisfying of the band's three releases, was the first to feature Albert's composed vocals and melodic piano, reminiscent of Jackson Browne or the early Tom Waits. "Tony started to pull back a bit towards the end of '71—it gave us the incentive to write songs and I came up with three, including 'Roadshow,' which was inspired by

Jackson Browne, with whom I'd already worked." The stark reality of its lyrics shows Albert under the influence of Jimmy Webb and might also reflect the fact that in the middle of February Mary told Albert some devastating news. She was expecting a baby in September.

This was not meant to happen. Mary knew that Albert would have been happier "if I had decided to become un-pregnant, but my circle of friends did not consider it a problem. While my parents may not have been happy they dealt with it, though it must have been difficult for them." Muff describes Mary's parents as "pretty unusual people: they had been out of Wales for some time so they didn't have the parochial attitudes of a small town in south Wales in 1970." They were always totally supportive of Mary and had brought their daughters up with the freedom to be the people they wanted to be. "They knew that I was seeing Albert. In any case my father was working abroad during part of the time—perhaps if he had been around he might have been more vocal than my Mum was. She had a family and a business to deal with and stroppy teenage daughter who was doing her own thing."

Mary's shock news shines a bleak light on "Roadshow," "a song about somebody leaving home and the kids, about things that were going on in my life," as Albert puts it, though his perception of how it came to be written is rather different from Tony Colton's. "I wanted him to write songs because with his genius he had to have some awesome material but he was very lazy: He'd admit that. He still is. I booked Advision, one of the most expensive studios in the world at the time, and I called him to a session." When he turned up I said, "Here's the deal. I've booked the studio this morning for you and me to write. And we're splitting the bill. That guitar came out of the case as fast as anything and three songs came together. 'Song and Dance' and 'Rhyme and Time' were two of them. He wrote 'Roadshow' at home—that song changed my writing style: I'm still trying to write my own 'Roadshow.' Forcing him to sit down and write when it's costing him money produced the goods—that's the gypsy in him." Today, Albert still finds it hard to write: "I prefer to use the piano more than guitar for writing because with the guitar I keep going off on instrumental tangents, rather than keep to the concept of the song. I haven't got the time or patience to sit down and work out lyrics, I want to play." But "he shone on Tracks," says Colton, "and I wish he'd continued."

The influential Chris Welch, reviewing Tracks in Melody Maker, loved the album. Welch recognised Albert "as a guitarist to rub shoulders in the big league. Since his days with Chris Farlowe's Thunderbirds, he has been quietly playing marvelous country and blues guitar. But now it should be proclaimed that Mr. Lee is also a singer of merit and a songwriter of distinction. Although he has been singing for some time, his voice here blossoms with a power and confidence that makes me think if only Albert wore a star-spangled top hat he might be a superstar."

Albert's distinctive vocal style comes as something of a surprise on the album. Although he had sung since the skiffle days he stopped when he joined Farlowe.

The week before Tracks was released in April 1972 Albert had acquired himself a piano. The band were playing High Wycombe Town Hall,[27] when at the end of the gig Albert noticed a Steinway grand backstage. A town hall porter told him it was about to be dumped. Albert rang the Council the next morning. A young female employee confirmed the porter's story and asked Albert how much he would offer for it. He gulped and suggested £50 as an opening gambit. "It's not in very good condition," the girl replied. Nevertheless, Albert said, he still wanted the piano, sent £20 as a deposit and three weeks later got the roadies—with the readies—to fetch it from High Wycombe. Later, Albert found it was an 1882 model; a new one would have cost about £3,000. It was an impulse purchase but Albert, the grandson of a fairground trader, was shrewd enough to obtain a receipt. It was fortunate that the innately disorganized Albert had kept it, for a year or so later the police called Lucy at Canberra Road inquiring about a piano which had mysteriously disappeared from High Wycombe Town Hall.

The bulk of the winter was taken up with recording *Tracks* and with the album safely in the can, the band embarked on an intensive promotional tour with Patto and Claire Hamill in the second half of March, in the midst of which Green Bullfrog's release went virtually unheralded. Then one of the rock magazines hyped it and the album became instantly collectable. Early in April, the band again worked with Johnny Harris, who had been co-commissioned with Bill Whelan[28] to write the score for the new Richard Harris film *Bloomfield*,[29] which in America was called *The Hero*. At Harris' request Colton and Smith provided three songs, "Hail the Conquering Hero,"[30] "Homing in on the Next Trade Wind," and "Distraction," which Albert sang. Albert contributed "Rhyme and Time," which Colton considers "should have gone into the film—it was better than our songs."

Tracks[31] received appreciative reviews but proved to be no more successful commercially than the debut album, despite being exceptionally well-crafted. In addition, the band were scheduled to be in the U.S.A. on a promotional tour but Capitol decided to promote the Raspberries, who had a hit single[32] and a debut album, and the tour was postponed until July. Another factor in the postponement was Tony Colton's five-week break, on doctor's orders, officially diagnosed with exhaustion. Actually, on his own admission, he was doing too many drugs. Albert told the press, "Tony Colton has worked himself ill. He's singing, writing and producing, and it all adds up." The band, now a four-piece, played the Odeon Theatre, Manchester, the Royal Festival Hall and the Marquee, as well as two shows for the BBC—*Sounds For Saturday* on BBC2 and a live radio performance on May 7 introduced by Andy Dunkley, "now bootlegged," complains Ray.

One evening in the middle of May, Albert took a call in Canberra Road. It was Jackson Browne—could he pop round that evening with "a friend?" "Sure," said Albert. He had a vague idea who the friend might be and rang Keith Nelson. "Fancy dropping round this evening, Keith? Jackson's coming over." Nelson duly turned up and he and Albert were idly strumming when there was a knock at the door. There stood Jackson Browne together with Joni Mitchell. Albert's hunch had been correct: Browne was, as the tabloids say, her "constant companion" and she had played the Festival Hall the previous Saturday night. Browne had recently recorded his second album, *For Everyman*.[33] "He played 'Redneck Friend' from the album on the piano," recalls Nelson. "Albert recorded the whole evening on his Vortexion but after about three hours—it seemed we jammed for ages—they said, 'We'd better go out and see if the cab's OK.' Joni and Jackson had a black cab sitting outside whereas we didn't have tuppence to rub together!"

Tensions were beginning to surface although the band was now successfully gigging as a quartet. The sound was tighter and the band's versatility showed. Keyboards were shared between Albert and Chas, and when Chas played fiddle, Ray switched to bass. The issue arose as to whether they needed Colton at all, although no new front man emerged. "Maybe it's that standing back thing with Albert," says Ray, "but he didn't take the reins and go up to the mike and say 'I'm going to do these numbers with Chas.' It was 'Well, I don't know.... What do you fancy, lads?'"

Albert, reluctant to rock the boat, acknowledged his personal debt to Colton. "He's the heart of the band and keeps everything moving. I need somebody to point me in a direction and give me a push, and Tony is ideal."[34] With the seven-week American tour impending "we thought we'd better get Tony back in," Ray recalls, "but we still wanted him to leave afterwards, when we'd be doing the last album, but once Tony's foot's in the door you can't shift it." In the event, Colton was fit again for the tour, which opened in Albuquerque on Monday, June 19.

The criss-crossing of America went smoothly considering the band was jumping from tour to tour. Heads, Hands and Feet worked with Procol Harum, the Allman Brothers, J. Geils in Central Park, Humble Pie, Edgar Winter and Jethro Tull at the Forum in Los Angeles, where, according to Ray, "they did an encore and got thrown off so had to promise not to do one again." Albert has a review of one of those shows. "It's a one-liner and it said 'the opening band Heads, Hands and Feet, *a West Coast band*, were easy to forget'—that shows how much they knew about us." The band also opened for Black Oak Arkansas, a Southern rock combo: They also fell prey to the customary hazards of life on tour, says Albert. "We were an English band on the road in America and the women were flying around all over the place." For Ray the whole tour was "glorious. It was almost gladiatorial in those big stadiums. It was pitch-dark, you plug your guitar in, the lights come up and the roar—there's no feeling like it. Les Paul said, 'If there is a heaven on earth, it's when you're up on stage and they're enjoying what you're doing.'" Tony Colton concurs. "For everyone in the band," he says, "the tour was fantastic. Greg Allman remembers us at the Fillmore when they chanted 'HHF' all through the Allman Brothers' act—he was pissed off about it. It was a magical time for us—when we supported someone we were hard to handle." It was an experience for Chas, too. "I loved it. I'd been over to Florida briefly before but that tour was great."

The tour itinerary reads like a Greyhound timetable—Albuquerque, Los Angeles, Houston, Chicago, New York, St. Louis, San Diego, Oklahoma—and a memorable stay in Denver, where as usual the band stayed at the Holiday Inn. After checking in, Chas was first in the bar, where he found the "filthiest couple of characters you ever saw. At their feet was this scruffy little dog [named Basil, Albert recalls, after Basil Rathbone]. They thought the world of it and with every round of drinks they would order it up a steak sandwich." Chas found out they were hillbillies from just outside Denver, treated with respect by the staff and from the way they were spending he thought they must be a couple of gold prospectors who had struck it rich.

When the hillbillies found out the Brits were musicians they decided to throw a party that night for the whole of the hotel. After the gig, "Me and Albert homed in on the grand piano and we rock 'n' rolled til the sun came up. Every now and then a couple more marguerites arriving." Albert remembers "those hobos in Denver. None of us had spent very long in the States at that time and to meet hippy guys and quasi-cowboys was exciting for us"—but not unduly so, Chas recalls. "Albert was a raver on his instrument but he wasn't a boozer. He liked a drop of Guinness but you couldn't get Guinness over there. He quite fancied a marguerite."

The party has a delicious coda. Next day, at the swimming pool, the hillbillies were quietly drinking beer. They livened up when they saw Chas.

"Hey Chas! You and Albert played great last night. What d'ya wanna drink?"

"I'll just have a coffee, if that's all right."

"Sure, whatever you want. Hey, waiter. Bring our friends a coffee."

With that he turned to his mate.

"Hey, Luke!" he said. "Ain't it amazing? No-one needs money anymore. This little ol' piece of plastic can get us a plane ride!" He had in his hand a credit card. "You just carry one of these little pieces of plastic, wave it a people and you can get anything you want! It sure was our lucky day when we found this!"

Chas was astounded. The hotel room, the drinks, the steak sandwiches for the dog, all the marguerites had been down to this credit card they'd found. "Finish your beer, Luke, c'mon, let's go." They whistled the dog, and off they went.

Such bizarre diversions notwithstanding, the tour was strenuous. The band flew everywhere, with early calls most mornings to catch the plane to the next gig. Chas, never a morning person, vowed each day to get an early night. "But we'd be somewhere like St. Louis. For one night only! How can I go to bed knowing there's probably some fantastic band playing in some club just around the corner? I couldn't do it. We'd be gone next day. I'd get no second chance." So Chas and Albert would ask around after the gig where the music was, and if "we got to sit in with the band, which happened most times—we made sure of that— our night was complete. Or almost. We usually ended up in the guitar player's or the banjo player's hotel room, singing and strumming 'til it was time to catch the plane to the next town."

If the band had any time off it was spent in Los Angeles, where they were based. A late-night club there was the Palomino, a country and western club, where Albert and Chas, both long-time fans of Rusty and Doug, saw Doug Kershaw, a wild fiddle-playing Cajun. They found out he was staying at their hotel "and that night me and Smiffy (Ray Smith) had a fiddle-playing, guitar-strumming session in his room. I remember (just about!) writing a song with him. Though I can't recall the tune. Albert was the first there and he quite happily sat there and played guitar all night with one and a half cans of beer." Unfortunately Ray sat on Kershaw's violin—"he was a walking disaster with things like that," recalls Albert—and Chas had to give the wild Louisianan his own fiddle. A more vivid memory for Albert was that Doug had a drinking buddy with him in the room, by the name of Chas Underwood, who wrote "Ubangi Stomp" for Warren Smith, recorded in Britain by Dean Shannon, with Albert on piano.

There was always someone to see in Los Angeles. Chas saw James Brown at the Forum— "he was great"—and Albert also met Phil Everly again, who took Terry Slater and him to Disneyland. "I'd met Phil in England in 1962. Phil asked if I was interested in joining Don and Phil's band, but I said, 'Oh, you're ten years too late'—I was involved with Heads, Hands and Feet."

There was always something to buy, too. Albert went berserk and bought "all the old gear I could find. I got my first maple-neck Telecaster—a '53. You couldn't get a maple-neck Tele in England. Guys used to go around to hotels in L.A. where bands were staying; they'd have a trunkload of guitars to sell, because they knew we all wanted such gear."

The tour wound up with ten days in Boston, where on Wednesday, August 2, the band played the Intermedia Studios. The following afternoon, Albert took a call in his room at the Holiday Inn. It was Mary's sister Lindy. "She told me Mary had gone into labor six weeks prematurely." At 11:40 P.M. on August 3, Mary gave birth to Cassandra at the Royal Free Hospital in Islington. That was not all. To everyone's consternation, a few minutes later Rebecca was born. Nobody knew that there was another baby. "The hospital was so busy telling Mum she was irresponsible having a baby when the father wasn't anywhere to be seen," says Rebecca, "that when I popped out it was a surprise to everybody, including Mum."

Albert was dumbstruck. "If my jaw dropped Lucy's must have dropped even further though she knew Mary was pregnant. It was a chaotic situation and I had no idea what I was going to do." His sister Vanessa remembers Albert phoning when the twins had been born. "He said, 'Oh, Lord! What am I going to do now?'"

It was a hard time for Albert, though of his own making. His parents were terribly upset that he appeared to be throwing his marriage down the drain, though his father's attitude changed once the girls were born. He realized that Albert could not totally abandon this relationship. Nevertheless, Keith Nelson recalls his father saying, "Stupid little shit. I'm going to box his ears." Although at first he felt that Mary was destroying the marriage, Albert's father eventually warmed to her. "It wasn't her fault," says Albert, "it was mine."

Mary concedes that "it must have been terrible for Lucy." The twins' arrival was devastating for her and worse was to come. "I'd taken the kids up to meet Albert coming back from America but he said he wasn't coming home—he was going to see the twins. So I had to get the train back to Charlton with my two." Albert had not worked out a plan of action regarding the families. "I was stuck between a rock and a hard place. It was very difficult."

The difficulty was compounded by the fact that Rebecca was very ill. At the hospital a young female doctor told Albert that "Becky had a problem and it was touch and go. It was a very tough time for me. I felt duty bound to Lucy but I wanted to be with Mary." Lucy was naturally bitter but Albert continued to live in Charlton when he was in England, visiting Mary and the girls who were living in a basement flat in Belitha Street, a few doors from Lindy. Tony Colton has a view on Albert and Mary: "It's a bit like the guy who leaves a note or phone number of a woman in his pocket—not meaning for his wife to find it on a conscious level but deep down he really needs to break the mold and move on. He can't do it himself and I think that's what the thing with Mary was."

Against this background of less-than-happy families, Albert was back in the studio in a fortnight recording British country/folk artist David Elliott's debut album[35] with Caleb Quaye, Nigel Olsson, Francis Monkman, Dave Mattacks and the whole lineup of Cochise, B.J. Cole's country-flavoured outfit. And Heads, Hands and Feet carried on gigging: the prestigious Queen Elizabeth Hall in September, Brighton Polytechnic Students' Union in October, the Greyhound in Fulham Palace Road and a two-week Norwegian tour in November.

Heads Hands and Feet were getting a name but were not making the charts. They still lacked the killer hit single. So "we did one," says Chas. "It was a good one too, as far as singles go. I got a credit for a share in the writing of 'Warming Up The Band.'" It received considerable airplay but it still failed to sell and Chas for one grew increasingly discontented. "I appreciated that it was a great band in a lot of people's eyes, but it still wasn't my ideal band."

This sense of frustration over the group's lack of acceptance affected the band's cohesion. The talent was there but they needed a charismatic personality to be the boss—as Chas put it, "Someone who would be impressed by, and work creatively with, the band product. Putting forward constructive criticism now and again, knowing from the heart what the band has got and only wanting the best out of them." The problem was that when Reg Locke began acting as manager under Tony Colton's direction the band had lost its figurehead. "Tony Colton has talent," says Chas, "but he wanted to do too much. A great songwriter and a great producer but he should have stopped there." For example, the band arrived back from the States and were suddenly signing contracts for Atlantic Records, which had always admired them. Capitol were losing interest, perhaps because rumors of growing tensions began to threaten future sales prospects in America. Ray Smith was less than happy: "I thought Tony was pushing it a bit."

The final album was recorded at Island Studios in the autumn of 1972. Entitled *Old Soldiers Never Die*,[36] it was an ambitious effort, according to Albert: "It had strings and everything." It featured "Stripes," a track which grew out of a gig in Bristol. "We'd got hold of some kind of acid," recalls Tony Colton, "and we all decided to do it, including Albert, who didn't do many drugs. That night, Albert played the piano like he had never played it before, long ringing notes instead of flowing arpeggios." Albert vaguely remembers the gig. "I felt dreadful in the dressing room, which was whirling round my head. I don't remember much about the gig, though they said I was great. I do recall that the piano was an old one on a sloping stage so I was kind of playing it uphill! After the gig we toured Bristol listening to Cat Stevens and I can't go there now without memories of flashing street lights and *Teaser and the Firecat!*" Colton wanted to hear him play like that again. "Normally he doesn't because his fingers are so restless on the keyboard. In the studio I asked him if he would take some acid and do that track—and he did." Albert also sang lead vocal on "I Won't Let You Down" and "Just Another Ambush" and dueted with Chas on "Taking My Music to the Man."

Despite the collapsing dynamics within the band, there are other fine tracks. "Soft Word Sunday Morning" is one of Colton's most heartfelt vocals and "Jack of all Trades" features a lusciously extravagant string arrangement. Albert's performance is consistently impressive and Chas displays his full potential. However the feeling is inescapable that the band knew it was all over and so these songs of life and love on the road are filled with a bittersweet sadness. It is perhaps apt that the final album track from Britain's finest country/rock band is "Another Useless Day." The album's sleeve notes carry more than a hint of an obituary notice: "Our very special thanks go to all the goodies and baddies who played their part during the lifetime of what was always more than just a band."

Chris Welch, reviewing the album in *Melody Maker*, admired the band's eclecticism but felt they were "at their best on the laid-back country music." He noted the orchestral arrangements "on the peculiar and decidedly showbiz 'Jack of all Trades'" and on "Soft Word Sunday Morning" and "Stripes." "There is however room for Albert to jam on 'One Woman,'" he goes on, "and to sing on the unusually constructed 'Just Another Ambush' which is the 'Old Soldiers Never Die' song which gives the album its title. This is one of the best performances featured and avoids the despairing, Procol Harum-ish declaiming typified by 'Stripes.'" It is indeed a strikingly ambitious album, imbued with a desperate end-of-term exuberance, on which Albert demonstrates his growing assurance as a vocalist of considerable authority and adds driving piano to tunes like "Another Useless Day."

Ray Smith asserts that there are a few Heads, Hands and Feet tracks still in the can—"'Other Peoples' Windows,' 'Nothin' Doin,' 'What I've Always Done' (which was Chas's first Cockney song, written for 'Tracks,' but we only used the intro),[37] 'Hard Road,' 'So Glad' and 'Here Comes the Whiz-kid.'" There were two last singles. "One Woman on My Mind" was released in November 1972, described as a "fine rock boogie, with Albert Lee rocking up a storm on geetar.... There's a kind of hillbilly flavor, and one suspects a certain amount of mountain dew was handed around at the session. Best release of the week, and let's hope it's a hit." In January 1973 "Dirty Heavy Weather Road," a tune from the Poet days, appeared but by then the schism had taken place. Heads, Hands and Feet finally split at the end of 1972 after the last-ever gig at the Patti Pavilion in Swansea.

The reasons for the split were complex. The band was supposed to be a democratic unit, but Ray Smith felt that Tony Colton regarded it as his band since he did most of the singing, writing and producing. Albert and Chas believed that the vocals should have been shared more evenly and would have preferred to have more country-oriented material. However, Tony and Ray had a leaning towards the hippie or contemporary sound and Pete Gavin preferred rock.[38] Everyone therefore was pulling in different directions and eventually each decided to pursue his own interests. Albert felt "a great sense of relief as I hadn't really enjoyed it too much and it's true to say that I hadn't been totally into the material the band performed." At the time, Reg Locke tried to put the traditional spin on the split: "The reason they have decided to stop gigging is that they are all talented musicians who are anxious to get involved in other things and this will give them the freedom to undertake solo projects." Ray remembers Reg getting flak from Colton, who initially felt that after Chas and Albert left he should have carried on: but then "Ahmet Ertegun called me to a meeting at the Beverley Hills Hotel. He wanted me to restart the band without Albert but I wouldn't do it. The dream was as it was—for me it certainly was more than just a band." Ray was devastated. "I arrived back home from the Norwegian tour and got a phone call saying that Albert and Chas wanted to leave the band. It was like the ground had gone from beneath me."

Chas and Albert had indeed been making vague plans for a new band. "We were all in transition," Albert remembers, "wondering what to do next." He and Chas had very similar tastes in music. "It was to be the band we'd often talked about. I wanted to be part of my ideal band—so did Albert. I wasn't interested in the fame and the glory."[39] Chas also wanted to work with Dave Peacock and soon rehearsals were under way with Peacock on banjo, Ian Wallace from King Crimson on drums and Steve Simpson from the Newport Jug Band, The Saddletramps and The Tumbleweeds on guitar. "They were all good players," says Albert. Ray Smith, who was part of these early rehearsals though he was airbrushed out of the embryonic line-up, played slide guitar and, recalls Albert, "had tuned it in some weird way, not with a normal open major chord as most slide players use but with a C6 steel guitar tuning on it and I wondered if it would work."

The new outfit naturally wanted a new name but Atlantic insisted on calling it "The New Heads, Hand and Feet." They saw Albert as the new guitar hero, up the front making a guitar noise, which he was reluctant to do. Atlantic wanted him to make a solo album and were uninterested in what kind of music the band would play. "They were turning up on gigs," complained Chas, "reporting back on … everything we did…. This is not how we meant it to be. What happened to the *band* we'd talked about? We wanted to play again and not be judged on 'hit potential.' We had more to offer than that. But I felt that it would be, in the end, up to us and I was willing to give it a real go…. But it never got that far." The band played a few gigs and went down well but Chas felt there was "no real spirit there—it never felt right from the start."

"More than just a band"—what is the legacy of Heads, Hands and Feet? "People say we never quite made it, but we did so much in just over two years," says Ray Smith. His songwriting partner Tony Colton continues to be amazed at "how many musicians in Nashville have a copy of our first album in their personal collections and still ask me what happened to the band. Looking back we were one hell of a band and on a good night we could blow anybody off stage."

One major reason for the band's never reaching either its commercial or artistic potential is ironically its appeal to a diverse public. Colton feels that the eclectic nature of Heads, Hands and Feet was part of its strength—"a patchwork quilt," as he calls it. While this is undoubtedly the case, it was also its weakness. The public's inability to pigeonhole the band diffused its impact and in appealing to several different clienteles, sometimes to the country people, then the rockers, then a bit to the folkies, the band, though critically acclaimed, never defined its own distinctive market. Albert feels that today. "I haven't listened to the albums for ages. The problem was that people haven't been able to categorize them." The most one can say, as he and Colton do, is that Heads, Hands and Feet were Britain's response to the Band.

Albert always found Colton "a likeable character," as did Mike O'Neill: "Although he had a strong personality I got on quite well with TC." Colton has mellowed somewhat from the driven workaholic of the early '70s, though still claiming that his energy pulled together the band's disparate talents into a cohesively creative whole. He is generous towards Albert, saying "He told me once that he didn't want to be a star at the front. He said, 'I know I'm going to be famous'—but in his own way and on his own terms—quietly famous—which of course he is—he's a quiet legend."

Then in January 1973, Steve Rowland, the producer, rang. Jerry Lee Lewis was flying to London to record an album and Rowland wanted the erstwhile Heads, Hands and Feet as the rhythm section. Albert would be working with the Killer.

Eight

California Dreaming

On January 6, 1973, Jerry Lee Lewis, "the Killer," arrived in London for four days of sessions for Mercury Records. Two days later he went into Advision Studios with a galaxy of rock musicians from both sides of the Atlantic. Lewis disdained rehearsal and had a proclivity for no-holds-barred arrangements: hence the resultant album[1] is frayed around the edges. Thanks however to the solid rhythm section provided by Heads, Hands and Feet, "the primitive sound of the 50s acquires a new, formidable muscle," wrote *Classic Rock*, "and Lewis plays piano boogie-woogies with flash and sparkle." Along with Albert, Chas, Ray, Pete and Tony, the sessions featured among others Tony Ashton, Andy Bown, Delaney Bramlett, B.J. Cole, Matthew Fisher, Peter Frampton, Rory Gallagher, Kenny Jones, Alvin Lee, Klaus Voormann and Kenny Lovelace, who in 2006 celebrated 40 years as leader of Lewis's backing band, the Memphis Beats. For Albert, seeing the man at work was a revelation. He and Chas deliberately positioned themselves behind him so they could watch his hands. "There were at least two or three cassette recorders under the piano running the whole time taping all his licks. We were totally in awe of him and he was on form playing great."

On the first day of recording[2] Lewis cut pounding versions of "I Don't Want to Be Lonesome Tonight," "Let's Get Back to Rock 'n' Roll" and "Sixty Minute Man," solid rock standards, with Madeline Bell leading the chorus on "Back to Rock 'n' Roll." On day two Lewis was late—as Albert recalls, "Each day he'd show up a little later with his cigars and brandy or whatever on the piano. It was very ad hoc—he'd just turn up and we'd kick a few things around." Lewis would canvass opinion in the control room for songs—"Sea Cruise" and "Headstone" were two such suggestions. Albert and the band had quickly become accustomed to Lewis's idiosyncratic working methods and most numbers[3] went down in one take. Directing solos, Jerry Lee said, "Take it, son." He never bothered to learn anyone's name. Owing to the lack of planning the set veered preponderantly towards early rock 'n' roll songs, like Chuck Berry's "Memphis, Tennessee" (complete with a yodel), "Down the Line" and "What'd I Say."

On the third day Lewis rose again. Tony Colton had tried for two days to get Lewis to do one of his songs. His perseverance paid off and Jerry Lee sang a couple of Heads, Hands and Feet numbers, "Music to the Man" and "Jukebox," though it cost Colton a couple of playful clips round the ear from the great man. The Colton/Smith songs were followed by a frenetic "Johnny B. Goode," "Singing The Blues," and a disappointingly throwaway "Whole Lotta Shakin' Goin On" (enlivened by Rory Gallagher's awe-inspiring slide guitar and a concluding snarl worthy of the Killer).

On the final day he cut a medley of hits—"Good Golly Miss Molly," "Long Tall Sally," "Jenny, Jenny," "Tutti Frutti" and a second "Whole Lotta Shakin' Going On"—that boogied with the frenetic excitement of a live show. The session continued with "What'd I Say?," featuring Lewis on electric piano, followed by "Proud Mary" and two instrumental versions of "Be Bop A Lula" and "High School Confidential." Finally, fifteen years after he first recorded it, Jerry Lee cut "a loud, drunken version"[4] of "Drinkin' Wine Spo-Dee-o-Dee,"[5] which as a single rose to 41 in the pop charts and 20 on country charts in the States.

"The Session" worked in spite of everything and everyone. Pearce pointed out that the most successful Jerry Lee sessions were those in which he was relaxed, but not too relaxed, sounding "as though he had drunk too much wine from the ole spo-dee-o-dee and did not care who was in the room with him. In London, seeing Jerry Lee Lewis in the studios was like being at a live concert. He had the assembled company stomping, including the 60-year-old tea-lady."[6]

In chronological age, only a few years separated the Killer and the British. For instance, Jerry Lee is only thirteen months older than Rolling Stones bassist Bill Wyman. However, there were many generational and geographical differences between Jerry Lee's entourage and the British players. Jerry Lee was fundamentally conservative on issues like how long a man's hair should be. "He can be the nicest guy," says Albert, "but he can be really ornery if he's not in the mood," and Chas has seen him act "quite frighteningly" to other people. However, between Chas and Jerry Lee "there was complete mutual respect and we liked each other. I first saw Jerry in 1958. Me Mum was a great piano player and she wanted me to play piano when I was a kid—and I can remember saying to her 'I don't want to. Boring kids play piano, I want to go fishing and play football.' I took up the guitar when I heard Lonnie Donegan, same as Albert. Going on tour with the Outlaws and Jerry Lee in 1963 was great because I was sitting right beside him, watching him for two months so he really taught me. On those London sessions, he was doing 'Bad Moon Rising' and I was sitting behind him playing bass, just singing along. I didn't even realize I was singing. He said 'Hey, get Chas a microphone. Get him to sing harmony with me.'" Jerry Lee clearly enjoyed the freewheeling chaos of the sessions. Perhaps in 1973 it was only in "swinging" London, far away from the country-drenched environs of the Nashville scene, that the Killer was able to work up such a sweat in the studio.

During that week in London, too, Lewis was beset with a harrowing personal scenario. His eldest son, Jerry Lee Jr., had been behaving strangely. The son of a bigamous marriage, who had seen his three-year-old half-brother Steve drown in the family swimming pool, Jerry Lee Jr. had been entrusted to record producer Eddie Kilroy, who shared a room with him at the Royal Lancaster Hotel near Hyde Park. "Junior kept pacing the floor. He walked back and forth, imitatin' his Daddy. 'I'm The Killer! I'm The Killer! I'm the great Jerry Lee Lewis!' One night he took about ten or twelve baths, said he couldn't sleep. He told me that he thought a little boy and a little girl from Ferriday were livin' in his belly.... It was a hard thing to take—only eighteen years old and already gone."[7] Sadly, after months in mental hospitals suffering drug abuse, Jerry Lee Jr. was killed in a car crash in DeSoto County, Mississippi, only ten months later.

For the first few months of 1973, Albert survived on session work such as the Lewis album. In late February, he had a hilarious few days at Rockfield Studios, Monmouth, working with folk-singer Carolanne Pegg, who had come to prominence in the late '60s with Mr. Fox, who, along with groups like Steeleye Span and Pentangle, were pioneers in blending traditional British folk music with electric instruments. She played fiddle and harmonium and was an accomplished singer, whose work in the view of some observers almost rivalled Sandy Denny's solo output and foreshadowed the early albums of Kate Bush. The sessions at Rockfield featured Albert, with Dave Peacock on bass, Alan Eden on drums and the banjo of Keith Nelson. The eponymous album,[8] produced by Fritz Fryer, Nelson's mate from his early bluegrass days in London, encompassed folk-rock, pop and some country-style elements such as electric piano.

The Rockfield Studio was based in a large country house with ample accommodation. It was just as well, for it was a real family occasion. Nelson's wife and eldest daughter were there and for the first time he met Mary and the twins, who, what with the studio staff and musicians' wives and girlfriends, did not lack child care. The house also boasted a vast kitchen, the domain of Paul the cook, an old friend of Fryer's from Blackburn. Paul, "larger than life and built like a rugby player," recalls Albert, decided to have Christmas dinner in March. After the thirty-strong company had had a huge meal, they decided to go down to the Monmouth Arms, "get really hammered," says Nelson, "come back and do a rock 'n' roll song in the studio." In the pub a lone local sat sipping a quiet pint—but not for long. Paul went up to the bar. "Thirty pints of Guinness, please" and in no time there were amps set up, dart games, guitars, banjos, with Albert on the piano. "We got so pissed," Nelson vaguely remembers. "Albert was dancing with my wife down Monmouth High Street: when Lucy heard of it she complained, 'He's never fucking danced with me!' and Mary wasn't very happy about it either. We got back to the studio and I could barely see, Dave Peacock could hardly sit on his chair and Albert couldn't tune his guitar." Events took a turn for the worse when Paul the cook fell into an argument with Alan Eden, whereupon Paul seized a trifle he had made for the Christmas dinner and threw it at him. As Nelson shrewdly observes, "the aerodynamic properties of a trifle are not great and the whole thing landed on the 20-grand mixing desk. They had to take every component out and clean it. We had all collapsed in a heap covered in trifle: Nobody could play a note." Kingsley Ward, who owned Rockfield, was laughing his head off. "Whenever he sees me today," says Albert, "he still reminds me how much fun that all was."

Another project Albert worked on was Jaki Whitren's self-penned album *Raw But Tender*,[9] dubbed by *Record Collector* "one of the most impressive debuts of the time." Possessor of one of the finest voices of her generation, Jaki Whitren was just eighteen when she was signed by CBS and introduced as the next Streisand. The album, a soulful collection of country-flavored folk-rock, featured Jaki on vocals, banjo and acoustic guitar: The rest of the band, assembled from Matthews Southern Comfort and Fotheringay, all had beards, including Albert, Pat Donaldson and Gerry Conway. Albert was impressed with her. "She was very intense, and when she did an overdub she was in tears at the end of one number. She was great but I never heard of her again."[10]

In September 1972, before Heads, Hands and Feet split, Reg Locke issued a press statement, "Albert Lee is right now working on a solo album," and in early 1973 Albert should have been working on the project for Atlantic. There was a problem, however. No one had thought to let Albert know and the album may have existed more in the mind of Ahmet

Ertegun as a potential money-making enterprise. Whatever the case, if ever a contract existed with Atlantic, as a result of being too busy with other people's gigs, Albert lost it. As he freely admits, "I've never been an organizing person—I just drift along with things."

Some of the things he drifted into, along with Steve Simpson, Chas and Dave, were a few gigs at the Nashville Rooms with the Tumbleweeds, one of the most popular bands on the London country circuit. They were sometimes nine-strong, including Ray Flacke and Keith Nelson, and always had a varied assortment of guest players. Albert also worked with Chas on a session for two Japanese brothers, Fuymi and Satsuya Iwasawa, who called themselves Bread and Butter. Their album *Images* was released only in Japan and must rank as one of the rarest albums that Albert has played on. He continued his session work with Eddie Harris, a jazz tenor sax player from Los Angeles, who was also signed to Atlantic. In the early '70s, although the heady euphoria of the Swinging Sixties had evaporated, London was still a rock music mecca with session musicians any self-respecting U.S. soloist wanted to work with. American writer Richard S. Ginell sums up Harris's album[11]: "most of the results aren't too different from what Harris had been recording at home at the time, with only a hint of a rock edge. If anything, the workmanlike Brits are too much on their best behavior—[Jeff] Beck plays with restraint and taste while Lee is jazzier and a bit flashier—making Harris seem like a wild man by comparison."[12] The album featured the pick of British talent—Albert, Jeff Beck, Steve Winwood and Ian Paice, the Deep Purple drummer. Bass player Ric Grech played on only one track, but would soon play a pivotal role in Albert's career when he bumped into Albert at a press reception for Teresa Brewer's single, "Music to the Man." The American star had just completed an album,[13] "Music, Music, Music," in London, with a reunited Heads, Hands and Feet rhythm section. "Music to the Man" was one of two Colton and Smith songs she recorded, together with "Another Useless Day." Albert was impressed with her: "she looked and sounded really good."

Bordeaux-born Richard Roman Grech, a fine, multitalented musician, had been a key player in Family, the British folk/rock band, and was a member of Blind Faith, the super-group successor to Cream, with Eric Clapton, Ginger Baker and Stevie Winwood, whom he later joined in a revamped Traffic. Grech was now living in Los Angeles and had joined the Crickets earlier in the year when they were "exploring the possibility of getting a little different sound," as Sonny Curtis puts it. He had met Albert in California the year before and at the press launch mentioned that the Crickets were due to tour Britain but that keyboardist Glen D. Hardin had to fulfill the last couple of dates with Elvis. "It would be great," he told Albert, "if you could play the first few gigs until he shows up." Naturally, Albert jumped at the chance—he was a huge Crickets fan.

Albert joined the Crickets at Ric Grech's farm near East Grinstead to rehearse. After playing a couple of songs, Albert was perplexed and inquired whether they sounded like that. "I thought they went this way," he said. For a moment drummer Jerry Allison was taken aback. "Albert knew them exactly like the original records: We'd been doing them for so long that we had got a bit loose. 'OK,' we said, 'Albert, teach us.' He knew the songs better than we did. He played 'That'll Be the Day' with a capo,[14] exactly like Buddy."

Albert's first gig with the Crickets was at the Speakeasy three or four weeks after he had he had formed the new Heads, Hands and Feet—and Chas turned up with Dave. Chas did not blame Albert. "It was what he wanted to do—though I admit I was choked at the time. All them months we'd talked about our Ideal Band together. Now I knew it was never going to be." Only a few weeks later Chas formed what has become much-loved and very successful musical partnership with Dave Peacock.

An indication of Chas's feelings surfaced at a smart birthday dinner one night in March 1973. Derek Lawrence was present and recalls that he had warned Chas about his language ("He's well-known for talking in the vernacular"). Chas behaved himself all through the dinner. The New Heads, Hands and Feet had recently held a drinks reception at the Revolution which Lawrence missed and when the cigars came round Lawrence asked Chas about it. Chas could restrain himself no longer. "Oh that ... Albert walked in, well late, said he was joining The Crickets ... and off he fucking chirped."

The gig at the Speakeasy went very well and JI[15] asked Albert if he would do the whole tour—for three or four weeks, often playing two workingmen's clubs in an evening. "We went up north and I showed up with Mary and the twins. The Crickets went along with it and I had a room in the hotel." A few days later Glen D. turned up, and, according to Sonny Curtis, "we got a lot of flak from the audiences because they'd come to expect that three-piece sound but we were now a four-piece—but it was the most fun I'd had. We were a real kick-ass rock 'n' roll band. Albert sang solos and his harmonies were fantastic." Glen D. was a little disconcerted—not only was there was another band member but he had a family with him. However, "we were drinking a lot and we became very good friends," recalls Albert. "I never detected any animosity from him but he'd just finished a tour with Elvis and wasn't really enjoying the small northern clubs." It must have been a culture shock for Hardin. He had been catapulted from the glitz and glamour of the Las Vegas Hilton with the world's biggest rock star to the beer and pickles of the Barnsley Miners' Welfare.

Late at night Glen D. would knock on JI's door.

"I'm going home, JI."

"OK," Jerry would reply, humoring him.

On one occasion Hardin actually got a cab to Manchester station, where JI found him in the café at four in the morning, bags packed, waiting to get to London to fly home. Hardin is an affable Texan with a keen sense of humor but he had had enough. JI persuaded him back to the hotel when Hardin discovered that in his anxious haste he had left a bag full of cash from the Elvis tour in the cafe. He managed to get it back.

At the end of the tour Albert and the Crickets flew to Los Angeles for the recording sessions which resulted in *Remnants*.[16] Albert, Lucy and the kids were staying with Sonny and Louise Curtis, just across the street from JI, who had Ric and Jenny Grech staying. Albert and his family became good friends with the genial Texans: "I'm glad to say that I was immediately accepted into the fold. I was—and still am—extremely proud to be an 'honorary Cricket.'" "The feeling's mutual," says Sonny. Albert was familiar with all of the albums[17] that the Crickets cut after Buddy Holly's death: "I used to sing 'Just this Once' and even had a copy of Sonny's 'Red Headed Stranger.'" Also in the band was Tonio K, aka Steve Krikorian. Born in 1950, Antonio Vladimer Stephen Michael Krikorian grew up in central

Opposite—Top: **Albert with the Crickets in 1973. From left, Tonio K, JI, Sonny Curtis, Ric Grech, Nick van Maarth and Albert. "Those photos are in JI's backyard, while we were doing that album," Albert recalls (photograph by John Livzey, courtesy Jerry Allison).** *Bottom:* **Albert and the Crickets, thirty years on. From left, Joe B. Mauldin, Sonny Cutis, Albert, and Jerry (JI) Allison, (courtesy the Lee family).**

Albert with his buddies, Jerry (JI) Allison, left, and Joe B. Mauldin (courtesy the Lee family).

California, where his father ran a ranch. After leaving college in 1970, Krikorian and Raik's Progress bandmate Nick van Maarth moved into a psychedelic bus parked behind Devonshire Studios in the San Fernando Valley in Los Angeles and began work on an album. At the same time the Crickets were recording in the same studio and liked what Krikorian and van Maarth were doing. By 1972, Krikorian, too, had become an honorary Cricket.

One Tuesday evening in July 1973 Don Everly called JI and invited him to the Sundance Saloon in Calabasas, a Los Angeles suburb on the historic El Camino Real west of the San Fernando Valley, where Everly was playing with a scratch band before wildly enthusiastic audiences. He had split up with his brother a little while before when their personal conflict finally erupted at the John Wayne Theatre at Knott's Berry Farm in Hollywood. Unhappy with Don's performance, entertainment manager Bill Hollinghead stopped the show midway through the second of three scheduled sets, whereupon Phil smashed his guitar and stormed off. Don performed the third set solo and caustically announced, in one of rock's most famous comments, "The Everlys died ten years ago." Albert thinks another factor was responsible: the brothers "were on a dead-end circuit, the same old gigs and the Las Vegas thing, which I know Don didn't enjoy."

Don was beginning to enjoy a taste of freedom—he had a tubular neon sign in his apartment saying "FREE"—but "was floundering around a bit," says JI, "figuring where he was going to go with it." JI told Don on that Tuesday night that Albert was there. "He's Phil's friend, isn't he?" Everly replied. Albert had met him backstage in England in 1963 but to Don, the brothers' friends and colleagues fell into two distinct camps—and still do today. However, that evening Albert sat in with Don. "Ron Coleman was playing bass, Al Perkins was on steel." It is a measure of Everly's volatility that he and his wife, Karen, loved Albert's playing and became close friends.

That summer, Albert was hanging out with his heroes, "guys I'd been listening to in the '60s on those great albums. Here I was playing with them in bars in Los Angeles! I thought—this is the place for me." Albert, Lucy and the two children, not wanting to outstay their welcome with the Curtises, took a room at the Heritage Motel on Ventura Boulevard in Sherman Oaks, just east of Calabasas, for $70 a week. This seedy hotel in west L.A. had cockroaches rustling over the floor, but Albert spent little time there. It was Lucy who had to cope with the children, the cockroaches and the vicissitudes of family life. Albert was recording in Canada when Wayne fell off a wall and cut his leg badly on a nail. "The medics wouldn't stitch it," Lucy recalls, "until payment could be guaranteed. I couldn't contact Albert so Sonny sorted it out." In August Albert took the family home to Charlton. The children were back at school but things were up in the air. Albert was living from week to week without a steady gig, but he did make an appearance on BBC Radio London with Keith Nelson, Chas and Dave doing a bluegrass session and interview.

All that uncertainty was dispelled when the Crickets' producer, Bob Montgomery, who had been Buddy Holly's original partner on radio KDAV's *Buddy and Bob Show* in Lubbock in 1953, playing mainly country and bluegrass, decided it would be a great idea if the band recorded an album in Nashville, the home of country music. Albert flew back to California early in September, sending his parents a postcard from North Hollywood: "Arrived safely. Flight was really tiring as usual. The boys have really nice houses and I have a nice room of my own. We haven't done very much yet. It's been a holiday weekend and everyone had just lazed about. Mind you, I think they laze about most of the time. Plenty of food, drink and TV. At the moment I'm really homesick. I think about all the things I should be doing. Still, when we get busy, it will pass. I hope you're feeling better, Dad. Look after yourself. I'll write again soon. Love Albert." This was just one of many cards his parents received while Albert was on the road. Before the days of satellite communications and the Internet it was his way of keeping in touch with Blackheath, for it was important to him to stay close to his roots.

The night before Albert left L.A. for Nashville, he had an historic one-off meeting with Gram Parsons, perhaps the single greatest name in country/rock. He and his manager, Phil Kaufman, dropped by at JI's. Gram and Ric Grech had written "Oooh Las Vegas" together and Parsons had introduced Grech to the Crickets after the *GP* sessions at the end of 1972. JI has good reason to remember the charismatic hedonist Parsons. "I woke up one morning, went into the living room and Gram had fallen asleep and burnt a hole in the sofa— he and Ric had been out rockin.'" That evening, recalls Albert, all the guys had a lot to drink and listened to the tapes of the *GP* album. Albert talked to Gram about Ian Samwell,[18] seeing him play with Country Fever and telling Parsons that he was playing music along similar lines. Albert told Parsons they were off to Nashville in the morning to cut an album and "we almost convinced him to jump in the Winnebago and come with us." JI was not happy with the idea, fearing that "he and Ric might rock a little too hard. Given the way things turned out, I wish he had." Instead Parsons, heavily back into drugs, headed out to Joshua Tree in the Mojave Desert, taking Grech's advice to "get himself sorted out there."

JI and Sonny, thinking that Albert and Ric would get a kick out of seeing the United States, rented a camper for the trip. Though Grech took it in his stride, the drive to Nashville was excruciating for Albert. "We did 1800 miles in about three days. It was a nightmare. I hope I never have to do that again without having a hotel or two on the way." Ric and Albert were "getting pilled up and drinking beer, because there was no stopping for a rest." The camper left the West Coast around midday and reached Barstow, in mid–California, about sundown, when Albert asked the tentatively hopeful question "Are we nearly there?" Sonny broke it to him as gently as he could, "We still have Arizona, New Mexico, Texas and Okla-homa to go." The Texans even considered putting Albert on a plane in Little Rock but he survived, despite their falling foul of the natives. "We stopped for gas in Shamrock, Texas. The van was taller than I thought it was and clipped the station awning stuck out over the road. We had long hair, which wasn't that common in Texas at that time. This young pump attendant started screaming and yelling and called his buddy, a policeman. We had wine in the van and who knows what else." Fortunately, Albert recalls, "JI and Sonny spoke the lan-guage and we narrowly escaped arrest, slipping the kid ten dollars for the damage."

When Albert arrived, he felt like death and crashed out in the hotel. The other Crick-ets had planned to stay out at the Loveless Motel but Rick and Albert wanted to be down-town as it was their first visit. The album, A Long Way from Lubbock,[19] was recorded at the Soundshop studio on Division Street. Albert vividly remembers one of the sessions: "One afternoon I did 'Rhyme and Time' and it came out really well: Bob Montgomery suggested taking an hour off at the Grand Ol' Opry. We went in the back door of the historic Ryman Auditorium and watched the Osborne Brothers on stage, then in the dressing rooms we met George Jones and Tammy Wynette. It was my only time at the original Opry and it would have topped it if I'd got on stage and played a song with someone, but it was a mem-orable day." Albert loved the Nashville music scene but according to Ray Smith, the town made him feel uncomfortable. "He told me they were all nutters, toting guns and he couldn't wait to get out of the place."

While the others flew back to Los Angeles, Sonny drove Albert back through Texas, hearing on the way of Jim Croce's[20] sad death in a plane crash. En route they stopped off at Sonny's mother's house in Meadow: the genial Texan said he had a present for Albert. Around 1955 or 1956, in pre–Cricket days, Buddy Holly had given a jacket to Sonny Cur-tis which Sonny's mother had been carefully looking after. "She wasn't best pleased," Albert recalls, "when all of a sudden this strange Brit walks in and Sonny gives it to him!" Albert was even more excited to find in the top breast pocket a scrap of paper with a phone or car number on it. "I like to think Buddy had actually written it: Even if he didn't, it's a cool jacket!"

On the day they arrived back, on Thursday, September 20, Albert and the Crickets learned of the death of Gram Parsons at the Joshua Tree Inn the day before. The strange circumstances of his death from drug and alcohol abuse and a bizarre funeral gave him an immediate cult reputation, based more on the legend than the music. Phil Kaufman "kid-napped" the corpse from Los Angeles airport and cremated it in the desert as Gram had wished, a departure now immortalised in the film Grand Theft Parsons. It is only now that his true significance in the field of country-rock is genuinely acknowledged. "Perhaps he'd be alive now if he had come with us," says JI, "but he certainly lived life to the full." Ric Grech, to whom Kaufman bequeathed Parsons' guitar and workbook, was deeply upset and Albert is keenly aware of a lost opportunity. "Gram and I had agreed at JI's that we should play together but it was not to be. I made up for it later by being in his ex-partner's band."

There was a postscript to the Nashville saga. Albert returned to England, to an unprepossessing music scene dominated by David Cassidy, the Osmonds and Sweet, to an autumn lived against the somber backdrop of the first oil crisis, petrol rationing, the miners' strike, and the three-day week. Then in December he took a call from Polydor: they were unhappy with some of the Crickets' tracks and asked Albert to fly back to Nashville to help out with some remixes. After a couple of days' work he flew back to New York, where the flight to London was delayed by bad weather. Stuck in the airport overnight, he eventually managed to change enough pound notes to find a hotel room.

The delay meant that next morning at Newark airport Albert fell into conversation with some characters "who looked a bit showbiz. They asked me who I was and I said I was going back to London to do some sessions." It turned out to be Herbie Mann, who was traveling to London for five days of recording with Albert and other British rock musicians. Mann was continually searching for new playing contexts for his flute and a day or so later was at Advision: The result was *London Underground*,[21] an album which was more rock-influenced than the soul and R&B-flavoured recordings Mann had been making in the late '60s. The highlight was the addition of Stephane Grappelli on Donovan's "Mellow Yellow." "With guitarist Albert Lee adopting a Django Reinhardt stance, the cut is reminiscent of the old Hot Club of France recordings in the '30s. There are a couple of damp clunkers here ('Layla' doesn't work), but for fans of late-'60s/early '70s rock, not a bad ride."[22]

Early in 1974 Les Walker, a British soul singer from Burnley, was at loose ends after his band Warm Dust had run out of cash, when Derek Lawrence, who had produced the last Warm Dust album, suggested a solo album, using some tracks he had already recorded. Lawrence pulled in several of the old faces and Walker was thrilled to meet and work with the likes of Jim Sullivan, Albert Lee, Chas Hodges, Dave Peacock, Steve Simpson and Ian Wallace on drums. "They were great people," Walker remembers, "Albert was an amazing player and a lovely feller. He arrived late for a session one day and apologized profusely, whereas I was just grateful that he was playing on my album!"

At that stage he and Lucy were still trying to mend their marriage but just before Christmas, when he arrived home from Nashville, he told her, "I'm not staying long." It was the last straw and she retorted, "Well, don't stay at all." She weighed only 84 pounds and was passing out in the street. She had to make a clean break.

In California, Tony Colton had been conscripted as producer for the Australian folk/country star Russell Morris. Colton and Ray Smith were still signed to Warner Bros., as was Albert. Colton's idea was to recruit the Heads, Hands and Feet rhythm section to play on it. After all, the band were all still mates and there seemed to be money flying around.

The project to all intents and purposes signaled Albert's final break with Blackheath and his irrevocable move to Los Angeles. The British musical landscape, dominated as it was by a plethora of bespangled, high-heeled, heavily made up glam rockers and sweaty, leather-clad heavy metal outfits, held little attraction for someone who had played with the Crickets and Don Everly and had experienced the burgeoning and beguiling country-rock scene of the canyons of California.

For Albert, in the spring of 1974, "Music was the most important thing but I had all this other stuff going on in my life. My marriage was pretty much finished. Going to the

States I was kind of running away from it all." Mary feels that only too keenly: "That sense of running away, of his caravan moving on, has always been in his nature. Although I was the final catalyst in their divorce, there had been other women and if it hadn't been me it would have been somebody else. Once Lucy had children and had to stay at home it was the beginning of the end of their relationship. In retrospect I was a stepping-stone on the way to Albert breaking out of one lifestyle and into another in America." Ronnie Bell agrees: "He did a runner—on the one hand he had Lucy with two children and on the other two newborn daughters and he couldn't handle it. And Chas and Dave wrote that song, 'Billy Tyler,' all about Albert. What made it easy for him was the fact that over there was this land of milk and honey saying 'Come! We can answer all your artistic needs.' He would never intend doing the dirty on anybody. He wanted a little space and then it would all be all right for everybody. Wishful thinking, as there would soon be another woman on the scene."

Built high above Sunset Strip in 1929, the prestigious Chateau Marmont at 8221 Sunset Boulevard was modelled on an actual chateau outside Paris. The outside chalets afford visiting celebrities extra privacy, and Colton and Smith, at Warner Bros.' expense, had taken chalet No. 3, where in 1982 John Belushi would spend his last day before succumbing to a drug overdose. They stayed there for about a month. "Wonderful," thought Ray. "Let's get Albert over." Then Pete Gavin arrived and it was Heads, Hands and Feet again—except that Chas was in England facing an action for breach of contract. Heads, Hands and Feet had not played the Fairfield Hall in Croydon as booked. Chas was the only band member they could get hold of and nearly lost his house. The others were all in sunny California and the memory of it still rankles. In fact Albert also received a summons—for £90,000. Lucy managed to extricate him by successfully claiming it was all Reg Locke's fault. She wondered "Why Albert?" and asked the hall's solicitor. "Because he's the one who's likely to earn the money."

By the winter of 1973 Don Everly, in search of solo stardom and artistic fulfillment, had left RCA and started work on an album for Lou Adler's Ode label. Don wanted Albert to play on it, but when he went into the studio early in 1974 Albert was still in England. Adler himself was at the production controls but after Everly had completed a couple of disastrous tracks he lost interest and palmed the project on to Tony Colton. "He thought I could pull it off and I did the best I could with it but ... I'm not proud of it at all." Indeed, he contributed only two songs: the rest were Colton/Smith compositions. Everly convinced himself the songs were great, although Colton knew they weren't.

While *Sunset Towers*[23] is clearly not an Everly Brothers album Albert likes it, although "it wasn't representative of what Don could do. He sang really well on it but knowing what a great and unusual writer he is, it didn't come across in those two songs." The backing weighs the vocals down and the album sounds overproduced. It arose from jam sessions every Sunday afternoon at Don's apartment in the Sunset Towers block on Sunset Boulevard and was recorded over a four-month period at A&M's studios. Roger White, the Everlys' chronicler, describes the album as "a fusion of American country-rock with British rock; a mixture of Don's country voice and Buddy Emmons' steel guitar with the heavy instrumentals common in British groups in the late 1960s and early 1970s."[24]

"Tony Colton, being the pushy kind of bloke that he is, took over everything," says Albert. "Don may have resented it at times but at the end of the day he could see that things were being accomplished. There was a little bit of head-butting there because Tony's that kind of guy. He likes to whip people into action but some people don't like it."

Don admits that he didn't have a good relationship with Tony Colton. "I didn't get along with him at all. I was fighting with this producer ... to get the project down. It was another painful experience [though] I did get vocally what I wanted on that album. Albert contributed a great deal. I think I'm happier with *Sunset Towers* than I am with *Stories We Could Tell.*"

Albert feels that Don's mental approach at the time could have been partly to blame. It was a time of transition for him. The Everly Brothers had been the most important vocal duo in pop/rock and the birth of his solo career was bound to be hedged about with hesitancy and insecurity. As Albert points out, "It took a hell of a long time to get the break-up out of his system." Elvis Presley had blended the raw excitement of black blues with mainstream white pop but it was the Everlys who stirred Appalachian country harmony into the rock 'n' roll soup. After so many years, the sudden loss of harmony, in both senses, inevitably brought with it stresses and resentments which both Don and Phil harbored for a decade.

Albert continued to work with the Crickets, who were recording an album with Waylon Jennings, who had met the Crickets in Lubbock in the 1950s while working as a DJ on radio station KDAV. Buddy Holly had produced his first single in 1958, and Jennings played bass on Holly's final fatal tour. With Duane Eddy producing, the trio added a tougher edge to the classic tracks, Albert adding his Telecaster to the Buddy Holly medley. "You can tell it's me by the rolling finger style figures on 'Peggy Sue!'" The album was recorded at RCA in Los Angeles and after the session, JI, Sonny and Albert went to a bar across the street on Sunset where dramatic news was unfolding live on TV. On that day, May 17, the police had surrounded a house where members of the Symbionese Liberation Army, including their former hostage, newspaper heiress Patty Hearst, were holed up. A massive shootout ensued and the building went up in flames.

The album[25] was not released until 1978, when in late March of that year, Waylon and Willie Nelson had the nation's no. 1 country single with the classic "Mammas, Don't Let Your Babies Grow Up To Be Cowboys," which won them a Grammy. The Crickets received a gold album but Albert was not paid for the sessions, "which was probably my fault. I think JI felt a bit bad for me and one day, when we were drunk at his house, he gave me an acrylic cube called the Buddy Award. Waylon had been presented with it for the hit single and he had given it to JI. I still have it."

That summer, 1974, Albert toured Britain again with The Crickets. According to Tonio K, "Albert would do these lightning fast, mind-warping guitar solos for the English audiences, who had come to the gig in chartered buses wearing their red shoes and their teddy-boy coats. Everyone would just sort of yawn through the solos, and then applaud politely at the end. But then, when he'd break into a note-for-note version of 'That'll Be The Day,' everybody would be on their feet. It was just obvious no one wanted to hear any new material from the band." The tour finished and so ended Albert's period of intense involvement with Buddy Holly's old band, although whenever the Crickets had something interesting on they called Albert. "I love to play with them: They were among my first musical influences."

One or two of the "interesting" occasions happened fairly soon after the U.K. tour, when Albert was in Los Angeles working with Don Everly. The Crickets opened for Waylon Jennings at a women's prison. "It was hilarious and the girls were sitting up on the bleachers in the gymnasium and when Waylon came on they all flashed their boobs at him." On another occasion, Waylon had a couple of Hell's Angels working on his crew and after the gig Albert and the Crickets were invited to a soiree at the Angels' Oakland Chapter. "It was quite an honor, everybody was well-behaved, hors d'oeuvres were all set out on trays and the girls told us there were even tampons in the ladies toilets!"

Albert was, in the meantime, trying to establish himself on the tough Los Angeles studio scene. He worked on one occasion at the Capitol Tower on a session co-produced by Glen Campbell, while at the same time continuing to gig informally with Don Everly every Tuesday night at the Sundance Saloon. "One night I turned up and Buddy Emmons was on pedal steel. I almost wet my pants but I got up and played: I was in heaven." Campbell, who had played his Telecaster on countless sessions in the '60s as well as briefly joining the Beach Boys, became a Sundance regular, and other players included John Hartford, Ron Coleman and Doug Dillard. Albert sat in with Jimmy Bryant twice at the Palomino, playing piano while Bryant played guitar with ex-Bluecaps guitarist Johnny Meeks on bass. "So I was surrounded by heroes!"

The following contemporary reviews capture the atmosphere of those legendary Tuesday nights: "Buddy [Emmons] was living in L.A. doing lots of sessions as always, but on Tuesday nights at a tiny funky little bar in Calabasas called the Sundance Saloon, the 'magic' used to happen a lot and all night long, too! Ron Coleman ran the Sundance Band, played bass or rhythm guitar, sang great and had the best phone book in town! A lot of the time, Don Everly would sing the lead vocals and play his old EB Gibson acoustic. Jackson Browne, Glenn Frey, Billy Burnette, Glen Campbell would sit in.... But on the special nights, the steel would be none other than Buddy Emmons and Albert Lee on his B bender Telecaster!... Between 200 to 350 people would pass through the club on any given Tuesday night. Harrison Ford used to hold down the end of the bar back before he became 'Indy,' and a lot of the Hollywood 'A' list people used to come out to be 'cool.' Oh yea, it was $2 at the door!"[26]

And "one night, the lead guitar was being wonderfully played by Albert Lee, who had just gotten his Evan's Pull-String Tele the week before. Harold Hensley was playing fiddle and after a few incendiary rides by Harold, he handed it over to Albert and what came next was burned into my music memory banks forever and ever. It was the hottest, cleanest, most musical, blazing Tele solo I've ever heard taken on 'Orange Blossom Special.'"[27]

In August 1974 Ray Smith and Tony Colton were living in a rented house in Encino, in the San Fernando Valley, north of Mulholland Drive. They had been there for a couple of months working with Russell Morris but were soon involved with mixing the Don Everly album. Albert was living either with JI or at the Heritage Motel but "they had a spare room and so I moved in. It was a really nice house with a swimming pool. Tony always had some scheme going and I never knew where the money was coming from. I assumed that Warner Bros. were paying."

Joe Cocker, the gravel-voiced rocker from Sheffield, was also in the canyons, and Reg Locke, through talking to Jerry Moss at A&M, ended up co-managing him. Albert had played on "Marjorine," Cocker's first single, along with Jimmy Page. Joe had a tour planned for the southern states and had got a band together—but they needed a rehearsal place. Locke contacted a real estate agent, Karen Kovar, who found them a ranch in Buellton, north of Santa Barbara. Karen lived in and was literally the Girl Friday, which was when she drove down to Los Angeles to buy essential supplies for the weekend—booze, drugs and—oh, yes—food. They had been up there for a couple of weeks when Reg stopped by in Encino with Karen. "We were going down to see Clapton play at the Forum," she recalls, "and we stopped by and we asked them if they wanted to come to the concert." Albert wasn't keen on the concert but he was struck by Karen. "She was kind of Reg's girlfriend but not," he says. "Anyway, I met her for the first time and thought, 'She's nice.'"

Cocker was in the studio finishing off an album at the Village Recording studios on Butler Avenue in west L.A. Up at the ranch the band had been getting drunk and stoned every night. There had been little rehearsing and excessive drink and drugs resulted in a major brawl. "I don't know what started the fight," says Karen, "but teeth were literally flying. Henry McCullough broke his wrist and left, drummer Jimmy Carstein had broken his arm—he'd dived off a hotel roof into a swimming pool and missed. Joe found a bass player, Greg Brown, on the street in front of the Roxy but he didn't even know how to change his strings and he lasted only a few gigs." With the tour a fortnight away, an urgent call went out from Reg Locke for a guitar player and drummer. As for the drums, Reg knew Pete Gavin was in town but at that time *Sunset Towers* was about to be released and Don Everly had some gigs booked which Albert was supposed to do with him. However when he received the S.O.S. from Reg Locke Albert reluctantly had to tell Don he had been offered the tour with Joe Cocker as the headline band. So Don put together a band with Lindsey Buckingham and Don and Albert remained on good terms.

Albert went up to Buellton and rehearsed for two weeks. "It was madness up there. Joe was drunk most of the time: I'd be trying to sleep and he'd be playing Ray Charles records at 4 in the morning full blast. He's a tremendous bloke with a great mind but if ever there was a candidate for an early grave it was him—I'm amazed that he's survived."

He had with him with a 17-year-old girlfriend, Susie Thomas, who became Micki Steele, the Bangles bass player. One day in Laurel Canyon she fell distraught on Ray Smith's shoulder: Albert had gone off with Karen. "Looking back, it wasn't very nice," says Karen, "but he seemed to have an instant attraction to me. He seemed like a nice guy and I thought he and Susie were a nice couple but it just sort of happened. Susie left that night and we were together after that."

These were the inevitable pitfalls of life on the road as a wandering minstrel. "Albert was the gypsy rambler with a roving eye," says Ronnie Bell. "It's very hard not to be when it's thrown at you like that. Where Mary was concerned it was an 'out of sight, out of mind.'" Albert admits, "I was a crazy guy at that time. I'd flown Lucy and the kids over the year before and felt very guilty that I hadn't brought Mary to the States so I took her on the road with Joe, without the twins." The problem was that Karen was also on the tour. "He suddenly came to me one night and said, 'I've got to tell you something. Mary's coming.' She'd bought her ticket and it was a done deal. Luckily we were on the East Coast so I went to my parents' house in New Jersey. I actually went to one of Joe's shows in New York and met Mary there. She stayed on the road for another week or so but he called me when she'd left and I went back."

Albert and Karen in the mid−1970s (courtesy the Lee family).

Albert now sees that period as part of his life which he wishes he had handled differently. He does not emerge from his relationship with Mary in a very good light and when she arrived back in England from the tour she finished it. "It was a waste of time and I moved back to Wales."

Joe Cocker and the Cock 'n' Bull Band[28] toured America twice during the autumn but Cocker was having a few problems. "Every night during the same song he would signal to me to do a guitar solo and rush back stage and throw up. He was nervous and jittery ... couldn't eat and was drinking a bottle of brandy a day. We had to try to keep it away from him before gigs." Nevertheless, he finished the whole tour. "What a great voice."

Between the two parts of the Cock 'n' Bull tour, Mick Weaver left the band to go on the road with Frankie Miller, and Reg Locke thought it would be a cool idea to decamp to the Bahamas to bed in a new line-up. Albert was far from impressed, as he wrote in a post-card home on November 20. He describes the trip as a "waste of time and money," whereas "it would have been better to have gotten together a couple of days before the tour rather than take an enforced holiday here. There's very little to do except swim and lay in the sun and dodge falling coconuts." Soaking up the sun on a Caribbean beach, he still had a message for his father: "Hope you're getting down to the Prince of Wales now and again." His Dad loved basking in the reflected glow of Albert's "celebrity" status.

Things had improved, however, by February 1975 when he told his parents[29] he thought the new band was "going to be great." He also let them know that the band would be leaving

The Cock 'n' Bull band in Australia in February 1975. From left, Albert, Phyllis, bassist Gordon Edwards, Joe Cocker, pianist Richard Tee, Marianne, guitarist Cornell Dupree and drummer Pete Gavin (courtesy the Lee family).

"about the 16 for Australia. We play in Hawaii on March 7 and I might be home during the second week in March." Albert loved Australia. A card from Sydney describes the weather as "fine most of the time" and like most visitors, he thought the Opera House was stunning.

Though his stint with Cocker had broadened his geographical horizons enormously, the only album Albert contributed to was *Stingray*,[30] playing a beautifully soulful solo on "You Came Along" by Bobby Charles. The album, produced by Mark Aglietti and Richard Tee and arranged by Peter Tosh, was recorded at Dynamic Studios, Kingston, Jamaica, though Albert overdubbed his solo in L.A. An attempt to blend Cocker's growling vocals with reggae, the experiment had mixed results—and reviews. "Using crack New York session men instead of Jamaicans somewhat defeated the purpose, but did work well in off-setting the reggaefied tunes.... The album's quality springs from the first-rate talents of his guest accompanists ... full of gems worth seeking out."[31] Those guest accompanists included backing vocalists Bonnie Bramlett and Deniece Williams, Richard Tee on organ and keyboards, Eric Clapton and Cornell Dupree on guitars and Steve Gadd on drums. "In short," wrote Cliff White, "the album has class."[32]

Short as his time with Cocker was, Albert's contribution to the band and the album brought him to the attention of Jerry Moss, the M of A&M. Moss, who was inducted into the Rock and Roll Hall of Fame in 2006, signed Albert to make his first solo album. Albert worked on the album, on and off, for the rest of the year and still chuckles about it today. "I'm still convinced that Jerry thought he'd signed *Alvin* Lee[33] because he was a little puzzled about some of the tracks I eventually presented to him."

Albert turned up back in Canberra Road as promised in the middle of March to face the music, in more ways than one. Lucy was pressing for a divorce. She felt that Albert wanted the best of both worlds, while the more charitable view was that he was desperate to keep everybody happy. She was consulting an attorney and "he kept saying, 'Please don't.'" Eventually Lucy prevailed and the couple were divorced in May 1975. Family problems apart, Albert still found time to play piano with Country Fever backing Marvin Rainwater at the International Country Music Festival at Wembley, "where I probably earned about a fiver."

Albert hung around Charlton over Easter, seeing his parents and the children, but by early May he was writing from Nashville, "The gig in Kentucky was only 40 miles from Nashville so I couldn't go back [to L.A.] without seeing it for a few days." He had played the first-ever U.S. Army Rock Festival at Fort Campbell, where 40,000 GIs rocked to Joe Cocker and Pure Prairie League. Albert spent most of his time in Nashville with Don Everly, doing a bit of fishing, but he hoped to be back in Los Angeles in a few days and "home some time next week"—for he had some sessions booked.

In London, in between bands, Albert played on *Squire*[34] by Lindisfarne's Alan Hull and on another outing with jazz flautist Herbie Mann. Despite its title, *Reggae*,[35] the album is largely a mixture of jazz, R&B and pop. Guitarist Mick Taylor, who six years earlier had replaced Brian Jones in the Stones, joined Albert, keyboardist Pat Rebillot and the eight-piece Tommy McCook band to create with Mann "some spirited and danceable, if a bit dated, music. Together they jam on The Beatles' 'Ob-La-Di, Ob-La-Da,' the traditional 'Rivers of Babylon,' Moe Koffman's old hit 'Swingin' Shepherd Blues' and an 18-minute version of 'My Girl.' The results are fun if not all that substantial."[36] That summer, too, Albert played some gigs, including the Floral Hall, Southport, with Aj Webber, a female folk artist from Bushey. He also played on the album *Aj Webber—Folk Girl*,[37] a tasteful offering reminiscent of Carole King's *Tapestry*, with tracks such as "Rhyme and Time" and Jimmy Webb's "The Moon's a Harsh Mistress."

Then, out of the blue, Albert got a call. It was the unmistakable Islington twang of Chris Farlowe. "'Allo, mate! Fancy doin' an album?" Apparently a wealthy gold merchant named Barry Parker had long been a fan and wanted to finance a live album.[38] Farlowe assembled quite a line-up: Albert, Jean Roussel on keyboards, Pat Donaldson on bass, Gerry Conway on drums, Chris Mercer on sax, Ron Carthy on trumpet, with backing vocals from Madeline Bell and Joanne Williams. The album was recorded at the Marquee on July 28 and at the Lyceum on August 6. "It was a great band and a lovely album," says Farlowe. "Barry wanted to put on a tour in November and December all over England so I asked Albert if he wanted to do it." It looked as if Albert would be home for a family Christmas—a chance for Karen to meet the folks.

First, however, Albert had his solo album to finish—and a session at Sunset Sound with Jackson Browne, playing on "The Only Child," an Eagles-flavored offering on Browne's *The Pretender* album.[39] With Jon Landau at the helm, who earlier in 1975 had produced Springsteen's classic, *Born to Run*, the album has a stellar cast—Bill Payne and Leland Sklar on piano, with vocal harmonies from Don Henley, J.D. Souther, Lowell George, David Crosby, Graham Nash and Bonnie Raitt. Albert admired Browne's reflective, literate songwriting, which echoed that of his contemporary L.A. songsmith, Jimmy Webb. Browne's laid-back folk-rock became the model for much of the music to emerge from California during the '70s, his intensely personal style tapping into the angst of baby-boomer America.

For most of the year, on and off, Albert had been working on his solo album. He had enough money from A&M to employ J.D. Maness, the renowned pedal steel player, and to fly Chas and Dave over to Los Angeles—"you can imagine how much fun I had with them and Pete Gavin." At the end of November he wrote to his parents that he had been in the studio "a couple of days so far and it's gone really well. We've done a great version of an old song called 'Give Me Your Smile.' Chas phoned his Mum up for the words. Weather is great but we don't get to see much daylight when we're working." Lucy had apparently told him his mother had been ill, for he begged, "Please make her go to the doctor's." He also apologized that he had not "had a chance to look for cowboy shirts yet. I'll probably go shopping with Chas and Dave soon."

Pleased as he was to be working with his old mates, Albert was dissatisfied with the final result of the sessions, "which was my fault entirely: I didn't really do enough preparation and made the mistake of trying to produce it myself." Mike Berry recalls Chas Hodges telling him, "We were hanging around and not getting in the studio. In the end, I had to say, 'Come on Albert, get down the bloody studio and let's do something!' Albert was so reticent about getting stuff down." In the event, the project was put on hold until 1978.

Albert's Christmas holiday back in Blackheath was important and enlightening. Important, in that his parents met for the first time the lady who would become, and has remained,

Los Angeles, 1975, in the recording studio. Rear, from left: Chas Hodges, Leo Fender, Tom Walker, Albert. Front: Dave Peacock and Sterling Ball (courtesy the Lee family).

Albert's wife. Karen had given him more self-confidence. "He didn't carry himself well but I encouraged him and made him feel good about himself"—and that Christmas his mother told her shy and self-effacing son, "You're standing up straighter." Important, too, for that was when Karen first met Abigail and Wayne, who remembers "sitting in the car outside Nan's and Grandad's. Dad was saying, 'I don't know if it's right,' but we went in and it wasn't a problem." Enlightening, in that it is "illustrative of the kind of guy he is and his dedication to music," says Keith Nelson. On New Year's Eve Nelson, who had to take anything that paid, had "a lousy gig with a not-very-good Irish band. They couldn't sing and their timing was chaotic." Out of the blue Albert rang Nelson, who told him he was playing in an Irish bar called the Coach and Horses at the bottom of Blackheath Hill. He warned Albert the gig would be terrible but had just set up the gear "when in walked Albert with a Fender amp and his Telecaster and his Dad with his accordion." The punters ignored the band's first set but it was all the same to Albert, who just got up and played. It was his Dad who stole the show. He asked Nelson if he could play his accordion in the break. "He blew us all off the stage," says Nelson. The Romany from Kidbrooke, with his Jimmy Shand songs, stirred the drunken Irishmen out of their Guinness-fuelled disdain, evoking vague folk-memories of a long-lost Celtic twilight of the soul.

At the turn of the year Albert was at a crossroads. He and Karen had been living rent-free at Joe Cocker's house in Malibu but Cocker had decided to fold the band, sell up and move back to England. With no permanent gig in California, Albert talked of getting a place in Wales. For him, as for Robert Frost, "Two roads diverged in a yellow wood."[40] Should he return home, where all the leaves are brown and the sky is gray, or should he take the road less traveled, and continue California dreaming on such a winter's day?

Nine

From a Deeper Well

Just after Christmas 1975, in Blackheath, with Queen's "Bohemian Rhapsody" in the middle of its seven-week run at U.K. #1, Albert was in a quandary, at a crossroads with no sign post. With no firm gig in place in the States, he was reluctant to return to California. However, "I knew I wanted to be with Karen." So when she said, "Let's go back to L.A.," the die was cast.

Soon after he got back the phone rang. It was Ron Coleman from the Sundance Saloon. Ron had built a copy of an Excalibur car, "a big gaudy two-seater," recalls Albert. "He knew I was a car buff and asked me if I wanted a drive in it down to Laguna Beach. He'd been invited to go and see Emmylou Harris." Albert had seen Emmylou and the Hot Band at the Palomino Club in North Hollywood the previous summer when he was recording with Chas and Dave. For Albert and his mates, the main draw that night was not the lady herself, however, but James Burton, at the time a Hot Band member. Albert had met Burton briefly in Las Vegas a couple of years before when he went to an Elvis gig with the Crickets. Furthermore, his old comrade from the Crickets, Glen D. Hardin, was on piano.

Emmylou Harris is now the most admired and influential female vocalist in modern country music, having explored trails long-untrodden across the landscape of American roots music. Early in 1976, however, she was relatively unknown. Born to a military family in Birmingham, Alabama, she lived much of her early life in Washington, D.C., and cut her musical teeth around the folk clubs of the capital and Greenwich Village, performing with artists like Jerry Jeff Walker.[1] Then in the spring of 1972 a chance meeting in Clyde's, a singles club in Washington, changed her life. A hippie kid from a rich Florida family, on the recommendation of Chris Hillman of the Flying Burrito Brothers, walked in and heard her sing "It Wasn't God Who Made Honky Tonk Angels." Gram Parsons knew, he just knew, that she was the singer he'd been looking for. He and Harris performed two songs together at Clyde's that night for five or ten paying customers.

Country-rock pioneer Parsons was a rocker who venerated both George Jones and Elvis Presley: Parsons' music fused country's fervor with rock 'n' roll's excitement and over the next eighteen months Emmylou became an acolyte. After Parsons' sordid death, with its lurid aftermath[2] in September 1973, she blended the essence of what he had taught her about the magic and mystery of real country music with her splendidly supple soprano. She surrounded herself with first-rate backing musicians and, she says, "was doing what I was doing because of Gram. He was the real driving force. He really helped me find my voice

137

because the idea of a folk artist singing country music was unusual. One song at a time I was trying to figure out what Gram would have done. I knew that he hated the term 'country-rock': to him, it implied something that was less than the sum of the parts. He was aiming for what he called 'Cosmic American music.' I knew that he loved the beauty of the traditional music, but infused it with his own poetry. A song like 'Sin City' has all the structure of those beautiful Louvin Brothers songs, but the words could have been written only by someone of his generation and his experience. The key," she continued, "was singing harmony with him and learning the phrasing, because singing with Gram required you to be extremely restrained and economical. I realize now in retrospect that that is a real signature of country music; the emotion is in the restraint; and I believe restraint intensifies emotion, especially in music." From her days with Parsons, Harris sourced, revived and later wrote high-class material, but as Hank De Vito says, "Emmylou could sing the phone book and it would sound great."

Following the trauma of the loss of her mentor, Emmylou Harris did a few shows with the Angel Band, her original band from D.C. However, when producer Brian Ahern was rolled in by Warner Bros. to record an album, she wanted "everything that had ever touched Gram. I wanted to keep the momentum going but it felt like there was a wheel missing— I'd just started to learn when I lost him." The studio band included drummer Ron Tutt, pianist Glen D. Hardin, bassist Emory Gordy, Jr. and lead guitarist James Burton, all members of Elvis Presley's backup band, and all of whom had played on Parsons' album *Grievous Angel*. Other familiar faces included Fayssoux Starling on backing vocals and Bernie Leadon on various stringed instruments. Warners' Los Angeles office had little hope that she would reach a mainstream rock or country audience and Emmylou agreed. "I felt it would be ignored because it wasn't a commercial pop record and it wasn't basic country, and it definitely wasn't rock 'n' roll."

Although she had recorded the album *Gliding Bird*[3] in 1969 for the small and short-lived Jubilee label, *Pieces of the Sky*[4] is seen as her major-label debut. The album announced itself with what became the Ahern/Emmylou formula for the next decade—a tasteful mix of traditional country's integrity, folk music's spirit, and country rock's panache. Neil Coppage, assessing the album in *Stereo Review*, vividly described Emmylou as being one of those "country singers who are aware of the world that lies beyond the honky-tonk at one end of Main Street or the church at the other (and all that triangulating Family Life in between)." The album even had a top-10 country hit in her cover of the Louvin Brothers' "If I Could Only Win Your Love" and contained a tribute to Parsons ("Boulder To Birmingham") and a version of the Beatles' "For No One." For all Warners' misgivings, Bud Scoppa, in his review in *Rolling Stone*, described it as "more of a country album than just about anything to come out of Nashville for years. Aside from having that miraculous voice, she has great personal charm made up in proportionate parts of intelligence, honesty and self-effacement."

Warner Bros., favorably surprised at the response to *Pieces of the Sky*, decided it would be worth putting some money behind a "hot band" and persuaded Emmylou to go out and find one. It did not take long. Both James Burton and Glen D. Hardin accepted, with the proviso that they could work around Elvis' increasingly rare live appearances. Emory Gordy signed on full-time as the bass player and Hank De Vito took the pedal steel chair. John Ware, formerly with Michael Nesmith's First National Band, "we found rehearsing with the

Bellamy Brothers next door," says Emmylou. "He came in and offered to sit in on drums." She had to pay their sizeable salaries out of her own pocket, but decided it was well worth it. She dubbed them the Hot Band—but she still lacked a vocal partner, a surrogate Parsons. Ahern, who also owned a publishing company, had stacks of cassettes lying around his office in Toronto and brought Emmylou to Canada to listen to material. "We listened for an entire day but I didn't hear anything I liked. He had one last tape and I heard Rodney Crowell singing 'Song for the Life' and 'Bluebird Wine.' And I said, 'Okay. Now we're getting somewhere. This guy has obviously listened to George Jones.'" Crowell, a 22-year-old vagabond from Houston, had no prospects at the time and welcomed the call from Ahern. "I went to Toronto and Brian and I flew down to Washington, D.C., where Emmy was playing at a club with her Angel Band," Crowell recalled. "After the gig, we stayed up all night somewhere in D.C. and played songs till daylight." Emmylou explains, "He was a Texas boy who had played in his dad's band, and could play whatever instrument was required. But he also had this great gift as a writer, because like Gram Parsons he was my age but had come to country from his roots, not as a sort of intellectual exercise. That day, he said, 'I've just written this,' and he played me 'Till I Gain Control Again.'"[5] The Hot Band was in business.

Elite Hotel,[6] released in December 1975, was the first outing for the Hot Band on vinyl and has the flavor of a group of session musicians gradually finding their shape as a cohesive unit, together with guest artists Little Feat pianist Bill Payne and singers Jonathan Edwards and Linda Ronstadt. The album moved a step closer to fulfilling the promise of commercial success hinted at in *Pieces of the Sky* and further acknowledged Emmylou's debt to Gram Parsons. Two of his most enduring compositions, "Sin City" and "Wheels," along with a rollicking live cut of "Ooh Las Vegas" are featured while other selections clearly reflect Parsons' influence: the Louvin Brothers' "Satan's Jewel Crown" and Buck Owens's "Together Again," in which Glen Hardin tumbles around the keyboard "as if caught between despair and reckless humor."[7] Emmylou stays true to her guru's vision while updating the musical vocabulary in which it was expressed. As Ron Krouse wrote in a contemporary review, "She has dissolved whatever was left of the barriers between the best of rock and country." Her purist stance, however, proved a commercial success as well. The album produced three top-five singles. Her interpretation of two of country music's most recognizable standards—Buck Owens's "Together Again" and Don Gibson's "Sweet Dreams" (a huge hit for Patsy Cline)—took Emmylou to the top of the country charts, establishing her in the vanguard of female country singers. The album rocked, too. The driving "Amarillo," a Crowell and Emmylou original, a boisterous take on Wayne Kemp's "Feeling Single, Seeing Double" and "Jambalaya," a Hank Williams honky-tonker, contrast with her readings of the Beatles ballad "Here, There and Everywhere" and the plaintive "One of These Days," the essence of subdued desperation.

The Hot Band was now gigging consistently, and James Burton's showy guitar work was a highlight of each night's performance, some people doubtless turning out not to hear Harris, but to admire the Louisianan's Telecaster technique. After about nine months in the Hot Band, Burton, who was also still contracted to Elvis Presley, was finding it increasing difficult to reconcile the conflicting gigs. While working with Emmylou was obviously pleasurable and fulfilling, and although he was allowed to work with the Hot Band when

Elvis did not require his services, it meant that the Hot Band could not play gigs when Elvis was working. The band had toured Europe with Burton in February and at that point, recalls Hank De Vito, "Glen decided he was going to quit Elvis, which he did, and he was going to work with Emmylou full-time come the spring tour in April. We were trying to get James to quit Elvis as well." In fact, guitarist John Beland of the Flying Burritos was asked by Presley's conductor Joe Guercio to replace Burton. Beland learned the show and met Presley but at the last minute Burton threw in his lot with the King. De Vito quotes, "His line was 'Elvis called me, personally. I gotta stay with him'"—and as Rodney Crowell recalled with a chuckle, "James went with Elvis, and Glen D. went with us. He liked us better."

That March, after the gig at the club in Laguna, Albert went backstage unaware he was walking into a new life.

"Hi, Albert!" said the genial Glen D. "We were just talking about you. What are you doing in the next two or three weeks?"

"Not much. I was just about to go back to England."

"Well," said the keyboard man, "James is just going off to play with Elvis and we need a guitar player to fill in."

Emmylou, unaware of Albert's work but forced to replace Burton, drafted Albert into her band on Glen D.'s recommendation, but she remembered thinking, "How do you replace James Burton?" "The psychology of having James Burton as your big gun meant that when I was out there I thought 'it doesn't matter if people don't like me or don't think I've got the goods, I've got James—worth the price of admission.' James was the star and was consummate at backing a singer. His playing made you phrase differently but at the same time he was always paying attention to what you were doing. I learned a lot about singing from him." Pedal steel ace Hank De Vito had similar thoughts. He had met Albert socially the year before at the Palomino but he "didn't know him as a player. I wondered how we would replace James Burton, who had been an icon for nearly 20 years. I would watch James play three notes and they were just the right notes—you didn't have to play anything else."

Albert thinks that "There were a lot of people that were kind of surprised. There's this English guy taking the place of James [Burton]—what's he going to do?"[8] As far as Harris was concerned his Englishness was irrelevant. "Albert upped the ante when we got into that rock edge and it wasn't because he was English. I was beginning to see that many people in England appreciated real country music—more than in the States where many saw it as being politically incorrect. You don't replace James but you get somebody who is just as good but with a completely different style. When you replace a musician you trust that they're going to bring something different to the mix. Albert brought a very muscular sound to the band, more so than James. He was more driving and rocking. Style is a product of your limitations. Albert could play a lot of the stuff James could play but not exactly like him. He could do other things that were extraordinary which added a different flavor to what I was doing." De Vito agrees: "Albert was much more our contemporary and had a lot more going for him. We'd have to egg James on to play sometimes. Albert took the great respect he had for James, as well as people like Jimmy Bryant and brought the '60s sensibility, which he'd picked up with the Thunderbirds."

As far as Rodney Crowell was concerned, "the day Albert Lee came on the scene, the Hot Band went from a group of subsidized musicians to perhaps the best country rock band of all time. Albert's musicianship was as dazzling as it was unifying." To Tony Brown, later a keyboard player in the band and vice president of MCA in Nashville, "the way James would bend strings was fascinating and the parts he would play on those early Emmylou records like 'Too Far Gone' and 'Together Again' were amazing, but he had not got Albert's fast fingers. I think Albert could do James but I'm not sure that James could have done Albert, especially the lightning fast playing that Albert did." It was not all sweetness and light. Drummer John Ware "was always friendly," Albert recalls, "but kind of officious and would annoy me by calling me 'Bertie.' He was more particular than the others in the band about me duplicating James's licks. Some of them were signature licks for the songs but after a while they got used to the way I was doing things and I put my own stamp on them." Albert's blistering and immaculately picked fretwork was bringing to Harris's music yet another dynamic. Whatever the technicalities, Albert soon realized that he was playing with a talented band "who played the kind of music I really loved. I thought 'This is great. I'm living in America now.'"

And he was. Karen and Albert had been staying in Joe Cocker's guest house on Malibu beach, which was for sale and due to be vacated at any time. "Suddenly I got this gig with Emmylou and within a week we were going on the road. We happened to look in the *Malibu Times*—there aren't a lot of properties about but we found this lovely little apartment on Bailard Road overlooking Broad Beach for $500 a month. We snapped it up, bought a lot of Joe's furniture, some of which we still have—the big old dining table, etc., and Karen moved the stuff in while I was on the road."

Albert's first gig with the Hot Band was in a honky-tonk, the Branding Iron, at 320 S.E. Street in San Bernadino. Burton had pulled out at the eleventh hour and as De Vito remembers, "We tried to get Bob Warford who had sat in the previous year but he was still playing with Elvis, too." There was no time to work on any orchestrated parts with De Vito: "We were just trying to get through a gig." Not that the lack of rehearsal seemed to matter. "He came in cold and floored everybody. He knew some of the material but you just had to tell him what key we were in and he'd take a lead and burn up the place."

During the first month of touring Albert was in limbo, not knowing whether he was a permanent member of the band or not. "At that point Glen D. and John Ware were still trying to persuade James to stay," says De Vito, "but Rodney and I thought if James is hemming and hawing, let's have Albert in." Albert hit it off with Rodney Crowell from the beginning: "We were both young outsiders living in Hollywood." Albert's innate good nature and his lack of ego enabled the "social and musical protocols to relax around Emmylou and we became an outfit," says Crowell. "Beneath Albert's innocent exterior beat the heart of a naughty boy and his willingness to let his hair down made life on the road downright vivid." Emmylou saw at once the quirky British humor of the slim fellow from south London. "He was very funny. He brought the Peter Cook and Dudley Moore tapes on the bus and they became part of our vocabulary." Hank De Vito recalls that aspect of life on the road: "The Hot Band was pretty much *A Hard Day's Night*—that movie thing. Lots of fun, lots of shenanigans, lots of energy. James was always the odd man out; he was of another period. Albert assimilated right into the humor. Everybody brought tapes with them and he always had the best and the craziest tapes." It was not only comedy: "He had some American country music I wasn't even aware of. He was a great guy to tap—Rodney and I were big Beatles

The Hot Band in 1976. Back row, from left: Rodney Crowell, Hank De Vito, Emmylou Harris, Albert. Front, from left: John Ware, Emory Gordy, Jr., Glen D. Hardin (courtesy the Lee family).

fanatics and he'd tell us that 'Lady Madonna' was based on 'Badpenny Blues' and he'd make us a tape of it. He was very knowledgeable."

That knowledge was hardly surprising. In London Albert had been buying rare imported examples of America's traditional music for fifteen years and had been assiduously absorbing the licks, chords and riffs of the genre. On the road, says Emmylou, "he was such a workhorse. I was next to him a lot of times in the hotels and as soon as he got in the room off the bus he would have his little amp and he'd start practicing. I thought he already knew everything and yet he never stopped playing the guitar—he loved it. He's never lost that exhilaration for playing."

From time to time, Wayne and Abigail would join their father on the road. Wayne remembers that "Emmylou was absolutely wonderful to me. She always made me feel really welcome and they treated you like family." The Hot Band on tour had the ambience of a traveling gypsy commune. As Emmylou recalls, "Glen D. is my favorite story-teller and the Hot Band was a real family, with the kids and all. I can't imagine being able to work unless

I really loved and felt supported by the people around me and I've had that from Day One. We took care of each other and you can't be away from your family if you aren't with another family. It's wonderful seeing Rodney, Emory and Albert becoming such good friends."

The Romany trait in Albert's traveling minstrel persona emerged on a trip to Canada early in Albert's days with the Hot Band. A gig in Toronto was to be the last before the *Luxury Liner* sessions and Hank De Vito remembers that Albert's work permit and his passport had expired. "The Canadians were going to deport him back to England. We were starting recording that week and if he'd been deported we wouldn't have been able to start the sessions. Fortunately we were still in Toronto airport and hadn't got out of Immigration. Brian Ahern contacted his lawyer: as none of the band members had gone through Immigration technically we hadn't got into the country. So Brian cancelled the gig in Toronto and everybody flew back into the U.S. That shows his gypsy side—he'd probably never even looked at his passport. Now Karen takes care of all that paperwork stuff he doesn't want to deal with."

Ahern and the band recorded 19 tracks for *Luxury Liner*[9] that summer; in the end, they included 10. Gems from the Parsons canon, now a standard part of a Harris album, included the title track, written by Parsons with his mid–'60s International Submarine Band, and "She," an exquisite ballad with overtones of Gershwin's "Porgy and Bess." A Carter Family classic, "Hello Stranger," a time-honored Appalachian folk song, has Emmylou and Hank De Vito's ex-wife Nicolette Larson interweaving the lyrics in the manner of Sara and Maybelle Carter. Emmylou's new friend Dolly Parton joined her in a pure reading of the Louvin Brothers' "When I Stop Dreaming." Rodney Crowell's "You're Supposed To Be Feeling Good" welcomed back James Burton, with Albert on acoustic guitar, and he and Albert sang backup on Townes Van Zandt's haunting border ballad "Pancho and Lefty."

This, Albert's recording debut with the Hot Band, remains "one of my favorite albums," says Emmylou, "because it was the turning point where the Hot Band left James and took off in the direction of Albert Lee. There's a real purity of focus to the album that I love.[10] Brian turned the title track into a vehicle for Albert, creating something that people had never heard in country music before. You can't deny the virtuosity of someone like Chet Atkins or all those other great players but since he could play rings round almost anyone with his fire and subtlety, Albert defined a style which gave the music credibility in the rock world. Now almost everyone is trying to play like Albert." Albert appreciated Ahern's rearrangement of Parsons's sparky but slight song: "'Luxury Liner' was nothing like the way Gram did it. Emmy always felt that she was carrying a torch for Gram's music and we recorded a great deal of his songs, giving them our West Coast sound. We were kind of mavericks. We'd taken a step forward but a step back as well. We were honoring the past. I wasn't really aware how important Gram was to Emmylou at that time although of course I was aware that she had worked with him."

The album also gave Albert a chance to show off his skills on the instrument at the heart of classic bluegrass, the mandolin. Emmylou admires his playing: "He creates a lovely sound and his solo on 'Hello Stranger' is quite beautiful. He plays it like a guitar player, more melodically—after all he's a gypsy."

But Emmylou and her producer Brian Ahern were determined not to make archivist recordings. *Luxury Liner*, like the first two albums, felt fresh and inventive, and they pitched pop and rock songs into the mix, accentuating the innate emotional links between the styles, which before the country-rock groundswell in the canyons of California in the late '60s, with Jackson Browne, Neil Young, Gene Clark and Gram Parsons in the forefront, had seemed worlds apart. Emmylou had sung Chuck Berry songs with her folk trio back in D.C. "It was great fun and I was very eclectic!" She was listening to a lot of rock 'n' roll oldies on the road and for the album she and the Hot Band enjoyed themselves laying down Chuck Berry's "C'est La Vie (You Never Can Tell)"—not without some effort, according to her: "I'm not a rock 'n' roll singer. It's great to play, but it doesn't come natural for me to sing. I hurt my voice when I consistently try to hit it really hard."

Released in January 1977, the same month she and Ahern married in Nova Scotia, *Luxury Liner* was something of a high-water mark for Emmylou. Forged into a cohesive unit by the constant road work, the Hot Band more than lived up to its name. Later that month the album was released in Britain, to a not unqualified chorus of approval. Although acknowledging that the title track showcased Albert's agility on the fretboard, Chas de Whalley, writing in *Sounds*,[11] complains of the paucity of "physical excitement in the way these boys play, there's no fire or exuberance there. It's all too professional and controlled. Sure, they play well. What do you expect from a bunch of guys with their musical credentials? But just like Albert Lee's twitching, clawpicking solo on the album's opener, 'Luxury Liner' itself, they find their operating level immediately and never deviate from it. Half of the beauty of country music lies in its capacity and propensity to laugh at itself from time to time. Emmylou Harris has forgotten this, I fear. On 'Luxury Liner' she takes herself so goddam seriously, she gets tedious and tiresome. I want to see the return of the twinkle to the school ma'am's eye." In contrast, John Tobler describes it as "a classically conceived album. The Hot Band, as hot as ever, with Albert Lee proving that he's at least an adequate substitute for James Burton, if a rather faster picker, and on occasion a bit more upfront, just fabulous, and will readily slide into the category labelled 'classic.'"[12]

Brian Ahern's studio in the Enactron Truck parked outside his home in Lania Lane, Coldwater Canyon, was busy that summer. In July, when Columbia Records sought a producer for actress-singer Mary Kay Place's debut album *Tonite! At the Capri Lounge—Loretta Haggers*, Ahern, much in demand in Los Angeles as a free-lance producer, was entrusted with the task. Place, who later appeared in the movies *The Big Chill* and *Being John Malkovich* and has played Surgeon General Millicent Griffith in *West Wing*, won an Emmy for her portrayal of wannabe country and western star Loretta Haggers on the cult late-night television soap-opera *Mary Hartman, Mary Hartman*. However, *Tonite! At the Capri Lounge* contained a Top 3 hit, "Baby Boy" and suggested that, rather like earlier TV creations, such as the Monkees, Place's music transcended the novelty of its origins. Place, it seemed, had broken free from the straitjacket of her trailer-trash TV character and when she came to cut her second album, *Aimin' to Please*,[13] Ahern whistled up virtually the entire Hot Band. Albert was joined on guitar by James Burton: "We'd switch back and forth. James would play electric some times and I'd played acoustic or mandolin." Glen D. Hardin and Leon Russell were on keyboards, Richard Greene on fiddle, with vocal contributions from Emmylou, Dolly Parton and Anne Murray. The album featured three original songs from Rodney Crowell, a subtle reading of "Save the Last Dance for Me" and a duet with Willie Nelson, the #3 Billboard hit "Something to Brag About." Albert remembers doing a TV show, *Saturday Night*

Live, in New York with Willie Nelson and Mary K. "After the show we went off to a Texas bar where we all got up and jammed and John Belushi did some Joe Cocker songs."

Jonathan Edwards, a folk artist and songwriter from Minnesota, was another visitor to the truck that summer. Edwards had spent the '60s and early '70s working the folk circuit of New England. After more than three years of working five and six one-nighters a week, in 1973 he recorded an energetic live album, *Lucky Day*, a song he wrote in the truck on his way up to live in Nova Scotia. Edwards had rubbed shoulders with Emmylou Harris around the folk clubs in Washington, D.C., and she invited him to Los Angeles while recording *Elite Hotel* to duet with her on "Wheels." That led to a deal with Warner Bros. and two albums produced by Brian Ahern—*Rockin' Chair*, which appeared in 1976, followed by *Sailboat*,[14] recorded at Enactron during that bicentennial summer. The album contains Hoyt Axton's beautiful border town love song, "Evangelina,"[15] which immediately became a favorite of Albert's. He cut a version on Eric Clapton's unreleased *Turn Up Down*[16] in early 1980 and later, a live performance appears on the Hogan's Heroes' 1993 album, *In Full Flight*.[17] With a couple of original tunes and covers of songs by Jesse Winchester, the Louvin Brothers and Rodney Crowell, the album has a back-up band with Ahern himself on acoustic guitar, Hank De Vito on pedal steel, Glen D. Hardin on keyboards, Herb Pedersen on banjo, Richard Greene (strings) and John Ware on percussion. Emmylou Harris reciprocates for *Elite Hotel*, providing supporting vocals and acoustic guitar. Edwards recalls that "Brian suggested that Albert play Telecaster and mandolin and he came in and just blew everybody away with his phrasing, ideas, melodies, and just straight out soulfulness. Albert took the touches that Burton established on *Rockin' Chair* and elevated them to a whole new level of brilliance. I became a huge fan."

Albert had been on the road or in the studio for most of the year with the Hot Band but by the early autumn he felt like a change of scene. He turned up in London as one of the superpickers on Lonnie Donegan's "Puttin' On The Style" album,[18] which emerged early in 1977. Despite the presence of skiffle fans Ringo Starr, Elton John, Nicky Hopkins, Rory Gallagher, Brian May, Ron Wood and Albert, American audiences were either baffled by the genre or completely oblivious to it as the album "was ignored, rapidly becoming a collector's item," wrote Bruce Eder in *All Music Guide*: "The record isn't bad, as Donegan does his stuff with this big name support, but overall it seems overproduced, a sort of skiffle supersession, a treatment to which the music doesn't lend itself"—a case, it seems, of Newcastle not wanting the coals after all.

In October he guested at the Bluegrass Club at the Three Horseshoes in London's Tottenham Court Road. According to David Wood, a blind guitarist and friend of Eric Clapton, the club had been started in late 1975 by Ernest Firkin from Walthamstow for his daughter Heather. "Albert would come and sit in with the house band and played at 180 picks a minute," Wood recalls. Bob Powel, the Canadian journalist and broadcaster, was also involved, and Pete Stanley, seen on BBC TV early in 2007 vainly trying to teach Frank Skinner, was also a regular on 5-string banjo.

Of greater significance than this foray into the somewhat esoteric world of British bluegrass was an interlude in which Albert joined his old mate Pat Donaldson from Country Fever and another acquaintance from session work in Soho in the early '60s, the Telecaster man Jerry Donahue, in Joan Armatrading's backing band. Armatrading, a distinctive singer-songwriter born in the West Indies but brought up from the age of 8 in Birmingham, England, had emerged on the critical radar in the mid-seventies when she teamed up with A&M. Her eponymous third album,[19] produced by Glyn Johns, included "Love and Affection," her signature song, and indicated a mature writer with a voice reminiscent of Nina Simone. With "Love and Affection" a Top Ten hit, and the album at #12, she began a British tour in Edinburgh.

Albert joined the band towards the end of the tour when, as a result of a booking error Jerry Donahue had to miss the last two gigs. "Needless to say, the blend of Joan with these superb session players (including Albert Lee) warmed even the hardest critics."[20] The singer appreciated the sound of Albert and Donahue playing together and asked Albert to play on the forthcoming U.S. tour. She was very particular about her band: "I only chose the best players to be with me on tour and Albert was a great musician. He could play anything. I mean, when he was with Emmylou he was more a country player, but my music is more eclectic, so he had to be adaptable and he was just outstanding."[21] It was during that tour that Albert made his only recording with the band, when on February 18, 1977, the band cut the *Live at the Bijou Café*[22] album in Philadelphia. Sean Mayes, Armatrading's biographer, notes that "Albert Lee's guitar is superb, though he draws our attention more than anything in Glyn John's production."[23]

A month earlier, on January 13, the tour had opened at the Civic Auditorium in Santa Monica, California, with folk/rock artist Al Stewart also on the bill. It was to become an important gig in Albert's career. A&M's Jerry Moss, the same man who eighteen months earlier thought he'd signed Alvin Lee, approached Albert and said "he'd really like me to work on the tracks I'd recorded in 1975 and he'd give me the money to do it." Although the tracks existed and he now had A&M's resources to finish the project, it had to be put on hold for the rest of the year. "I spent a lot of time with Emmylou during '77 so it didn't happen till '78 when I enlisted the Hot Band and Emmy's husband Brian Ahern to do it. I should have toured with it on release but fell into Clapton's band. While I didn't get full value out of the record, I had great fun making it."

As soon as his brief stint behind one leading female artist was over, Albert was back in Britain with another. There could hardly have been a greater contrast in almost every way, however, personal or professional, between the two performers. In April, Emmylou and the Hot Band played a special session on BBC's influential *Old Grey Whistle Test* at the TV Theatre in London's Shepherd's Bush.[24] The show took its name from the adage that if the gray-haired doorman whistles your tune it's a hit; it did not pay undue homage to the pop charts but focused serious critical attention on developments in the album and music worlds. Two bands usually played live in a largely unfurnished studio—a one-band special was particularly prestigious. Emmylou thoroughly enjoyed herself—*The Old Grey Whistle Test* was wonderful—singing a ten-song set[25] which climaxed with "Luxury Liner" and "Ooh Las Vegas." Launched in 1971 with Heads, Hands and Feet doing "Warming Up The Band," the show had achieved cult status among aficionados of a wide range of musical styles but it was under the aegis of presenter "Whispering" Bob Harris that the program's halcyon years arrived in the mid-'70s. Bob Harris had an understated but authoritative manner and a genuine feel for the music which gained him both a wide viewing audience and respect among music professionals like Emmylou: "He's a nice guy and very knowledgeable." For his part,

Emmylou and Albert live at the International Festival of Country Music, Wembley, March 1977 (courtesy the Lee family).

Bob had admired Albert's playing for a decade, since the Thunderbird days at the Flamingo. "Albert's unique in the sense that you can put him into almost any musical context from the big concert on stage to the pub band round the corner and he would look completely at home and contributes so much in a very unobtrusive way. A lot of guitarists step forward to the front of the stage and get their foot up on the monitor but he just doesn't do that. When you watch Albert playing on stage, it takes a little while for the brilliance to soak through because he's making it all look so ridiculously easy and comfortable."

That spring the Hot Band were touring with nine-time Grammy award winners Asleep At The Wheel, a Western swing outfit originally out of Paw Paw, West Virginia, and according to Emmylou, "a crazy bunch." Nonetheless, band leader Ray Benson has kept the flag of Western swing flying for over 35 years and in that year, 1977, they were voted Best Country & Western Band by *Rolling Stone* magazine and named Touring Band of the Year by the Academy of Country Music.

For 23 years impresario Mervyn Conn promoted the annual Country Music Festival at Wembley Arena, introducing the British public to the world's leading country music artists. Every Easter thousands of fans packed Wembley for the three-day International Festival of Country Music. Performers of the caliber of Johnny Cash, Don Williams, Billy Jo Spears, Tammy Wynette, Slim Whitman, Kenny Rogers, Boxcar Willie, Freddy Fender and Conway Twitty were among the roster of Nashville's finest who appeared down the years. Conn booked some British, European, Canadian and even Japanese acts (fiddler Tokyo Matsu with her show-stopping number, "Rocky Top") to dovetail with the American stars on the main stage, while mounting a separate Best of British program in the nearby conference center.

Conn ran the festival for 23 years and George Hamilton IV once said, "If it was not for Mervyn, none of us would be here." He was, however, always the target for complaints: some centered on the authenticity of some of the acts—he booked the Osmonds one year—and eventually several local acts spoke out publicly about the lower-than-union rate payments they were offered for their appearances.[26] Keith Nelson pulls no punches: "Mervyn Conn was a very rich asshole. He used to have to pay the U.S. artists but guys like Albert and myself got paid nothing for doing that festival." Thus, when Emmylou and the Hot Band were booked to appear at the Festival at Easter, Albert told her, "Make sure you do him over good. I want to get paid for all the ones I did for free."

They did, and on the Sunday night went down a storm. Second on the bill was none other than Don Everly, in his first live appearance in two and a half years, coinciding with the release of his third solo album, *Brother Jukebox*.[27] "There was a great deal of speculation," writes Roger White, "as to what Don would perform considering his often reported objection to singing the Everly hits. Albert Lee knew that Don wanted him to play, but it was not till the morning of the show that asked Albert if he wanted to sing on 'Bye Bye Love.'" Albert gulped and thought "Oh, God!" The Festival had its drawbacks but for many years the Wembley show was the biggest of its kind and the only one to benefit from national television coverage. Albert had never dreamed that he would one day be an Everly brother but "all of a sudden I was up there doing it with Don in England on TV." Singing for fun to a packed Sundance Saloon on a Tuesday night was one thing; being half of the most famous vocal duo in pop history in front of ten thousand people and a live TV audience was something else. Considering Don's reluctance, Albert was a little surprised that Don sang all the old Everly songs, "but he knew people expected to hear them. He was very nervous and needed support. He'd had his brother there for years and looked on him as a necessary evil as he'd always wanted to be a solo singer. So he was happy to have me there and his way of thanking me for it was to give me one of his guitars." As White has noted, "After two or three years away Don didn't feel quite the same way about the old hits.... 'It was like reading the same book over and over again and always knowing what was coming next.'"[28] Nevertheless, Don's return to the stage was a triumph and Mervyn Conn invited him back the following year.

Following the Wembley dates and the euphoria of being a stand-in Everly brother, it was down-time from Emmylou for a month or two, at least as far as touring was concerned. At the Enactron truck, Brian Ahern was putting together material for the album which became *Quarter Moon in a Ten-Cent Town*.[29] He and Emmylou had been stockpiling a discrete range of recordings over the past year which gave the pair an opportunity for a change of direction with the new album. More eclectic than the previous three, it was her first record to eschew any overt references to Gram Parsons. The conscious decision to branch out was reflected in two new songs—"Easy from Now On" and "Leaving Louisiana in the Broad Daylight"—and a vigorous attack on Delbert McClinton's dissolute honky-tonk song "Two More Bottles of Wine,"[30] another country #1, with Albert contributing on piano. "I think Delbert's is still the best version. I love the lope on his. I remember doing that track in particular. It was in E flat, not a good key for me, so we slowed the tape down so I could play it in D. By that time we'd moved the Enactron Truck—they'd taken over an old paint shop on Magnolia Boulevard in North Hollywood. Brian built a big new studio and it became Enactron Studios. He still had the truck outside so he rented it out and did overdubs there."

That summer, in Albert's last few months as a Hot Band member, Rodney left to do his solo album and Ricky Skaggs joined the band. Crowell's debut solo album, *Ain't Living Long Like This*,[31] on which Albert joined Emmylou, Ricky Skaggs, Willie Nelson, Nicolette Larson and Mac Rebennack (Dr. John), was noted more for its quality than its quantity, nine songs only making up a set which, when released the following year, nevertheless received critical acclaim. Rodney Crowell would soon leave the Hot Band for a solo career and marriage to Rosanne Cash, but his parting gift to Emmylou was the vividly cinematic ballad of life on the road, "Ain't Living Long Like This." A deeply satisfying album, with the Hot Band at the top of their game, it marked Emmylou's tentative emergence from the shadow of her musical mentor[32] and "unlocked the door to her heart." A fine duet with Willie Nelson on Martin Cowart's "One Paper Kid" indicated perhaps that Emmylou had realized that country and soul were kindred spirits, not competing radio formats.

Emmylou and Albert at Enactron Studio (courtesy the Lee family).

Taking time out from the demands[33] of the Enactron truck, down at the Palomino club in North Hollywood's San Fernando Valley, Albert played with another hero, Jimmy Bryant, albeit that the great man was on fiddle. It was in just such a venue, in 1976, that Steve Fishell, now Albert's producer for the Sugar Hill label, met him for the first time. "It was only a honky-tonk in west L.A. Albert loves to throw his amp in the back of the car and drive wherever it takes, down the corner or 50 miles, to go jam with a little band." Fred Wallis, the proprietor of the music store, introduced Steve to Albert. "How can you not have heard of Albert Lee? He has the hands of Eric Clapton and the ideas of James Burton." Steve still has this vision of him "coming in with his long shaggy black hair and his Music Man amp. The band was transformed just by having him sitting in with us. Any other player would take time to find their place within the band's structure but he became the leader. We played 'Peaceful Easy Feeling' and he played this devastating solo with such wonderful ideas—it wasn't just about technique. It was about melodic structures, not just the alphabet but complete musical sentences.[34] At the end of the number there was an extraordinary moment when the entire club stood up and applauded. Everyone felt we had heard this magic moment. This was a jaded sit-down L.A. bar with a fireplace, not a dance club, perhaps a cynical, 'Come and entertain us' crowd."

Likewise, Rodney Crowell recalls "the fun we had performing semiregularly as Rodney and Albert at the Sweetwater in Redondo Beach, California. Albert's playing was not to be

The Cherry Bombs in early 1979. From left: Rodney Crowell, Emory Gordy, Jr., Albert, and Hank De Vito (courtesy the Lee family).

believed." It was at those devil-may-care, just-for-fun gigs that Albert began to hit his straps as a singer. He and Crowell shared the vocal responsibilities, with Albert doing "That's All Right, Mama" and "Rock Island Line." On other occasions, "when Emmylou wasn't touring," Hank De Vito says, "or was with child, since we were all living in southern California, we'd do weekend gigs as 'Rodney Crowell and the Hot Band.'" However, the band soon realized that some of the audience were expecting to see Emmylou and decided not to use the name, although it was essentially the same line-up. "So we became the Cherry Bombs," says Hank. "Guests would come down and sit in. One of the most exciting nights was when Albert brought along Lonnie Donegan with his D18 and he got up and we did 'Rock Island Line.' You never knew who Albert would be dragging down."

Sometimes Emmylou herself would turn up, just for fun. "I loved to see the camaraderie between Albert and Rodney. I still wish they could have been a group because Rodney was comfortable in the background and Albert was more than just a sideman so they were great standing side by side. Some of the Cherry Bombs shows I saw down at the Sweetwater were incredible—just what music should be, I thought. If Albert is polishing somebody else's star but still being up there in the spotlight, he's happy with that." The band played the Sweetwater and clubs like Laguna Beach, with a basic core of Larry Londin on drums, Emory Gordy on bass, Tony Brown on piano, Hank De Vito on steel and "depending who was available," Brown remembers, "Albert would play or maybe Vince Gill—the guitar player was the moveable part. The band was like the way Albert played, which was freestyle, not too structured, unlike Western swing where you have to observe the written parts and it's difficult to sit in. Richard Bennett, who also played with the Bombs, was much more of a swing player than Albert or Vince." Albert loved this free-wheeling approach to music-making. After all, as Hank pointed out, "He was born to be a rock 'n' roll man. It's the gypsy, the poshrat."[35]

Albert had always expressed that gypsy strain in his heritage by playing on the road with musicians he liked. That summer he had a good time with singer-songwriter Jesse Winchester on a short tour, of which both men have vividly enjoyable memories. "Aside from his wonderful playing," says Winchester, "what I remember best about Albert was his exhaustive collection of hilarious tapes—mostly outtakes of famous musicians in the studio: Bing Crosby forgetting the words to a song and improvising with profanities, an orchestra of nuns, the Troggs trying to record a follow-up to 'Wild Thing.' I recall all of us sitting in hotel rooms, laughing at those things till we cried." Albert found Winchester "a really nice guy, though a bit quiet. Then once onstage he'd do this crazy dance to the 'Rumba Song,' totally out of character."

If Lonnie Donegan has claims to be the most influential performer in the history of British rock, then there can be little doubt that the single greatest icon in American popular music was Elvis Presley. On August 16, 1977, he was discovered on the floor of his bathroom in Memphis by a girlfriend, Ginger Alden, dead from what was medically described as "cardiac arrhythmia due to undermined heartbeat." According to President Jimmy Carter, his death "deprives our country of a part of itself. He was unique and irreplaceable."[36] Although he had done his best work two decades earlier, Presley was the first rock star and along with Frank Sinatra, defined popular music in the twentieth century. By coincidence, Emmylou and the Hot Band were booked to play in Memphis on the day of his death.

"When we flew in we were besieged by the media, especially Glen D.," remembered Crowell: Hardin had of course played keyboards with Presley until a few months before. The following morning, remembering his friends back in England, Albert bought all the newspapers for Elvis fanatic Jackie Lynton before flying home.

By the fall of 1977 Albert's primary commitment for nearly 18 months had been touring and recording with Emmylou and the Hot Band. That winter, the close season for life on the road for most rock bands, Albert began to turn his attention to the long-standing commitment to Jerry Moss, left on the shelf for a while and revived in Santa Monica nearly a year before. He was aware that Moss had been somewhat unimpressed with the results of Albert's work with Chas and Dave in the fall of 1975. "Maybe he thought it was too country or maybe he really did think he'd signed Alvin instead of me. He again said, 'I'd really like you to finish that album' and gave me some more money to go back into the studio."

Before recording began at the Enactron truck in the spring of 1978 Albert had left the Hot Band. "The basic tracks for *Hiding*[37] were done in a matter of days—a week and a half maybe. There were a few tracks that didn't make it." From the 1975 sessions, when Albert played virtually everything but bass and drums with Chas Hodges and Dave Peacock, only two basic tracks survived—"Now and Then It's Gonna Rain" and "Come Up and See Me Any Time"—and these were re-recorded, co-produced by Albert and Richard Digby-Smith. "The rest was new," says Albert. "Brian was a meticulous producer and always got great sounds though I'm not too sure about some of my vocals." As Albert pointed out in the sleeve notes of the reissue, "You have to realize that I was just a sideman when I made these albums and didn't have the confidence or the vocal chops I have now." Thom Jurek, writing for the *All Music Guide*, concurs, somewhat harshly, "While Lee's singing leaves a bit to be desired here, it doesn't detract, either."

Albert had played some of the tracks recorded in 1975 to the Hot Band "and they loved them, especially 'Country Boy,' and the album opens with perhaps the definitive version of Albert's signature tune, with Ricky Skaggs, who had a #1 hit[38] in 1984 with the song, helping out on fiddle, and Emmylou on backing vocals. The track sets the tone for the album, packed with varied instrumental ideas on fiddles, acoustic guitars, mandolins, bass and piano, shot through with Albert's tastefully incendiary Telecaster."

For the recordings Brian Ahern enlisted the services of the entire Hot Band—Ricky Skaggs, Hank De Vito, Emory Gordy, Glen D. Hardin and John Ware, together with backing vocals from Emmylou, Rodney Crowell and Don Everly on Hodges and Peacock's "Billy Tyler" and Mark Knopfler's "Setting Me Up." Don joins Albert in a quasi–Everly Brothers treatment of the title track, Steven Rhymer's beautiful ballad, which also features a lyrically perfect solo from Albert. Session stalwarts and old friends Pat Donaldson (bass), Buddy Emmons (steel guitar), Jerome Jumonville (horns), Mickey Raphael (harmonica), Bruce Gary (drums), and Gerry Conway (drums) also helped out in the studio on three Crowell tunes, covers of the Louvins' "Are You Wasting My Time?," John Reid's "Now and Then It's Gonna Rain," and "Setting Me Up."

It was in effect Albert's first solo album, albeit with a little help from his friends, and rather touchingly, he gives special thanks to Don Everly, Emmylou, Chas and Dave, The Crickets, Lonnie Donegan, Sterling Ball, Karen Kovar and Lucy and dedicates the album to his children.

During 1978, apart from the work in the studio on his own album, Albert found time to contribute to sessions for significant recordings by other artists such as Nicolette Larson, Marcia Ball, Tonio K and Guy Clark. Larson had made her name as a singer with Commander Cody and the Lost Planet Airmen in the early '70s before drifting into the canyon scene in California and into the musical ambit of Neil Young. She had appeared on Young's "sensuous, drunken and loud"[39] *American Stars and Bars* album the previous year and her eponymous solo debut for Warners included a cover version of Young's "Lotta Love," which reached #8 on Billboard Magazine's Hot 100 chart in February 1979. The album[40] starred the great and the good of L.A. session players—Albert, James Burton, Bill Payne and Klaus Voorman—and featured on backing vocals the Doobie Brothers' Michael McDonald and Linda Ronstadt.

Marcia Ball, a Texan blues singer and pianist reared in Vinton, Louisiana, has earned a huge reputation as a kind of female Jerry Lee Lewis. According to the *Minneapolis Star Tribune* in a somewhat overwritten critique, "Ball is the bayou queen of the piano, steeped in blues and honky-tonk. When revved ... she's a rollicking dynamo spewing heat-seeking triplets from the ivories while her horn-driven band wails. She's also a subtle songwriter and a formidable singer with a wisp of huskiness edging her Cajun–Texan twang." In 1970, when she was just 21, she formed a progressive country band called Freda and the Firedogs in Austin, Texas. When the band broke up in 1974, Ball launched a solo career and recorded a single that signposted her future direction. One side featured Patsy Montana's "I Want to Be a Cowboy's Sweetheart," the first song by a woman to sell a million copies on the country charts, backed by New Orleans R&B singer Irma Thomas's flag-waving "Done Got Over." On the strength of the single, Capitol Records signed her and recruited Albert and Nicolette Larson, among others, to record the bluesy, country-soul flavored *Circuit Queen*[41] but Ball's heart was not in singing about rodeos and big rivers and the album died a death. "[The future] wasn't going to be country for me," said Ball, paying all due respect to the venerable genre. "It was going to be R&B, New Orleans style. I didn't want the cowboy shirts; I wanted spangles and high heels."

"We did the Guy Clark album in Nashville," remembers Albert, "at American Studios which Waylon [Jennings] part-owned. That was when Rodney showed me in a battered guitar case Scotty Moore's Super 400, so I had my picture taken with that." Clark, now regarded as one of the great American songwriters, sees himself as merely a patient craftsman and the quintessential Texan, although he has lived in Nashville for more than 20 years. Almost invariably described as a country act, he has always thought of himself as a folk singer, "doing traditional English and Irish ballads and all that kind of thing. A lot of what I do is steeped in that traditional kind of approach and I usually put at least one blues-influenced tune on each album." A painstaking craftsman, he is rarely content with an easy couplet and takes time to breathe life into his gaunt, hard-bitten but irrepressible characters. Jerry Jeff Walker was a particularly enthusiastic supporter, recording superb versions of two Clark classics, "L.A. Freeway" and "Desperadoes Waiting For A Train," in the mid-'70s.

Rodney Crowell, Steve Earle, Richard Dodson, Emmylou Harris, Townes Van Zandt, Nanci Griffith, Joe Ely, Lucinda Williams and Lyle Lovett have all worked with him in the recording studio, and on-stage, his tall, rangy good looks and ruggedly vulnerable persona added to the appeal of his striking songs. A louche charm and a dry sense of humor did the rest. His debut LP, *Old No. 1*, appeared in 1975, followed a year later by *Texas Cookin'*. The 1978 album,[42] produced by the late Neil Wilburn, was the most experimental of the three, featuring touches of cello, harpsichord and clavinet, as well as the traditional country stringed instruments. Don Everly, Rodney Crowell, the Whites and the then-unknown Kay Oslin contributed background vocals; and as well as Albert, the instrumental cast included such luminaries as Buddy Emmons and Mickey Raphael.

Apart from the Guy Clark album, Don Everly would work again with Albert when he visited Britain in March to play the Wembley Festival. Backed on this occasion by a British group, Barbary Coast, his Wembley performance was followed by a nine-city British tour with the late Marty Robbins. Barry Fletcher of Barbary Coast remembers the tour: "I got the feeling that there was another half of Don there somewhere. He clung to Albert Lee like nobody's business." Albert backs up that comment: "Don was very nervous. It surprised me he never drank when he was doing a gig.... I think he would've eased up a bit if he had had a beer before he went on."[43]

The Wembley dates were, of course, merely a prelude to Albert's recording commitments, which occupied most of the year, but Keith Nelson recalls an outing to hear Gordon Lightfoot at the Santa Barbara County Bowl in early June. Nelson remembers, "he had a band with him and the gig was terrible. Albert was really depressed about it as he had been a fan of the Canadian troubadour for many years and had always admired singer-songwriters like Lightfoot, as well as Jimmy Webb, Jesse Winchester and Rodney, of course." Albert also liked to listen to classical music. "When you've had a Fender amp stuck up your ass all night and you come home from a gig you'll probably listen to classical music because it's very calming," says Nelson.

Albert had the opportunity late that month to record a Rodney Crowell song for George Jones's double LP, *My Very Special Guests*,[44] a collection of 37 duets with country music's premier league performers. Jones was not even present at the sessions, as it was recorded during one of his legendary "no show" periods: He added his vocals later. Despite this, his duet with Emmylou Harris on Crowell's "Here We Are," with Brian Ahern producing and the Hot Band as her trusty support, is magical. "He doesn't need any smoke screens," says Emmylou. "He just sings from the heart. He taught us all how to sing country music."

From working with a long-established superstar in June, albeit vicariously, a month later Albert had a hand in recording an album[45] which upon its release in February 1979 had critics queuing up to herald the emergence of a major new talent. Steve Krikorian was an honorary Cricket, following his work on their albums five years before but had now adopted the name of Tonio K., references to Kafka's hero Franz K and to the Thomas Mann novel *Tonio Kröger*. His first solo album, *Life in the Foodchain*, featured an all-star lineup that included Albert, together with Earl Slick, surf guitar king Dick Dale and the Band's Garth Hudson on accordion, for the album was recorded at the Band's studio not far from where Albert was living, on Bailard Road in Malibu. Producer Rob Fraboni had been at the helm for the Asylum debut of Bob Dylan with the Band, whereupon Dylan invited him to be the sound consultant for the Dylan/Band Tour in 1974. A year or so later Fraboni designed and built Shangri-La Studios in Malibu to Dylan's precise specifications.

Fraboni coaxed a hard-rocking, stripped-down sound from the seasoned band of studio professionals and the album received critical acclaim, most famously from Steve Simels of *Stereo Review*, who proclaimed it "the greatest album ever recorded." While he restrains himself from such hyperbole, Mark Derning for *All Music Guide* called it "a masterpiece. The unexpected political bias and anti-capitalist stance that dominate many of the lyrics come across as eloquent, passionate and compelling" and he concludes, "cut like a chainsaw while also managing to be pretty damn funny."

Although Albert's solo career led to his gradual departure from the Hot Band in 1978, his guitar graced Emmylou Harris's Grammy award-winning *Blue Kentucky Girl*,[46] released the following year. The fifth of her albums since the death of Gram Parsons, it had a more acoustic, unadulterated country atmosphere with Harris pouring her heart and soul into every vocal performance. On *Quarter Moon in a Ten-Cent Town* she was too closely involved in the mixing and the more musically focused approach taken on *Blue Kentucky Girl* was a reaction to her overinvolvement. "We just said, 'We're going to make a pure country album,'" Emmylou recalls. She also felt she had something to prove to those purists who felt that "the only reason I was a success on the country charts was because I was more pop. So I thought, 'Right, let's see if we can do just a country record. No Beatles songs. Just very, very pure.' That's what we set out to do."

While she steered clear of the mixing desk, Emmylou was at the helm in other ways. She played acoustic guitar on every song but two and made particularly astute song selections. It was the recipe as before—a mix of classic country songs, this time from the Louvin Brothers and Leon Payne, new material from neo-traditionalists like Rodney Crowell and Willie Nelson, and one rock oldie, the Drifters' "Save the Last Dance for Me," which became a top five country hit. She had always had an innate ability to source songs to which she can bring something special, keeping annotated song lists in notebooks for reference when it came time to record and showing that traditional country songs could hold their own in a contemporary setting. Relatively new songs, such as Jean Ritchie's "Sorrow In The Wind" (1960) and Dallas Frazier's "Beneath Still Waters" (1967), which hit #1 on the country singles chart for the fourth time, sound as if they could have been written fifty years earlier. She extracts from Gram Parsons' nostalgic paean "Hickory Wind" the bitter-sweet sorrow beneath the superficially romantic veneer.

Although all ten songs come from different writers, they cohere around metaphors of nature and themes of desire or separation. The harmony singing is particularly fine, utilizing high-class accompanists in Don Everly, Glenn Campbell, Dolly Parton and Linda Ronstadt. The Hot Band, augmented by guests James Burton, Tony Brown and Ricky Skaggs, make thoughtful contributions that coalesce into an effortlessly textured whole. Albert and James Burton trade electric guitar duties throughout the album, with Albert playing mandolin on the title track and on "Save The Last Dance For Me."

It was the last album Albert would record as a member of the Hot Band; by the end of 1978, he had left, as it seemed, for a solo career. Yet in three short years his guitar playing, rooted in British skiffle and R&B while infused with the essence of Buck Owens' Telecaster, the lyricism of Chet Atkins and the rockabilly riffs of Burton and Burnette, had been a major factor in an extraordinary musical phenomenon. Emmylou Harris had made traditional country music acceptable to a rock audience. "She gathered about her a bunch of fine musicians like the Hot Band," wrote Penny Valentine, who "gave her a credibility with a rock-reared audience that was almost condescending. Country music is by nature lyrically simple: the music of poor whites, agricultural workers, red-necks in bars who blame all their problems on someone else, it's inherently limited in its power of expression. It's this rural quality, this simplicity, that Emmylou purveys in a way that contradicts the sophistication of her appearance."[47]

Albert came home to London for Christmas that year, as Ray Smith remembers. "It was the last time I played with him. At Harrow College I played slide guitar with Chas and Dave with Mickey Burt on drums. Albert played knockout guitar and Tony Colton got up and did two numbers, 'Nothin' Shakin' and 'Tryin' To Put Me On.'"

Early in the new year Albert found himself in London, "a little bit at a loose end. Emmylou had found herself another guitar player. I was beginning to wonder 'What next?' After all, I couldn't really expect to walk right back into her band." The Hiding album was due out early in the new year: "I should have put a band together and gone on the road to promote my record but I didn't seriously think about it. I hadn't fronted a band before so it would have been all new to me."

But he got a call from Glyn Johns, who had been working with Joan Armatrading. He was in London producing the Lost in Austin[48] album with the Texan blues guitarist Marc Benno and asked Albert to sit in on the sessions. "Eric Clapton was playing on it," Albert recalls, "with his bass player Carl Radle. Jim Keltner was on drums and Dick Sims was playing keyboards. I knew Eric from the mid–'60s when we used to play the same circuit as Farlowe." "That's where we made our bones as players," says Clapton. "We'd be playing seven nights a week, doing the Rikky-Tik circuit and all the clubs round London."

Albert and Eric met up again in late January when Albert played on Chas and Dave's Live at Abbey Road album.[49] The famous Studio 1, no doubt still haunted by the ghosts of George Martin and the Beatles, was fitted with a real stage, two specially-installed bars and the best sound equipment in the world, and seven hours of tape recorded a Cockney rock 'n' roll party for 1500 people over two snowy days in north London. People had come from all over the capital and thanks to Stuart Colman's announcement on BBC Radio London, coach parties had been organized from pubs in less time than ordering a round in most of them. With John Darnley, an A&R man from EMI, co-producing with a less-than-sober Tony Ashton, the performances are rumbustious, and, if a little rough round the edges, convey the raucous atmosphere of a no-holds-barred, Friday night rave-up in an East End boozer. Eric Clapton, an early Chas and Dave fan, was there and was instrumental in luring Ashton from his duties on the second day, spending a good deal of time and money at the bar. It was a real family occasion, as Albert's son Wayne recalls: "At half-time I got up and played drums with Chas's Mum Daisy playing piano. Chas went on to bass, Dad played guitar and Dave played banjo. I was only ten and 'Master Lee' got a mention in the sleeve notes!" Albert contributed some tasteful Telecaster solos amidst the pounding boogie piano ("Breathless," "Sea Cruise," "I'm A Rocker"), a Chet Atkins–style offering on the country-shuffle "Better Get Your Shoes On" and some pyrotechnic picking on "Rufus Rastus." The standout performance, however, is his incredible rendering of "12th Street Rag." "Albert's playing is superb," writes Chas in the 2005 CD insert. "We think he was at his best when he was with Chas and Dave."

Eric Clapton's U.K. tour had started in Glasgow in November, with his band down to a four-piece, "which meant that Eric had to do all the guitar solos with no foil on rhythm, although fans were rewarded with some of his best playing of the '70s."[50] Albert knew that on certain numbers Clapton liked having another guitar on stage. "He told me he had done a British tour without a second guitar and that he'd missed having that option. He asked me to come on the road." Eric Clapton suggests that it might have been the idea of his manager, Roger Forrester.[51] "It was so obvious it evaded me—it was too close."

However it came about, for Albert it was a chance to play with the world's highest profile rock guitarist. It would do the solo album no harm "and besides, it would be fun and regular money. How could you turn that down? So I said, 'Sure.'"

The dice had rolled again[52] and Albert was off down another road.

Ten

Further on Up the Road

In February 1979, shortly before Albert went off up the road with the Eric Clapton band, *Hiding* was released, "a good way," Albert thought, "to promote the album. It didn't really work—it didn't sell that much, not bad, but not great."

The band rehearsed for the world tour at Ascot racecourse, difficult for Albert to reach from Charlton for he had no car in England, but "they rented a nice Ford Ghia for me." One day at rehearsals Albert told Eric he had sold his old Les Paul. "He told me he'd got one somewhere, but of course he was drunk."

The next day Clapton brought one in. "I gave him my Les Paul Custom because those guitars were made with very low, slim jazz frets which were difficult to bend. They are quite hard to find and I was very disappointed when I tried to play it because it didn't suit my style. I knew it would suit Albert because he plays up and down as much as he does sideways." Albert still has the Les Paul: "There's a lot of history to that guitar. It's a black custom model with three pickups, the one with the 'woman' tone[1] he used on the Cream and Delaney and Bonnie albums, playing it through a twin-amp."

The tour opened at the City Hall in Cork on March 8. Roger Forrester, Clapton's manager, loved winding up band members, including Eric, with practical jokes. "When I got to my room in the hotel," recalls Albert, "there was nothing in it. A settee was standing against the wall and there were rolls of carpet all over the floor. Roger had set this up. 'Here's your room, Albert! Welcome to the band!'"

A contemporary review[2] of the gig in Sligo gives a graphic account of what Albert could expect from an evening on the road with the world's leading rock guitarist:

"Anyone who stood in the old Baymount in Strandhill on March 13, 1979 realized that Eric was in bad shape. Probably in the height of his drug and alcohol days, Eric stumbled through his set, often handing lead guitar riffs off to country guitar legend, Albert Lee. It is hard to believe that, given his state on the night, [Clapton] would outlast the hall in which he was performing. Alas, Eric is here and the Baymount is gone!"

The band ended its pre–U.S. warm-up tour with a St. Patrick's Day concert at the National Stadium in Dublin. The set included "Knockin' On Heaven's Door," "Watch Out for Lucy," "Lay Down Sally" and from the *Hiding* album, Albert stepped into the spotlight for Mark Knopfler's "Setting Me Up." At the time Albert was using a cream-colored Telecaster with black binding, a copy made by Phil Kubicki. "I have two of his guitars, and they're excellent. The first one was given to me by Seymour Duncan, a really good friend who's stood by me over the years." In the mid–'80s, when Ernie Ball's Music Man company produced a signature model for Albert, he wanted Seymour Duncan pickups in it.

At the end of March the tour opened in Tucson, Arizona, and Albert had his first real taste of the rock 'n' roll lifestyle. "They were very generous: They flew Karen and me first-class—and they were always buying us presents. In Ireland, somebody had this expensive Nakamichi cassette deck with American ADS speakers, in an aluminum Halliburton case, a system probably worth about $2,000 at the time. When we arrived in Tucson, everyone was presented with one, and I still have it." On March 27, Eric married Pattie Boyd at a little Spanish church in Tucson—and Albert's cassette system was used for the music at the wedding reception.

The band began their 40-date American tour the following night and "Eric insisted on Pattie joining him on stage, so he could sing 'Wonderful Tonight' to her. The crowd loved it as he introduced his wife—but she was crimson with embarrassment.... The newly wed guitarist performed beautifully, kicked along by a great band—Albert Lee, Carl Radle, Dick Sims and Jamie Oldaker."[3] Albert's country-rock background came into its own on songs from *Backless*,[4] Clapton's recent country-flavored release—"Tulsa Time," "If I Don't Be There by Morning," "Early in the Morning" and "Watch Out for Lucy." It also became clear that Albert's ability to handle both rhythm and occasional lead guitar duties gave Clapton more options. The tour received rave reviews all along the line, and Muddy Waters' presence on stage was a rare privilege for the paying public.

Muddy Waters, the father of Chicago blues, was Clapton's idol and the man most responsible for introducing the electric guitar into the genre. "It was great having him on the bill," recalls Albert. "Muddy was like Eric's big father figure and a lovely man." Clapton once claimed, "His music changed my life, and whether you know it or not, and like it or not, it probably changed yours, too." The music of Muddy Waters lies at the roots of rock 'n' roll and his influence is so deep and so wide that a legendary British rock band, a well-known music magazine, as well as a Bob Dylan tribute, took their names from the title of one of his songs, "Rollin' Stone."

From Tucson, Albuquerque, El Paso, Dallas and on into Alabama and Georgia, the early part of the tour wound through the southern states, working its way steadily eastward. "In Atlanta, on one of his nights off, Clapton attended a B.B. King show, joining King onstage for an improvised blues encore. The duet had the crowd on its feet. Despite all his recent work in a country vein, Clapton could still trade licks with the best of the blues-men."[5] However, the erratic quality of his playing was noted in Tuscaloosa, Alabama, when a local review observed that on Otis Rush's blues lament "Double Trouble," Clapton's performance was "mediocre at best, but Albert Lee really pulls off a long, jazz-tinged solo that's worth a listen."[6] The caravan came to rest in Providence, Rhode Island, at the end of April, after a month on the road, and before resuming the tour at Pentecost, Clapton and the band flew home for a three-week break.

By the time Clapton took the stage at the Civic Center in Augusta on May 25, Carl Radle, Dick Sims and Jamie Oldaker were no more. Clapton had severed a five-year association with the "Tulsa Tops," as he called them. Roger Forrester was concerned, says Clapton, that "all of my musicians in the last four or five years had been American. The logistics were tough because we could only really hang out when we worked. We couldn't rehearse material because we had to fly them over and financially it was difficult." Furthermore, they were "getting out of it again, and I was the lead," says Eric. "I was trying to get straight, but I was drinking maybe two bottles a day of whatever I could get my hands on."[7] As Shapiro has pointed out, Albert's arrival threw into relief Eric's growing unease, demonstrating to him "that although American musicians may be closer to some of the music, they are not necessarily the right kind of people to play in a rock band and keep company with."[8] On the road, Albert and Clapton "became soul brothers" (in Eric's words), and there were perceptible tensions in the band between the two Englishmen and the Tulsa boys. Roger Forrester was trying desperately to keep things together but in the end Clapton got Forrester to dismiss them by telegram. "Later I had to face the guilt of Carl checking out.[9] I blame myself to some extent because I didn't take responsibility for firing them face to face."

For these reasons Clapton wanted to form a band made up of fellow British musicians "and for this he turned to a rhythm section of bassist Dave Markee and drummer Henry Spinetti—two rock-solid session musicians he had worked with in the past, most notably on the Pete Townshend-Ronnie Lane *Rough Me* album—and former Joe Cocker keyboardist Chris Stainton. He kept Albert Lee as his second guitarist. In assembling an all-British band Clapton hoped to achieve a tighter unity."[10]

Albert, the new boy on the block, was surprised. "I thought 'Wow, what's going on here?'" but he had no expectations of how long it might last. "I was very excited to be playing with Eric and it certainly kept me on my toes"— and he was receiving rave notices. In Augusta, the first gig with the new band, a local aficionado assessed the best performance of the evening as "Albert Lee's take on the Dire Straits classic 'Setting Me Up.'"[11] From Portland, Maine, through upstate New York, Ohio and into Michigan, where Johnny Winters

Albert with his Les Paul Custom guitar, a gift from Eric Clapton, in the early 1980s (courtesy Jackie Nelson).

joined Clapton and Muddy in Saginaw, the long tour pressed on into June, traversing the breadth of the country. With an itinerary sounding like the lyrics of "Route 66," the band played dates in Wichita, Kansas, Omaha, Nebraska, South Bend, Indiana, and Salt Lake City, reaching the west coast in Seattle. Two concerts in New York marked the end of an exhausting month: the band had played 23 gigs in five weeks. At the end of it all, Albert remembers being summoned to Roger Forrester's hotel room where "he gave us huge video-cameras and recorders which were totally new then. They weighed a ton and you had to carry them on your shoulder."

Albert flew home to Blackheath, where one day, "I was at my folks' house when Welsh rocker/producer Dave Edmunds called. I didn't know him very well but he wanted me over at Eden Studios in west London." Albert had given Edmunds "Sweet Little Lisa": "We were cutting tracks for Emmylou at the Enactron truck and in one of the bedrooms Donivan Cowart had a little recording set-up doing demos with Hank [De Vito]. They'd written this song and I put a guitar solo on the demo, which I sent to Dave. Later he cut the track with Nick Lowe, Phil Lynott and Huey Lewis and got me in to do the solo"—now regarded by many as among his finest recorded work. "It was kind of fun to play. It stands out for a lot of people who wonder how I play it but it was easy: Using my Fender B-bender there are licks on there that you couldn't do otherwise." There is a live version on *In Full Flight*, the 1993 live recording, but by then Albert had grown "a bit fed up with it after the early Hogan's Heroes days. Dave did it at a real fast pace and we had slowed it down to more of a Chuck Berry feel. Every now and again someone will call out for it and we think, 'Oh, well, why not,' but it suits if done faster as Dave did it."

Released later that year as *Repeat When Necessary*,[12] the record contains four classics apart from "Sweet Little Lisa"—Elvis Costello's galloping "Girls Talk," which contains one of *the* memorable rock lyrics, Graham Parker's relentless "Crawling from the Wreckage," the comic "Creature from the Black Lagoon," and De Vito's country-rocker "Queen of Hearts," later a hit for Juice Newton. As Stephen Erlewine wrote for *All Music Guide*, "It is an energetic, old-fashioned rock 'n' roll record that ranks as Edmunds' last great album."

In late August, Brian Ahern was holding sessions at the Enactron truck with a heavily pregnant[13] Emmylou Harris for what became the *Roses In the Snow* album,[14] released the following April. *Quarter Moon in a Ten-Cent Town* and *Blue Kentucky Girl* had mined a rich seam of country music, incorporating Louvin Brothers classics, new work by the likes of Rodney Crowell and Townes Van Zandt as well as the Gram Parsons canon and some modern pop songs, but this back-to-the-roots album was something of a landmark in Emmylou's career, as she ambled serenely through traditional country and bluegrass pastures. "After *Quarter Moon* we started doing the bluegrass stuff and we brought in Tony Rice and Jerry Douglas because we were trying once again to push the envelope a bit by going into something with stricter parameters but the album doesn't have the cohesiveness of *Luxury Liner*." Apart from two numbers, Albert played mostly mandolin and with accomplished support from Tony Rice on lead acoustic guitar, Dobro ace Jerry Douglas, Emory Gordy on bass, and Ricky Skaggs on fiddle, the venture was not such an off-the-wall departure as it might seem. Emmylou had met Ricky Skaggs and Jerry Douglas in D.C. around 1974 "sitting around John Starling's living room [Starling was a founding member of the Seldom Scene bluegrass band]. I put together the first Angel Band and played clubs where Seldom Scene played and we

would get together after shows and jam. Ricky was the bluegrass prodigy and had been playing with Ralph Stanley. Instead of overdubbing fiddle, I wanted to record with a fiddle so
we brought Ricky out and he became part of the band." The only concession to modernity
was a rendering of Paul Simon's "The Boxer," a respectable but odd inclusion which is
markedly out of sync with the rest of the selections. As Marc Greilsamer writes on Amazon,
"Among the set's peaks are Flatt and Scruggs's 'I'll Go Stepping Too,'[15] with Rice, Skaggs,
Lee (on superb electric guitar), and Dobro master Jerry Douglas turning up the instrumental heat, and the spiritual 'Jordan,' with Harris, Skaggs, Rice, and Johnny Cash engaging in
buoyant four-part harmonies."

Albert was back in England in September for the second leg of Clapton's world tour,
and, as was becoming the norm for him, he was seldom out of the studio for long.[16] Almost
immediately after he arrived, he found himself with keyboard virtuoso Geraint Watkins and
pedal steel man B.J. Cole on Stuart Colman's *It's Rock 'n' Roll* studio session on Radio One,
with Welsh pop rocker Shakin' Stevens. Recorded at BBC Maida Vale, these sessions remain
unreleased, but the following February CBS decided to give Stevens another crack of the
whip after three singles on CBS subsidiary Epic had failed to ignite. Mike Hurst, Stevens'
producer, used the same musicians when at Eden Studios Hurst and Stevens laid down
some rock 'n' roll tracks including a cover of Buck Owens' "Hot Dog." Bass player Stuart
Colman[17] remembers Albert at the session and later produced him in Nashville. "He is the
ultimate stylist. In the studio, I would throw anything at him and he'd put a lick around it
so tastefully, until it ended like a Les Paul fretboard exercise. He always seemed to hit the
right note." Benefiting from Albert's rockabilly licks, "Hot Dog"[18] reached #24 in the charts,
and Albert joined Stevens on a short spring tour. Colman recalls a gig "at a theatre opposite Centre Point in Tottenham Court Road. On the Sunday night, Albert did 'Country
Boy' first and his little electronic gizmo packed up. Its battery had died and the guitar packed
up completely. Albert was annoyed at himself for not checking the batteries so he calmly
plugged his guitar straight into the amp and carried on—a true professional."

Also that month, B.J. Cole, the pedal steel maestro who had been part of the Black
Claw sessions in 1968 with Albert, was producing an album with Hank Wangford and "I
got him to do a couple of numbers—I think his solo on 'Jenny' is particularly fine." The
album, *Cowboys Stay on Longer*,[19] is a typical example of Wangford's wry and idiosyncratic
take on country music. Wangford, in real life gynecologist Dr. Sam Hutt, was a friend of
Rik Grech and became something of a medical guru to musicians, notably Gram Parsons.
Recorded at Sarm East Studios, Aldgate East, London, together with Cole and Albert, it
featured Andy Fairweather Low, John "Rabbit" Bundrick, who later played keyboard with
The Who, Pete Wingfield, of whom much more later, Fairport Convention's Dave Mattacks
on drums and Geraint Watkins. Including a honky-tonk-style "Whiskey on My Guitar," with
a smoothly rockabilly solo from Albert and a startling country cover of the Troggs' "Wild
Thing," the album has a quirky freshness "at a time when American country music was still
searching for the bland and inoffensive and denying the harder roots of the music."[20]

At the end of September, Clapton's new English band played a debut concert at Stoke's
Victoria Hall, a low-key warm-up for the six-month world tour. Clapton appeared clean-
shaven, in dark suit, white shirt and tie, a throwback to his days with the Roosters in 1963.
Steve Turner, writing in *Melody Maker*,[21] discerned that Clapton was striving to recapture

the days when he was merely a "laborer musician" and sensed that "with Albert Lee on guitar, Dave Markee on bass, Chris Stainton on keyboards and Henry Spinetti on drums you're on your way to recapturing that feel.... On Sunday you did a similar thing with Albert Lee and his 'I'm Just A Country Boy' [sic] likewise went down a storm." Turner was not totally uncritical: "Now that you've changed the barnet[22] and the band, isn't it time to take a few more risks with the music?"

The new band's first tour was a characteristic stamina test for Clapton's entourage, with dates spanning Europe and the Far East. Opening at the Stadthalle in Vienna on October 6, and with concerts scheduled in Yugoslavia and Poland, Clapton felt "he was finally breaking through. The first performance in Poland, at Warsaw's Palace of Culture, was uneventful, though the huge audience, composed largely of Polish dignitaries and people with connections, was slow to respond to Clapton and his band."[23] Albert remembers some young U.S. Marines in the front row: "I played 'In The Halls Of Montezuma' which went down a storm. They came backstage afterwards and invited us back to a party at the U.S. Embassy with some American girls—it was good fun."

The next evening, October 17, in the Halo Sportowo (the Sports-Show Hall), an 11,000-capacity music venue, was an entirely different story, Albert recalls. "We'd only done about 20 minutes. The kids were very excited, jumping up and down at seeing this rock hero. The police were striding about trying to make them sit down." During his career Clapton had found that playing ballads or slow blues could calm volatile situations but in Poland, where fans were thrilled at seeing him play anything, the ruse failed. "It wasn't really a riot," says Albert. "The police were overreacting to the kids, who were having a good time. Then they whacked a few and the tear gas came." Clapton watched in horror as young people were beaten and dragged away by their hair, whereupon he and Roger told the band to get off the stage. In the ensuing mêlée, some of Clapton's road crew were

Eric and Albert in Yugoslavia, late 1979 (courtesy the Lee family).

knocked about and the band's sound system was badly damaged. After the show, Clapton sat in his hotel room and wept; he was emotionally drained "and uncertain about his power as an internationally known entertainment figure."[24] In fact, the opposite was the case. In late 1979, Poland was in social and political ferment: Any mass demonstration of enthusiasm or unity was seen as subversive. Because of the potentially liberating impact on young Poles of this taste of Western music the police had cracked down hard. The year before, Lech Walesa, a shipyard electrician in Gdansk, had organized the illegal underground Free Trade Union of Pomerania and Pope John Paul II had visited his homeland in the summer, voicing obliquely veiled criticism of the regime. The Communist Party's monolithic grip on power was beginning to show terminal cracks.

In such an atmosphere Clapton refused to play the second show. "The Poles blamed the management for everything and Roger Forrester was forced to forfeit the fee."[25] The tour left the country as quickly as it could, returning to an England where Geoff Barton, in *Sounds*,[26] was describing a New Wave of British Heavy Metal, exemplified by bands like Iron Maiden and Hawkwind. Nothing summarized more definitively the musical landscape which Albert found less than conducive to his brand of country-tinged guitar-playing. There were lyrical oases in the heavy metal desert. In October Don Everly joined the Crickets and Albert on the show that climaxed the Buddy Holly Week arranged by Paul McCartney. "It was fun," remembers Albert. "Bob Montgomery and Karen came over, too." Maria Elena Holly was also there and at the end of the show Don joined Paul McCartney to harmonize on "Maybe Baby."

The second leg of the world tour approached and the band flew into Japan at the end of November, a tour which Clapton approached with mixed feelings. "The audiences are invariably generous and appreciative but the pitfalls still exist—ill-health, the feeling of being something of a freak in the tightly closed society they are so proud of ... but all in all, it never fails to work out"[27] and gigs in Kyoto, Osaka, Hiroshima, Kokura and Osaka led to two nights at the Budokan in Tokyo.

In Tokyo, the two concerts on December 3 and 4 were recorded and the subsequent double album,[28] produced and engineered by Jon Astley, appeared in May 1980 and reached #3 in the British charts. Clapton, however, declares that he is "not a big fan of live albums. I like Ray Charles live albums and good jazz like Coltrane. I don't ever consider myself to be the kind of stature that can stand up and do it well. I very rarely make a live album that I can listen to but I understand and respect other people's wishes in that. It was all right, but." By contrast, Albert thinks the album stands the test of time. "I heard *Just One Night* not too long ago for the first time in 15 years and thought, 'Boy, that's pretty good, you know.' I played piano, too, and Chris played organ, which was fun. I also sang on nearly everything—like 'All Our Past Times.' Eric was very generous letting me having my solo spot. He would sit behind the amps while I did 'Country Boy' and yell 'Come on, Albert.' I did it at the Budokan but it got left off the album. If it had been on it I would have earned a few more bucks instead of making more for Mark Knopfler."[29] As he told *Vintage Guitar*, "There were some things I did on the Clapton albums where you might think it was all Clapton ... the solo on the live version of 'Cocaine'; it's so un–Eric-like," he chuckles, "and I'm quite proud of that. I'm glad Eric gave me the chance to do it."[30]

Inside the Budokan, "thousands of young Japanese chanting Eric's name made for a great atmosphere, and the sort of welcome Eric has grown to love from that country. 'Lay Down Sally' was as contagious as ever, with Eric's playing carrying stacks of gusto, and Albert Lee broke out on 'If I Don't Be There By Morning,' along with some great keyboard work by Stainton on 'Worried Life Blues.'"[31] Schumacher has reservations: "The double album, which *Rolling Stone* less than happily labeled 'the definitive document of Clapton's post–*461 Ocean Boulevard* era,' caught the essence of the highs and lows of Clapton's work in the latter part of the decade. ...'Just One Night' revealed Clapton's all-English band to be a talented, technically refined unit, adept at handling the framework of Clapton's music but not especially creative when it came to improvising or breaking new ground."[32]

Nonetheless, the album is a rewarding one. Clapton's first love remained the blues and the album includes work by artists like Maceo Merriweather ("Worried Life Blues"), Otis Rush ("Double Trouble"), J.J. Cale ("After Midnight," "Cocaine") and Robert Johnson ("Rambling On My Mind"). His playing on these standards remains as lyrical and emotional as ever and more importantly, Clapton introduced a seven minute-plus rendering of "Further on Up the Road," which became a major feature of his live sets.

Marc Roberty enters a caveat: "Guitarist Albert Lee was a session veteran and without doubt the finest country style guitar player Britain has ever produced"[33] and Shapiro stresses that "Albert Lee and George Terry were very different players—Terry's hard edged rock/blues style gave way to Lee's highly talented but essentially unobtrusive country playing."[34] The band had a problem though. Basically, Spinetti and Markee were session musicians and "were unable to jam quite so readily as the Americans. They were certainly exceptional musicians, but they hadn't grown up amid the jamming culture that so many American rock musicians take for granted. As a result, the arrangements of Eric's songs on *Just One Night* lacked the improvisatory nature of previous albums and often sounded regimented and cold as a result."[35] For Roberty, the album's high spots were "'Setting Me Up,' Albert's solo spot" and "'Blues Power'—always a live favorite with Eric and fans alike, this number cooks with a vengeance. Albert's lilting piano intro quickly lets way to a fast-paced version which is counted in by Eric. He rips out a lengthy wah-wah solo driven by Albert's piano."[36]

The final verdict comes from Clapton himself: "I didn't really want to record it. There's a natural shyness about me when I'm playing onstage. For me it's something that should happen only once, you know, and then it's gone. The album was one show. We did two nights and recorded both. I think they chose the one I didn't like."

Albert was back in California for Christmas with Karen and a letter written from Bailard Road, Malibu, to his old Blackheath band-mate Johnnie Haylock in mid–January gives a revealing insight into his preoccupations at the time. "Here are the photos as promised. [These were pictures of the early band playing the cinemas, etc.] ... I haven't done very much since I arrived back which is the way I wanted it for a while. Tomorrow I'm going to New Orleans for a few days to do some recording with a couple of French guys. I must admit I'd rather have stayed at home and recorded locally. I'm sick of traveling at the moment— still, you have to take the work when it comes.... I may be back in London in a few weeks to record with Eric Clapton and hopefully play with Don Everly and Emmylou at the Wembley Festival. I'll get in touch if I'm there." His letter has a charming sign-off, indicating his continuing attachment to his south London roots: "I'm really glad we found each other after all this time." Albert did indeed play with Don Everly and Emmylou Harris and Ricky

Emmylou Harris, Albert and Ricky Skaggs at Wembley, April 1980 (courtesy Graham Barker).

Skaggs at Wembley, following a date with them and rockabilly outfit Matchbox in Paris and a gig with Commander Cody at Dingwalls in Camden Lock, London.

Albert had referred in his letter from Malibu to recording again with Eric, sessions which took place at Surrey Sound in Leatherhead. By this time Clapton had recruited ex–Procol Harum singer, keyboardist and writer Gary Brooker. Brooker had bought the Parrot Inn, in Forest Green, not far from Clapton's home and for two or three years had been playing blues with Eric in the pub. "By the end of '79 we were almost like a pub band, playing for fun and we saw ourselves running a band together," says Clapton.

It was Clapton's idea, says Albert, to make "a band album with everybody singing." Brooker wrote several songs and "we all used to chip in with ideas" but Roger Forrester had a problem with that. He was not keen on other people singing, as Clapton observed. "He and Gary went toe to toe several times. It was like sibling rivalry over who was going to get

Opposite: Top—Don Everly, Karen and Albert backstage at Wembley, 1980. *Bottom*—Albert's Dad, Don Everly, Albert and John Derek at Wembley, 1980 (courtesy Graham Barker).

my attention or approval." Although Clapton had an abundance of new material to consider, the songs, when recorded, sounded lethargic even by Clapton's nonchalant standards. In all, the group recorded thirteen songs over a two-month period, including numbers with Gary Brooker and Albert Lee on lead vocals, but "The sessions produced some fairly uninspired results. It is difficult to pinpoint blame; maybe it was Eric simply being lazy, maybe it was the band being too laid back, or perhaps Glyn Johns in his role as producer was not assertive enough."[37] Clapton maintains that "we cut a lot of interesting tracks but they never saw the light of day." The album, to be called *Turn Up Down*,[38] was sent to various RSO executives. "It was rejected outright as being too eclectic." RSO wanted a hit—and something with the Clapton stamp on it. As Albert put it, "The powers that be thought there was too much Brooker and not enough Clapton."

Clapton's new line-up, the late 1979 band plus Gary Brooker, opened a 13-date U.K. tour at the New Theatre, Oxford, on May 2, taking in Brighton, Newcastle and the Hammersmith Odeon, London. Cockney rockers Chas and Dave were great favorites of Eric and they opened most dates. "It was like a pub band and we traveled very rough," says Clapton. "My drinking was going strong and it suited my perspectives then. I don't remember very much about that period." On most nights Chas and Dave invited Albert to join them for their finale which on occasions appeared to niggle Clapton. "He was genuinely choked and it surprised us," says Dave. "We'd known Albert since the early '60s and he was our pal. So it felt right and I know Eric would now recognize Albert as one of the finest guitarists in the world." Clapton feels that "Albert Lee and I were the most stimulating pairing but in a very different way, more comradely"[39] and does not recall harboring any resentment towards them or Albert for him playing with them: "His playing's so different I couldn't consider him a rival," says Eric. "He was there to complement my playing and vice versa. Any time I'm with a good player with a true personality and feeling in his playing, I always find I stretch myself to keep up and I love that element."[40]

The tour ended, as most of Clapton's British tours did, at the Civic Hall, Guildford, a stone's throw from Hurtwood Edge, Clapton's country home in Surrey. Guitar ace Jeff Beck, who had replaced Clapton in the Yardbirds, joined him on Robert Johnson's "Ramblin' On My Mind," but even his presence failed to add much luster to an end-of-term gig, described in a local review as "an otherwise eminently forgettable performance." Clapton always threw an end-of-tour party at Hurtwood Edge to which he invited the great and the good in the world of rock and showbiz. On this occasion, Albert remembers, "my Mum and Dad came, too." The next day Vanessa asked her mother who had been at the party. "She said she'd met various people from the band. 'I was talking for such a long time to this really nice young man. Then his wife came and spoke to me and she was ever so nice, too. They were telling me about their house and what he'd been up to.' She turned to my Dad and said, 'What was his name, Dave?' My Dad said, 'It was George Harrison, you silly old fool!'" Abigail, too, remembers the occasion well. "I had a crush on Eric Clapton and used to sit on his lap. Fleetwood Mac were there, and Ginger Baker, who fancied me dressed up as a showgirl. I even pinched Billy Connolly's bum!"

For the rest of that summer Albert had a couple of recording dates, one with Byron Berline in L.A. and an interesting session with Paul Kennerley in Nashville, as well as being committed to a few weeks at Compass Point in Nassau recording the new Clapton album. None of these, however, were as significant as the one on August 18 in Malibu.

Eric and Albert at the Hammersmith Odeon, May 17, 1980 (courtesy Graham Barker).

George Harrison and Albert at Hurtwood Edge, Eric Clapton's home, in May 1980 (courtesy the Lee family).

It was all Clapton's fault, apparently. With Karen in the wings at a gig, Eric would say, "Albert Lee, ladies and gentlemen! The lovely Karen is here with him tonight and they're gonna be getting married soon." "She put up with it for a week or so," said Albert. "Then she said, 'Right, we're getting married.' In those days we used to stay in one place for a week at a time, in some really nice places. We'd fly in and out, get a cab to the airport, jump in a helicopter and fly to the big airport—real rock star stuff." Karen found "a lovely little church near our hotel but it would have been frighteningly expensive to fly people in 'cause it was very remote. It would have had to be a small wedding with just the band there." So the couple were married after the tour at Malibu Presbyterian Church.

Abigail and Wayne flew over for the ceremony with their mother. "I was a bridesmaid at Karen and Dad's wedding. Mum was OK about Dad getting married and trusted Karen with us kids." Unfortunately a few days before the ceremony Wayne fell off his skateboard and was rushed to hospital in Santa Monica, where blood was found in his urine and his spleen removed. With no National Health Service to fall back on, the operation cost $5,000. Fortunately "I had it, just after the tour." He could not quite run to a new suit, however, and Albert hardly cut a sartorial dash at his wedding. "I looked pretty scruffy, but I had a nice light-colored corduroy western jacket, tan pants and cowboy boots."

Albert had invited Don Everly to be his best man but he preferred to stay in Nashville. "He didn't want to come back to L.A., where there were too many bad memories. Sterling Ball was best man and for a long time, he ribbed me about being best man by default." That summer Karen had found a rented house halfway up Malibu Canyon in Calabasas for drummer Gerry Conway and his family. "It was very spectacular—a great big wooden house with a huge living-room the size of a nightclub," recalls Conway. He was an old friend of Albert's and offered to host the reception. "It was a brand-new property and we loved it," says Albert—so much so, the Lees now live in it!

It was an all-day party and, of course, an impromptu jam. "The whole accent of the day," Gerry Conway recalls, "was people dropping by, singing a few songs and playing. We had all the instruments set up, including the back line. Rodney Crowell, Rosanne Cash,

Albert and Lonnie Donegan at Albert and Karen's wedding reception, August 1980 (courtesy the Lee family).

Albert and Rodney Crowell at Albert and Karen's wedding reception (courtesy the Lee family).

Emmylou, the whole of the Hot Band, Tony Brown, Freebo[41] was playing bass—it was just amazing—all day long." By about midnight everybody was beginning to wilt: Conway remembers Albert saying, "It's funny Lonnie didn't come by." At that moment the door-bell rang and there he was, Lonnie Donegan. "He walked straight in, strapped on my '58 Stratocaster." The party had acquired a second wind "and we zapped through his entire set—a memorable day." A year later, when Gerry went back to England to work with Jethro Tull and the house was vacant, Albert and Karen asked the owner about renting it, but he was ready to sell. "Luckily we had some money and put down a deposit and moved in late in 1981."

The cedar-wood house stands at the crest of a steep drive in a small residential neighborhood just off the Malibu Canyon Road. One of Los Angeles's best-kept secrets, Monte Nido is a quiet, wooded community of laid-back rural serenity. The main room, dominated by a massive fireplace built of huge sandstone boulders and a vast picture window with a breathtaking view of a rugged, barren hillside, is haphazardly strewn with the paraphernalia of an artistic life. Books on almost every conceivable subject line the walls and are piled on the floor. Albert's den, on a half-landing overlooking the room, represents the accumulation of four decades of a life in music—guitars, a Korg keyboard, amplifiers, shelves and boxes of CDs and vinyl LPs, posters, photographs, the odd gold disc or two, awards, and a 1950s British railway sign listing all stations to Blackheath he picked up for ten dollars in a Canadian antique shop. The huge oval dining-table is submerged under a mountain of newspaper and magazine articles, mail, CDs, receipts, Post-it notes and invoices. In the hall, just inside the front door, stands an upright piano which belonged to Joe Cocker, and in the elegant cedar wall, which stretches twenty feet above one's head, another enormous window allows the late summer sun to trace a mesh of fine filigree in the dust of a Californian afternoon. The whole house exudes a gloriously Bohemian aura: to those who live there, people, good wine, books and music mean more than life's boring minutiae.

Albert continued to be in demand as a session player in Los Angeles and had had time before his nuptials to join Byron Berline, the Oklahoma fiddle virtuoso and denizen of the Sundance Saloon on *Outrageous*,[42] a pleasant but undemanding set of original tunes. Berline was a veteran L.A. session man on albums by the Flying Burritos, Gram Parsons, Emmylou, James Taylor and the Nitty Gritty Dirt Band. Along with Albert, James Burton and a youthful Vince Gill on guitar, J.D. Manness on pedal steel and Leland Sklar on bass, Berline led the gang through a set which varied in style from bluegrass to western swing. Albert was also achieving recognition among the country music fraternity, coming third in the Best Country Guitarist category in the readers' poll in *Guitar Player* magazine.

All in all, it was a heady summer—marriage to Karen, the acquisition of a 1980 Triumph TR8 and an appearance as Jim Younger on Paul Kennerley's ambitious song-cycle, *The Legend of Jesse James*.

Kennerley, an ex-ad agency hack from London, was a part-time musician and writer who had come to prominence in 1978 with *White Mansions*, a musical saga based on the American Civil War. Glyn Johns had taken up the project and had recruited Clapton's rhythm section, Waylon Jennings, Ozark Mountain Daredevils John Dillon and Steve Cash, together with Jessi Colter and former Eagle Bernie Leadon for the recordings. At the same time, Johns was circulating copies of Kennerley's songs for his second project, *The Legend of Jesse James*.[43]

White Mansions attracted negative reviews in the States, which Emmylou Harris ascribed to "people who still cannot stand the South being looked on sympathetically." *Jesse James* has more historical focus and narrative momentum, and Emmylou was convinced of the album's merit from the first. "I felt it was brilliant, a masterpiece. Albert gave me the tapes of the demos while we were in London doing the Wembley Festival. He said, 'I'm doing this project. Listen to this and tell me if you...' I said, 'Oh, Albert, if you're doing it and it's good, I'll do it.'" Emmylou offered Glyn Johns Ahern's Enactron studios. "I thought it was one of the best things I'd ever heard and I got very excited about it. I hoped it would come to pass." She rounded up Rodney Crowell, Rosanne and Johnny Cash as cast members, together with Bernie Leadon and Emory Gordy. Levon Helm of The Band plays Jesse with Emmylou as his wife and Johnny Cash his older brother. Charlie Daniels plays Cole Younger with Albert as his brother Jim, singing "Have You Heard The News?" and "Hunt Them Down." "We'd get so excited at the end of a tracking day that we all wanted to go out on the road together," says Emmylou. "When I was up at the Midnight Rambler recently, Levon told me it was the best thing he'd ever been involved in."

Recorded at Enactron Studios in Los Angeles and Quadrafonic Sound Studios in

Nashville, produced and engineered by Glyn Johns, the album does not evoke the sense of a lost cause, of a community devastated by an apocalyptic conflict, which *White Mansions* captures so eloquently, but expresses in vividly direct lyrics the bitterness of the Confederacy's defeat. There is a tragic inevitability about its hero's fate. In 1882 Missouri hired a horse thief for $10,000 to rid the state of an embarrassment, and Jesse James was shot at the age of thirty-five by a guest in his own home. The album has something of the epic sweep of a John Ford Western: as Brian Hinton has commented, "The project feels like a movie for which the pictures have been lost."[44]

Nonetheless the two albums are a remarkable achievement "for an unknown tunesmith a continent away from Music City."[45] Yvette Charbonnet grew up in Clay County, Missouri, "right up the road from the James Farm," and reviewed the album on Amazon. "The voices sound as if they are truly Missouri locals ... singing in a southern rock style that will have you swilling sweet tea out of a mason jar. If you like hog callers and mules, tobacco and whiskey culture ... [you'll] realize the Civil War really started on the southern Frontier in Missouri."

When the suits at RSO refused to put out *Turn Up Down*, Clapton took the rejection badly. His drinking intensified and he was now drinking a bottle of brandy a day. "I was a functioning alcoholic where I could do it, but I don't remember much about it. I needed it on a daily basis and I drank through everything. Some of it I remember and some of it I don't."

In July, he traveled with the band to the Compass Point Studios in Nassau. Why the Bahamas? Why not? "Comfort. And good vibes," says Clapton. "I'd fallen in love with the Caribbean anyway and any excuse to go there and try and mix it with work was good." The legendary American producer Tom Dowd had been engaged to coax and cajole another album out of an increasingly flaky guitar maestro. Dowd had worked with Eric before, having been the engineer at Atlantic studios in New York on Cream's *Disraeli Gears* album in May 1967. He had subsequently produced *Layla and Assorted Love Songs* for Derek and the Dominos in 1970 and had pioneered work in binaural stereo recording. Later his design of the eight-track console modernized the recording industry. Having worked on classic records for artists including Ray Charles, Aretha Franklin, Otis Redding, John Coltrane, Dizzy Gillespie, Thelonious Monk, Rod Stewart, Lynyrd Skynyrd, the Allman Brothers Band and Dusty Springfield, he commanded the respect of the world's most celebrated musicians.

The first and last Clapton studio album[46] to feature his all–British band of the early '80s, it turned out to be the final record of his 15-year association with Polydor, which therefore had no reason to promote it. The album's production gave considerable prominence to Albert and Gary Brooker, who brought to it more of a blues-rock feel than the sound of the '70s created by the *Tulsa Tops*, one of whom, Carl Radle, had died in May. The album is dedicated to him and "most of it is very bluesy," says Clapton. "It took a long time to make that album because I was totally fed up with writing ditties and pleasant melodies, and I thought it was time for me to reconnect myself to what I know best."[47] Clapton had written six of the nine selections, most of which reveal "an underlying sadness and I didn't know where it was coming from. Perhaps I was starting to recognize my problem on a very subconscious level and I think it was coming into the music, which gave it a kind of power."

The high spots are a straight Muddy Waters blues, "Blow Wind Blow," "I Can't Stand

It," a top ten hit in the States, and "Catch Me If You Can," with Albert and Eric independently conversing on the solo. There are disconcerting hints in the title track of the soft-rock which began to creep into the Clapton sound in the 1980s and the album, while it is professionally performed, does not show Clapton or the band at their absolute best.

With *Another Ticket* due out in the New Year, the band set out before Christmas to fulfill dates in Scandinavia, playing much the same set as in Japan the year before, with the addition of "Layla" (possibly at Tom Dowd's suggestion), Brooker's "Home Lovin'" and inevitably, "A Whiter Shade of Pale." The tour opened at the Brøndbyhallen in Copenhagen at the end of September. After the gig, in the early hours, Eric and Albert came across a fellow riding a bike with duck-whistles on a string round his neck. "We stopped him," recalls Clapton, "and he gave me them."

The incident illustrates the playful element in Albert's relationship with Eric, whose madcap irresponsibility on occasions gave Albert the license to indulge the "naughty school-boy"[48] in his own nature. "I've gotten up to all kinds of mischief over the years. It's all part of being on the road. Eddie Offord, the engineer for Yes and Heads, Hands and Feet, had turned me on to duck calls, and I introduced Eric to them on that first tour. He loved them so much one of the minders went out to this hunting store and came back with a load of them and real shoulder-holsters to keep them in. After the gig in Atlanta, Eric and I were really drunk and we were playing all these silly tunes to this honeymoon couple in the hotel elevator. They had no idea it was Eric Clapton! We very soon became 'the Fabulous Duck Brothers'—I was Peking Duck and he was Bombay. I showed up at rehearsal one day and all of our cases had 'Fabulous Duck Brothers' stenciled on them." In September, Clapton left RSO to set up his own WEA-distributed label, Duck Records.

Some of the other mischief that Albert stumbled into stemmed from his inability to resist any opportunity to play music, with or without a guitar. Back at the hotel after gigs, Albert and Chris Stainton would head for the piano in the lounge, and, billed as Rubbish and Landrover,[49] play an impromptu set of rock favorites until one or both retired, overtired, overemotional and overrefreshed.

The Scandinavian excursion, with a quick dash to Ireland at the end of January and a date at London's Rainbow in February, was in essence a warm-up for a major tour, set to begin in Seattle in early March to promote *Another Ticket*. In the meantime, Christmas 1980 was overshadowed by the murder of John Lennon. It had been a sad three months. In September, Led Zeppelin drummer John Bonham had died after a heavy drinking session and after a long battle Jimmy Bryant had succumbed to lung cancer in Moultrie, Georgia. He was 55. Albert paid this tribute in *Guitar Magazine*: "I loved his technique, the incredible speed and definition in his playing, and his choice of notes. It was kind of country swing without being too far out. He was getting this great sound out of his Telecaster when a lot of people playing that type of music would have been playing on a hollowbody Gibson."[50]

Another Ticket was released in February and immediately the first single, "I Can't Stand It," received a lot of air play. The commercial prospects looked promising and on the day the tour opened at the Paramount Theater in Seattle the album reached #18 in Britain. In the States, both album and single hit the Top Ten in May. All seemed well, until in Madison, Wisconsin, Clapton came off stage doubled up in agony. On arrival in St. Paul, Minnesota, he was rushed to the United Hospital where one of the doctors examining him pronounced, "he could die at any moment." He had been taking pain-killers for stomach ulcers and drinking brandy as well. It was clear that Clapton was physically near death as a result of his alcoholism: "The ulcers were the size of golf-balls apparently. I didn't know whether people were exaggerating or coloring the story but they said I was on my way out. I don't know if that was true"—but it was obvious that the tour had to be canceled. "We hung around for a few days and got part of our fee," Albert remembers, and Gary Brooker adds a characteristically acerbic touch—"The tour T-shirt was called 'Just 60 nights' but we crossed out the 60 and put 7."

Clapton had had a frightening intimation of mortality but was in that insane denial which afflicts every alcoholic. "When they spoke to me in my convalescence and said, 'We're ready to let you leave hospital now but you've got to do something about your drinking' I said, 'What are you talking about? I'm English—you people don't have the first idea about drinking.' So I carried on for another year after that." With no promotion the album sank rapidly without trace and then as he began to recuperate, Clapton was hospitalized again, this time with injuries from a car accident.

With his main employer sidelined and in rehab, Albert returned to the session scene. Emmylou and Brian Ahern were recording constantly and "sometimes tracks which we cut in a particular period for a particular album ended up being pieced together with other bits." So it was that during 1981, both *Evangeline* and *Cimarron* appeared. *Evangeline*[51] is "a scattershot affair, encompassing rock, folk and bluegrass which stands among Harris's few disappointing efforts," according to Jason Ankeny, of *All-Music Guide*. While this verdict is a trifle harsh, the album does lack focus and perhaps tries too hard to be all things to all men. The title track is a version of Robbie Robertson's "Evangeline," a song that Emmylou also recorded with The Band in 1977 for their triple album and movie, *The Last Waltz*. Albert plays guitar on "How High the Moon," "Oh Atlanta," "Mr. Sandman" and piano on "Bad Moon Rising."

Cimarron,[52] like its predecessor, comprised for the most part outtakes from other recording sessions, suffered from similar criticism—the lack of a unifying sound. However, the album sold well and Paul Kennerley's "Born to Run" (not to be confused with the Bruce Springsteen song of the same name) was a top-ten country single. It offered Emmylou's now-customary melange of country favorites, songs borrowed from the pop/rock arena, and singer/songwriter discoveries. Particularly memorable were two other country Top Tens, Karen Brooks and Hank De Vito's "Tennessee Rose" and "If I Needed You" (a duet with country great Don Williams), written by Townes Van Zandt. From the pop mainstream, Harris covered Poco's "Rose of Cimarron" and "The Price You Pay," originally on Bruce Springsteen's double album *The River*.

Albert worked with another country great in that summer, when Rodney Crowell produced *As Is*[53] for Bobby Bare. Featuring Albert and Ricky Skaggs, the album was a down-to-earth collection of good songs highlighting Bare's wily, understated charm. Bare had had a Top Twenty hit in 1963 with Mel Tillis and Danny Dill's "Detroit City," but unlike many of his contemporaries, he possessed an intense musical curiosity and a love of great songwriting from an eclectic range of music. He was among the first country artists to record songs by a new wave of writers who were blurring the lines between country and folk, including J.J. Cale, Gene Clark and the Rolling Stones and later Guy Clark, Rodney Crowell and Billy Joe Shaver.

From working with an American great Albert found himself alongside the man who, with Davy Graham and more recently Richard Thompson, has carried the torch for British folk-guitar for nearly half a century. At Silverlake Studio, Los Angeles, in June, Albert did an album with Bert Jansch. Entitled *Heartbreak*,[54] commissioned and produced by guitar retailers John and Richard Chelew, the album featured Jansch on lead guitar and vocals, backed up by Albert on guitar and mandolin, Randy Tico on bass, Matt Betton and Jack Kelly on drums, with Jennifer Warnes ("Up Where We Belong") on backing vocal. It was a strange hodgepodge of tracks, including "If I Were a Carpenter," "Wild Mountain Thyme" and "Heartbreak Hotel" and while Albert appreciates Jansch as a player, he thinks it "an odd pairing." He and Jansch did a U.K. tour around that time and "we were double-billed, which was very uncomfortable for me. There were people coming along to see me and I was just tinkling away behind him. At the Half Moon in Putney, Jeff Beck came to see me and was a bit disappointed that I didn't get to rock."

More to his taste, and just before he was due back in Europe for the now-recovered Clapton's autumn tour of Scandinavia, Albert played on Rodney Crowell's eponymous third album.[55] Crowell, who also produced, assembled a top-flight crew of musicians; as well as Albert, Rosanne Cash (who was his wife at the time), Booker T. Jones, Vince Gill, Emory Gordy, Jr. and Tony Brown all appeared and while the album was not to be the hit that *But What Will the Neighbors Think?* turned out to be, it has some great songs. His original versions of "'Til I Gain Control Again" and "Shame on the Moon," his existentialist masterpiece, together with "Stars on the Water," "Victim or a Fool," and "Old Pipeliner" confirmed Crowell as a major talent whose clever, prickly songs were gourmet dishes compared to the standard fare on offer in Nashville at the time.

In Gothenburg, Sweden, in mid–October, the 1981 tour resumed as if nothing had happened with Clapton superficially recovered and apparently determined to enjoy himself. At the Vejlby-Risskovhallen in Århus, Denmark, he introduced himself as the sax player and played it for the encore! Albert was, however, finding the venues uncomfortable. In a postcard home from Oslo, he wrote, "Hi! The tour is going quite well. We're playing mostly ice stadiums so it's a bit cold on stage."

Ten days in Japan brought the band home for Christmas and the inevitable end-of-tour presents from management. Albert wanted to reciprocate and buy Eric something. He had retained his passion for Breitling watches and back home at the end of the tour, he saw a Breitling for about £170 in a jeweler's window in Woolwich. "It was a newer Breitling, slightly thicker with a date on it. I was earning good money at the time so I thought I'd buy one for Eric. Then I thought 'No—I'll get myself one as well,' so I bought two, gave one to Eric and I wore the other one for quite a while. My Dad still had the original one."

With Clapton still in early recovery, there was no tour scheduled until June 1982, followed by sessions for another album penciled in at Compass Point in Nassau in late summer. His band members thus were free to pursue individual projects and in March, Gary Brooker released his debut album for PhonoGram, entitled *Lead Me to the Water*.[56] Brooker wrote several new songs for the album, recording some in London, with George Harrison on guitar (repaying a favor as Gary played on his post–Beatle album, *All Things Must Pass*) and Phil Collins on drums. Clapton's rhythm section—Henry Spinetti and Dave Markee, plus Chris Stainton and the man himself joined in, too. "Then I went to San Francisco to play with a lot of people I'd never worked with," Brooker remembers, "and I thought, 'I need a friendly face here.'" He rang Albert in Malibu and asked him to come up and do some sessions. "So Karen and I drove up for a couple of days and we did four or five songs at the Crescendo Studios in Russian Hill."

Although produced by Brooker, the album includes technical contributions from Tom Dowd and Glyn Johns. With one of the most distinctive voices in British rock, Brooker expands beyond "A Whiter Shade of Pale" into a more eclectic range, from unsentimental rockers like "Mineral Man" and the rustic "The Angler" to the meditative "Cycle" and "Sympathy for the Hard of Hearing." Brooker managed to get a couple of the Surrey Sound tracks from Roger Forrester and recorded "Lead Me to the Water" and "Home Lovin'."[57]

Albert committed himself to his own solo project when in the spring of 1982 he signed a one-album deal with Polydor, recording his second solo album at the Enactron Studios and United/Western Studios, Hollywood. The album[58] is virtually a Cherry Bombs reunion, as Rodney Crowell was at the production desk, Larry Londin on drums, John Hobbs on keyboards and Emory Gordy on bass with Vince Gill on rhythm. "The albums are quite different," says Albert. "The second one is more rock 'n' roll." He is not wrong. If *Hiding* was weighted more towards the country half of country/rock, then this eponymous offering has more of a rockabilly tinge. Hank De Vito's "Rock 'n' Roll Man," compete with brass backing, Australian rocker Johnny O'Keefe's "Real Wild Child" and Rodney Crowell's flag-waver, "One Way Rider," not to mention "Sweet Little Lisa," the opener, lend an altogether more up-tempo feel to the album. Albert's particular favorites are the country-style track, Don Everly's "So Sad," on which he plays piano, and "Pink Bedroom" by John Hiatt, who also features as composer on a calypso-flavored "Radio Girl." Crowell believes that "had Albert concentrated on his voice in the same way he approached guitar playing he might have been Don Everly and John Lennon's equal." While recording the album he recalls Joe Cocker dropping into a session and commenting on how much he liked Albert's teen country sound. Albert himself chips in with a self-penned number "Your Boys." The Raven release includes a bonus track from Mrs. Gordy, as Patty Loveless sings DeVito and Kennerley's "Blue Side of Town."[59]

History repeated itself, however. Albert did not tour with his new album, though he did sing "Pink Bedroom" on the upcoming Clapton gigs. Despite Crowell's assertions, Albert was still unsure of himself as front man and did not feel he had what he called "the vocal chops" to lead a band and headline a tour. Indeed, it is this innate reticence which has prevented Albert from achieving the recognition which many of his musical colleagues believe he deserves as one of the world's great guitar players. He is, as Tony Colton so shrewdly observed, a "quiet legend." Yet he was gaining some measure of national appreciation in his adopted country. Every year between 1982 and 1986, *Guitar Player*'s Readers Poll voted Albert Best Country Guitarist, and he was permanently inducted into the magazine's Gallery of the Greats.

Having just finished work on the solo album, Albert was enlisted to join bassist Leland Sklar and pianist Bill Payne of Little Feat in working on an excellent album for Oklahoman songstress Gail Davies. Produced by Davies in Nashville, the album[60] blends Californian folk-pop with the commercial hard edge of modern country, including a version of Joni Mitchell's "You Turn Me On (I'm a Radio)" and the Top Ten hit "Round the Clock Lovin'."

By June, Clapton had begun the slow process of recovery, attending Alcoholics Anonymous,[61] leading the band in a "very spirited performance" in Minneapolis and taking them from Detroit through Buffalo, New York; Portland, Maine; Augusta, Georgia; and on into Florida. At the Sportatorium in Miami on June 30, Clapton performed "I Shot the Sheriff" and "Blow Wind, Blow" with Muddy Waters. It was the great man's last live appearance: he died the following April in Chicago.

Apart from his guitar, his piano, and his devotion to his family, Albert's other passion is his small but much-loved collection of vintage sports cars. To his Triumph TR8, he added the pièce de résistance in the summer of 1982 when he bought a 1961 Ferrari. "I was pretty flush at the time because I'd had the advance from Polydor for the album." Albert kept the news of his purchase from Clapton for a while—"I didn't know what his reaction would be." In the strand of society that Albert came from, it was considered rather "common" to flash your money around—and buying a Ferrari would be a bit too showy; "I never thought I'd be in that league." Albert would have preferred an old Jaguar, an XK140 or maybe an E-type, but in the event Clapton was "overjoyed. I remember sitting on the beach in Nassau reading the handbook, which was like gold-dust—a reprint of the owner's manual." Albert still tunes the car himself. "It's pretty tricky because you can't get leaded gas. At one time you could buy cans of real lead to add to the gas but you can't get that now. I've been using another additive which didn't do it much good. It's not difficult to tune it but you have to think laterally."

Albert with his first car, a 1948 Rover, ca. 1964 (courtesy Georg Grimm).

Albert at the wheel of a Mercedes 540K roadster at Harrah's, February 1990, with Karen and four-year-old Alexandra in the back (courtesy the Lee family).

Albert and his Ferrari, ca. 1982 (courtesy the Lee family).

Albert's eponymous album came out in August but even had he been inclined, with studio sessions booked in Nassau with Clapton, he was unable to promote it. In the Bahamas, the first few days in the studio proved to be unproductive and lethargic, despite Eric's improved health. Clapton was aware of a feeling of paranoia: "I felt the thrill had gone and the band sensed it, too." He was in the early stages of recovery when the euphoric buzz of the alcohol had not yet been replaced by a creative clarity and sense of purpose. He had been writing but had little material and had "powerful personalities in the band, Gary being one, who did have material and the album started to go in his direction." Brooker accepts that there was "a lot of friction between the players. Dave Markee went all religious and started frowning at us if we swore. It caused a lot of bad vibes." After a fortnight, "without a single track completed to his satisfaction, Clapton was convinced that something radical had to be done."[62]

Clapton had called in Tom Dowd to produce the album. "He had been a stalwart of mine for ten or fifteen years and he was getting outraged by the situation." He confronted Clapton: "Just be brutal. Fire them all, they'll understand." Brooker, while acknowledging Dowd's qualities as a producer, felt "he wasn't even getting the best out of Eric." With the album in crisis, Clapton's manager, Roger Forrester, flew in from England, prepared to act as Clapton's hatchet man if Eric wanted him to do the dirty work. He need not have worried. "This was my first work in sobriety and I was in very bad shape. I had no confidence whatever but Tom was the pivot. He said, 'This is your record and you have to start owning up to that.' So I sat them all down and fired them myself—one of the first respectable things I had done in sobriety. It was a no-win situation, but most accepted it. That was a lesson learnt from before when I allowed Roger to fire the American guys." Albert felt "sad for them while being happy to be still involved." Ray Coleman believes that Albert was retained "partly because his style complemented Clapton's work—and also because having such a lauded player in the band was quite a coup for Eric."[63] Albert had survived his second purge.

With the band reduced to Eric and Albert, Dowd summoned the cavalry from Miami. Eric was back to working with Americans and within twenty-four hours, Donald "Duck" Dunn, the bassist for Booker T and the MG's, drummer Roger Hawkins, who was part of the legendary Muscle Shoals musicians, and Ry Cooder, arguably the best young slide guitarists in the business, formed a studio band which "was Clapton's best as a solo musician."[64] Chris Stainton returned to the fold and with two technically skilled guitarists like Cooder and Lee to keep him on his toes, Clapton began to warm to his task with significantly more gusto than he had during his soft-rock phase in the '70s. Albert believes Cooder was drafted "not only so he could play slide guitar but so that Eric could pick his brains. Like Emmylou Ry has the ability to find great old songs and put his own stamp on them. He was a little reticent in coming up with ideas like that, but he was quite happy to play on the record."

A postcard to Kidbrooke Park Road on October 7 described the Americans' arrival. "We now have American bass and drums. They are session players and of course very good. We're having a great time in the water. Roger has even bought a mask to snorkel with." After the Americans arrived, Albert was flabbergasted to find that Forrester and Dowd wanted the band in the studio at 10 in the morning. "I couldn't believe it. Who wants to record in the morning? We never used to go in till the afternoon. I used to have a quick breakfast and jump in the water at 9, have a snorkel and run to the studio. It was so much fun—but once I went out a bit too far. I looked at the shore and thought 'I don't know, it's a long way.' I started to panic but I just told myself to relax. I got back OK but I could have easily died."

In the studio there was a new sense of discipline and purpose: The dynamics had altered. "The first day they came in," Clapton recalls, "we set up and played 'Crosscut Saw' as a kind of jam all day. It was the first time I'd been stretched for several years, simply because I'd been playing with people who were laying back, and the more I laid back, the more they laid back: whereas this rhythm section counted themselves in and started playing and I didn't have to be there. If I wanted to get in on it, I had to work fucking hard. And that's when I decided I was getting back to where I should be." Coleman observed, "Cooder's roots, like Eric's, skirted jazz, and the communication between the two men, musically as well as out of the studio, was firm. As a master stroke, the talent of Albert Lee was deployed to the concert piano, while Roger Hawkins spent a complete day buying a new set of skins for his drums to achieve a very special sound Eric required."[65]

Within a few days the album was complete: For Albert, however, the satisfactory conclusion of a difficult period professionally was marred by a phone call from Wayne. Assuming his father had heard the sad news, Wayne said, "Ain't it a shame about Grand-dad?" For a moment Albert was unsure whether he meant his own father. But no, Albert's grandfather had died. "I was very upset and got back to London in time for the funeral. Poor Dad was in a state."

"Money and Cigarettes"[66] was Clapton's first release on his own Duck label, set up a year before and is "a telling statement about his powers of survival and recuperation"[67] with little of the anodyne pop that blights much of Clapton's other work in the '80s. It sold poorly, however, despite Ry Cooder encouraging Clapton's innate penchant for slide guitar, Delta blues, and good time rock 'n' roll. There are some old blues covers, the best being Sleepy John Estes' upbeat "Everybody Oughta Make a Change," but none of the other tracks are especially memorable and some Clapton originals are threadbare: for instance "Ain't Going Down" is a thinly disguised reworking of "All Along the Watchtower." Some of Clapton's most dexterous playing can be heard on "The Shape You're In," a rockabilly rave, featuring exhilarating interplay between him and Albert, who also sings backing vocals.

After his grandfather's funeral in Blackheath, Albert stayed close to his family's native heath for a subdued Christmas. His father was still coming to terms with the loss of "fat grand-dad," whom he—and Albert—had loved dearly. Before returning to America in mid–January for the *Money and Cigarettes* tour, he did join Eric on Chas and Dave's TV *Christmas Show*, singing "Country Boy" and dueting with Clapton on "Goodnight, Irene."[68]

In January, the month in which Billy Fury, arguably Britain's finest rock singer, died of heart failure at the age of 41, the band spent two weeks in Seattle rehearsing for the tour, which opened at the Paramount Theater on February 1. Albert confessed in a postcard home that the band felt "a bit nervous but it went well." Tragedy had struck during rehearsals when "Duck" Dunn heard that one of his sons had been killed in a car accident. Naturally distraught, he flew off for the funeral but made the first show the day after.

The tour set featured much of *Money and Cigarettes* and Clapton gave Albert the space to showcase his solo album on "Sweet Little Lisa" or "Pink Bedroom." As the tour wound south and east through San Francisco, Phoenix, Austin, Houston, St. Louis, Philadelphia, Atlanta, Washington, D.C., Worcester, and Hershey, Pa., *Money and Cigarettes* reached #16 in the American and #13 in the U.K. album charts. The tour hit Europe in late March, playing dates in Germany, Holland, France, Italy, Ireland and Spain, ending in Britain with concerts at London's Hammersmith Odeon, the Apollo in Manchester and the traditional end-of-tour bash at Guildford's Civic Hall. It was quite a party. Phil Collins and Jimmy Page joined Clapton on stage for "Cocaine" and "Further on Up the Road," and Irish folk/blues man Paul Brady, Chas and Dave, and Collins stepped up for a rousing finale on "Roll Over Beethoven," "You Won Again," "Matchbox" and "Goodnight Irene."

Back in Blackheath that June for a breather at the end of one of Clapton's marathon tours, Albert was playing at the Tunnel Club one Sunday lunchtime, where his old schoolmate Mo Clifton caught up with him. "He remembered me," says Mo, "and we started keeping in contact again. He's such a lovely guy. He's never changed. He's always been the same bloke from when he was 14." True enough—he had almost come full circle, playing guitar in a small venue close to his roots.

All seemed normal as Albert took the stage in Jones Beach, New York, on July 7 for the second half of Clapton's U.S. tour. Yet his days in the band were numbered. His last hurrah was a mini-tour of southern Europe followed by a trip to Israel and then to Egypt. With no hint of his impending departure, Albert sent a postcard home from Milan at the end of January: "Well, we didn't get to play at La Scala but we played a huge circus tent down the road. The crowds are great, the weather is cold, I'm having trouble finding car parts." Albert was searching for a distributor cap for his vintage Ferrari, but "they didn't have them even at the factory. Eric was going to look at his car—the black Boxer—on the production line and we had a fantastic tour of the factory." A week later, Albert was in Cairo, which "wasn't quite how I imagined it. Hundreds of locals picnicking around the base of the Pyramids, playing football! Forcing you on to a camel or a horse then trying to take you for all you've got! Anyway it's an experience I wouldn't have missed. Big old hotel with good Indian restaurant. Jerusalem next."

"It was the last thing I did," he recalls, "because when I called at Forrester's office to pick up my tour money," the manager told him, "'Sorry, boy, but Eric won't be needing you on the next album.'[69] I know he was trying not to drink. Maybe he felt I was having too much fun playing but I'd never tried to steal the limelight. I thought Eric and I were mates"— but Albert was philosophical. "I'd realized four years before that Eric likes to change the guys around him just to make life more interesting—but I was very disappointed." Despite this, he had no regrets. "Eric was always very gracious; he gave me lots of space and lots of solos, and he let me do 'Country Boy.' It was a great time."

Over the previous year, the Everly Brothers had started to talk to each other again and for Albert, as one door closed, another door opened.

Eleven

Walk Right Back

In the late '50s and early '60s, the voices, the quiffs and the lyrics of the Everly Brothers beguiled a teenage generation. Their songs—three-minute flights to high-school heaven—captured the Appalachian folk, bluegrass and country sounds of their Kentucky boyhood and expressed adolescent angst in a richly harmonized form of rock 'n' roll. After the Knott's Berry Farm cataclysm in 1973, when the plaintive and flawless harmonies turned sour, both Don and Phil ploughed solo furrows of erratic quality with varying success. In the ten years since their dramatically public schism, the brothers had met only once—at the funeral of their father, Ike, in 1975—and eyebrows were raised on both sides of the Atlantic when late in 1982 rumors spread that Don and Phil were considering working together again. Don had mentioned the possibility of a concert to Albert, who was surprised that they were talking at all. Phil explained, "There is a desire on both our parts to do it which is brand new.... I don't want to end my life on negative terms with my brother. It's important that Don and I get back together and sing together. The main reason is that if my Dad was still alive it would please him greatly and I think it will please us too."[1]

The reunion concerts were initially scheduled to take place in February 1983 but were postponed several times as the scale of the project escalated. "It's wound up being very complicated because there's obviously been more interest than even I expected," Phil clarified. "Don and I would probably be better singing together in the back garden of his home or my home but as we had a public parting I think we should have a public gathering." Eventually the Everlys "settled 'the big Southern feud,' as they both called it, with a bear hug when they finally met in Nashville in the early Summer 1983."[2] On that occasion they went into a studio with some session musicians. "They got together," said Terry Slater, "so that they could exercise their voices and learn the songs again." Slater had first met the Everly Brothers on a British tour in 1963, when he was a guitarist with one of the supporting acts, the Flintstones. He became Phil's bass player in the mid '60s and wrote "Bowling Green," a U.S. Top 40 hit in 1967. By 1983, as head of A&R at EMI, he had signed EMI's publishing deal with Queen and was instrumental in the negotiations which resulted in the reunion concerts, finally arranged for September 22 and 23, 1983, at the Royal Albert Hall in London.

Independent of each other, Don and Phil decided on London's premier music venue. "It's a special place for us," said Don. "We have very fond memories of the Albert Hall. It was the last place we appeared with our Dad." The 7,000 seats were sold out, rapidly snapped up by fans who had given up hope of ever seeing the Everlys on stage together again.

The Everlys flew to London in early September for ten days of rehearsals with the musicians booked to support them. The band's line-up had been the subject of intense conjecture. "Each of us has a group," said Phil, "and I could happily sing with Don's people and I'm sure he'd he just as happy with mine. Then there are people who have said they'd like to be involved. I have to keep an open mind and leave it to the natural flow of events." Eventually it was decided to leave it to Terry Slater: "It was complicated because there would be so many people who would've been offended if we'd picked others."

There was one name at the top of both the brothers' lists and a month before rehearsals began Slater called Albert in Calabasas. He said, "The Everlys are doing a couple of concerts at the Albert Hall. Would you like to be in the band?" Albert had heard all sort of rumors about the people likely to be involved. "Dire Straits and James Burton were mentioned, but though I hadn't seen Phil in a few years I had always had a good relationship with him. I think in the end they wanted someone on the stage they felt comfortable with and my name came up."

Joining Albert in the rehearsal studio were Martin Jenner on guitar and steel guitar, Mark Griffiths on bass, Graham Jarvis on drums—three of Cliff Richard's band whom the Everlys had never met—and Pete Wingfield on keyboards. Wingfield had been around the British blues scene since the early '70s, working with Mike Vernon after Blue Horizon Records folded and playing on numerous sessions with artists like B. B. King, Freddie King and Lightning Slim. It was the first time he had met Albert, although over a decade later he was to become a close colleague in Hogan's Heroes. In 1982, Wingfield had worked with Stuart Colman in London on Phil Everly's eponymous album, on which Phil had recorded some duets with Cliff Richard. One of them, "She Means Nothing to Me," became a Top Ten hit in Britain.

For ten days, Don and Phil, determined to make the shows memorable, spent three hours each day with the band, working to get the act together. "They decided to do what they always did best," says Terry Slater, "and that's their hits ... including some, which was nice, that they'd never ever done on stage before." Both brothers had included several of the hits in their solo acts but, "in line with their differing musical tastes, their approach varied enormously and it must have been a problem to return to the disciplined style required of harmony singing."[3]

"The rehearsals were hard work," Albert remembers. It hardly helped that on the second morning the band found that somebody had broken in overnight and stolen half the gear. "They'd lifted my amp, which was incredibly heavy, over a wall. Then someone heard some kids talking in a pub and we got everything back that day." Still, it was an inauspicious start and things were not gelling. "We were really depressed. Then Phil didn't come into the rehearsals for a couple of days and seemed happy enough to leave things up to Don, who, on his own, was just like the old Don we've come to know and love over the past ten years with his varied vocal phrasing. But the minute Phil came in and walked up to the mike Don keyed straight back into the tight vocals necessary to make the harmony come through."

All was not immediately sweetness and light, however. "By the time of the split there was extreme tension between them which ten years of non-contact was unlikely to have eased. It was a softly softly reconciliation, with close friends creating an important buffer."[4]

Their approach to each other had nonetheless changed. "We don't argue now," said Don. "The trouble was that I blamed the Everly Brothers ... but now I can't use that as an excuse for my unhappiness. At this point the brothers come first and the act second." Phil believed there to be "creativity and power in a disagreement which helps make the end product good.... It's a process we're better able to handle now whereas before it was divisive."[5] As Pete Wingfield, who was to work with them for over fifteen years, observes, "The two brothers are very different types. They do however realize that together they are more than the sum of their parts."

On the night of the first concert Phil and Pete Wingfield had dinner in the hotel restaurant overlooking the Albert Hall. Phil pondered on how they had the nerve to do the concert without any warm-up shows, but thinks "we did it the honest way. We told the TV people that we were going to go out there for real—a real reunion—and it was."

During rehearsals there had been much discussion about their entrance. "They thought they would come out to the guitar riff of the opening number like they always had done," says Albert. Someone suggested they come on with no introduction: Don was not so sure. "Do you think there'll be a big enough response?" "Are you kidding?" replied Albert. "They'll go mad."

In the event it was a calculated piece of staging. When Don and Phil surprised everyone by appearing unannounced—Phil from high to the left of the stage, Don from the right—the applause which rolled like a tidal wave around the circular arena became a prolonged standing ovation which visibly surprised them. Perhaps they had merely forgotten how it was. It had been a long time. Each had a black Everly guitar slung around his neck. But it wasn't the trademark Everly Gibsons they carried, but new handbuilt Ike Everly guitars made by Robert Steinegger to Phil's specifications.

"You had to half-close your eyes, but then it all came back: 1958, *The Perry Como Show*, two boys with strange faces, perfectly greased quiffs and matching tuxedos, hoisting identical black-top jumbo guitars and sharing a microphone as they chopped the chords and sang in siren harmony about how Johnny had kissed the teacher." Thus wrote Richard Williams in *The Times*, reviewing the video of the concert in 1985. "Filmed and recorded for posterity, it may not have carried the cultural punch of that flickering black-and-white performance on a nine-inch screen 25 years ago, but it certainly felt like history of some sort being made."

In the late 1950s, on that black-and white screen, it was difficult to tell Don from his brother Phil, but by 1983, Don, at 46 the elder by two years, seemed more intense, thicker-set and more noticeably taking the melodic lead lines on most of the material. In contrast, Phil's open face had acquired an almost everlasting smile. Their between-song patter, while it still had the folksy flavor of down-home Kentucky, revealed nevertheless a genuine pleasure at being on stage again—and at being welcomed as the stars they undoubtedly were.

Furthermore, the shows were not the truncated act that the Everlys were occasionally criticized for in the early 1970s. Each show lasted for well over two hours and included practically every major hit of the Everlys' career. At the end of each concert Don and Phil received a tumultuous standing ovation and did three encores. On the second night they acknowledged the band by insisting they shared the applause.

Indeed, Albert and the other musicians had given the brothers "superbly idiomatic

The Everly Brothers (Phil at left, Don at right) reunion concert, Royal Albert Hall, London, September 1983, with Albert in the background (courtesy the Lee family).

accompaniments, ranging in the first section of the show from the rampaging rock riffing of 'Love Is Strange' through the subdued teenage melodrama of 'Take a Message to Mary,' to the unsullied poignancy of Don Everly's 'So Sad.'" [6] Albert had welded together within a very short period a reasonably tight outfit he felt the band was understandably "nowhere near as slick as it was a few years later." Phil, however, thought they were "sensational. They made it a delight."

For Albert, the concerts were the fulfillment of a lifetime ambition, not only to play behind Don and Phil, but to help recreate some of their greatest songs. "The Everlys sang great and it was fun being in the middle of it"—a typical Albert understatement. To have his family there as well made it a really special night. Whereas his father was like Albert writ large, his mother suffered a mild form of agoraphobia. "It was the last gig she ever came to. Wayne and Abigail were there, too." The night was memorable for Wayne in more ways than one. He dropped his backstage pass and someone snatched it up. It is the one pass missing from the vast collection he has accumulated down the years—"and it would be from one of his most important gigs."

The two concerts[7] were a remarkable triumph for the brothers. They had recaptured their power and sang as much for each other as for the audience, for whom they verified the ineluctable truth—that in the tension which existed between them lay the genius of their music. "It's as if the lyrics of such as 'When Will I Be Loved,' 'Bye Bye Love,' and particularly 'Love Hurts' and on this night of reconciliation 'Let It Be Me,' are directed as much to each other as any next party."[8] They had enthralled an audience of "aficionados, ageing rock 'n' rollers, today's pop stars and young people experiencing their music for the first time."[9]

Albert was, of course, nominally still a member of Clapton's band, but while Eric was largely engaged that autumn with the ARMS charity concerts at the Albert Hall (only two days before the Everlys), Albert and Karen had time for a European break with Don and his girlfriend Diane Craig. Albert was able to indulge his love of Italian food and in a post-card from Florence he waxes lyrical about the holiday: "The photo shows the most famous bridge in Venice. The only one the Germans didn't blow up when they were retreating!"—and in a reminder that while you can take Don out of rural Kentucky, you can't take Kentucky out of Don, Albert remarks, "Don and Diane have gone south for another week.... I don't think they've really enjoyed the cities as much as we have."

After Christmas in Calabasas, Albert and Karen had their last taste of the rock lifestyle with Clapton on the mini-tour in January. Apart from the memorable visit to the Ferrari factory, the band traveled by Citation jet, which had only six seats: no room therefore for Karen and Eric's then wife, Pattie, who followed them round on the train. Then Albert came down to earth with a bump in early February when Roger Forrester delivered his bombshell. His services no longer required, Albert had time and opportunity to assess his options. A postcard home at the end of the month reveals what they were. He tells his parents he would not be back till the end of March as the Everlys recording sessions[10] had been postponed. "I'm going to Nashville mid–March to record with Emmylou. That's good news!"

The March session in Nashville resulted in Emmylou Harris's *The Ballad Of Sally Rose*,[11] country music's first concept album. It marked a significant departure for Emmylou in that all the songs were written by herself and husband-to-be Paul Kennerley. Loosely drawing on her relationship with Gram Parsons, it was however, says Emmylou, "a made-up story, in the sense that I made it more linear and more obvious to give it a dramatic push."

The album, which she co-produced with Kennerley, tells the story of Sally Rose, a singer from a small town whose lover and mentor, a hard-living, hard-drinking musician who dies. It has a poignancy and vibrant immediacy which reflects its semi-autobiographical nature. The usual suspects—Albert, Emory Gordy, Vince Gill, Hank De Vito and Larry Londin—provided accomplished instrumental support, augmented by Ray Flacke and Waylon Jennings, and additional harmony came from Dolly Parton, Linda Ronstadt and Gail Davies on several of the songs, many of which flowed into one another to create a continuous narrative. Harris herself described the album, which was a commercial flop, as a "country opera." In an interview with BBC Radio 2 in 2006, she related how the album's relative failure meant she had to work "for money" again, producing such predictable but success-ful albums like *Trio* (1986) and *13* (1987). She felt the lack of success of *Sally Rose*, thus far her most personal album, very deeply, believing that "Country music must constantly evolve if it is to have any credibility. Groups that recreate the past, like rockabilly groups, are inter-esting, but you have to bring something else to it." In a reference to Albert's work, she says, "It's those musicians who bring different influences who are unique."

The influences to which Emmylou was referring have been as diverse as the musicians and minstrels, hobos and heroes, writers and renegades who have poured their talents into the crucible of the American popular song. Some brought their unique voices—Bessie Smith,

Billie Holiday, Sinatra, Little Richard, Roy Orbison and the Everlys; some articulated a poetic vision—Cole Porter, Jimmy Rodgers, Woody Guthrie, Joni Mitchell, Bob Dylan; still others exerted an irrepressible charisma—Robert Johnson, Louis Armstrong, Ray Charles, Jerry Lee Lewis and Elvis. And then there were the players, those who expressed their uniqueness through their mastery of an instrument—Benny Goodman, Art Tatum, Bix Beiderbecke, Charlie Parker, Earl Scruggs and Chet Atkins. Albert, a disciple of Atkins, Jimmy Bryant and James Burton, brought with him his innate Britishness, his Romany heritage and an intuitive feel for the roots of American country music.

Albert's tools, his guitars, were first his Hofner, then the Futurama and Bob Xavier's Les Paul Custom, followed by Eric's gift of the Gibson Les Paul. At the back of all these however was his '53 Fender Telecaster, with its inherent simplicity and clean, cutting sound. Albert had met Leo Fender a few times—"he was a really nice old guy. There's a theory that his hearing wasn't quite as good as it should have been. That's why the Fender guitars sounded so bright." Albert was not keen, however, on the guitars that Fender was making for Music Man, a company founded by Tom Walker. "They seemed so big and clunky. I still preferred my Telecaster." At Music Man Walker designed the amplifiers and Fender made the guitars, but in 1980 Leo Fender left to found the G&L Guitar company with George Fullerton. In the late '50s, Walker had been a sales representative for Fender, a job on the road which brought him into contact with Ernie Ball.

Ball had grown up in Santa Monica, California, where his father sold cars and taught Ernie Hawaiian steel guitar. At 19, he successfully auditioned for the pedal guitar slot in the band led by Tommy Duncan (former lead singer for Bob Wills and the Texas Playboys). For a year they toured the Southwest until the Korean War broke out and Ball enlisted in the U.S. Air Force Band. After leaving the service Ernie returned to the honky-tonks of Los Angeles, where he worked on a popular weekly show on KTLA Channel 5, a job which trebled his earnings and enabled Ernie to make his name in the L.A. music scene.

In the late 1950s the rock 'n' roll guitar boom was exploding, and in 1958 Ball opened a small music shop in Tarzana, a few miles from Hollywood. "We were the first store in the state, maybe in the country, to sell only guitars." He sold Fenders, of course, but he noticed that guitar students were having difficulty pressing down the third string of the Fender #100 medium gauge set, which were the most popular electric strings of the day. He mentioned the problem to Tom Walker and asked him to tell Leo Fender about it. Tom reported back that Leo wouldn't allow lighter gauge strings on his guitars because they caused string buzz, so Ball talked a string manufacturer into making him some custom medium gauge sets with a 24 third string instead of a 29.

More and more musicians began to buy a set of guitar strings, throwing away the sixth string, and then buying a banjo first string,[12] enabling notes to be bent. Ball felt there should be a rock 'n' roll string set manufactured in these lighter gauges. Again, Fender refused to discuss it. Neither would the Gibson guitar company. So Ernie Ball produced the first set of his Slinky strings (Regular 10–46), selling them initially only in the Tarzana store. As demand for Ball's strings continued to grow, in 1967 he sold the retail store and moved the string business to Newport Beach where his sons, Sterling, David and Sherwood, helped out in the warehouse after school. After graduating high school Sterling joined the Ernie Ball Company full time as a traveling road rep and phone salesman. During the 1970s Sterling

Albert and a Gibson Jumbo, mid–1980s (courtesy the Lee family).

Ball gave Ernie Ball products a global presence, setting up distributors in Europe, Japan and Australia and earning a reputation as an accomplished bassist and a shrewd businessman with a solid network of music industry contacts.

Sterling Ball ultimately became a key figure in artist and dealer relations, and later in the design of the Music Man instrument line and by the early 1980s, Ernie and Sterling felt that the market was ready for a finely crafted American made electric guitar, even though most guitars were being manufactured in Japan, Korea, and Mexico. They believed that with a union of modern technology and old world craftsmanship they could successfully build high-quality electric guitars and basses in the USA.

After Fender left Music Man Walker continued to produce amplifiers for a while, but "the amp market was a little dodgy at the time," Albert remembers, and on March 7, 1984, as Albert recorded *Sally Rose* with Emmylou, Walker sold Music Man to Ernie Ball and the company became Ernie Ball Music Man. "Ernie didn't want to mess around with the design of the amps because of the way the market was going," recalls Albert, "but when their new amps came out I got one. I was immediately in there on the ground floor so that I've now probably got about 15 Music Man amps all shapes and sizes—they're just great amps. They haven't made them in many years now but they're really tough, like tanks, really, and it's only recently that I stopped using them. I use Fender Tonemaster now."

The acquisition of Music Man's name and reputation, allied to his creative flair, gave Ball the impetus to redesign some guitars. Chief designer Dudley Gimple, together with Sterling Ball, sought the ideas of some leading players. Brian Ball, Sterling's son and now Music Man's chief of marketing and artist relations, notes that Albert "was a guinea pig for the Silhouette guitar before his current model was prototyped as the original Axis-named guitar in 1987, or later the Albert Lee signature model. While we were prototyping the Silhouette, we tried several different neck profiles and bridges"—but Albert didn't like the way the Silhouette played. "I needed "more of a Fender bridge where the strings are spaced so as to facilitate my finger-style playing. But with the Fender bridge the neck was too slim and the strings fell off the edge of the finger-board." Ball's solution on both the Silhouette and Albert Lee signature model was to "make the neck wider than the typical Telecaster neck, which had been Albert's main guitar. We put a Gibson-type bridge on it which was slightly narrower." Albert is still not entirely certain whether his signature model was a turning point in the design of the instrument. "Steve Morse put in his tuppence-worth and so did I," he recalls. "Nevertheless, the guitar became much more playable for me."

Ohio-born Steve Morse made his name with his band the Dixie Dregs and was one of the newer guitarists on the scene in the late '70s and early '80s. "He was very interesting and technically brilliant," says Albert, who had become aware of him in 1982 when Morse won the *Guitar Player* Best Overall Guitarist poll. "I bought two or three Dregs albums, and he just killed me. I particularly liked the country cuts, like 'Pride o' the Farm' on 'Dregs of the Earth.'[13] That just took country playing in another direction yet again." The Steve Morse Band began in 1984 as an offshoot of the Dregs, recording *Stand Up*,[14] released in 1985. It was a highly experimental work, using electronic drums and guitar synths. As well as Albert's rockabilly picking on "Rockin' Guitars," guest players like Peter Frampton, Eric Johnson, Alex Ligertwood and the Dregs' own keyboard man T. Lavitz contributed their talents.

Around Easter that year Emmylou was in Britain for the Mervyn Conn Festival and a short European tour. She asked Albert to put together a backing band, so he recruited Pat Donaldson on bass, drummer Gerry Conway, Pete Wingfield and an old friend from the Country Fever days fifteen years earlier, Gerry Hogan, on pedal steel. "We'd just done Wembley when Pete Wingfield called me. Dave Edmunds was producing the new Everly album and they needed pedal steel on one track. I'd worked with Dave in the '70s when he mixed some things for Fatso, which was me, Roger Rettig and what's now Hogan's Heroes."

The success of the reunion concerts had earned the Everly Brothers a major recording contract with Mercury/PolyGram, and in January 1984 it was announced that Don and Phil would record an album to be produced by Dave Edmunds. A devotee of '50s rock, Edmunds had established a successful career in the '70s with his band Rockpile, marrying a genuine feel for rockabilly to Everlys-style vocals. Phil and Don met Edmunds in New York in December. "We have a lot of respect for his work," said Phil, "and we share a similar appreciation of basic rock 'n' roll." Edmunds had struck up a friendship with Don in 1979 at the Buddy Holly Week and seemed a natural choice for the job, but in the early '80s he was more influenced by the synthesizer sounds of his new producer, Jeff Lynne of ELO, and was mildly surprised when he was asked to produce the comeback studio album. He accepted, however, believing "in saying yes to most things and seeing what happens, because that way it spurs you on to do things you wouldn't otherwise do."

In early April Don and Phil traveled to London to record the album at the Maison Rouge Studios, where Edmunds had assembled a high-quality group of British session musicians. Along with Albert and Gerry Hogan, he recruited Phil Donnelly on guitar, Pete Wingfield and Richard Tandy on keyboards and John Giblin on bass; Terry Williams and Gerry Conway shared duties on drums. Edmunds had chosen the venue because of its atmosphere and the fact that it was expensive.[15] "That sharpened your sense of perspective. It's a job and you get things done."[16] Edmunds confessed to feeling nervous "but everybody ... was determined to give 150 percent." He felt a little in awe of Don and Phil, "which wasn't a good thing because it colors your judgment and attitude." Albert sensed the awkward atmosphere. "I don't know if the Everlys really got on with Dave Edmunds. It was an odd situation. How can you tell the Everly Brothers how to sing? They didn't like being told what to do. Poor Dave had that thankless task. You have to let them do what they do. They'll find it if they're in the right mood."

The problem was they weren't. In a manner indicative of their idiosyncratic way of working, when Don went into the studio and started singing Phil stayed in the control room. Edmunds was hoping they weren't going to do the vocals separately, so he asked Phil to go out, too, but he just refused. Don felt his way around the song for a while and when Phil was ready, and not before, he went out and joined in. "They don't talk to each other at all in the studio. They just look straight into each other's eyes and sing ... and suddenly it clicks.... It's fascinating to see it. When they hit their stride it's genius working."[17]

The album has several striking songs, and one in particular, Paul McCartney's "On the Wings of a Nightingale," rivals the best of the early hits. In contributing the song, McCartney repaid the debt to the Everlys owed by the Beatles, who were huge fans.[18] Though the song became a worldwide hit and a perennial favorite in the Everlys' stage act, initially the brothers "weren't enthralled at the demo," recalls Albert. Other stand-out tracks are the country-tinged "The First in Line," anchored by piano and pedal steel guitar, "The Story of Me," a Jeff Lynne tune, and three songs penned by Don. One of them, "Asleep," is the second best song on the album, and another, "You Make It Seem So Easy," has lyrics that shined a light on the decade-long split which tormented the brothers.

Phil has no compositions on the album. "He was reluctant to pitch his songs," says Albert. "They are different from Don's. Don has always written deeper songs while Phil's are more straight-ahead pop."

Expectations were high for *EB84*,[19] for the album is a strong set of songs, and the critical (and mildly commercial)[20] success of *Nightingale* suggested a return to form. However, while here and there Dave Edmunds managed to capture the Everly harmonies, the album is both a triumph and a failure. The sleeve notes claim that the duo wanted a contemporary sound, but in striving for the new, Edmunds was forgetting that there was nothing better than Phil and Don Everly, a couple of acoustic guitars, and one microphone between them.

The brothers were limited in the time they could give to the recordings as they were scheduled to return to the USA to start rehearsals for their first tour in eleven years. Don casually remarked to Albert, "D'ya wanna join us? We're going on the road." After rehearsals in Nashville, the Everlys played forty-two major venues in ten weeks in the USA and Canada at such prominent venues as the World's Fair in New Orleans, the Pier in New York City and the Greek Theatre and Pacific Amphitheatre in California.

Don and Phil had hoped to keep the reunion band together for the tour but the commitment of three of them to Cliff Richard necessitated a search for substitutes. Don suggested Phil Donnelly from his Dead Cowboys band on guitar, together with Nashville session drummer Larrie Londin. With John Giblin, who played bass on the album, unable to tour, Pete Wingfield recommended Phil Cranham, the bass player with Hot Chocolate. Cranham had seen the reunion concert on TV. "I thought it was great but never thought I'd end up working with them. I knew Pete as he used to play on Hot Chocolate's albums; he called me and asked, 'Do you want to do a 10-week tour with the Everlys?' Did I! Any number of American bass players in Nashville could have done the tour, but the Everlys were in London and as they're big Anglophiles, I got the gig."

Albert, Pete and Phil Cranham remained the nucleus of the Everlys band for the next 18 years. Tragically, Larry Londin died of compilations arising from diabetes in August 1992 and was replaced by another Dead Cowboy, Tony Newman (formerly of Sounds Incorporated, Nashville Teens and Jeff Beck). When Donnelly left to join Nanci Griffith in 1986, Albert missed the laid-back Irishman. "He was a mad, but an all-round great character with real style. He was good fun but could be a bit wearing if you were leaving at 5 in the morning and he was larking around. There was some politics going on—a couple of members weren't happy with him." He was replaced by noted steel guitar player and songwriter Hank De Vito, and "he jumped at it. He's not a good road-dog though"—and as Pete Wingfield points out, "A lot of those tours were in the States on the bus."

Albert found the hours on the road "really boring" and Phil Cranham remembers him as being "quite quiet on the tour bus, listening to classical music or reading a huge biography of Leni Riefenstahl[21] or Percy Grainger[22]—or he would sometimes put on one of his vast collection of comedy tapes." Pete Wingfield remembers Albert as "good bus company. He's a witty guy and so was Phil Cranham. We could all have gone on one bus but obviously Don and Phil have separate buses. It's difficult when you have two bosses who aren't getting on. You learn to keep your head down and get on with it." Albert never took sides: His view was that whatever friction there was between the brothers was their affair. His focus was always the music and he would not have wished to intrude on a private quarrel.

For all the boredom and the grind of the road, there were compensations. After a gig everyone would be in a good mood and back at the hotel, Cranham recalls, "we'd have a couple of beers at the bar and if there was a piano then Pete W., who was drawn to it like a moth to a flame, and Albert would do a roaring four-handed boogie-woogie. Pete would sit on the right and Albert on the left, then they'd swap sides halfway through. Phil Everly loved it."

The reunion tour was a triumphant success, the gigs frequently recapturing the breathtaking atmosphere of the Albert Hall concerts. For the first couple of gigs, the Everlys played two halves but they reverted to one set as it soon became evident that promoters could sell out two shows a day. Albert put his own stamp on the solos while staying faithful to the guitar licks of the well-known songs, although on "Bird Dog" he played the lick from the re-recorded version. Having the same musicians on the road as in the studio proved most effective on the newer songs like "I Know Love," "You Make It Seem So Easy," "You Send Me," "Born Yesterday" and "Brown Eyes."

A review in the *Seattle Times*[23] early in August gives a flavor of the live concerts. The show started 40 minutes late because of a three-hour truck breakdown between Seattle and Spokane and there was a poor sound system. On this occasion the gig was not a sell-out, as the 6,000-seat arena was less than half full. However, "Any fans of the Everly Brothers who missed their show last night at the Seattle Center Arena can kick themselves right now, because it was better than anyone had a right to expect. Don and Phil Everly harmonized as sweetly as ever, with maturity adding just a touch of deepness to their voices ... Part of the reason the show was so satisfying," the review went on, "was the backing band, which obviously was a source of some of the Everly spirit and pride. Albert Lee, the great British rock guitarist, added stunning solos to 'The Price of Love,' 'Gone, Gone, Gone' and 'Lucille' and recreated the original solos of other songs with understanding and respect."

After the American leg of the tour Don and Phil played dates in fifteen British cities, and for the whole band it had been an intensely rewarding professional experience, which Albert thought might last twelve months—"but it ended up lasting for eighteen years during which time I worked on practically everything they did." Each year from 1984 to 2001, he, Phil Cranham and Pete Wingfield joined Don and Phil for three or four months. "We'd

Albert with Phil, left, and Don, right, in the late 1980s (courtesy the Lee family).

Don and Albert feel the cold in Nashville in the 1970s (courtesy the Lee family).

start in July and stay there till Labor Day in the first week of September," Cranham points out. "We might come back and do a week in Lake Tahoe or Vegas—then perhaps a U.K. tour in the autumn or winter." That winter, when Bob Geldof begged, coaxed and bullied his fellow artists into the studio to cut "Do They Know It's Christmas?" and when the Clash were performing benefit shows for Britain's striking miners, Albert stayed around after the Everlys tour. Gary Brooker, his old mate from the Clapton days, had taken to organizing a Christmas party at the club in Chiddingfold, a delightful village near his home on the Surrey/Sussex border, at which an impromptu band of reprobates from the music business would play for fun and for charity. He had invited Albert to join the merry band—"Eric was one of them," Albert recalls. "We talked about cars and he was friendly but a little guarded. He'd fired me after all, less than a year before."

The Everlys were scheduled to do a second reunion album with Dave Edmunds, again at Maison Rouge in the spring, but before then Albert enjoyed one of his occasional excursions into other musical forms, working with two outstanding instrumentalists in Los Angeles.

A Cajun accordionist from Louisiana, Jo-El Sonnier, had made his name as a child prodigy and sought to carve out a career in California and Nashville as a session musician

Karen Lee, Don, Abigail, Wayne, Albert and Karen Everly, at the Hammersmith Odeon in April 1978 (courtesy Graham Barker).

but with little success. He had almost abandoned the accordion when Merle Haggard invited Jo-El to open for him on the road. This positive change of fortune sparked a return to California and by the end of 1984, Sonnier had a Grammy-nominated recording to his credit with *Cajun Life*. In Los Angeles he worked in a band with Albert, Californian guitar, banjo and mandolin maestro David Lindley, British drummer Ian Wallace and Canadian Garth Hudson, perhaps the most talented musician in the hugely influential and much-respected outfit The Band. A multi-instrumentalist, but best known as a keyboard player, he became part of the California music scene after the Band folded in 1976. In 1980, he composed and played the score with the title "Our Lady Queen of the Angels," for an exhibition at the Museum of Science and Industry in Los Angeles to mark the city's two hundredth anniversary.

Hudson played a few gigs with Albert in Jo-El Sonnier's band, which he recalls as "a distinct pleasure. Albert listens to the other players when he plays.... He watches your hands and knows where you're about to go and then adjusts what he plays accordingly. This makes playing with him effortless and fun."

Another outfit that inhabited much the same musical landscape as Hudson and The Band were Creedence Clearwater Revival, the most popular rock band in the USA in the late '60s, with their brand of riff-based revivalist rockabilly. As a counterpoint to the wave of trippy psychedelia which was sweeping the States, especially the west coast, CCR flew the flag for American roots music and a more gritty, denim and beards, stripped-down sound. After the band's demise in 1972 amid a welter of artistic dissension, lead singer and writer John Fogerty began a solo career, releasing a couple of albums. Legal wrangles meant he had a decade in the wilderness but by early 1985, he was primed for a comeback to the live stage.

Fogerty's return to live performing took place on January 31 at the Chaplin Stage on A&M Records' Hollywood lot. The show was filmed for an MTV special but the real rationale of the concert was more significant: "it was a chance for Fogerty, under the most controlled conditions—the invited audience of about 200 was filled with sympathetic Warner Bros. employees, friends and musicians—to feel once again what it's like to stand onstage and play rock 'n' roll."[24]

Fogerty had assembled a stellar band—Albert played his Telecaster, with Booker T. Jones on keyboards, Donald "Duck" Dunn on bass, Steve Douglas on saxophone and Prairie Prince on drums. In a relaxed and informal setting Fogerty and the band wandered on to a low stage and romped through a selection of R&B covers, none of which appeared on his hit album *Centerfield*. "He's an incredibly powerful singer, and it was real fun," Albert recalls. But he did not play on the album and when Fogerty went on the road, it was with another band.

In 1985 the Everlys in essence repeated the pattern of the previous year's work, six months of touring the USA, Australia and Europe, preceded by recording an album in the spring.

The second reunion album,[25] again recorded at Maison Rouge with Dave Edmunds at the helm, is one of the best of the Everlys' career. It contains material as varied as "Arms of Mary," the 1976 hit for Britain's Sutherland Brothers, a teenage reminiscence that the brothers convert into a reverie of innocent yearning, a track from Dire Straits' "Brothers in Arms," "Why Worry," which Knopfler wrote with the Everlys in mind, "Abandoned Love," a previously unreleased Dylan song which has Liam O'Flynn of the Chieftains providing Irish pipes, and the pounding rock of "Always Drive a Cadillac," by the gloriously named Larry Raspberry, where Don and Phil's harmonies weave through each chorus. The single from the album was the opening track "Amanda Ruth," "a blistering start to the proceedings, with some great guitar work from Mr. Albert Lee."[26] The title track, written by Don, is a moving song of loss and spiritual dereliction which took him three or four years to write, containing a decade's pain in its lyrics. His brother suggests the song "points out that we're all like children. Do any of us really grow up?"

Again there are none of Phil's songs on the album. Don chose most of them and many of the arrangements are his, though he felt he should have spent more time on them. "It was a little bit of a rush job."[27] Certainly Mercury was anxious to cash in on reunion fever with a second album but while the rush may have been exacerbated by Edmunds' brisk approach, "Don and Phil must take a portion of the blame."[28] Albert recalls that all the albums were recorded in the same way. "We'd all go into the studio, Don and Phil would show up, sometimes just Don. We'd work at a song for an hour or two, then Don and Phil would disappear and return later, unhappy with what they were hearing. We went through this a number of times and we said, 'Hey, guys, you should stick around and make sure it doesn't go in a direction you don't want it to.' It was a very difficult way to try to make a record."

Roger White has the impression that recording *Born Yesterday* "re-opened some of the sores between the brothers."[29] Yet Phil Cranham, who played bass on the album, remembers that they were "getting on fine in early 1985—there's a lot of rubbish talked about them fighting all the time. As long as I've known them their relationship has been pretty steady. They disagree sometimes but on the whole they've survived very well all those years." And Jay Cocks, writing in *Time*, had the feeling that "the emotional weight of their new album ... comes from the sense that matters have been settled."

Whichever view is correct—and both may contain a measure of truth—an album which was critically acclaimed, which *Time* magazine named as one of the Top Ten albums of the year and which was nominated for a Grammy in the Best Country Performance by a Duo or Group, was a commercial failure. The reunion fever had abated and the media had moved on.

By then, so had Albert. In April, he played on L.A. singer-songwriter Rick Densmore's unissued album with Glen D. Hardin and Sneaky Pete Kleinow, and in June Ricky Skaggs, the bluegrass fiddler and guitar-picker, took Colton, Smith and Lee's "Country Boy" to the top of the country charts. He had rung Albert because "he wanted to do a video but couldn't get permission from Island. I called them and said it was a big deal." Albert didn't even feature in the video, which would have been quite an experience: Skaggs describes renting a subway in Times Square, New York, "from midnight until 4 A.M. or 5 A.M. Bill Monroe was in it and so was Mayor Ed Koch. The song topped the charts and Island were astounded—they had their first country hit and took me out to lunch."

Of greater significance however was his first solo instrumental album,[30] recorded in July at One on One Studios in North Hollywood. "Tony Brown said I could do what I wanted so I did," says Albert.

In the late '70s, Brown had been thrilled to play with Albert in the Cherry Bombs. "If you needed something to kick a show in the ass, Rodney would get Albert to do 'Country Boy' and the roof blew off. I had to remind myself that this English dude had written one of the best country/bluegrass/rock 'n' roll songs ever written." Brown had also played on Emmylou Harris's *Blue Kentucky Girl* and been a Hot Band member. In 1984, he arrived at MCA in Nashville and producer Jimmy Bowen told the keyboard man he would welcome any new ideas. "That was about the time Windham Hill emerged," said Brown, "with Liz Storey and Will Ackerman—New Age music: great musicians improvising and people paying good money to listen to it on a Sunday afternoon drinking a nice glass of Chardonnay. I'd hear jazz musicians in the studio—transplants from California learning to play country music."

Tony Brown began to think that "after all these years Albert must have some great instrumental things to say. I'd heard his guitar of course but I had no idea what a piano player he was. He'd played on Rodney's "Til I Gain Control Again' and I figured he would be a rocker like Glen D but the piano is almost classical. He's a very graceful, gentle and calming person to be around yet within those fingers is that blistering pace."

Soon Brown had signed up Dobro ace Jerry Douglas, bass virtuoso Edgar Meyer and the ex-Crusaders jazz-rock guitar maestro Larry Carlton. Called the MCA Master Series,

Brown remembers it as "more than just mainstream country music. It was fun and we had a very successful launch. Carlton, Douglas and Albert were the lead horses and brought a lot of credibility to the Series. I'd told Jimmy Bowen, 'We won't pay producers $40–100,000 to make the record. We'll tell musicians, Just go and do anything you want to do, no restrictions and make it as inexpensive as possible.' I wanted every musician do their own stuff, to make it where they wanted, in their bedroom if they liked, and to be a creative expression of their personalities."

Albert's creative input was not confined to playing guitar, mandolin and piano—and writing five of the eight tracks. He co-produced it with Bradley Hartman for Poshrat Productions, his own label, with Jim Cox on keyboards, synthesized banjo and steel guitar, Greg Humphrey and Sterling Ball on bass and the aptly named Chad Wackerman on drums. Special thanks were expressed to Karen Lee, Sterling Ball and Tony Brown for their encouragement and Albert did not forget to "raise a creamy pint to: Ernie Ball, Tom Walker and Seymour Duncan."

Present at the recordings was Albert's son, who would join his father for the sort of vacation most British youngsters could only dream of. "That summer I watched Live Aid on TV in the studio," Wayne recalls. "It's only in my latter years that I've realized some of the people I've met. To me they were just Dad's friends. Once when I was a little kiddy I got locked in Jimmy Webb's bathroom at his house in L.A. and he had to break the door down to get me out. Then every summer I would join Dad and the Everlys for a lot of their tour. I started off in the band bus, got bored and went with the crew. Sparky, the sound engineer, taught me so much about sound that eventually I was setting up the front-of-house sound for the gigs. I have been very lucky and these people have been a good influence."

The disc received fulsome critical acclaim, both from guitar fans and the wider music industry. The *Lincoln Journal* wrote, "Lee shows his versatility and flair, playing guitar with breakneck speed, without losing feeling, all his work is amazingly crisp and clear" and BAM[31] described *Speechless* as "one of the finest guitar albums of the decade." The album benefits also from some jazzy piano from Jim Cox, notably on "Bullish Boogie," and ends with two reflective piano compositions from Albert, "Romany Rye," on which he pays homage to his roots, and "Erin," a tune born of the Celtic twilight. "Speechless" was nominated by members of NARAS for a Grammy Award for Best Country Instrumental Performance: Albert received "a nice telegram from Jimmy Bowen, the big noise at MCA. There's a lot of politics in these things but I was overjoyed I got nominated."

He was overjoyed for another reason. Karen was due to give birth early in the new year to their first child, and she would therefore miss an Australian tour with the Everlys. The band's line-up for the tour saw significant changes, enforced by the absence of Pete Wingfield and Larry Londin, in demand as the leading session drummer in Nashville. "He was so big he could afford to do other things," Albert comments. "Most players are scared at losing what they call their 'accounts.' We had two great guys, Ron Kruzinsky from L.A. on drums and ex–Small Faces' Ian McGlagan on piano. We rehearsed in L.A. without the Everlys— the first time they met the new band was before the gig in Honolulu."

On the Australian tour, at the Sydney venue, Albert met Andrew Pattison, an expat Brit and Everlys fan who had started a folkie/coffee lounge/music venue in Melbourne in 1978 called The Troubadour. By the early '80s it had become the pre-eminent acoustic music venue in Australia, featuring most of the touring international acoustic acts. Pattison ran a winery and a music festival and few years later Albert ... but that's another story.

By Christmas, via some British dates with Don and Phil, Albert was back in Calabasas with a now heavily pregnant Karen. While at home Albert would eat what Karen, a committed vegetarian, was eating, but "when we went out I'd have steak and eggs and burgers." Albert, whose mother used to cook pork strips and pour the fat on the vegetables, had a constitution tried and found wanting after a life on the road where regular meals were a luxury. "On the way to gigs we'd have a fry-up and a Mars bar and before the gig fish and chips and a couple of pints of beer which I wasn't used to drinking. On stage I often felt a bit sick and a couple of times I passed out, once at the Flamingo." In an exquisitely ironic twist, given their subsequent history, "Eric was there and got up and played for me." In the mid-'80s Albert's cholesterol count was exceptionally high, and he decided to source his protein—fish, nuts and cheese—from outlets like the farmers' market each Saturday, at the

intersection of Calabasas Road and El Canon Avenue. "It was a very easy transition. I immediately started to feel better and now if I eat the wrong thing I feel sluggish—but I still miss a roast lunch on Sunday!"

New Year 1986 came and went and with Karen due to give birth at any time, Albert was on tenterhooks. In 1979, on the album *Blue Kentucky Girl*, Dolly Parton and Linda Ronstadt had accompanied Emmylou Harris on Rodney Crowell's "Even Cowgirls Get the Blues." That January they joined forces again on what was to become a million-selling album, *Trio*. Work was due to begin on January 19 at The Complex in West Los Angeles, and Albert was worried. "I didn't want to miss out on the recordings but I wanted to be at her birth." In the event Alexandra arrived a week before, on January 12—"and each day I'd come in the studio and the girls would ask me if I'd named that baby yet."

The album[32] attracted very mixed reviews, despite the luminous studio personnel, which included Ronstadt's producer, George Massenburg, and Emmylou's musical con-

Dolly Parton and Albert, January 1986 (courtesy the Lee family).

Albert's children, Alexandra, Wayne, Rebecca, Cassandra, and Abigail, backstage at Wembley in 1990 (courtesy the Lee family).

sultant, John Starling, together with the three vocalists and Albert, Steve Fishell (pedal steel guitar), Ry Cooder (tremolo guitar), Herb Pedersen (banjo), David Lindley (mandolin), Mark O'Connor (viola), Bill Payne (piano), Kenny Edwards (bass) and Russ Kunkel (drums).

The three women went for a traditional, acoustic sound on work by writers as varied as Jimmie Rodgers, Porter Waggoner, Kate McGarrigle and Phil Spector. As *Mojo* put it, "The 3 first ladies of country settle on down-home musical virtues and songs of suffering womanhood."[33] On the other hand, Alanna Nash, writing in *Stereo Review*,[34] sees in the pursuit of an old-fashioned feel "the reason for the album's funereal pacing, something most apparent in the songs in which Ronstadt takes the lead." She even takes them to task on the inclusion of the Teddy Bears' 1958 hit, "To Know Him Is to Love Him," which she describes as "lifeless and weighted down." Nonetheless, the song was one of three Top Ten country singles, along with "Telling Me Lies" and "Those Memories of You," "a strong and mournful bluegrass tune in the best Bill Monroe tradition."

While *Trio* may not have been a masterpiece, even Nash concedes that it is "a gorgeous sampler of female harmony singing and thrilling instrumental solos—particularly those by guitarist Albert Lee and fiddler Mark O'Connor—as well as a monument to perseverance and a celebration of enduring friendship. In today's world," she concludes, "perhaps that is rarer than a masterpiece after all."

The warm reception for *Speechless* the year before encouraged Tony Brown to commission a second solo instrumental from Albert, and while Karen nursed young Alex in Calabasas he recorded *Gagged but Not Bound*[35] at the Sunset Sound Factory on Selma Avenue in Hollywood, where since the 1960s dozens of great names have worked, including Jackson Browne, the Flying Burritos and Brian Wilson. Other tracks were laid down at Avatar, Sounder and The Village, a 22,000 square-foot converted Masonic Temple on Butler Avenue in west L.A.

Gagged but Not Bound, so-called in an ironic reference to its instrumental format, was produced and arranged by Jim Cox, the virtuoso keyboardist who embellished much of *Speechless*. With accomplished help from Jimmy Johnson, Jerry Scheff and Sterling Ball on bass, John Ferraro and Paul Leim on drums and Steve Douglas and Jim Peskin on saxophones, Cox masterminded the sessions from his seat at the keyboards and even found time to add some rebel yells with Albert on "Walkin' After Midnight."

Albert opens up with an insightful acoustic version of the traditional tune "Flowers of Edinburgh," then moves through the gears into an eclectic mix of country, blues, jazz and bluegrass. He pays homage to standards such as "Don't Let Go," where the Stax-flavored horns lend a jazz-funk feel to Jesse Stone's tune "Tiger Rag," Duane Eddy's "Forty Miles of Bad Road," and "Midnight Special." There are a couple of original tracks, "Fun Ranch Boogie," co-written with Sterling Ball, and "Monte Nido," a solo piano composition named for the small community where Albert lives, south of Calabasas just off the Malibu Canyon road. The piece has ethereal overtones of George Winston, one of the outstanding American composers of non–classical music. Born in Michigan but raised in Montana, Winston describes his style as "rural folk piano," and many of his atmospheric pieces evoke the essence of a season and reflect natural landscapes. His 1980 album *Autumn* became the best-selling album in the New-Age Windham Hill catalog.

Only "Schon Rosmarin," Fritz Kreisler's waltz tune, and Cox's own "Oklahoma Stroke," an odd mix of rustic hoedown and a theme for a TV detective series, fail to inspire on what is otherwise a crisp showcase for Albert's talent. He offers the customary thanks on the sleeve notes to Cox and engineer Mark Howlett, to Tony Brown, Seymour Duncan and Ernie Ball for their continued support, "and to Blake Morris for helping me overcome a fear of Italian engineering."[36]

However brightly the MCA Master Series blazed, it proved to be as ephemeral as the desert flower. "One day just before I began a short tour, I went to order some CDs and was told they'd been deleted six months before, which was a bombshell. If I'd known I'd have stocked up! Now, whenever Karen sees one on eBay, she buys it."[37]

Although in the first years touring with the Everlys there was regular money while on tour, inevitably there would be some down-time, perhaps "a couple of months when I wasn't doing very much and we'd have to watch the pennies." Hence, Albert would take other work. In September 1986, when Duane Eddy and the Rebels were the opening act for Huey Lewis and the News, Albert played the first part of the tour, sharing the lead guitar slot with Arlen Roth, who recalls Eddy saying that "Albert and I were his favorite guitarists!" Three years before, Albert had toured Texas with Eddy and went to Lubbock. "It must have been around the time of the ARMS tour as Eric, Jeff Beck and Jan Hammer were in the audience I also played with him at the Baked Potato, a tiny little jazz club on Cahuenga Boulevard in North Hollywood. It was great fun. Steve Douglas was on sax and Don Randi, who owned the club, was on keyboards."

Working with another of his teenage idols was an entertaining experience for Albert, who values greatly the time he spent playing guitar with men who were his heroes in his formative years. Chet Atkins was another idol, and in November 1969 when Country Fever backed Nat Stuckey and Connie Smith on a European tour, Atkins appeared on the two final London dates. In January 1990 Albert, together with Steve Morse and Buddy Emmons, recorded some sessions in Nashville with Atkins for the French guitarist Marcel Dadi. *Nashville Rendezvous* appeared in 1991, and a second album came out in 1992, with Albert on five tracks. Six years later Dadi was killed when TWA flight 800 blew up over Long Island. Albert had been on stage with Jimmy Bryant, perhaps his biggest hero, on two occasions, once in 1973, when Albert played piano for him, and again at the Palomino Club, where James Burton was also on stage. That winter, in February 1987, when Eric Clapton began his annual series of concerts at the Albert Hall, Albert renewed his acquaintance with Burton, when Seymour Duncan organized a charity concert for Childline at the Town and Country Club in London. "Albert played and you knew it mattered," recalls Mike Berry. "The others were very flash with little substance. Whereas Burton played the solos off his hits, which was nice, with Albert you knew he felt it." Dave Gilmour was also on the bill. It was the first time Albert had met Pink Floyd's hugely gifted Fender player and writer, whose playing he admired greatly.

In the autumn, Albert played a number of British dates with the Everlys, with Larry Londin, Phil Cranham and Hank De Vito. By then, De Vito had had enough of touring and at his last gig—at the Albert Hall—he ceremoniously tore up his band jacket.

At the same time, Gerry Hogan was about to run his fourth steel guitar festival in Newbury. He had left the full-time music business in the late '60s to go to university and joined IBM in 1971, though he still played pedal steel semi-pro and "Albert was very good about riding me into sessions and keeping me abreast of all the old chaps." The festival was in trouble. "We couldn't make ends meet: We weren't getting enough people just on steel guitars alone. I was ready to chuck it in but my wife knew how much it meant to me so she said, 'Why don't you bring a guitar player in to attract guitar buffs who want to play steel as well? You could kill two birds with one stone.'" Gerry thought for a moment and then picked up a metaphorical pebble. He chose his quarry with precision and loaded his slingshot. He took careful aim and fired.

Albert had another gig.

Twelve

"A Band of Heroes"[1]

Side One

The pedal steel guitar, with its sweeping glissandos and its almost palpable tug at the heartstrings, expresses perfectly the pain, the loss and the misery at the heart of traditional country music. Yet the roots of the instrument lie not in the American South but in the blue Pacific, where in the 1880s, according to legend, Joseph Kekuku, a Hawaiian schoolboy, discovered the sound while walking along a railroad track strumming his guitar. Picking up a bolt lying by the track, he slid the metal along the strings and, intrigued by the sound, taught himself to play using the back of a knife blade. Apocryphal or not, by the end of the century other Hawaiian musicians had adapted the Spanish guitar and began to play it flat on their laps, fretting it with a slide instead of their fingers.

Hawaiian groups were a big hit at the 1915 Panama-Pacific International Exposition in San Francisco and from there the sound of the Hawaiian guitar spread throughout the United States. Soon hillbilly musicians like Jimmy Tarlton and Cliff Carlisle began imitating what they heard and saw. As players experimented, seeking to develop its capabilities, the steel guitar became heavily modified. More strings were added, then additional necks and as the guitars got heavier, they were placed on legs, changing from lap steels to table steels. Finally in the early 1950s pedals and knee levers were attached to the strings, allowing the player to change tunings as the guitar was played.

Against the backdrop of such an exotic history, the small market town of Newbury in Berkshire became the unlikely epicenter of pedal steel in the British Isles when in 1984 Gerry Hogan started a steel guitar festival at Burgchlere School. At the time, Hogan was playing with Brian Hodgson, Peter Baron and Mike Bell in Fatso, a band which had arisen as a consequence of one of those intricately connected and faintly incestuous webs which have delighted music anoraks down the years.

The original Fatso comprised Hodgson, John Halsey on drums, Roger Rettig and Billy Bremner, who went on to Dave Edmunds' Rockpile and the Refreshments. "I'd first met Pete Baron in 1972 working with Roger and Billy in Marty Wilde's band," Hodgson recalls. "After we left Marty Wilde, we formed a Crosby, Stills and Nash–type band called Compass, with a drummer called Pete Kershaw who used to be in Honeybus." When Pete left to join Liverpool Express and John Halsey went off to work with Roy Harper we called up Peter Baron. Adrian Legg, our steel player, was busy. Roger Rettig had been taking steel guitar lessons from Gerry Hogan and "we got Gerry to come and play on our regular Sunday night gigs in Kenton," recalls Pete Baron. Thus Compass became the mid–'80s Fatso via Panhandle, a band Hogan had run for a while of which Hodgson and Baron were irregular members.

Peter Baron, from Northwood, had made a name in the mid–1970s playing jazz nights at the Busy Bee Transport Café at Junction 5 on the M1 highway, where a husband and wife team ran gigs in the tiny grill room. "A year or so after I'd met Brian and Roger, I met a pianist called Mike Bell, who was doing a six-night a week residency at the Busy Bee and I used to deputize for his drummer. Mike was a good bass pedal player so you could do gigs without a bass guitar. We decided to play a bit of jazz and R&B and began to gig together." After a stint with Marty Wilde, Baron joined Elkie Brooks's band for about a year in 1978, enjoying a top 5 hit with "Don't Cry Out Loud." Then Hodgson asked him to fill the drum seat in Fatso, "and we became synonymous with humor as much as anything else, working a lot with the satirical and surreal song-writer Neil Innes, ex–Bonzo Dog Do Dah Band, on *The Innes Book of Records* and *Rutland Weekend Television*—and when our regular piano player couldn't do a gig I recommended Mike."

Mike Bell remembers Fatso with affection. "I joined with Gerry Hogan around 1978, post–Neil Innes, but he was involved in producing us. Brian had written some songs and we were about to record them when Pete K went, which pissed Brian off." Baron's admiration for Mike Bell's playing was reciprocated. "When Pete turned up I was blown away because he could do stuff other guys couldn't do. Ordinary drummers who read music perfectly played in a kind of jazz style, like Oscar Peterson's drummer Ed Thigpen. What they couldn't do and Pete could was the Steve Gadd stuff and the back beat, as on Stevie Wonder's 'Mr. Know-it-All.'"

For the 1985 Festival Buddy Emmons was the headline star. Since the mid–'50s, when Emmons worked with Little Jimmie Dickens, Ernest Tubb's Texas Troubadours and Ray Price's Cherokee Cowboys, his virtuosity had taken the pedal steel guitar to new levels of performance. Fatso seemed a natural choice as his backing band. "Roger and Gerry were very country-oriented," says Mike Bell. "Brian was basically a rocker. Pete and I were the youngest and came from a slightly different school. Good music is good music, however." And it seemed to work. "Halfway through the set," says Hodgson, "Buddy said, 'Sometimes the bands we play with aren't too swift. This time I guess we really got it right.'"

After 1985, Fatso metamorphosed into Hogan's Heroes at Brian's instigation. Gerry Hogan had just done an interview for *Guitarist* magazine, in which he had expatiated about his steel-playing heroes from the States. The title of the article was "Hogan's Heroes," and Hodgson seized on the name. "Great—we'll call ourselves that." Hogan was concerned in case the TV series sued but in the end Brian assuaged his fears.

By 1987, the festival was in trouble. "We couldn't make ends meet on steel guitars alone. My bank-manager said to me 'You've got to hit this on the head. This is ridiculous.'" Gerry was about to throw in the towel when his wife suggested he broaden his customer base. "Get a name guitarist to help put bums on seats," she said. The first choice, everybody's hero, was Albert.

Pete Baron had first seen Albert with Farlowe and the Thunderbirds at the Fender Club at the Conservative Hall in Northwick Park. "I'd have been 15 or 16. The first time I ever played with Albert was in 1980 on a recording session just off York Way north of King's

Cross for a guy called Tom Newman, who produced *Tubular Bells* for Mike Oldfield. Albert turned up to play the guitar solo on one of the tracks: he and Eric were working that week at the Rainbow in Finsbury Park. As was often the case in Albert's story, 'neither of us ever got paid a cent—the guy who was financing it got busted for flogging cocaine.'"

When Gerry rang Albert his reply was totally in character. Never wanting to say "No" to people, he said "Yeah. I'd love to do it." He was certainly attracted by the idea while being genuinely worried, daunted at first by the prospect of fronting his own band. "He might have sung the odd song here and there," says Brian Hodgson, "but he'd always been the archetypal sideman, which is crazy when you think of his talent."

Nonetheless, Albert drove to Newbury for a six-hour rehearsal on a Thursday in a village hall opposite Gerry's house. Brian found Albert apprehensive, but Gerry had put together a bunch of songs which he thought Albert could do and which the band had already woodshedded.[2] Albert looked at the set list and said, typically non-committal, "That's all right—yeah.... Well, yes, I suppose I could do that." Whatever suggestions he may himself have had, there was already more than enough material. Gerry Hogan rehearsed with the steel player on Friday: the show with Albert was due on Saturday and Sunday. Albert called Gerry on the Friday evening.

"Everything all right?" Gerry asked.

"Yeah, yeah. What time do you want me there?"

"The show starts at 2 but you won't be on till the evening so come whenever you like."

Albert asked again, "Are you sure you want me to front this thing?"

"Oh, yes," Gerry reassured him. "Absolutely. You can do it."

"Oh, I'm not so sure. I've never done it before."

"I'm telling you. You're the man. People come to see you and they will be amazed at your singing. A lot of people think you're only a guitar player."

"Well. I don't know. I'd be happy just to ... if you want to get somebody else..."

"No. I want you up there."

It was a big step for the quiet, reticent, south Londoner. Chas Hodges, who has known Albert for over forty years, observes that he was always reluctant to take responsibility, to see himself as the leader. "In the '50s," says Gerry, "we were brought up not to put ourselves forward, to think carefully and not to be thought of as a big-head." Friends in Blackheath remember Albert in the early skiffle days playing guitar solos with his back to the customers—who had expressly come to see him. "When he used to sit in with us at the Red Cow, he would want to stand at the back," Gerry recalls. "We had to push him out the front," says Pete Baron. "He'd sung the odd song with Heads, Hands and Feet, Country Fever, Don Everly and Clapton. What he hadn't done was two hours out front on his own."

"So we did it," recalls Brian, "and everybody had a ball." Albert thoroughly enjoyed himself. "It was easier than I thought and came together quite easily. The time just flew by and I didn't use lyric sheets at all." Afterwards he said to Gerry, "I wonder ... Can you get some more gigs?"

While Gerry was busy networking that winter, drawing on his European contacts, Albert flew halfway round the world in February. Andrew Pattison, the ex-pat Brit and Everlys fan whom Albert had met in Sydney a couple of years before, had booked the Byron

Berline Trio to appear at the Troubadour in Melbourne in the mid–'80s. The trio included a youthful Vince Gill, and in 1988 Pattison booked Gill again, this time with Rodney Crowell. At the last moment Rodney had to cancel, so Vince gave the promoter other names, which included Albert—and Pattison instantly said, "yes."

Albert loved the trip, remembering particularly a song by Vince and Guy Clark called "Jenny Dreamed of Trains," which later appeared on Gill's hit album *High Lonesome Sound*. Albert and Vince stayed with Pattison and his wife, Ann, who kindly did her visitors' laundry. In a country where most things are larger than life, Ann observed that Albert's brief underpants were "the smallest men's' underpants she'd ever seen," which Vince thought hilarious. In the mid–1990s Albert played acoustic guitar, plus mandolin and harmony vocal, on a traditional song, "Anachie Gordon," on a CD called *Everything Possible*, for Pattison's then-girlfriend, Melbourne folk singer Meg MacDonald.

Gerry's networking had borne fruit, meanwhile, and the Heroes had been booked for Mervyn Conn's Wembley Festival on Easter Monday. At a loose end on the Sunday night, the Heroes, with Albert, found themselves at Chas and Dave's pub, the New Pegasus in Newington Green, north London. It was a serious old rock 'n' roll venue, dark and dingy,

Hogan's Heroes at the New Pegasus in April 1988. From left, Gerry Hogan, Albert, Pete Baron, Brian Hodgson and Mike Bell (courtesy Graham Barker).

Albert and Willie Nelson at the New Pegasus, April 1988 (courtesy Graham Barker).

but as the papers observed the next day, "some people knew where the best gig in town was last night." Nobody had seen Albert play in England since he had left for the States, except with the Everly Brothers, and the fans were queuing down the street. Not only that, Willie Nelson was top of the bill at Wembley, and he and his band dropped by the Pegasus and got up and sang with the Heroes, who still talk of that gig in deeply nostalgic tones. "It was an unbelievable night," says Pete, "one of the great ones."

Just after the Newbury Festival, Albert had asked Gerry Hogan if there were any other gigs to make the trip from California more worthwhile. Early in 1987 Gerry had been asked to produce a Yugoslavian band in Zagreb but as his work at IBM precluded spending a month in the studio Brian Hodgson did it. The band then asked if the Heroes would go out with Albert for a week's tour after the Wembley Festival. It was an interesting time to be visiting the former Yugoslavia, a patchwork of conflicting nationalisms held together by Communist rule and Tito's charisma. Economic crisis and increasing centrifugal forces based on centuries-old ethnic tensions were beginning to threaten the break-up of the federal republic. Interesting or not, it was hardly an auspicious time for Albert to mention in a TV interview in Zagreb, Croatia's capital, that his wife, Karen, was half Serbian. "Her full name is Kovacevic. That kind of went down badly." The band was, however, well-received, and Gerry came up with an agent who booked some gigs in Denmark and Norway towards the end of the year, after Gerry's Pedal Steel Festival in November.

"The first tours were always messy," says Pete Baron, and the story of the first Scandinavian odyssey reveals just how chaotic they were. The band was due to fly from Copenhagen to a gig in Oslo but owing to a strike at Oslo airport had to travel by rail. "We'd played the night before till God knows what time but we made the nine o'clock train in the morning," says Gerry Hogan. "We had to change in Gothenburg, with all our equipment, got to Oslo at 7 o'clock and played at about 10."

The next day the band was booked for a gig in Jutland and the agent had organized a ferry crossing from Gothenburg to Fredrickshavn and a train to Aarhus, about two hours away. "First of all, there's no lift on the ferry," recalls Gerry, "so we had to lug our stuff up the gangway. There was nowhere to put it safely so we put our stuff in the cloakroom with everybody's coats, etc. The restaurant was closed that day so we ended up in the piano bar and had a few beers and some crisps." At Frederickshavn the train was about a mile away from the ferry terminal. Gerry describes loading all the gear on to a supermarket trolley and "racing with this thing along a cobbled street. My steel guitar is top-heavy and Mike's piano was six feet wide." Mike Bell remembers it as "pretty dangerous. We were the worse for wear—I'd been drinking and playing the piano on the boat." With half an hour to catch the train, everybody was running, including Albert, and the tour manager was offering helpful advice—"You've got to hurry." Pete Baron thought the fellow "a total doughnut. He'd spent a con-siderable amount of time on the

Albert at Wembley, April 1988 (courtesy Graham Barker).

train showing me pictures of his girl-friend in a porn magazine. We got to the station just in time to see the two rear lights of the train disappearing in the distance. The guy asked helplessly, 'What do we do now?'"

"This is your gig," said Gerry. "*You* tell us what we do."

"We're going to have wait here until the 7:30 train in the morning."

Gerry, a mild-mannered individual but with a low threshold for incompetence, backed the fellow into a corner. "You must be joking. This is the middle of November. You've got to find us a hotel."

"Oh, no. I can't."

"I'm telling you," he said, his face a few inches away from the manager's. "This is Albert Lee here. It's not some tin-pot local guitar player and you will find us a hotel."

The man saw sense. He rang his boss and checked the band into a guest house. Over the two weeks, Pete Baron suspects "they made money and we didn't, or if we did, they made a lot more than us, which was not an unusual story."

In spite of dramas like these, at the end of it all, at Heathrow, Albert said to Gerry, "I really enjoyed that. Can we do it again?" Gerry took a straw poll. "Everybody else was keen so Brian and I started to work on dates for the following year."

In the spring Albert had spent a busy seven weeks among the blue-rinses and Bermuda shorts in Florida, doing three corporate shows a week for IBM in Fort Lauderdale and working five days a week in the studio, recording the Everlys third post-reunion album.[3]

Some Hearts received mixed reviews. While some critics found it disappointing and overproduced, others thought it an excellent album, with tracks exploring the pain of love. The brothers supplied seven of the ten songs, with Phil having a significant input. His song "Brown Eyes," about his second wife, is the outstanding track, too short, however, to make it a viable single. Albert and the band found it difficult to recreate the magic of Phil's demos in the studio, and "he wasn't happy about how we did them."

When Don writes he has a clear idea of what he wants. "I write from the first four bars.... There's always a rhythm guitar thing. That's always been my style and guess it always will be."[4] This is evident in the title track in which the brothers' harmonies are interwoven with Albert's acoustic guitar solo. On the rest of the songs, the Gibson is swapped for the synthesizer, which suggests Phil's influence: "I believe in high tech. I've always liked synthesizers. High tech is like the echo we used in the fifties. That was all we'd had available then."[5]

Some Hearts was produced jointly by Don and Phil, for reasons which Phil explained: "We wanted to set our own pace. Besides, most of the songs are our own and more personal so we didn't need to hear an outsider's interpretation."[6]

Bassist Phil Cranham's view is that while *Some Hearts* had some good songs, "they tried to do too much and some of the tracks lost their way a bit, straying too far from the original demos." For that reason, the album had been a struggle to complete, and in the end drummer Larrie Londin is credited as associate producer, "which is something he really didn't want to do," Albert explains. "It really was like pulling teeth. They didn't record for a while after that."

In any event, the project lost focus. Mercury did not see any of the brothers' songs as commercial and tried to push the only recognizable track, Brian Wilson's "Don't Worry, Baby." "This led to a falling out between the Everlys and the record company and to the extent that promotion of the album was minimal."[7] Don now acknowledges his own self-indulgence: "I had written things and I didn't think about the commerciality of it. I didn't think of anything but just this vision I had in my head." Phil was less analytical: "I never think about it.... Once I've cut something I just move on." So did Mercury, which dropped the Everlys the following year and since 1988 there have been no new albums from Don and Phil.

For the summer tour, Buddy Emmons had been drafted for the road-weary Hank De Vito. For Don, the addition of Emmons gave the concerts more of a country flavor because "the voices and the steel guitar go so well together. When Buddy came aboard he said, 'What should I do?' and I said, 'Fill holes.'" Of course, the king of pedal steel did so much more. Don loved the acoustic country blues medley with Albert accompanying the brothers on mandolin: "I'd like to do a show where we do an hour or so unplugged with Buddy and Albert ... and let everyone hear the voices and the lyrics."[8]

Just after the 1988 tour was over, Don happened to be listening to a TV news report about the fire department in Central City, Kentucky, and their need for a two-way radio system. Don immediately called Phil and the two donated $7500 to the cause. The citizens of Central City wanted to express their appreciation and a committee made up of several businessmen met Phil, his road manager and sound man and the idea of a concert took shape.

Thus, on August 25, 1988, approximately 10,000 fans gathered to hear the songs which made the Everlys great. Over the next fourteen years, the Everlys played what became known as the "Homecoming" gig in Central City on Labor Day weekend, and Don and Phil set up the Everly Brothers Foundation, endowing a music scholarship for local musicians. The annual gig was a fund-raising event to support that cause and "anyone who has heard the Everly Brothers sing 'Kentucky' knows the emotion they convey in the song of their home state."[9]

Although the family moved to Chicago soon after Don was born, Don and Phil are plainly Kentuckians by birthright. Their great-great-great grandfather settled there, probably from Ireland or Scotland, and became a substantial landowner, although their musical roots lay in the poverty of the coal-mining families in which their grandfather, a left-handed fiddler, was raised. The concerts featured a number of Kentucky-born or related artists such as John Prine, the Kentucky Headhunters, Thom Bresh, the son of Merle Travis, and special guests like Duane Eddy and Sonny Curtis.

Albert, Phil Cranham and Pete Wingfield were of course part of the Labor Day celebrations in the Everlys' backyard, and a few weeks later Don returned the compliment. After the finish of an Everlys U.K. tour, he stayed in England for a couple of days and sat in with Albert and Buddy on a couple of London gigs with Hogan's Heroes, at the Borderline and New Pegasus. "They were fantastic gigs," recalls Gerry Hogan. "Two of my best nights ever." Buddy Emmons stayed on for Gerry's Steel Guitar Festival, which also featured Dewitt Scott, who organized the huge annual steel festival in St. Louis. Albert reckons Scott "kind of invited himself as he knew Buddy—and poor Gerry had to foot the bill!"

Following the Heroes' Baltic saga, Albert had a busy Christmas. Apart from Gary Brooker's Christmas bash in Chiddingfold, there were Heroes gigs at the Two Worlds Pub, Plumstead and Ronnie Scott's in Soho. That year, the Heroes had played with Willie Nelson, Don Everly and Buddy Emmons, but the real highlight, just before 1989 hove into sight,

Albert and Buddy Emmons at Newbury in 1988 (courtesy Graham Barker).

was when Lonnie Donegan guested with the band at the Tramshed in Woolwich. That same day Albert had recorded "Try Me," "Function to Function" and "Hold On" in a session with Chris Farlowe, produced by Tim Hinkley.[10]

Albert ran across his old comrade again at the Borderline Club in Manette Street, Soho, in early February when Farlowe turned up at a gig with Biff Baby's All Stars. An ad hoc assemblage of L.A. players, the All-Stars kept the same line-up for nearly 20 years—Albert and Sterling Ball, his brother Sherwood, Jim Cox on keyboards and John Ferraro on drums. That night, Wayne Lee recorded the whole gig. "It was unreal. Farlowe sang and I did a couple of numbers with Biff Baby's All Stars."

Hogan's Heroes (left to right, Brian Hodgson, Roger Rettig, Pete Baron, Albert Lee, Gerry Hogan) at Kensington in October 1988 (courtesy Graham Barker).

It had been an unusual winter for Albert in that he had spent much of it in Britain but he was back in Nashville in March playing lead guitar and mandolin, with backing vocals from Vince Gill and Rodney Crowell, on Patti Loveless's third album, *Honky Tonk Angel*,[11] one of the more impressive female country albums of the late 1980s. The wife of Albert's old Hot Band mate Emory Gordy, Loveless combined a shy, Kentucky innocence with a powerful tenor and the album was a commercial success. "Timber, I'm Falling in Love," a catchy, upbeat song, made #1 in the Billboard country charts, and "Chains" and "Blue Side Of Town" were also hits. "That album changed her career," said producer Tony Brown, "and a lot of it was built around having Albert on the sessions. I thought 'Who would make her sound different from Reba McEntire or whoever?' So I brought in Albert and Leland Sklar, a mixture of Nashville and Los Angeles musicians."

More or less at the same time Albert contributed to three tracks on Dolly Parton's *White Limozeen* album,[12] notably on the hit "Why'd You Come in Here Lookin' Like That?" After a period when she had been accused of selling out to mainstream pop, Dolly appeased traditionalists with a genuine country album, produced by Ricky Skaggs. Albert also appeared on three tracks on Skaggs' own *Kentucky Thunder*,[13] his best since *Don't Cheat in Our Home Town* in 1983, which also featured Albert. Skaggs wanted Albert to join his band but he felt that it would be a sideways move, talented as Skaggs was. In a significant aside which sums up his career, revealing his sense of loyalty and his acknowledgment of a lost opportunity,

Albert adds, "At the time, I was with Eric—but I did waste my time in not putting my own thing together."

Skaggs, whose bluegrass, honky tonk, and pop sound stood at the heart of country music in the early to mid–1980s, clearly admired Albert's work, as did Andrew Hardin, singer-songwriter Tom Russell's fire-breathing guitar slinger for more than 20 years. Hardin first met Albert in the summer of 1989 in Toronto, where Russell was producing Sylvia Tyson's *You Were on My Mind* album[14] and recalls Albert "naturally playing lead on most things, but 'Truckers Café' was a remake of the original by the Great Speckled Bird, Ian and Sylvia Tyson's old band. The new version had me and Albert dueling. I got smoked, of course. It was one of the most exciting experiences of my life." Three years later, Tyson's *Gypsy Cadillac*[15] featured Albert (also on mandolin and piano). Sylvia Tyson herself adds, "Albert remains one of my favorite people, a lovely man, and a wonderful player. Unlike a lot of guitar greats, he's also very supportive: Whatever he plays is totally distinctive, but totally appropriate and integral to the arrangement." And in 1995, Hardin asked Albert to play on his first solo CD, *Coney Island Moon*.[16] "We recorded Albert's tracks at Mad Dog studio in Burbank: he appears on 'Burnt Siena,' a fast Danny Gatton-ish track, and 'Big Rig Country,' a Bakersfield-style guitar trade-off."

Albert, sought after by players like Skaggs and Hardin, by the early 1990s had become

Albert at the Borderline, circa 1988 (courtesy Graham Barker).

the doyen of session guitarists in country music. "He's put on a pedestal by most young guitar players," said Tony Brown—players such as Brad Paisley, a West Virginian guitarist and singer and one of the most respected of the new breed of country performers. "Albert and I have become real close friends and anytime I'm in L.A. he'll sit in for the whole show! It's fun ... the audience think he's some new band member. They don't realize Albert's the reason we all play Teles!" Tony Colton, speaking in the ASCAP building in Nashville, thought "the best guitar players in the world are in this town. In the 40-odd sessions going on this morning you can go six or ten deep before you find a bad player and 99 percent of them are trying to be Albert Lee—including the ones at the top of their game. He influenced a whole style of playing."

Apart from the studio commitments in Toronto, Albert was back on the road again that summer with the Everlys and as was becoming customary, one of the children would join him. In a postcard from Southeastern Pennsylvania in mid–July, Albert mentions he would be busy till the end of October and that "Cass will be with me in a day or two. I'm looking forward to it." Cassandra, nearly 17, spent three weeks with the Everlys and her father. While she enjoyed the musical side of the tour, "she felt uncomfortable," Albert recalls with regret, "as I hadn't really got a relationship with her. In the end I sent her home. I felt bad about doing it but if she wasn't happy." Against that backdrop, a rather plaintive note from Cassandra appeared in *Superpicker* that November: "Dear Bill, Thank you very much for sending us the magazines. They contain so much information about what Dad has done and is doing that we don't get to hear about. It's pretty strange having a magazine all about my father." It was also pretty poignant that she couldn't hear it from the man himself.

In late July, Nanci Griffith's album *Storms*[17] was released, with contributions from Albert, who sang harmonies on two songs, "If Wishes Were Changes" and "Listen To The Radio," Pat Donaldson, Jerry Donahue, Bernie Leadon and Phil Everly. Disappointed by the lack of commercial success, with her appeal falling between the rock and country audiences, Griffith had moved from Nashville to MCA's pop music division in Los Angeles to work with the eminent producer Glyn Johns, who aimed the album at American radio. *Storms* was a sonic landmark in Griffith's career and in a somewhat hyperbolic review, Lindsay Planer notes that her "crystalline-toned resonance weaves almost hypnotically through her realistic and acoustic-based neo-folk Americana."[18] Despite, or perhaps because of, reviews like that, the album failed to attract country audiences. Nevertheless, it became her best-seller, reaching the album charts in the U.K. and Ireland, where she had regularly toured.

In mid–August Albert played the Everlys' Homecoming Festival, where he met up with Duane Eddy once again, along with John Prine, New Grass Revival and Sonny Curtis. At the end of the month he had an unbelievably hectic week. On August 31 he drove the Ferrari up the California Route 14 to Lancaster, 70 miles from Calabasas, for another Everlys gig. The following day he drove 170 miles up the coast to San Luis Obispo to play a "great gig" with Biff Baby's All-stars in a small bar, and a couple of days later, closer to home at the Long Horn Saloon in Canoga Park in the San Fernando Valley, he did four hours on a hot and sticky night with the Doo Wah Riders, whose style is high energy country with a Cajun twist. The Riders, based in Studio City, California, have been riding their own patch of the musical range for the last 20 years and are still playing county fairs, rodeos, bars and honky-tonks throughout the West.

On September 7 he did some overdubs with Brian Ahern for Rick Densmore, a singer-songwriter from L.A. who had moved back to California from Texas in the mid–'80s after performing with Lucinda Williams, Townes Van Zandt and Willie Nelson, and the next day Albert left for Australia with the Everlys to do a Legends of Rock package show.

The two-week tour, which starred Jerry Lee Lewis, Bo Diddley, Chuck Berry, Lesley Gore and Mary Wilson, was "a bit of a zoo," Albert recalls. "Chuck stole the show each night, although the music was terrible. At the first gig he simply got his guitar out of the case and started playing a quarter of a tone out. He'd never rehearse and would walk on stage expecting the band to know the tunes. The Everlys for some reason didn't go down too well. We got polite applause but not much compared to the rapturous yelling Chuck was getting." The tour package was "fundamentally wrong for the Everlys. Theirs is not a raucous nostalgia act but a blend of musical styles."[19] Albert had time for a couple of days R&R in Monte Nido before leaving for Las Vegas.

The three-week date at the Desert Inn with the Everlys was not Albert's favorite gig—"three days is long enough to be in Vegas!" And to cap it all, he had driven there in the Triumph, which broke down when the radiator blew. On the last date of the gig Albert used his 1953 Telecaster, a rare outing for his much-loved guitar. He also used a mandolin which Keith Nelson had found him up in Carmel, a Gibson F4 dated 1913. It was a rare time altogether for Albert, for, with the Everlys at a TV tribute to Tennessee Ernie Ford at the

Roy Rogers with Albert at the Tennessee Ernie Ford tribute concert in November 1989 (courtesy the Lee family).

A chip off the old block: Albert and Wayne with Hogan's Heroes bassist Brian Hodgson (courtesy the Lee family).

end of October, he could be sighted in a tuxedo. He took as his guest John Bryant, Jimmy's son. Bryant and Speedy West had played together on many of Tennessee Ernie's great Capitol recordings of the early '50s.

At the end of the '80s and early '90s, Albert's working life had acquired some sort of annual pattern, dovetailing tours with the Everlys and dates with Hogan's Heroes while being much in demand as a session man. When he flew into Heathrow in early November it was against the background of a Europe in cataclysmic change. On November 7 MTV beamed live into East Berlin, two days before the Wall came down, and on the 11 Joe Cocker performed a free acoustic show at the Wall. For the first time, Albert decided to use the Ernie Ball/Music Man Axis prototype on the Heroes tour, though he felt it was "not too easy to handle." After dates in Ireland and a tiring trip to Inverness, with flights delayed by fog, there was a lively gig at the Borderline, where son Wayne sang "Johnny B. Goode" and "Bony Moronie" and special guest Gary Brooker did "You Win Again," "Hit The Road, Jack" and "Little Queenie."

Following a gig in Strasbourg the autumn then took on its familiar shape with gigs all over Britain, except that Albert dropped "So Sad" and did Phil's "Brown Eyes" at the piano. Albert's old mate from Thunderbird days, Ricky Charman, appeared at Corby, and Keith Nelson sat in and did "Foggy Mountain Breakdown" at the Royal Standard in Walthamstow. The highlight was again two nights at the Tramshed in Woolwich, where following the appearance of one British legend Lonnie Donegan the year before, another turned up, this time local boy Marty Wilde, who did a couple of Elvis numbers—"Little Sister" and "Baby, Let's Play House." On the previous night, Malcolm Hutton, who had admired Albert's playing at the Melody Café in Lee Green nearly three decades before, bumped into Albert's Dad in the restroom. "He'd had a few beers," recalls Malcolm. "Bursting with pride he said, 'That's my boy, Albert! Fuck Eric Clapton!'

Albert at the Tramshed, Woolwich, in December 1989 (courtesy Graham Barker).

Above—Hogan's Heroes with Marty Wilde at the Tramshed, Woolwich, in December 1989. *Right*—Albert at the Tramshed, Woolwich, in December 1989 (courtesy Graham Barker).

It cracked me up. He was really pleased that his boy had come back to play in the area where he was born."

Albert flew back to Calabasas for Christmas for a session with Lonnie Donegan, cutting a song called "The Last Of The Eight-wheelers," written by Brian Hodgson, who also produced the album, before taking off on January 20 for a 7 to 10 day solo tour of Australia. The tour had been organized by Andrew Pattison as a double bill with a virtuoso Australian guitarist Tommy Emmanuel. "Albert found it a bit competitive," says Pattison. "He'd comment, 'I keep hearing my own licks being played back to me at twice their original speed!'" The tour was sponsored by the Australian guitar manufacturer Maton, which wanted to make an acoustic signature guitar for Albert. "I told them I had a deal with Music Man but they produced a prototype." Albert and Minnesotan country singer Joe Sun were the only overseas acts. Tommy and Albert also played a small club in Cairns where Albert enjoyed a short break, snorkeling on the Great Barrier Reef.

It was a brief respite, for within a week, he was playing Harrah's in Lake Tahoe with the Everlys, for whom Duane Eddy was opening. "It's working well," Albert wrote in a postcard to Blackheath. "It's a big jump from the tropics to the snow but it's nice not having to travel for a week. The big news is I will be touring with Linda Ronstadt this year. The Everlys don't appear to have much lined up so it's just as well. I will have a much higher visibility in her new band and the money will be better too."[20]

Twenty miles from Lake Tahoe is Reno, where along the banks of the Truckee River is the massive car collection of the late gaming pioneer and avid collector Bill Harrah. Opened after Harrah's death in 1978, the museum displays more than 200 cars from 1892 to the present. "We had a great trip there in 1990," says Phil Cranham. "A British guy was the curator and Albert, Karen and I blagged our way in. We were having a laugh and at the end of the tour the guy asked us, 'Do you want to have a drive of something then?'" Out came a '55 Thunderbird and the ultimate statement in power and style in the mid-'30s, a Mercedes 540K roadster, which used to lead all the parades across the Golden Gate Bridge. "It's a $2 million car at least," said Phil. "Albert took it round for a lap with Alex in the rumble seat."

By 1990 Talmadge Holt Farlow (always known as Tal), who made his name in the Red Norvo Trio and with Artie Shaw in the '50s with improvisations based not on scales but exclusively on chords and whose fast, bebop-influenced style and the occasional use of percussive finger-tapping had made him a jazz legend, had become a sign painter and something of a recluse. However, in April 1990 he was persuaded out of self-imposed retirement to join Albert and Dobro king Jerry Douglas on a tour sponsored by the U.S. State Department. The tour went well. "Tal was the jazz player," recalls Albert. "A big fan of Tal asked me 'Do you play

Albert at the Cunningham, New Addington, in December 1989 (courtesy Graham Barker).

jazz?' 'No, not really,' I said. Tal turned to him and said, 'Yeah, he plays jazz.' That was a great compliment coming from him." In a card from Columbus, Ohio, Albert reported selling lots of CDs and T-shirts and in the previous week seeing "an Amish town, a Klan rally, a pro-drug rally, sun, snow!"

All this must have seemed a world away to his parents at home in Blackheath, but Albert always kept in touch, and he would be seeing them soon, as he says in a card from Nashville on April 20: "A quick visit to Nashville for some great clubs. I'll be arriving in London on May 6." Many colleagues in the business have wondered why he never moved to Music City. In the same card he hints at a reason: "It's a nice place to visit. I don't know if I'm ready to move yet!" Yet much of his work was there, and as Tony Colton pointed out, "the town was made for him—on his own he changed the style of guitar-playing here." On the other hand, Karen was very much a Californian, he had a stylish home in Monte Nido and the work was not exactly drying up in L.A.

He was in Nashville for a number of sessions, the first with ex-pro footballer and singer/songwriter Mike Reid, playing on three tracks on his debut album.[21] Reid had studied classical piano and taken a music degree while playing college football and if it hadn't been a knee injury that took him out of the NFL's Cincinnati Bengals, hits like his own "Walk On Faith" and Bonnie Raitt's "I Can't Make You Love Me" would not have seen the light of day. Another debutante was Jann Browne, whose album *Tell Me Why*[22] would earn her a nomination as Female Vocalist of the Year by the Academy of Country Music. Produced by Steve Fishell for Curb, Albert played on "Ain't No Train" and "You Ain't Down Home," with Glen D. Hardin, James Burton, Emmylou, Wanda Jackson, Byron Berline, Iris DeMent, Rosie Flores and New Grass Revival. Browne's roots lay firmly in traditional country, and discovering she had little taste for the politics of the major-label music industry, she became disheartened, as many have, and moved back to California.

The curse of Carlene Carter's career is her heritage as part of country music's royal family—granddaughter of Mother Maybelle, daughter of June Carter and Carl Smith, stepdaughter of Johnny Cash and half-sister of Rosanne Cash. After three moderately successful albums, the weight of expectation was almost too great, and after her divorce from British rocker Nick Lowe in the '80s she descended into substance abuse, returning to the studio after seven years to record her comeback album, *If I Fell in Love*,[23] which attracted much critical attention and yielded two top-5 country hits. Produced by her old friend Howie Epstein (of Tom Petty's band, the Heartbreakers), it featured Albert, in company with other elite West Coast session musicians Benmont Tench, Jim Keltner and James Burton, with background singers Dave Edmunds, Kiki Dee and Levon Helm. Three years later, Albert joined Buddy Emmons and David Lindley on her *Little Love Letters*[24] album. Again produced by Howie Epstein, it was less constrained by traditional country and was an accessible mix of ballads and country-rockers, including the top-5 hit "Every Little Thing."

As promised, on May 6 Albert landed in London with Karen about midday for a tour with Hogan's Heroes. Jet-lagged and with no time for rehearsal or sound-check, Albert played a gig that night at the New Pegasus and then set off on the usual British dates, plus one with Chris Farlowe in Berne, Switzerland, and a TV show in Baden Baden, Germany, with the Blues Brothers Band, including Steve Cropper and Donald "Duck" Dunn. Mike Bell recalls the tours being "pretty grueling. Once, I remember doing a gig in East Berlin followed the next day by a trip across to Switzerland and then back to East Germany. Seven-hour journeys around Finland and Sweden were commonplace. There's a popular myth that being a touring musician is a glamorous life style. Far from it. You turn up at a club at four in the afternoon after you've been on the road all day long. It's a miserable place to be—you can't go to the hotel because you've got to set the gear up. One cold late afternoon waiting for a sound check in a deserted and dingy club, a little voice from the corner—it was Sonny Curtis—was heard to say: 'Whatever happened to the romantic view of the gig?'"

However sordid and cheerless the venues were in the cold light of day, the British tour was doing good business. In Newcastle-under-Lyne, the Heroes played in Bridge Street Live, a funky cellar with about 250 people crammed in a venue only big enough for 100. At the Weavers Arms in Newington Green Road, Islington, Chris Farlowe and Bugs Waddell were special guests, and Keith Nelson played banjo on three numbers.

There were TV dates, too. The Heroes filmed a slot on Jools Holland's *The Happening*[25] for BSkyB at the Astoria, Charing Cross Road. Albert thought the show "a bit of a shambles—jugglers, some guy playing bagpipes, a female whistler plus Craig Charles, an awful obscene Liverpool comedian. Neil Innes was rubbish, unusually, but the girl singer, Kym Mazelle, wasn't too bad. We went down well though." Another TV show, in a series of six for Frontier Films to be called *Town and Country*, was recorded at Limehouse Studios, Wembley. Rodney Crowell and the Dixie Pearls was the headline act, John Prine was master of ceremonies and accompanied Albert and the Heroes on "Be My Friend Tonight." Albert was suffering from a heavy cold, but "we got on with it—if Don Everly got a sniffle

Romany roots: Albert in Ireland, June 1990 (courtesy the Lee family).

we'd cancel the gig and disappoint 2,000 people." Albert's cold had improved by the time they got to Ireland in early June, a trip which included a visit to the castle owned by the parents of Phil Donnelly's girlfriend. Out on the estate Karen took the classic picture of Albert sitting on the steps of a gypsy caravan.

That photograph encapsulates Albert's Romany heritage, of which his children are very proud. "Dad gave us all a photo album of our grandparents, great-grandparents and my great-great-grand-dad at a fair," says Wayne. "He was trying to make sure that we were all fully aware of our heritage." When Wayne was very young he would hear Uncle Tommy, his great-grand-dad's brother, talking Romany, "and it was 'Wow! They're from another country!' Dad wasn't embarrassed about it but Grand-dad wouldn't often use the language in front of anybody else, in case they couldn't understand him—it would have been impolite. Being a traveling musician is obviously in Dad's blood." Perhaps, but that summer, on the Everlys tour he wrote from Royal Oak, Michigan, "This tour seems to be harder than before, lots of overnight runs. I don't sleep very well on moving buses. We'd arrive sometimes at the hotel at six or seven in the morning: I'd grab a bit of breakfast if the kitchen was open and then crash out for a couple of hours."

That summer saw the Everlys caravan roll from Atlantic City, where Albert watched England scrape past Cameroon to reach the semi-finals of the soccer World Cup in Italy, to the City of Industry, California, the Homecoming gig in Central City, Kentucky, to come to rest in New Orleans.

Karen was finding it increasingly difficult with a young child to join Albert on the road but on November 8, 1990, she and Albert arrived in London for a short Hogan's Heroes tour. "We wanted to bring Alex but it would be hard work at the gigs"—especially in sweaty, smoky London pubs like the Half Moon Pub in Herne Hill when the Heroes were joined by Hayden Thompson, one of the original rockabilly singers who recorded for Sam Phillips' Sun Records label in the mid–'50s. Equally difficult might have been Woolwich's noisy Tramshed just before Clapton started his stint at the Royal Albert Hall. Taking the stage, Albert quipped: "Eric gets to play 24 days at the Albert Hall and I get to play one day at the Tramshed!" Rough justice, especially when the venue is named for you.

Side Two

He spoke with *Musician* magazine (May 1991) about his touring life.

"I thought about it a lot. I've been on the road since 1960 and a lot of my friends became millionaires, guys that I just played with, like Jimmy Page and Eric Clapton and Steve Howe. But I have no regrets, really, because if I haven't made any money in this business, I have nobody to blame but myself. I have the ability but chose not to go in that direction. That has held me back, but I've enjoyed it. I think my playing is getting better and I seem to be working more, so I can't complain. If it just carries on like this, I'll be happy."

For a while it *did* carry on like this until June, at the end of an Everlys tour in Canada, when Albert decided to cease working with Don and Phil. "I don't know why. Maybe I got a bit fed up." Perhaps that feeling of a lack of self-fulfillment had led him to pursue other musical ambitions. The session work was flooding in and over the next year there was the prospect of more work on the road and in the studio with Rodney Crowell. For a while Ray

Flacke replaced him, and in July Albert found himself in Nashville with Karen, doing over-dubs for Grammy-nominated[26] bass guitarist Steve Wariner's next album[27] and rehearsing with Crowell for a short tour, along with Larry Byrom (guitar), Jim Horn (sax), John Leventhal (guitar and keyboards), Michael Rhodes (bass) and Eddie Bayers (drums). Albert revealed in a card from Nashville: "We went to Don's house tonight. I'm glad we spent some time with him; apparently he's been unhappy since I gave him my notice. I have to make a decision on the European tour with Hogan's Heroes set for Sept-Nov"—a no-brainer, as Mike Bell asserts: "We all used to say, 'You have to remember that Albert's a gypsy'—what they meant was he doesn't want to settle down. He wants to do gigs." And Albert was beginning to do a few with Rodney.

The pair played a show in Kansas City with K.T. Oslin, who in 1987 had become the first female songwriter to win the Country Music Association's Song of the Year award, and then in Chicago, with Carlene Carter, one of the neighborhood festivals the city holds each summer. Also appearing were the Sun rhythm section—D.J. Fontana (Elvis's drummer), and Paul Burlison, the guitarist with the Johnny Burnette Rock 'n' Roll Trio, one of Albert's early influences.

At the end of July the final program in *Bringing It All Back Home*[28] was broadcast on BBC2. It featured a lyrically ethereal Albert with Davy Spillane on the haunting "Equinox," recorded at Cowboy Jack Clement's Studios in Nashville in February 1990. On the same show The Everlys[29] performed "Don't Let Our Love Die" with piper Liam O'Flynn, Nashville fiddle virtuoso Mark O'Connor and acoustic bassist Roy Huskey Jr.

Having decided on his trial separation from Don and Phil, Albert was able to look forward to spending most of August at home—a relative concept, however, for Albert. On the tenth he and James Burton played a tribute show for Leo Fender in Anaheim and a few days later worked on recording with Biff Baby's All Stars. Vintage cars are one of Albert's passions and at Laguna Seca each year "there's a tribute to a driver or a marquee. In 1990 [Formula One racing driver Juan Manuel] Fangio was there and I'll never forget the huge smile on his face as he drove round in a Lancia Ferrari. I got to sign some pictures of him in W196, the streamline one, with all the dents in the front."

One of the new creative consequences arising from Albert's departure from the Everlys' stable was the chance to work more with Rodney Crowell. In mid–September Albert returned to Nashville for a rape crisis show with Lari White which raised £15,000 and to do overdubs for Crowell's new album, *Life Is Messy*. He also played a show with Crowell in Philadelphia, with Asleep at the Wheel, the Forester Sisters and Carlene Carter.

The other openings arose from the constant demands for Albert to appear on sessions in Los Angeles as well as in Music City. Michelle Shocked's *Arkansas Traveler*[30] features an amazing array of guest musicians including Pops Staples, Doc Watson and Gatemouth Brown. "It was a tribute," she says, "to the fiddle tunes I'd played with my dad and brother in East Texas. I wanted to pursue the hidden roots of that music." Albert joined Levon Helm, Garth Hudson, Tony Levin, Jerry Marotta and co-producer Bernie Leadon on "Secret to a Long Life." Katy Moffatt was another Texan roots singer whose 1990 album, *Child Bride*, had attracted attention. She toured during the '70s with Leo Kottke, Jerry Jeff Walker, J.D. Souther and the Allman Brothers and worked with Willie Nelson, John Prine, Tom Russell and Rosie Flores. At the end of September, together with her brother, Hugh, Katy recorded "Dance Me Outside,"[31] a cut above the average Nashville factory output. Buddy Emmons contributed some tasteful steel and Dobro and Albert played acoustic guitar on "Dark End of the Street" and "Right Over Me," on which the superlative interplay between Albert and Buddy underscores the somber nature of the song.

Albert stayed in Nashville for the CMA Awards Show, which he opened with Bill Monroe, Earl Scruggs, Vince Gill and others as well as playing "Restless" with Mark O'Connor's New Nashville Cats. Three days later he flew to London for an autumn tour with the Heroes. The band were still getting gigs but "once he was here we had to keep working," Pete Baron points out. "An agent got involved in '91–'92, a guy called Martin Looby from Rotherham, and he introduced us to some connections in Germany when we didn't have any decent ones—but we were still playing dodgy gigs for dodgy pay. Martin's heart was in the right place but he got in financial trouble and it still wasn't as well organized as it could have been."

After three days' rehearsal in a club in Willesden the Heroes left for Switzerland at the start of a 53-date tour. New numbers in the set were "Your Boys," "Now and Then It's Gonna Rain," "Hey Doll Baby," "Brand New Heartache," "Only with You," "Highwayman" and "Restless." The itinerary encompassed those parts of the U.K. which other tours tended not to reach, in venues big and small. The band had fun at the Cavern in Liverpool, despite not getting on till nearly midnight. The volume was ultraloud for such a small club and a ridiculous smoke machine set off a fire alarm. Just across the Mersey the band played the Floral Hall in New Brighton, a gig reviewed by a local paper:[32] "Albert Lee cuts a curious figure on stage—Marc Bolan haircut, long purple shirt, drainpipe jeans and cowboy boots. It's his red and white guitar that attracts the spotlight. It stays absolutely motionless through Lee's mesmerizingly fast solos…. I just wish someone could have found the nerve to dance on the seats. Next year perhaps?" At the Stoker in Coventry there were frequent power cuts as the city commemorated the fiftieth anniversary of the Blitz, prompting Albert to remark, "I thought the Germans were coming over again!"

A regular gig at the King's Hotel in Newport was the subject of a piece by Paul Lewis in *Country Music People*:[33] "Albert was ever the musician's musician…. Swapping places with regular piano man Mike Bell halfway through the show Albert then pounded out a furious version of 'Real Wild Child' which perversely (for such a guitar-slanted event) damned near stole the show. Nothing, however, could ever quite topple the majestic 'Country Boy' at an Albert Lee concert, and indeed this bravura showpiece was included in its usual end-of-set position. Lee's playing is at times, unbelievably nimble, but it's always involving, emotive and supremely tasteful." Then a diverting European tour through Ireland, France, Germany, Switzerland and Holland was climaxed by a night at the Rolls Royce Social Club in the Starlight Rooms in Crewe, leaving Albert time to make it back to Calabasas for a quiet Christmas—and a riotous New Year's Eve when Biff Baby's All-Stars, with Steve Lukather and Jay Graydon, played a wild, loud night at the Trancas Bar in Malibu.

Between January and May 1992, Albert worked with Rodney Crowell on Lari White's debut album, *Lead Me Not*,[34] with Bill Payne, Eddie Bayers, Jerry Douglas, and Jim Horn. None of the album's three singles broke the Top 40, as it fell between country and cabaret. The album certainly had an eclectic range, from an uptempo country/rocker, "Where the Lights are Low," to a torch ballad, "Just Thinking," and from Latin-flavored pop, "Made to

Be Broken," where Albert gets some lovely string sounds from the Korg keyboard, to fervent gospel, "Good Good Love." In February Bo Windberg of the Spotnicks was in L.A. to cut a new album[35] for a Swedish label and Albert, now an honorary Spotnick, did a couple of overdubs. He also did some overdubs for Mike Reid's next album and worked on an instructional video[36] with DCI, a Nashville-based company, which had begun educational video programming in 1980 under the direction of Gil Gilliam.

There were reminders of his past that spring when Ronnie Bell[37] visited him in Calabasas and archivist Roger Dopson reported in *Superpicker* that the BlackClaw/Country Fever album was selling very well. It had taken only three months to reach break-even and was now showing a profit. Another visitor to Calabasas was Bert Jansch, who recorded "Heartbreak Hotel" and "If I Were a Carpenter" in Albert's front room, a logistical challenge, as every inch of floor space was taken up with two huge sofas, a Bluther grand piano, guitars, amps, box files and books. These songs, along with an interview, were broadcast on April 2, 1993, on BBC Radio 2 as part of the program *Acoustic Routes*. Albert also spent a lot of time working on his vintage Ferrari, the 1980 Triumph TR8 or the 1963 Fleetwood Cadillac, a present from Sterling Ball. "I like working on cars, but it's not good for my hands. If I change the oil I make sure that I'm not working for a couple of days in case I get a little bit of oil on my hands. With using the stuff to get the oil off, you take all the natural oils off your hands and they don't feel right." Albert had also just been given a NADY wireless stage unit. "I used it once: the guys at Audio Technica are big fans and it would be nice to have an updated one."

He had been estranged from the Everlys for eight months. Actually, Albert points out, "It was only for one tour when they did a few gigs opening for the Beach Boys. The truth was that I missed doing it and they missed having me." In March Albert's innate pragmatism surfaced and he was back with Don and Phil, at Bally's Grand in Las Vegas, and went on to do more gigs in Chicago and Cleveland in mid–May.

Hogan's Heroes had been a working band for nearly five years but had never yet committed any of the repertoire to disc. As Mike Bell complained, "I was with them 12 years and in all that time we made one album—and that was a live one over which we had little control." What became *In Full Flight—Live at Montreux*[38] was never in fact intended to be a live album. In 1990 the band had done a gig in Schaffhausen, Switzerland, when one Jimmy Duncombe approached Pete Baron. "He asked me to play in his band. In the end I was commuting to Switzerland every weekend and eventually he got the Heroes gigs in Zurich and Basel and then in June 1992 the Montreux Jazz Festival."

Duncombe, in a shrewd finesse worthy of a consummate bridge player, secured for the Heroes the rights to the video and the live recordings, whereupon Martin Looby, through his connections in Germany, found a fellow—Günter Kuch—with a recording studio in Stuttgart. "When we dropped in," says Mike Bell, "we found they were keen for us to do a studio album. We left it to Albert. 'Well, yeah, mmmm, yeah.' He wouldn't actively say 'No' to anything but he wouldn't do anything about it. He used to say, 'I haven't got time to go into a studio for three weeks—I'm working.' That got to me because it's hard to come by success in the music industry. When any other band would have given their right arm to be in that situation it was frustrating to go into that record company knowing jolly well he wasn't going to do an album. There was so much he could have done. He was too busy earning a living to make a fortune."

There were also differences in the band's musical direction. Bell saw Albert as more than a country musician. "He's just a wonderful player. We used to kick off with Little Feat's 'Let it Roll,' which was hair-raising. Pete and I wanted to do more of that and some Don Henley stuff and Albert was interested. We were ambitious and felt that Albert could have been the next Eric Clapton but he didn't do anything about it. The conservative elements were Gerry and Brian—Gerry didn't like it and Brian was frightened of it. He's a very good bass player but he's a bit uncomfortable outside the box—no bad thing as there were enough flair players in the band. In soccer terms he was an old-fashioned center-half who held it all together at the back. It was a great privilege to play with Albert but musically it got stale and it got loud."

The Montreux album represents the Heroes' first incarnation at their peak, opening with "Sweet Little Lisa," and including "Cannonball," featuring some high-class jazz from Mike Bell, "The Highwayman," Albert's homage to Jimmy Webb, and the first commercial live version of "Country Boy."

On returning to England, Albert had a pleasant day in leafy Banstead, recording for Deep Elm Records with Jerry Lee's sister, Linda Gail Lewis. Then, on July 7, he became part of the sequel to possibly the greatest-ever rock film when he appeared in *The Return of Spinal Tap*,[39] a video centered on Tap's performance at the Royal Albert Hall. Albert, who found the Pythonesque nature of the surreal parody intensely funny, played lead guitar on "Break Like the Wind." He is very proud of his involvement in the project and recalls with amusement that Nigel Tufnel (Christopher Guest) used a left-handed Music Man guitar.

Four days later a memorable tour ended for the Heroes in Koblenz, and Albert flew back for a 30-date Everlys tour in Canada and 18 states, ending at the Central City Homecoming. During the tour, Albert was in Wheeling, West Virginia, when he heard that Larry Londin, widely regarded as the greatest drummer in country music, had passed away at the age of 48. He had been in a Dallas hospital with a heart complaint, his diabetic ID was removed and when doctors unwittingly gave him an injection of blood thinning agent he lapsed into a deep coma. Larry had worked with Albert on his Polydor album and in a note in *Superpicker*, Albert remembered "his demeanor, enthusiasm and love.... I feel very fortunate to have spent eight years with him on the road with the Everly Bros. He is irreplaceable and I'll miss him." He looked forward to getting back to Calabasas: "Just a week or so then I'm home for a few days."

En route home through Maryland, Kentucky and Illinois, Albert played in a second rape crisis show in Nashville and after five days at the Las Vegas Hilton with the Everlys, he was home at last. Just to relax, as he did every weekend when he was free, Albert played at the Agoura Valley Inn, a few miles west along the Ventura Freeway, with Ron Coleman,[40] John Hobbs on piano, and occasionally J. D. Maness, and on October 25, he did a charity show with Rodney Crowell and Biff Baby's All-Stars in San Luis Obispo at $125 a ticket.

Albert enjoys working with younger players like Steve Morse, Steve Lukather and Brent Mason and in November he did an overdub with Frank Zappa's son Dweezil, who claimed to have been "getting into a lot of southern influences, listening to Albert Lee and Steve Morse." He had been working for a year on a half-hour guitar piece featuring many players from different styles. Albert's solo lasts a minute "and I don't know if it was ever released. Dweezil's become a really fine guitar player himself." In the new year Dweezil and Steve Lukather guested with Albert and Biff Baby's All-Stars at the Palomino.

As much as Albert is now respected by younger players he still feels very fortunate to have played with so many of his own heroes. He had just arrived back in England in early December when Phil Cranham called. Duane Eddy was playing Wembley the next night in a rock 'n' roll package with Jerry Lee, Little Richard, Bobby Vee, Lloyd Price, Little Eva, Chris Montez and Johnny Preston. Albert rang Duane, who said, "Yeah, come on down and bring your guitar!" It was a memorable gig. Albert had just finished his set with Duane Eddy when in the warren of dressing rooms backstage Jerry Lee's roadie came up to him. "Albert! Come and say hallo to Jerry Lee." Albert was always somewhat nervous being around him— Lewis's volatile nature is well-known in the business—"but it was great just to say 'Hallo' to him." Then his manager took Albert aside. "The guys have been drinking all afternoon. I'd really appreciate it if you would play with Jerry." It was a golden opportunity. "I did the whole set and they let me do some solos. Came the encore and Little Richard walked on. So there I was playing behind Jerry Lee and Little Richard." The skiffle boy from Blackheath never dreamed he would ever be playing with them.

Peter Baron has indicated that the Heroes' itineraries in the early years seemed thrown together and gigs booked by someone with either a warped sense of humor or only a sketchy knowledge of basic geography. That December, gigs in Ireland were being cancelled or switched at the last minute. Normally, Albert enjoyed the Guinness and the fun but the effort wasn't really worth the trouble. "It was horrible. They had just changed the licensing laws so you could drink much later and we'd play to a bunch of drunks who were just there for the late drinking. Ireland has changed a lot. Now we get on stage at 8 or 9 and they've come for the music." After a couple of nights at Gary Brooker's Christmas bash, where Wayne and Bill Wyman guested, Albert left for home the next day.

Over the Christmas he worked on the house and tinkered with the Ferrari but by the first week of 1993 he was back in the studio, first with Swiss viticulturist and blues aficionado Paul MacBonvin and then with Canadian singer-songwriter Charlie Major, recording *The Other Side*.[41] Major wrote about working-class life in songs reminiscent of Bruce Springsteen's blue-collar anthems, and his debut album, produced by Steve Fishell, was the Canadian Country Music Association's 1994 Album of the Year and produced the Single of the Year in "I'm Gonna Drive You Out of My Mind."

In the following week Albert drove his Ferrari from L.A. to Las Vegas for a gig at the Hilton with the Everlys, epitomizing the quintessence of the rock 'n' roll lifestyle and highlighting how far the quiet lad from south London had come. Despite his misgivings about the city, the gigs were going well: He describes them in a postcard to his parents as "easy work. We may do this twice a year." He also reveals that "Sterling is going to put out my guitar with my name on it at last. I'm happy about that."

The week before, at NAMM, the annual convention of the National Association of Music Merchants, the Ernie Ball Company had announced they were to name the Axis Prototype Guitar which Albert had been using for several years as the Albert Lee signature model, and in August, Guy Wallace of Music Man issued a press release announcing "the long-awaited Albert Lee Model Guitar."[42]

Part of Albert's deal with Ernie Ball was—and remains—the huge number of guitar clinics and workshops which he holds throughout the States and in Europe. In March Music Man's distributor in Australia, Pat Bonham, arranged a two-week tour for Biff Baby's All-Stars, including Albert and Steve Morse, who enjoyed playing with Albert "because he's just such a natural musician. Very intuitive."[43] They recorded a spot for a late night TV talk show, *Hey, Hey, It's Saturday,* in Melbourne before gigs in Sydney, Adelaide,[44] Fremantle (where Albert had dinner with Hank Marvin and Martin Jenner), Newcastle and Brisbane, followed by a few days' holiday on the Barrier Reef. Back in Calabasas he was home for 24 hours before flying to Nashville for a week doing overdubs for Holly Dunn's album, *Life and Love and All the Stages,*[45] and a couple of tracks for Telecaster genius Arlen Roth's new album, *Toolin' Around.*[46] Roth recalls, "The playing and ideas Albert used on the title track opened up new ideas for me, and his unique approach never fails to bring me joy, and new inspiration." Albert had met Roth on the Joan Armatrading tour fifteen years before when Roth was on the road with African singer Tony Bird. He also played lead on five tracks for the Brother Phelps album *Let Go,*[47] whose title track was a Top Ten country hit. Brother Phelps was actually the nickname of the minister father of Doug and Ricky Lee Phelps, who had been the core of the rock-oriented Kentucky Headhunters. Finally he did several demos for British song-writing stalwarts Tony Colton and Roger Greenaway.

On April 8 Albert arrived in London with the Everlys for a 34-date European tour. John Firminger, reviewing an early gig at Sheffield City Hall, describes "a night of wonderful music, proving that when they feel like it, Don and Phil are simply untouchable. Whilst some songs still tend to be faster than the original, the dynamics and interplay between the brothers and their band still make them exciting." After all, "The Everlys are, first and foremost, showmen."[48] Firminger records that a "jazz-swing piece gave each member a chance to solo whilst a furious 'Tiger Rag' showed why Albert and Buddy Emmons are so highly revered.... Don and Phil delivered a surprising and refreshing finish with their encore 'T For Texas.' The old Jimmie Rodgers blues yodel was transformed into a driving rockabilly as the boys and the band blew up a storm. It was a great ending."[49]

The tour ended in Rotterdam and from then on Albert's summer was the usual Everlys roadshow, working from Winnipeg eastwards to Radio City in New York at the end of July. A music presenter from Radio Slovenia working in New York, in a quaintly worded review, thought "Dion was very good, Everly Brothers not. Especially bad were their high voices, but fortunately they had a wonderful backup band which was led by you know who, Albert Lee! In the Everlys' time out, Albert Lee and the band played for about 30 minutes. They were outstanding and I wished, sorry to say, that Everlys won't come back on the stage." From New York they headed west through Tennessee, Missouri, Utah, New Mexico, ending in San Diego at the end of August.

Martin Looby had managed to put together an autumn tour for the Heroes with Gordon Giltrap[50] and on November 6 Albert flew into Heathrow with two new Albert Lee model Ernie Ball guitars: one was to use on the tour and one was for Paul MacBonvin. After rehearsals with the Heroes, Albert drove up to Pebble Mill to record the final show in the Radio 2 series *British Country.* The tour was again a marathon, comprising two dates in Switzerland, 23 in Germany, one in Finland, shared with Andrew Hardin and Tom Russell, two in Sweden and 11 in Britain. Fortunately for the band, it was split into two halves by Albert's commitment in Los Angeles to a recording project with Herb Pedersen, the ex-Desert Rose Band banjoist, guitarist and singer.

The second half of the tour took in Aberdeen via Ireland followed by a concert at the

Wembley Conference Center, entitled A Celebration of the Guitar. It featured (allegedly) Albert and the Heroes, James Burton, Snowy White, Gordon Giltrap and others, but it turned out to be a disaster. The afternoon overran, the Heroes did not go onstage till 6:30 P.M. and then only for a 20-minute set and when they opened the evening concert they performed only two numbers. Owing to a reported back problem, the other headliner, James Burton, never even left the States! Albert flew home after the tour, changed suitcases and flew on to New York to do nine clinics for Ernie Ball, finishing in Charlotte, North Carolina.

Albert was back at the Agoura Valley Inn in December and over the coming months the house band evolved into Albert, Ron Coleman (bass and guitar), John Hobbs (piano), J.D. Maness (steel) and Joe Pollard (drums), occasionally supplemented by Rosie Flores. At the end of January Wayne also played piano and sang a few numbers. "I only knew one or two songs they were doing. They'd just yell out a key and you'd feel your way through it, which was a good education."

Albert spent a quiet Christmas and New Year but in January 1994, he did some sessions with Maureen McCormick, Marcia in *The Brady Bunch*, and with Randy and Rachel Parton (Dolly's brother and sister). Their producer was Herb Pedersen, with whom Albert played a short bluegrass set at the Inner Circle at the NAMM show where Albert was working for Ernie Ball on their stand talking guitars and signing autographs. Wayne learned a lot about his Dad on the Ernie Ball seminars he didn't know before. "It's not like a father and son thing—we're good friends. He asks me my opinion on things he plays and sings and he'll ask me 'Can you think of any songs we should do?' I find that quite a privilege. Once we went on a clinic tour, just jumped in his van and went 'round California."

The focus of Albert's summer in 1994, when the jamboree that was the soccer World Cup came to the U.S.A. to be met with a wave of mildly curious indifference, was a month at the Desert Inn, Las Vegas. After that endurance test Albert did California dates and in August played in Canada, Atlantic City and the Kentucky State Fair, finishing in Green Bay, Wisconsin, playing for the Packers' Alumni.

There are gigs which have passed into folklore, sweaty, pounding blues nights in tiny pubs and sun-soaked festivals which have ascended into heaven on clouds of sweet-smelling oblivion. Others, like the Wembley rock package in 1992, featured improbable line-ups of stellar magnificence. One such was organized at the Ryman Auditorium on September 12 by the W.O. Smith-Nashville Community Music School on the tenth anniversary of its Masters Series Concerts. Joe Orr, of the *Nashville Banner*, describes the school presenting Rodney Crowell, Emmylou Harris and Vince Gill "in a band which re-created the heyday of the California country sound during a two-hour concert.... 'I'm back with some of my very best friends, remembering some of the happiest times in my life,' Harris told the audience as she introduced 'Together Again.' In a master stroke that set the stage for the entire evening, Crowell ... began the concert with Gram Parsons' 'Hickory Wind.' After a verse, Vince Gill came in, then Harris and the rest of the band.... Albert Lee, the British guitarist ... supplied guitar runs so inventive and speedy that Gill seemed to stand by in awe!" A month later Albert recorded with a German country band, Autumn Leaves, and the same evening played Hooter's (the Everlys' tour manager's club) with Don Everly, Buddy Emmons, fiddler John Hartford and Tony Newman in another of those unforgettable gigs, described by Stuart Colman as "a genuinely special occasion."

The highlight of Hogan's Heroes short autumn tour was a show on Ulster TV. As Mike Bell had begun to work occasionally with Dr. Hook's Dennis Locorriere, Wayne stood in for him on keyboards. "When I got there Dad said, 'We'll probably only get you to do 'Country Boy' but we were sitting in the canteen when a chap came up and said, 'I've been listening to your CD and I really like this other song' and I panicked. Dad quickly talked through the song with me and told me what key I'm doing a solo in and that was it. I went on and did it."

Along with his annual summer sojourn with the Everlys and the Hogan's Heroes autumn tours, one of Albert's fixed points was the annual visit to L.A. of Paul MacBonvin. In January 1995 he was back to record tracks for his CD *The Bridge* at Mad Dog Studios in Burbank. Albert was back in Burbank, at the Red Zone, later in the year working on Rosie Flores' best-known album, *Rockabilly Filly*,[51] for which producer Greg Leisz enlisted the aid of Albert and James Intveld as well as 1950s rockabilly pioneers Wanda Jackson and Janis Martin (the female Elvis). Flores romps through a sparkling bunch of her own new tunes plus Patsy Cline's "Walkin' Dream," Butch Hancock's "Boxcars" and Gene Vincent's "Bop Street." Sandwiched in between the sessions was the annual Everly progress. As Albert wrote to Keith Nelson from Minneapolis in October, "Still on the road. I haven't been home in four months. Next weekend, thank goodness. I'll be over later in the year." And he was. A week before Christmas, the Heroes were at the New Morning in Paris.

Bill Wyman left the Rolling Stones in 1993, "pursuing other creative interests," as the jargon goes in the business. He married Suzanne Accosta, launched his Sticky Fingers restaurant chain, worked on archaeology and photography and began to write. When his thoughts again turned to music in late 1995, it was not with any very earnest intent. "I just fancied playing a bit of bass, but not in a commercial sense. I decided to try to get back to our traditional roots. I began jamming at home with Terry Taylor and then we thought it would be fun playing and singing old raunchy blues numbers with other musicians. I put the word out and events snowballed."

Wyman approached vocalist and Hammond organ king Georgie Fame and Peter Frampton, an old friend Wyman had known "when he was a fourteen-year-old guitar prodigy. I got in touch with Gary Brooker and Andy Fairweather Low—both of whom had been involved in Willie and The Poor Boys, my 'fun band' of the late 1980s. I wanted a pianist who could play early jazz and blues and found the extraordinary Dave Hartley. I was introduced to Beverly Skeete, who had worked as a backing vocalist for artists such as Chaka Khan, Jamiroquai and Elton John. We then contacted Martin Taylor, a brilliant melodic jazz guitarist, who was ideal for anything that needed a 1930–40s bluesy-jazzy style." There was just one final piece in the puzzle—a lead guitarist as comfortable with rock as he was with country, as adept at blues as he was with jazz-funk, who preferably sang a bit.

Just before Christmas, Bill Wyman was doing Gary Brooker's charity gig at Chiddingfold Club. Albert turned up, did three numbers, and Wyman was knocked out. "I didn't know Albert's number so I rang Bob Harris at the BBC for it." He asked him to join the Rhythm Kings on some recordings during 1996. Bill Wyman had found his missing piece.

Thirteen

All Kings Is Mostly Rapscallions[1]

The former Rolling Stone, the bass player whose inscrutable face and detached immobility only served to highlight Mick Jagger's vocal contortions, had found the last player in his band of all the talents. For Albert, Bill Wyman's call added one more patch to the colorful quilt of his eclectic but unfocused career. Booked for some sessions with Wyman in April, he flew back to Calabasas for Christmas, working at the Guitar Centre in Hollywood with Steve Morse and Steve Lukather, both owners of Ernie Ball signature model guitars, and at the Ernie Ball stand at NAMM. However, he was back in Europe at the end of January for a mini-tour of Finland with Hogan's Heroes, playing gigs in towns with names like Scrabble tiles on a bad day—Joensuu, Oulu, Ylla and Kuopio. Driving conditions were dangerous, with icy roads in Lapland, where the bus hit a deer. It was the kind of tour which was beginning to convince Mike Bell that life on the road was not for him: "I got fed up with seven-hour bus trips to play to three Lapps and an elk."

On Sunday, February 4, 1996, Albert flew back from Helsinki, via London and Chicago to Nashville, where he was in a studio the next morning. Back in Hollywood, Ron Coleman had set up some dates with Rosie Flores under the name the Sundance Band. Gigs in late February at the Sugar Shack in North Hollywood, the Cowboy Palace in Chatsworth in the San Fernando Valley and in Bakersfield followed a fun night with Biff Baby's All-Stars at the Agoura Valley Inn.

Meanwhile, Albert continued to discharge his commitments to Ernie Ball. On March 25, he had just begun a series of guitar clinics in Las Vegas when he received some shattering news. His beloved father, Dave, the man whose love of life had enriched Albert's childhood, who had bequeathed his Romany heritage and love of music to his gifted son, whose boisterous accordion and pub piano had enlivened many a night in the Dover Patrol, had died in Herne Bay. He and Phyllis had been reluctant to leave Kidbrooke Park five years before but "Dad was very ill," recalls Vanessa. "I nursed him in Blackheath for a while but I had roots in Herne Bay and I persuaded him to move so I could look after him." Albert flew to Phoenix to stay with his in-laws, and his father's funeral was postponed to enable Albert, "always the quintessential pro," according to Arlen Roth, to fulfill clinics in Tucson, Palm Desert and San Marcos. On Monday, April 1, he flew to London to join a host of mourners at a small, overflowing chapel in Herne Bay. The day after the funeral was Good Friday, traditionally a time when the Lee family got together: that Easter was a somber one for everyone, but especially for Albert. His father had been a pivotal figure in his life, prepared on the one hand to indulge his son's unique talent but also not averse to commenting caustically on Albert's more quixotic behavior; in the relative peace of the north Kent coast out of season he spent several quiet days with his mother at the bungalow in Beltinge Road.

Work, however, was never far away and a few days after the funeral, Albert recorded "about a dozen tracks" for Bill Wyman. That spring, the Sex Pistols announced their comeback tour, the Beatles' *Anthology, Volume 2* hit U.K. #1 and Take That topped the singles charts with the Bee Gees' "How Deep Is Your Love?" (their final single before a split which broke the hearts of countless teenage girls). Music was in one of its cyclical changes. Rap, world music, independent labels and a new slant on R&B vied with boy bands and the nostalgia market for attention in an expanding world of radio, TV and online music outlets. For musicians of Albert's vintage, who were reluctant to hand in their dinner-pails and retire either to the canyons of California or their mansions in London's stockbroker belt, a return to their roots made artistic and commercial sense. The baby boomers whose musical tastes had been weaned on a diet of rhythm and blues, delta blues, rockabilly, Motown and good-time dance music now had healthy disposable incomes: back-catalog compilations, tribute bands and nostalgia tours mushroomed. Anybody who had been anybody, and even some who never were, made a steady living from "solid gold" '60s tours because, as Chuck Willis once said, "If it's in the blood, you gotta keep doing it."[2] Wyman, hooked nearly forty years before by Chuck Berry in the film *Rock, Rock, Rock!*,[3] took a refreshingly ad hoc approach to the material: "We began to record anything that came to mind. The benefit of working in this way—apart from the spontaneous atmosphere we created—was that I could pick and choose musicians for the particular style I wanted for each track. The result of these early sessions became the first Rhythm Kings CD,[4] which sold much better than we had anticipated."

Before returning to California at the end of the month, Albert played a couple of Heroes gigs and traveled northwest to Egremont, on the western fringe of the Lake District, working with local artists at Music Farm Recording Studio. Tom Tyson, the owner, had been Gene Pitney's bass player in the early 1980s and was keen on promoting new talent: "Most of my clients are semipros and are delighted to have Albert play on their tracks. He is a producer's dream to work with: He will come up with licks that are so tasteful and so right for the song, and his feel is second to none. He can play three notes and they mean everything! As a person I find him warm and generous with a lovely laid-back sense of humor."

Four days later, he was at a clinic at Whitstable Rugby Club organized by Phil Hadler, the owner of FSC Music in Tankerton. Hadler had seen Albert at the Hammersmith Odeon with Clapton and when he heard that Albert was in Herne Bay, only a mile or two away, he called him and set up a clinic. "We sold over 400 tickets in ten days and they were queuing to get in, which amazed me," Hadler recalls. "The next day, he came round for dinner. Jane and I set him up with his favorite wine and he talked about people who had been our heroes for years. It was the most enlightening dinner I'd ever had." He and Albert had a lot in common—mainly amplifiers. "He was using his old Music Man amp for years which he likes very much, but they were aging and they were noisy on stage. I had strong connections with Fender and said 'What you really want is a Fender Tonemaster.' I think he's got three now. We modified a couple of cabinets for him for use with the Rhythm Kings because while he was very loud at the front the band couldn't hear him at the back, regardless of the monitoring.

So we cut slots in the back of a Tonemaster amp so that the sound would also go backwards. You can't just take a board off because the whole thing is made like a shell." Hadler has now become a close friend and colleague of Albert, booking the odd flight, organizing transport and generally ensuring that life for Albert in and around Herne Bay runs smoothly. "I bought AlbertLee.co.uk for his birthday. It's a simple business and diary page. If he's got a problem he calls me and I like that."

Over the next month Ernie Ball certainly got his money's worth from his investment in Albert's signature guitar. Following some studio sessions with Peter Sarstedt in Tim Goodman's small studio in California, Albert set off for nine clinics in ten days in Michigan, Illinois and Minnesota. On the way to Minneapolis he took a detour to Albert Lea, the hometown of Eddie Cochran, staying at the Albert Lea Hotel and buying the T-shirt! He rolled across the plains through South Dakota and Kansas then drove 500 miles to Dallas, staying with a cousin, and after clinics in Dallas and Houston flew home, having driven 2,400 miles in ten days.

Rockabilly star Rosie Flores had been an old pal of Albert's from the Sundance Saloon two decades before, and in June 1996 Albert featured on a reissue of her eponymous 1987 debut album on Warner Bros./Reprise Records plus six bonus tracks from contemporaneous sessions. The reissue,[5] produced by Pete Anderson, attracted mixed reviews. For AMG reviewer Eugene Chadbourne,[6] the unreleased numbers had "more bite, partially due to the better pickers on board, such as guitarist Albert Lee," and while going back to her roots paid off artistically, Chadbourne felt that the album would not "make anyone give away their Patsy Cline or Kitty Wells records."

In late June there was a disappointing trip to the Koblenz Music Festival with Hogan's Heroes, where heavy rain produced a meager turnout. Albert did a number of clinics, including one at the at Paradise Wildlife Park in Broxbourne, Hertfordshire, where the audience included Chas and Dave, complete with vocals by peacocks (the feathered ones), and at the Roebuck in Lewisham, organized by Tony, of Tune-In Guitars in Hither Green. Before the gig, Colin, Tony's assistant, noticed a figure in a long drover's coat and hat shuffling into the shop. He asked Tony, "Do you think we'd better get rid of the old guy in the corner?" "Actually," replied Tony, "that's Albert." Colin should have recognized him from the video but it was a 15-year-old photo.

Albert's summer was a curious one, a mixture of the familiar and the faintly bizarre. The customary Everly Brothers coast-to-coast tour began in Mission Viejo, California, and took in Las Vegas, the Santa Clara County Fair in San Jose, the Win River Casino, Redding and the California Mid-State Fair, Paso Robles. Gigs at Harrah's were followed by Eugene, Oregon; Minnesota; Wisconsin; the iconic Surf Ballroom in Clear Lake, Iowa; Missouri; Ohio; and Massachusetts before the customary Homecoming finale in Central City, Kentucky.

When one reads in a film magazine that "negotiations are under way for so-and-so to appear in a movie based on etc. etc.," or in a music paper that "discussions are taking place regarding the possibility of X recording an album with Y," it's a dime to a dollar that it will never happen. These publicity puffs are all part of the fantasy world in which make-believe and reality become so intertwined that Tinseltown's movers and shakers believe they have only to wish for something for it to be so. In September such pie-in-the-sky negotiations involved Albert, when it was loosely put about that he was to appear in a movie, playing the part of a band leader. The film, with the working title of *The Bouncer*, was to be based on a book by a neighbor of his, Stuart Goldman, telling the true story of an aging bouncer and how he copes with life. It never got off the ground.

Albert ventured further into the world of the silver screen that summer when he cut tracks for the film *Cous-cous*, directed by Umberto Spinazzola. Billed as a comedy in which an acid-jazz band, three Asian teenagers, a rapper, a sound technician, a 70-year-old grandmother and an exotic showgirl together celebrate music as a unifying force, it became such a cult movie that nobody can remember actually having seen it. It was so memorable for Albert that he cannot even recall having recorded the tracks.

Clearer in his memory was beginning work in the U.K. in October for another Paul MacBonvin CD, recording "Real Wild Child," "Memphis Killer" and "Your Boys" with the Heroes, and "The Highwayman," when Albert played piano. The album had a long gestation period and was not completed till March 1998.[7]

By then Albert had been honored at the British Country Music Awards in April 1997, receiving the Lifetime Achievement Award. Later that summer his son Wayne was married to Sharon, the daughter of Ray Stiles, the bass player and Albert's colleague in Mike Hurst and the Method. "The in-laws knew each other before we did!" says Wayne. "They didn't get us together though—it was just one of those things." With the wedding scheduled for Saturday, July 26, Albert was on the usual summer tour with the Everlys. He played the Thursday night gig and flew back on Friday. At the wedding reception Albert played "Let It Be Me" on piano for the first dance, flew back and played at the Everlys' concert on Sunday night!

Earlier in the year Bill Wyman had asked Albert if he would like to do some gigs. After a few rehearsals the band was on the road. "We only did three cities—Hamburg, Amsterdam and London. It was great fun and I hoped it wouldn't be the last tour." Albert's old mate Mike Warner welcomed him to Germany on October 10; the Rhythm Kings played the Paradiso in Amsterdam three days later, and on Wednesday, October 15, Linley Lorenzo caught the band at the Forum, Kentish Town, London. He could not remember "having such a great night out. It was like watching a band play in your own living room—the ambience was so relaxed. Though half the audience probably had arthritis (given their age), though it didn't stop them jumping around."

Before a few days off in Herne Bay over Bonfire Night, Albert played a few clubs in the Shetland Isles with the Sheila Henderson band. Sheila Henderson was a nominee in no less than three categories in the 1999 British Country Music Awards: for British Female Vocalist, Rising Star and Album. Albert wrote the sleeve note for her last album and labeled her band "a world class act." He then flew back to California for a date in Los Angeles with Nanci Griffith and the Crickets but was back in England a week later to do a country show for BBC Midlands and a short tour with the Heroes. The gig at the Maltings in Farnham, Surrey, was described by Roger Mezzone, a fan who had traveled from Villeneuve sur Lot, in southwest France. He was surprised that most of the 200 to 300 or so people present remained seated. "I was once again reminded how reserved English audiences can be even with a player of this caliber on stage." Rockabilly legend Dale Hawkins, there to see the show, joined the Heroes in an impromptu performance of his swamp-rock classic "Suzie Q"[8] and "Sweet Home Chicago."

Albert with Danny Gatton in Nashville, June 4, 1993 (courtesy the Lee family).

When Grammy-nominated guitarist Danny Gatton shot himself in his garage in October 1994, at the age of 49, music lost one of its most innovative and influential players. Gatton's playing fused jazz, blues and rockabilly, and he would execute intricate passages with bewildering clarity and speed. His favorite guitar was a 1953 Fender Telecaster, one of which Albert owned. Indeed, Gatton's soubriquet was the "Telemaster." In January 1998, Albert, together with Vince Gill, Jerry Douglas, Rodney Crowell, Steve Earle, Arlen Roth, Rodney Foster, Brent Mason & the Nashville All Stars, John Jorgenson, and other special guests, played special tribute concerts at the Birchmere Club, in Alexandria, Virginia, to raise funds for Gatton's daughter, Holly, to continue her college education. Arlen Roth recalls that he and Albert "shared the joy of playing with James Burton and countless others. Both times, he and I played our signature duet from 'Toolin' Around,' entitled 'Rollin' Home.'" John Jorgenson, who made his name with the Desert Rose Band and is one of the pioneers of the American gypsy jazz movement,[9] remembers Albert playing "brilliantly. Good energy just exuded from him, and the crowd reciprocated with a standing ovation."

The year 1998 was exceptionally varied and busy for Albert: he toured Britain and Europe with the Heroes from February until April, played Las Vegas with the Everlys in

May and Australia in June, was back home for a breather in August, then did a Bill Wyman tour in early autumn. "At that time we had a guy called Mike Franklin, or 'Porky,' who was doing our sound," recalls Pete Baron. "He ran a company called Porky Pig PA and tried to get gigs but he didn't really do much better than Martin Looby."

Porky was receiving suggestions for venues from Sue Hargreaves, a fan since the early '90s. "Laura, my sister-in-law, used to run the Everly Brothers Fan Club, so I had met Albert before. I got involved because I was frustrated that I could never find out where they were playing. So I produced a sheet for people to write names and addresses on as a mailing list. Then one day the band had gone out to eat so and a friend and I decided to sell the merchandise for them. I'd often volunteered to do it before. After that every time I went to a gig I did the merchandise and I used to coincide my holidays with when the band were touring."

At about this time Pete Baron decided he had more than enough free time, bought himself a computer and entered the world of music management, setting up an office at home in Willesden Green. "Brian and I started with blank sheet of paper. At this point I barely knew the names of venues, let alone telephone numbers." The two musicians had no experience of hustling for work but "over the next two or three years," says Baron, "we put a few dates together and it got easier each year."

In 1998, too, Hargreaves, an accountant in industry whose involvement with the band for three or four years had merely been a hobby, had a heart attack and was forced to give her job up. "I then started booking gigs for them. Pete still handled the contracts but I did a lot of the logistics—hotels, travel, etc." With her solid background in commercial office practice, she was ideally placed to undertake the administrative links with venues. "I arrange the fee and the terms, collect the money and still do the merchandise. In effect I'm the tour manager. Albert always introduces me as his manager and sometimes as 'Mother Superior.'"

At the end of February Owen O'Connor, who for some time ran an unofficial Albert Lee Internet news page,[10] described the last night of the Heroes' Irish tour, at the delightfully named Purty Loft in Dun Laoghaire, the ferry port south of Dublin. "Albert's mike was disconnected for the first verse. Unfazed and professional to the last, Albert played on and joked afterwards that the first verse 'was like the second only not as good.'" The Heroes shared the limelight with Peter Baron singing a couple songs and as usual Albert climaxed the set with "Country Boy," this time segued onto "Tiger Rag." O'Connor had the impression that while "he feels obliged to perform 'Country Boy' and gets fed up with introducing it, he still seems to enjoy playing it ... and seemed genuinely surprised at the audience's reaction to the song." Included in the set was another Jimmy Webb song, "If You See Me Getting Smaller," and a medley of tunes from the *Speechless* album—perhaps a recognition of the album's reissue on CD.[11] For the anoraks, O'Connor records that Albert played "a new version of his Ernie Ball/Music Man signature model. This one had a metallic blue finish with pearloid pickguard and a whammy bar (which he was not afraid to use)."

On the whole Albert felt the European tour had gone well, though "it was hard work. We played nearly every night and traveled 11,000 miles in a rented minibus and trailer." He was also acting as part-time roadie: "To speed things along we helped with the gear every night." Although he always carried his own equipment, after a few weeks he began to feel twinges in the wrists and elbows. In addition, he got the flu halfway through the tour and had to cancel a couple of shows. He was, though, able to indulge his love of Italian cuisine when he played a guitar festival in Soave—"memorable and great fun—lots of wining and dining and terrific hospitality."

Equally memorable for Albert was an early gig in the Everlys' annual trek around North America. On April 29 the Everlys performed on the stage of the Ryman Auditorium in Nashville for the first time in four decades. The night began, appropriately enough, with an introduction by Chet Atkins, who discovered the brothers at a Knoxville fair in 1954 and persuaded the Everly family to move to Nashville a year later. Albert was deeply touched by the whole evening: "it was a thrill for me to be on that stage with them all and Buddy Emmons, my favorite musician!" A local review noted that "when The Everly Brothers opened their historic return to the Ryman Auditorium last Wednesday night with the sweet, supple harmonies of 'Kentucky,' it made perfect sense. For the brothers, whose roots are in the coal-mining region of the Bluegrass State, the concert was about home and heritage."

A week later Albert encountered a less pleasant aspect of life on the road. In Grants, New Mexico, the equipment truck was broken into in a motel parking lot. Albert lost his 1913 Gibson f4 mandolin blacktop, serial no. 14481, and a Musicman HD130 head. Phil Cranham was lucky—"it was the only time I'd ever lost an instrument and it was a replaceable bass, a green Music Man, not my favorite one." Truck drivers normally backed their rigs up against the wall of the motel so that it is impossible to open the back up. On this occasion, says Cranham, "he had forgotten to and some kids must have busted the lock and helped themselves to what was accessible, including Don and Phil's Steinegger Everly guitars and two monitor speakers." A few months later, Albert contacted some pawn shops in the area and Don did eventually get his back. "Somebody had pawned the guitar for about $80 and it's worth a good five or six grand. Phil's is still out there somewhere. It says Everly on the headstock and anyone with any idea would know it's valuable. It's got a dent in the neck because on stage Phil and I used to do a dance during 'Lucille' on stage and one night I clunked into him!"

Despite the loss of these valuable instruments, the Everlys had dates in Australia in June at venues as varied as the Twintowns Service Club in Tweedheads, New South Wales, the Melbourne Hilton and the Sydney Hilton. Back from the Antipodes, during July, Albert took the chance of a bit of a break to do some work on his cars and clear the brush round the house. Coyotes were becoming a serious menace in southern California as the exurban sprawl of Los Angeles encroached on their habitat. Increased human contact emboldened the coyotes, and they became a regular sight on the steep hillside of the canyon behind Albert and Karen's home. They had lost one or two pet cats to the coyotes and clearing the brush and dense weeds reduced potential cover for these canine predators. Chester, the present incumbent in Monte Nido, is made of sterner stuff. Spitting and snarling, this feisty feline sends the coyotes slinking away back into the canyon with their tails between their legs.

Then Ron Coleman called. He'd secured the Sundance Band a headline slot at Ronnie Mack's Barn Dance. Since 1988 singer-songwriter Mack had championed the Los Angeles alt-country scene, and every Tuesday night at El Cid on West Sunset Boulevard still gives country rock and roots acts a voice. A fortnight later, at the end of August, Albert had a great time at the Agoura Valley Inn playing with his old friend Dave Edmunds.

"He loves to throw his amp in the back of the car," says producer Steve Fishell, "and drive down the corner or 50 miles, to go jam with a little band." In a revealing interview with Canadian journalist Dave Veitch in 2000, Albert expresses no regrets about his career. "I'm generally a quiet kind of guy. Maybe my career might have taken a different turn if I had been more extrovert. But the music was always the thing for me." Albert's clear-sighted self-knowledge, appealing as it is, has sometimes irked Karen. "He'd play with whoever picked up the phone but he would never pick it up himself. I've had to push him and you get tired of pushing. He would have loved for the Eagles or The Band to call him and say 'Come join us' but he wouldn't get a band together himself. From time to time it *has* got to me that he doesn't have that drive."

That lack of affectation, or the instinct for self-promotion and personal ambition, to which Gerry Hogan and Chas Hodges have referred before, can be seen in his approach to a workshop he was doing early in October in Crewkerne, Somerset, not far from Keith Nelson. "He stayed with me. He was driving a rusty old Austin Princess he shared with his Dad. I wasn't having him turn up in that heap so I said, 'Albert, I'm your roadie and we're going in the Mustang.' He'd be quite happy to carry the gear in himself—he doesn't have a pretentious bone in his body."

Albert was over in Britain rehearsing with Bill Wyman for a more expansive European tour, following the release in October 1998 of the Rhythm Kings' second CD.[12] The core of the band had stayed the same, but as Wyman points out, "it's like a football team, with subs on the bench if anyone is injured or unavailable. We've all been mates for years and we know the music inside out." Everybody had an individual career "and while there's a bit of cash there's not as much as they would get with the bigger acts—but we're a democratic band with everybody pitching in and being given equal weight." The flexible element appealed to the band, says Wyman, "enabling people to do things different from what they would do in their careers. I get Albert to do songs he wouldn't dream of doing in his own band."

The three-week tour of Northern Europe and Scandinavia played to packed audiences and received rave reviews. In mid–October, at the Paradiso in Amsterdam and in Aarhus, Denmark, local reviewers mention Albert and Martin Taylor's final guitar battle on "Tear It Up," in which "they ended up both playing the same guitar at a rapid speed before a cheering crowd." Roland Clare, who for some years has been responsible for the Procol Harum website, described how "Martin Taylor unplugs, goes round behind Lee: they jointly play the one guitar, two hands strumming, two hands fretting. I haven't quite fathomed the geometry of this feat. Suddenly the song cranks up a semitone, and plays out in F major ... a splendidly exciting finale."

From the sublime, one might say, to the ridiculous, as Albert and the Heroes undertook the "Not Fade Away" tour of Ireland with Mike Berry and Dave Edmunds the following February. It was fun to tour with his old friend. Berry had come to prominence with his 1961 hit "Tribute to Buddy Holly" and recalls that on "Not Fade Away," "there's a little tag on the guitar solo that nobody ever does. You remember every little nuance of it because that's what made it for you in the first place and for the first time in 40 years I heard a guitarist play that solo properly. Albert smiled—there was an unspoken recognition." However, the trip holds bad memories for Albert. "It was a disaster. Shows were canceled and we didn't get paid." The tour was also Pete Wingfield's first with the band as Mike Bell was on the road with Dennis Locorriere. "He had been to see us a few times," says Brian Hodgson, "liked what he saw and said, 'If ever you need a stand-in.'"

In England, despite very little radio exposure, the Rhythm Kings' *Anyway the Wind Blows* had reached #5 in the jazz and blues charts. It was time to conquer Britain and around Pentecost, after a brief stint with the Everlys in California, Albert returned to Britain for three days of rehearsals with the Rhythm Kings for a 22-date British tour. On May 29, Gary Brooker's fifty-fourth birthday, the tour opened at the Assembly Rooms in the sedate spa town of Royal Tunbridge Wells, featuring an "amazingly fluent solo from Martin Taylor" on "Walking One and Only," which contrasted with the electric solo from Albert, "the only player retaining a rock-star haircut, which he doesn't shake about while playing!" Albert took the vocals on "Jump, Jive and Wail," with Georgie Fame and Brooker joining the female vocalists for five-part harmonies.

The following night, Albert returned to his native heath at Blackheath Concert Hall, a gig described as a "shared triumph ... when Bill Wyman's Rhythm Kings took the place by storm and blew away the last traces of cobwebbed complacency at the halls at the top end of Blackheath Village."[13] The tour was not a totally triumphant progress, as the gig in Stoke-on-Trent disappointed local Dave Lee. "The jazzy music early on was quite dull and played with little enthusiasm. The musicianship was good, but there were far too many musicians, and so a lot of the time the sound was just a mush of noise." Perhaps the band was at the mercy of an inadequate sound system. The tour wound up with July dates at the Edinburgh Jazz Festival and Chester Music Festival.

Albert had worked with Don and Phil earlier in the year at the Galaxy Theatre in Santa Ana, where long-time Everlys fan Jerry Lee (no relation), who had worked as a radio DJ for many years in L.A., Cleveland, Houston and St. Louis, noted a rare excursion for Albert into Western swing. "He and Buddy Emmons did the late '40s hit by Bing Crosby, 'I'll Make the San Fernando Valley My Home.'" In August, Albert "enjoyed" a week in Las Vegas with the Everlys and on the Monday after the shows, Phil married his third wife, Patti Arnold, at Caesar's Palace, where they would have been slightly better dressed than in January, when the dress code at Phil's sixtieth birthday bash was sweatshirts and Reeboks. Pete Wingfield played the piano at the ceremony, to which most of the band and crew were invited.

Events around the end of the month epitomized Albert's eclecticism as a player. On the one hand, he worked with rock and blues legends from the late 1950s, recording with the Crickets in Nashville and opening for Ray Charles in Ohio. He then appeared on an Aerosmith tribute album, *Not the Same Old Song and Dance*,[14] featuring famous rockers covering classic Aerosmith songs: Albert plays "Back in the Saddle" with Mark Slaughter, Rudi Sarzo and Frankie Banali.

Albert certainly clocked up some air miles in 1999: In September he was back in the U.K. on a three-week "Rave On" tour with Hogan's Heroes with Mike Berry guesting at some shows and Pete Wingfield again on piano. Pete had experienced unremitting touring with the Everlys—and of course, he knew Albert well: "It's the road-dog that's the real man, the relentlessly slogging gigster—but, there's nothing to beat playing live and that makes up for all the traveling." Mike Bell was working again with Dennis Loccoriere but while he had not handed in his notice, the Heroes had made the change and Bell did not blame them. He accepts that he had become hypercritical: "Albert has a brilliant temperament on the road and felt I shouldn't make a fuss. The killer reason for my leaving was the smoke—and as I'd given up drinking I hated the smell of stale beer. Furthermore we played in a lot of flea pits which were unnecessarily loud. I once said to Wayne, 'Is your Dad deaf?' 'Of course he's fucking deaf! You don't think he'd play that loud if he wasn't, do you?' In small cheap clubs the back of the PA is thin and it physically hurt as I was sitting right next to it." But for a while Bell was reluctant to leave the band as he was earning regular money.

In 1960 the Ford Consul taxi carrying rockabilly legend Eddie Cochran back to Heathrow crashed into a lamp post at Rowden Hill, Chippenham, Wiltshire. In the last decade the Eddie Cochran Rock 'n' Roll Weekend at the end of September has become a regular event in the Chippenham calendar. In 1999 a panic-stricken festival organizer had rung Brian Hodgson. The headlining Blue Caps' rhythm guitarist, Paul Peek, was ill. Could he suggest a substitute? "Well," thought Hodgson, "Johnny Meeks, the Blue Caps' lead guitarist, and Albert were old mates"—and as it happened, Albert had a few days free before flying back to join the Everlys. So Albert and Brian joined the Blue Caps on stage. "These guys were just a riot," recalls Hodgson. "Albert and I asked, 'What are we playing?' and they'd say, 'You'll be all right.' We hadn't a clue what they were going to do or what key they were going to do it in—and probably they didn't either. It was a hoot."

It had been a year in which Albert had virtually become a trans-Atlantic commuter, crossing the pond seven times. And after the Everlys' dates in Lake Tahoe, Las Vegas and in Laughlin, Nevada, where they sold out all four days at Don Laughlin's Celebrity Theater, he was not done yet. Albert had always relaxed by doing what he loved. Before leaving California for a short pre–Christmas tour with Hogan's Heroes he did some gigs with Biff Baby's All Stars and with a friend, singer-songwriter Mark Insley.[15] "Albert loves the old country stuff," he says. "He'd have the audience jumping out of their seats in utter amazement. He's so clean, so right when he's live. The guy's on fire."

The year 2000, Albert's fortieth as a professional musician, began with daydreams of Internet fortunes, instant stardom for boy bands like Westlife and global notoriety for rap artists such as Eminem. There was recognition, too, for more established stars, as Eric Clapton became the first musician to be inducted into the Rock and Roll Hall of Fame for the third time, Santana won eight Grammys and the best-selling album was the Beatles' 1. For Albert, a short tour with Hogan's Heroes was very much business as usual—with a notable exception. In March at Tom Tyson's Music Farm Studios the band recorded seven tracks for a new album, Tear It Up, before Albert began a European tour in April with the Rhythm Kings. The line-up comprised the usual suspects, except that Henry Spinetti, Albert's old friend from the Clapton days, sat in on drums for the British leg of the 42-date tour of Germany, Holland and Britain, which finished in Newcastle on July 3. The band had a month off in May, enabling Martin Taylor to run his International Guitar Festival at Kirkmichael in South Ayrshire and Albert to play at it with the Heroes!

Twenty-four dates in five weeks completed the year's commitment to Bill's band of old mates. It had been an easier year yet Albert had never considered slowing down, let alone retiring. "I don't think he'll ever retire," says Karen, "and I wouldn't want him to. I'd love to be able to afford to retire. There's a lot of financial insecurity in our lifestyle. I knew long ago that money and security lay in writing but I couldn't get him to write—it was like pulling teeth. I should have persevered and come up with lyrics. I'd say, 'You go and sit at the piano

Albert and Karen, mid–1970s: "You should really write more..." (courtesy the Lee family).

and do it' and he'd say 'I'm thinking about it.' I would respond, 'Writing's hard work: Inspiration's not going to strike while you're watching television.'" In addition, Albert never learned to read music. "I regret it now because I know I could have done a lot had I been able to read—especially in Los Angeles where there's tons of TV and movie stuff. And I haven't got the patience to work at a lyric for days on end." In any case, as Karen points out, "he loves the traveling minstrel bit. When he's home he's out every weekend somewhere doing a gig."

As 2001 ushered in the new millennium, Albert began his fifth decade in the business doing what he had done for over twenty years—Christmas at home with Karen and Alex, visiting her folks in Arizona, tinkering with the cars and getting ready for the NAMM show and that year's All Star Jam. It happened on January 19 at the Coach House in San Juan Capistrano, with Sterling Ball on bass, Steve Lukather, John Ferraro, John Petrucci and Vinnie Moore, who writes, "Albert is the king of country guitar, and during the big finale five guitarists were onstage at once playing Albert's tune 'Country Boy.' Each guy had a different style and is totally unique within his own field. Imagine Albert Lee's guitar neck being about three feet to your left, and Morse's guitar neck being around one foot to your right. Talk about having a good seat. Whew! It was astounding."

The Rhythm Kings' tour, which began at the Paradiso in Amsterdam in May, followed its standard progress through Denmark, Norway, Sweden, Germany, Spain, and France, with a month off in June. While Albert took a break in Calabasas, he learned with sadness that country music had lost one of its icons and he had lost a boyhood idol he had come to honor as a friend. On June 30 Chet Atkins lost a long fight against a brain tumor; he was 76. Atkins had adapted Merle Travis's finger-picking style, enabling him to play melody and rhythm simultaneously, and he became virtually the house guitarist at RCA studios. His unique playing can be heard on Hank Williams' "Your Cheatin' Heart," Presley's "Heartbreak Hotel" (where he played rhythm to Scotty Moore's lead) and the Everlys' "All I Have to Do Is Dream." In the 1950s, Atkins and producer Owen Bradley created the "Nashville sound," which was "a successful attempt to put more pop into country"[16] with artists like Don Gibson and the Everlys. Nine days earlier John Lee Hooker, one of the blues' most significant performers, had died at 83. His distinctive guitar style exerted a powerful influence on younger rock and blues players, featuring repetitive, often arrhythmic, riffs in open tuning.[17]

The prestigious Cambridge Folk Festival in Britain at the end of July was followed by the Rhythm Kings' first North American tour, encompassing 17 dates from New Jersey through New York, Pennsylvania and Ohio. Within six weeks, the world had changed forever. When the twin towers collapsed on September 11 in almost unimaginable scenes of impending Armageddon, the occasionally frivolous and often superficial world of popular music was put in its proper perspective. Many artists canceled gigs while others took part in a multinetwork telethon, *America: A Tribute to Heroes*, opened by Bruce Springsteen with his unrecorded anthem "My City of Ruins."

That month, Gib Guilbeau, a country/rock singer with an impeccable pedigree (Flying Burrito Brothers, the Gosdin Brothers, the Byrds), recorded a CD[18] with Wayne Moore, Darrell Cotton and Ernie Williams, with whom he had worked together in several bands during the '50s and early '60s. The highlight of the CD was a song Gib wrote together with John Beland years before, "We Shall Rise Above it All," with Albert playing guitar and piano. "It seemed a perfect song for the time," Gib recalls. Albert had worked with Gilbeau earlier in the year when Dawn Hopkins (a Women's Professional Billiards Association touring professional and part-time songwriter) produced a CD of mostly original songs written and performed by WPBA touring pros. Most of the songs on *The Other Side*, which is not available commercially, were recorded in Gilbeau's studio and Albert played guitar, mandolin and piano on the album. He also contributed to *Guitars for Freedom*, a CD with tracks by Jimi Hendrix, Santana, Jose Feliciano and others, released by Angels on Earth, a nonprofit "music for healing" organization, with all the proceeds going to the American Red Cross, the NY Firefighters' 9/11 Disaster Relief Fund and Mayor Giuliani's Twin Towers Fund.

Against the background of a world still reeling from the magnitude of 9/11, Albert began recording in Burbank the following month for Paul MacBonvin's new CD,[19] titled *Ainsi La Vie* ("That's Life"). There were two tracks with the Heroes, "Que Des Souvenirs" and "Lewis Boogie," with Albert on piano and producing, and "Kentucky," with Albert on mandolin and vocals. Earlier, in March, the band had produced MacBonvin's CD *On the Boulevard*[20] at the Fab Studio in Charrat, in the Rhone valley, Switzerland.

At the beginning of 2002, Albert and the band entered their fifteenth year together. What had begun for Albert as a diffident one-off to help out an old friend had become a musical symbiosis with which he now felt utterly at home, "but it had taken several years for that to evolve," says Pete Baron. Hogan's Heroes had always been a touring band and though Gerry Hogan feels that none of them enjoys the traveling very much "you go with what's happening." Considering the band lived in each others' pockets on the road, "we still have a laugh," says Gerry. "Pete Baron and I are the cynics, Brian is the main man with the ready quip at the right time—and Pete Wingfield does the *Times* crossword. Albert? It's very difficult to get him actually to have an opinion on anything." Albert's easy-going, affable and unassuming nature sometimes leads him to seem disengaged, in his own world. Perhaps his noncommittal stance is a reluctance to cause offence: His political views have encompassed the American spectrum: "I've always thought of myself as a Democrat but I've become more and more right-wing."

The band's name has caused problems down the years. "At Whelan's in Dublin," says Brian, "they managed to get three spelling mistakes in Hogan's Heroes, including the apostrophes. Wingfield got out his pen and changed it: We call ourselves the apostrophe police! We're often like grumpy old men on tour: In the end I think we're the ones who are out of step."

In January the band set off a 56-date anniversary tour beginning at one of the band's favorite venues, the tiny Fleece and Firkin in Bristol. By early February the tour had reached Holland and via Germany, Switzerland, Belgium, Ireland and Sweden ended up in Norway, in a village "way up above Trondheim which has a rock 'n' roll party every year," recalls Sue Hargreaves. It was another of those Norse sagas[21] which gave the lie to the sybaritic glamor of the rock 'n' roll lifestyle. "We'd been in Ostersund the night before and we'd left some of the gear there. After driving all day in very thick snow to this remote village the band didn't get on stage till nearly 2 in the morning and everybody was plastered: They kept inviting us to sample their vicious home brew, with moose to eat. We got back to the hotel about 5 or 6 A.M. and had to leave about 9 to drive back to Ostersund for the rest of the gear. Then we drove to Sundsvall just in time for them to go on stage."

In February, there was a rare event: The band's second CD, *Tear It Up*,[22] was released. Arguably the most rewarding of their three albums, it finds the band in party mood. Their maturity enables them to play relaxed yet effervescent Buddy Holly covers, "Take Your Time" and "Rock Around with Ollie Vee," a jazz-jump number from the Rhythm Kings' repertoire, "Jitterbug Boogie," and even a revival of "Singing the Blues." A Chuck Berry standard, "Back in the USA," is followed by Floyd Cramer's "Last Date" and "On the Rebound" and the impassioned rockabilly of Gram Parsons' "Luxury Liner." Albert sings unpretentiously but movingly on Jimmy Webb's poignant ballad "If You See Me Getting Smaller" and Rodney Crowell's "Til I Gain Control Again." Peter Baron steps up to cover "Country Comfort," Elton John's paean to the rural life, and the album climaxes with Albert's take on rockabilly legend Johnny Burnette's "Tear It Up." A self-penned guitar vignette from Albert, "Down to the Wire," provides a thoughtful coda.

It was a festive summer for Albert—in May the Heroes played what proved to be Gerry's final Steel Guitar Festival in Burghclere and an enjoyable festival in Switzerland. Then Albert had two gigs which happily combined his love of sports cars when first, in August, he was asked by Eric Clapton to join him and Gary Brooker, Andy Fairweather-Low, Dave Bronze and Henry Spinetti to form the Ferrari Band, playing at the Ferrari-Maserati Festival at Brands Hatch, Kent. Second, in early September half a world away, Albert played with Earl

Scruggs, sandwiched somewhat bizarrely between Los Lobos and the 21st Century Doors at the California Speedway in Fontana. While at home in California, he worked on sessions for his Sugar Hill album, *Heartbreak Hill.*

George Harrison and Albert had been long-standing friends, united as much by their mutual love of motor racing and offbeat humor as by their prowess as guitarists. At London's Royal Albert Hall, on November 29, 2002, exactly one year after George's passing, Eric Clapton assembled an all-star cast in a tribute concert. "I started with a nucleus of Henry, Dave Bronze and Gary Brooker. Then the jungle drums began to work and Albert got wind of it," Clapton recalls. Albert was in Britain fulfilling a series of pre–Christmas dates with the Heroes. "He applied to me saying, 'If you need any help, please let me know.' That's the mark of a gentleman. He's making himself available, 'but I won't be offended if you don't want me.' I called him straightaway." Clapton was the musical director for the show, which closely echoed the late Beatle's tastes—Indian music, comedy slots from the Monty Python gang and a stunning set composed almost entirely of Harrison songs. Guests of honor were Harrison's widow Olivia and their son, Dhani.

For the rock section of the evening, the house band consisted of Albert, with Jeff Lynne, Andy Fairweather-Low, Gary Brooker, Henry Spinetti, Dhani Harrison, Chris Stainton, Jim Keltner, Ray Cooper, Jim Capaldi and Dave Bronze. The band was joined throughout the evening by Jools Holland, Sam Brown, Billy Preston, Paul McCartney and Ringo Starr. Michael Kamen added orchestral arrangements to much of the set with a string orchestra. The overall effect was an aural tapestry in which friends of George Harrison wove their diverse strands, coming together to remember him by playing his music.

The platinum disc for sales of the CD and DVD of the *Concert for George* hangs on the wall of the house in Monte Nido: Albert is quietly but rightly proud of it. Yet he would have derived as much pleasure from the Heroes gig the following night at the Rayners Hotel in Rayners Lane, south London. Bill Wyman believes that Albert "does too many of these little gigs and cheapens himself a bit. If you can see him in a pub in Newcastle then psychologically you don't think of him as a huge star. I don't know anybody else who does those gigs who's a quality musician and a quality singer—but we all need money so he might do it for that reason." Karen would like Albert to "pick and choose his gigs a bit more. When you're more scarce people pay you more to come out. But it's his choice."

So why does Albert still drive almost 200 miles each day to a gig? "That's what you do if you're a musician, and he still has the latent Romany wanderlust in his veins," says Pete Wingfield. Pete Baron agrees: "He feels strongly about his roots, but the gypsy part of him takes him to the next place all the time." In his sixtieth year Albert's travels took him through Ireland, Holland, Germany, the Czech Republic, Northern Ireland, France and Spain, where Karen joined him before they visited his mother in Herne Bay.

His album[23] of songs associated with Emmylou Harris, Paul Kennerley and Rodney Crowell was released in October. Recorded at the Lair in Los Angeles, the Sound Emporium Studios and Scruggs Sound Studios, both in Nashville, it features such luminous back-up stars as Vince Gill, Rodney Crowell, Buddy Emmons, Brad Paisley, Patty Loveless and Earl Scruggs. Thoroughly engaging as the CD is, with Albert leading the young pretenders Gill and Paisley on an incendiary rampage through "Luxury Liner," it is Emmylou Harris's sleeve-note which is most memorable: "When St. Peter asks me to chronicle the highlights of my time down on earth, I'll be able to say (with pride if that's allowed) that for a while I played rhythm guitar in a band with Albert Lee."

I first saw Albert live that year, 2003, at the Komedia in Brighton a week before Christmas. A fortnight earlier, the Heroes had played the New Morning in Paris and through the good offices of their friend Yves Farge, together with Christine Badier at the New Morning and technical support from countless others, the complete show was recorded for a Heroic Records DVD.[24] The Komedia gig had the same set and the same atmosphere. From Pete Baron's rat-a-tat on the hi-hat, his count-in to Pete Wingfield's rockabilly intro to Albert's ringing cadence as he launched into "I'm Ready," I hadn't heard a live band willing to rock 'n' roll all night for years and at once I was back in 1956. Those chords, those lyrics, that piano, the chiming guitar and the sheer brio of it all—they were an unbroken chain stretching back to those days of youthful innocence, to the sheer excitement of a music which expressed our hopes and fears and which came from a world of blue skies, golden sands, pretty girls, shiny cars and the open road. Here, on stage in Brighton, was a man who had grown up through the same time and was still playing that vibrant music and singing those simple, direct and engaging songs.

I needed to know more of the man and his music. What else had he done? What was his story? In 2003, Albert told *Guitar World*, "I gave an English rock edge to the country music idiom." What did that mean? I needed to research his roots and his records and the idea of a book was born. It was an absorbing journey, digging through countless names of musicians, producers, managers, studios, albums, concerts, festivals, tours, arguments, reviews, dates and places. In time, however, the minutiae will fade and we shall be left with the memories, the man and his music.

It is a story whose final chapter has yet to be written. For Albert Lee, the beat goes on.

Epilogue

A Stopping Place

May 14, 2007, was the four hundredth anniversary of the Jamestown settlement in Virginia. That historic event marked the permanent physical arrival in North America of British settlers, who brought with them their belief systems, their farming practices and their culture. Over the next 300 years the church music, folk ballads, work songs, the jigs, reels and dance tunes of the common people became an integral part of the multifaceted evolution of North American music.

That music gradually absorbed elements of other traditions—from Africa, Latin America and different parts of Europe—but the link with the original British settlers informed and underpinned its evolution. By the early years of the twentieth century, while the music of the New World, speaking through blues, Cajun and the wailing strains of infant jazz had a voice intrinsically its own, the mountain music of the Appalachians, vaudeville comic songs and street ballads of cities like New York and Chicago were still recognizably rooted in the structures and themes of the Old.

Almost all the protagonists of the new American music were quintessentially American and the early rock 'n' roll singers, like Elvis Presley, Jerry Lee Lewis, Carl Perkins, Johnny Cash and Johnny Burnette, came from the South and had their origins in country music. In fact, rockabilly, which contributed so much to rock 'n' roll, was an offshoot from a style of country music, dominant in the decade after 1945, which developed in the roadside bars and honky-tonks of California and the rural South.[1] The honky-tonks provided raw entertainment for thirsty workers, evolving a harder sound which became as much urban as rural by the mid–1950s. The music was less romanticized, with a string bass, rhythm guitar chords and drums providing a pounding beat which would overcome the noise of the bars. Electrified steel or lead guitars and sometimes a piano were later developments.

While honky-tonk was increasingly reflecting the life of the urban South and helping to create the conditions in which rock 'n' roll could emerge, the songs of Hank Williams, perhaps the first real American pop star, were more rural, part of an older tradition. Rockabilly performers like Carl Perkins and Johnny Burnette sang of truck drivers, traveling hobos and the railroad and fused the urban elements of honky-tonk with the country styles of Williams and the earlier, hugely influential Jimmie Rodgers. While their voice was expressed in the new urban genre, its roots lay in an older, southeastern tradition of hillbilly, a term used originally to describe the traditional music of the people of the Appalachian Mountains. This tradition was characterized by fiddlers and string bands, both essential elements in Celtic and gypsy music. "That's how country music evolved, a combination of blues, Irish music and bluegrass," says Albert. "A lot of country players would trace their early influences to blues. The stock blues and the country riff are two different things, though, but when they merge you get a wonderful approach to playing guitar."

Albert's heritage lay in the Romany tradition of the extended family, the open road, the caravan and the communal camp-fire, elements not far removed from the freight-car hobo and the railroad worker, the itinerant farm laborer and the wagon trains of the New Frontier. When James Burton left the Hot Band, Emmylou Harris sought another unique stylist of the Fender guitar, "something I thought would be impossible. And along comes Albert Lee, a skinny, half-gypsy Englishman whose blistering solos and passion for American music knocked us all off our feet." While she recognized that Albert played with what is in his blood, as Eric Clapton has said, "He's a mixture of Django Reinhardt and James Burton and many others. He's not simply the greatest country player—he's unique and doesn't fit into a box."

Albert himself considers that he "gave an English rock edge to the country music idiom." The musical historian Jules Combarieu has described music as "the art of thinking with sounds." Albert, however, is not a cerebral player. Heads, Hands and Feet guitarist Ray Smith notes that Albert has the instinctive technique of the gypsy virtuosi, his musical thinking inevitably colored by his cultural roots and the early British skiffle and American rockabilly which suffused his formative years in south London. "He put all the elements together," says award-winning singer/songwriter Buddy Miller,[2] "and made something new, which is a rare thing. He inspired me to find my own voice. He is as big an influence on country guitar as there ever has been." It's a view echoed by long-time colleague in the Everlys band, bassist Phil Cranham: "He is the benchmark country guitar player of his generation."

Having said all that, Johann Sebastian Bach thought that "all one has to do is hit the right notes at the right time and the instrument plays itself." Tony Colton recalls Albert saying something similar: "The day I realized that whatever note I landed on was only a semitone away from the right one was when it all fell into place." Dolly Parton was always "so touched when he started to play. It would just run through me like some kind of liquid magic." That almost effortless ease was stressed by Steve Trovato, who teaches in the guitar department at the University of Southern California. "He has a gift for spontaneously composing solos which are fast but which possess a melodic continuity. He's almost the John Coltrane of country guitar. Most players play solos that are canned licks and ideas but when Albert performs, he seems to be merely channeling the music from a higher place. His solos are seamless, unending, melodic and flawless." Buddy Miller puts it thus, "every note is his own and oozes brilliance, heart and integrity ... and is just out of reach." Steve Morse cannot remember Albert playing a bad solo, or the same one. Typically self-effacing, Albert claims he never plays "the same thing exactly the same way twice because I usually forget what I did. I just wing it and sometimes it works. A solo is like a little extra color—like a nice painting above the fireplace."

Yet for all his pre-eminence as a player, Albert has not become "big-time." Drummer Tony Newman remarks that he "retains an element of adolescent enthusiasm. He hasn't become a stick-in-the-mud. He has no restraints musically and is great at improvising stuff.

At school we were taught classical music. You can hear influences of it in the Beatles—big theatrical playing. Country guitar-picking is traditionally structured and stays within the confines of the culture yet his solos can be grand and all-encompassing." Albert's attitude is that "you've got to get out there and play with a rhythm section or a band—that's where you really get your chops and feel together." Emmylou Harris stresses the importance of that communality of expression: "Music is a great thing because you almost have to have company to make it. It is communication and collaboration."

Yet while all the crop of young guitarists in Nashville know and respect Albert, he remains well below the radar in Britain. Pete Wingfield identifies three reasons for this low profile for a man who, as Buddy Miller put it, "is responsible for most of the good players in Nashville playing like they do … whether they know it or not." Wingfield thinks there is the confusion between Albert and Alvin Lee of Ten Years After. The music he chooses to play has a small but devoted following, and thirdly, "he is an unpushy sort of bloke."

Albert would accept all of that. "I didn't have the success that a lot of English players had. You often ask yourself: 'What if this happened or what if that happened?' Looking back, I feel very fortunate in what I've done."[3] In an interview in 1981, he revealed that he didn't think he had ever been successful. "I've always just played for myself because I've enjoyed the music."

August 2007. Calabasas is a long way from Canvey Island, and for Albert, Kidbrooke Park Road seems a hazy and distant memory. Forty-seven years, thousands of gigs, countless albums and innumerable recording sessions mark a career in music which has defined a whole genre in guitar-playing. Yet Pete Wingfield half-jokes that Albert will worry if there's no gig in the next 48 hours. "When he says he likes to be at home and not on the road I don't know if there's an element of double-bluff and he's just saying that because he feels it's what expected. But what you see is what you get with him." There is still a powerful element of the wandering minstrel in Albert, but as the Pretenders' James Honeyman-Scott observed in 1981, "If you're a pro you don't stop playing, you just carry on doing what you do. It's what defines you."[4] Albert would concur and would happily accept that "as long as I have a roof over my head and can feed my family while playing music that I enjoy, I'll be happy." For him, the "stopping place" is wherever he happens to be, for he is a man at ease with himself.

Appendix A:
Albert Lee's Family History

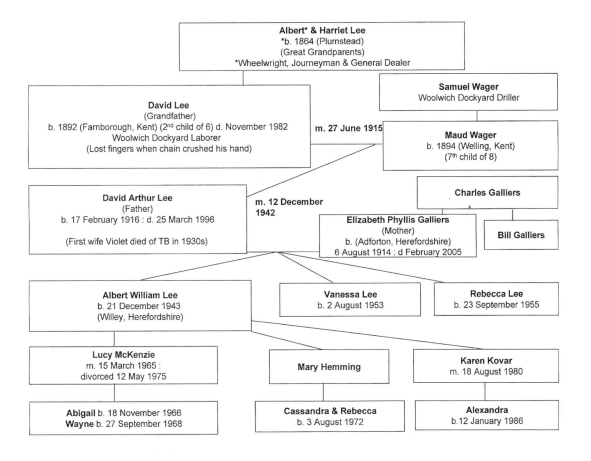

Albert* & Harriet Lee
*b. 1864 (Plumstead)
(Great Grandparents)
*Wheelwright, Journeyman & General Dealer

David Lee
(Grandfather)
b. 1892 (Farnborough, Kent) (2nd child of 6) d. November 1982
Woolwich Dockyard Laborer
(Lost fingers when chain crushed his hand)

m. 27 June 1915

Samuel Wager
Woolwich Dockyard Driller

Maud Wager
b. 1894 (Welling, Kent)
(7th child of 8)

David Arthur Lee
(Father)
b. 17 February 1916 : d. 25 March 1996

(First wife Violet died of TB in 1930s)

m. 12 December 1942

Charles Galliers

Elizabeth Phyllis Galliers
(Mother)
b. (Adforton, Herefordshire)
6 August 1914 : d February 2005

Bill Galliers

Albert William Lee
b. 21 December 1943
(Willey, Herefordshire)

Vanessa Lee
b. 2 August 1953

Rebecca Lee
b. 23 September 1955

Lucy McKenzie
m. 15 March 1965 :
divorced 12 May 1975

Mary Hemming

Karen Kovar
m. 18 August 1980

Abigail b. 18 November 1966
Wayne b. 27 September 1968

Cassandra & Rebecca
b. 3 August 1972

Alexandra
b.12 January 1986

Appendix B: Press Release from Ernie Ball Music Man, August 17, 1993

Ernie Ball Music Man Unveils Albert Lee Model Guitar

Whether it is his legendary work with Emmylou Harris, Rodney Crowell, Eric Clapton or his own solo work, no picker has been more influential in recent years than "Gallery of Greats" guitarist Albert Lee. Ernie Ball Music Man is proud to announce the long-awaited Albert Lee Model Guitar. The body, made of premium quality southern ash, utilizes Music Man's uniquely angular Axis prototype body style. It is contoured front and back for balance and comfort, and comes in a dazzling translucent pink burst finish. Albert has specially selected three Seymour Duncan single-coil pickups with 5-way switching mounted to a white pickguard. Music Man's strings-thru-body standard bridge is made of chrome-plated hardened steel with vintage-style stainless steel saddles for maximum sustain. The neck is figured maple with matching maple fingerboard, and an oil-finished playing area. It has a 25½ inch scale length, 22 special profiled frets, 10 inch radius fretboard, 1⅝ inch width at the nut, and 2¼ inch width at the last fret. Additional neck features include Music Man's exclusive 4 + 2 headstock configuration for straight string alignment, full-length truss rod with easy access adjustment wheel, 5-bolt neck attachment with sculptured neck joint, and recessed neck plate. The tuners are Schaller M6La. Albert's strings are Ernie Ball RPS nickel wound gauges .010 .013 .016 .026 .036 .046.

Chapter Notes

Introduction

1. Quoted in Nick Tosches, *Country—Living Legends and Dying Metaphors in America's Biggest Music* (New York: Charles Scribner's Sons, 1977 and 1985), 28.

2. Tosches, 19.

3. Tosches, 20.

Prologue

1. Vanessa Lee, Albert's younger sister.

2. "Dookering" means telling fortunes in Romany. Information from Vanessa Lee.

3. Traditionally the word referred to Gypsies or vagrants. The first recorded use was in 1847. Though sources agree that the word derives from "pike," the *Bloomsbury Dictionary of Contemporary Slang*, which gives "pikie" as an alternative spelling, indicates that the "precise origins of these terms (and the American term 'piker') are unclear because of the convergence of two similar senses of 'pike': the first is turnpike, a road on which a toll is collected; the second is an archaic British English verb meaning 'to depart or travel.'"

4. "In the 1881 Census most Travelers and Gypsies in Kent were described as 'peddlers, hawkers or general dealers.'" From Simon Evans, *Stopping Places: A Gypsy History of South London and Kent* (University of Hertsfordshire Press, 1999), 20.

5. Evans is responsible for the Romany Roots web pages on the website for BBC Radio Kent and author of *Stopping Places: A Gypsy History of South London and Kent*.

6. Gorgio: a gypsy word for a nongypsy, from the nineteenth century Romany.

7. Evans.

8. Adapted from a paper by Mary Mills, M. Phil., Ph.D., July 1996, quoted on www.gmt2000.co.uk.

9. "During 1966–1976, the five east London boroughs—Greenwich, Lewisham, Newham, Tower Hamlets and Southwark—lost 150,000 jobs, 20 percent of all the jobs in the area." In Jonathan Schneer, The Thames: England's River (Little, Brown, 2005), 267.

10. Charles Jennings, *Greenwich* (Little, Brown, 1999), 148–9.

11. "Elvis Presley was a Gypsy, Da.... He never admitted it, but he was a Rom." Esma Redzepova, quoted in Garth Cartwright, *Princes Amongst Men:*

Journeys with Gypsy Musicians (Serpent's Tail, 2005), 98.

12. John M., July 2003, quoted on www.beerinthe evening.com.

13. Evans.

14. Ibid.

Chapter One

1. The *Times*, December 21, 1943.

2. The *Daily Telegraph*, December 21, 1943.

3. A Greenwich resident, quoted on the BBC website www.bbc.co.uk/dna/ww2.

4. Andrew Blake, *The Land Without Music: Music, Culture and Society in Twentieth Century Britain* (Manchester, UK: University of Manchester Press, 1997).

5. Christopher Booker, *The Neophiliacs* (London: Collins, 1969), 32.

6. Arthur Marwick, *The Explosion of British Society, 1914–62* (London: Pan, 1963), 119.

7. Booker, 84.

8. This piano is now in Llandeilo, in the home of Albert's daughter Rebecca. Underneath the lid one can still see where Albert scratched his initials, incurring his mother's wrath.

9. Mo Foster, *17 Watts? The Birth of British Rock Guitar* (London: Sanctuary, 1997), 61.

10. Shawn Levy, *Ready, Steady, Go* (London: Fourth Estate, 2003), 3.

11. Quoted in Levy, 4.

12. Shakespeare, "As You Like It," Act 2, Scene 7.

13. "I Love You Because," "That's All Right, Mama," "Harbor Lights," "Blue Moon Of Kentucky."

14. Ian Cawood, *Britain in the Twentieth Century* (London: Routledge, 2004), 330.

15. Born during one of the most dramatic thunderstorms for many years. Their mother was a great fan of Daphne du Maurier.

16. Booker, 37: "In August and September the film 'Rock Around The Clock' provoked a series of riots much worse than the slight disorders of the previous year, in the most violent of which a mob of three thousand Teddy Boys rampaged through the South London streets for several hours, leaving trail of broken shop windows and overturned cars."

17. Booker, 32.

18. John Baines, interview.

19. *Melody Maker*, January 19, 1957.

20. Lionel ("Basher") Berry retired and lived a long life, dying a few years ago at the age of 101. Around his one hundredth birthday, on a special day at the School Clubhouse in Kidbrooke, he was reunited with many of the boys on whom he had inflicted physical punishment.

21. Quoted in Spencer Leigh and John Firminger, *Halfway To Paradise: Britpop, 1955–1962* (Folkestone, Kent, UK: Finbarr, 1996), unpaginated.

22. Quoted in Leigh and Firminger, unpaginated.

23. Booker, 38.

24. Iain Chambers, *Popular Culture: The Metropolitan Experience* (London: Routledge, 1986), 158.

25. In 2004 Allhallows escaped a grim end when government consultations finally agreed it would not be necessary to demolish the village to replace it with a parking lot for the third London international airport at Cliffe.

26. Quoted in Leigh and Firminger, unpaginated.

27. Larry Portis, *Soul Trains* (College Station, TX: Virtual Bookworm, 2002), 213.

28. Chambers, 158

29. Booker, 38.

30. *Melody Maker*, August 24, 1957.

Chapter Two

1. According to school records he retired in December 1958 to be replaced by W.L. Garstang. His conversation with Albert was one of his final as head.

2. *Melody Maker*, November 8, 1958.

3. Albert recalls meeting him years later at the Palomino Club in Los Angeles and was so star-struck that "all I could do was to stammer 'Hi, Mr. Robertson!'"

4. Quoted in Spencer Leigh and John Firminger, *Halfway To Paradise: Britpop, 1955–1962* (Folkestone, Kent, UK: Finbarr, 1996), unpaginated.

5. Quoted in Leigh and Firminger, unpaginated.

6. Lennon, "Life is what happens while you are busy making other plans."

7. Shawn Levy, *Ready, Steady, Go* (London: Fourth Estate, 2003), 4–5.

8. Christopher Booker, *The Neophiliacs* (London: Collins, 1969), 38.

9. A.W.E. O'Shaughnessy (1844–1881), quoted in Booker, 106.

10. Booker, 79.

11. Richard Aquila, *That Old Time Rock and Roll: A Chronicle of an Era, 1954–1963* (Chicago: University of Illinois Press, 2000), 21. Aquila is professor of history and director of the American Studies Program at Ball State University, Indiana.

12. Ian Cawood, *Britain in the Twentieth Century* (London: Routledge, 2004), 330. Cawood is a research historian at Newman College of Higher Education, Birmingham, England.

13. Philosopher, writer, sociologist, author of *The Outsider*, 1956.

14. Booker, 92–93.

15. Stanley Cohen, *Folk Devils and Moral Panics* (London: Routledge, 1972), 155.

16. Levy, 5.

17. Ibid.

18. Mick Kemp, an early Blackheath friend, in an e-mail to the author.

19. Formerly Dave Wombwell.

20. Andrzej Olechnowicz, *Working-Class Housing in England Between The Wars: The Becontree Estate* (Oxford, UK: Oxford University Press, 1997), 206.

21. Ibid.

22. Melinda Bilyeu, Hector Cook and Andrew Mon Hughes, *Tales of the Brothers Gibb* (London: Omnibus Press, 2003), 23.

23. Ibid, 25.

24. The only time that name was used. Albert explains: "Delroy's was a rock 'n' roll club in Belmont Hill, Blackheath. We'd go there on Friday nights to listen to the latest rock 'n' roll records. We thought Delroy's sounded American and cool." A little later they became Johnny Lane and the Cruisers.

Chapter Three

1. Albert, Bugs Waddell and Tony Walter, according to Pete Frame, *The Complete Rock Family Trees* (London: Omnibus, 1979), 25.

2. *Melody Maker*, January 2, 1960, 1.

3. Quoted in Spencer Leigh and John Firminger, *Halfway To Paradise: Britpop, 1955–1962* (Folkestone, Kent, UK: Finbarr, 1996), unpaginated.

4. *Melody Maker*, March 12, 1960, 8.

5. *Vintage Guitar* magazine, interview, March 1999.

6. Paul Burlison, whom Albert met in Chicago in July 1990.

7. In 1957 Gibson had changed the layout of the Les Paul Custom model by installing three new humbucking pickups to replace the previous pair of single-coil types, as well as a modified three-way switch to provide what Gibson described as a "much wider range of tone coloring." It is also a very attractive instrument, having block fingerboard inlays and a fancy split-diamond headstock inlay.

8. Later a colleague in the Nightsounds and Country Fever and—almost—Heads, Hands and Feet.

9. Later a colleague in Heads, Hands and Feet.

10. The same Terry Kennedy who had worked with Tony Walter at Noel Gay.

11. A new model would have cost $375 then.

12. Also known as Jimmy Little, whose "When My Little Girl is Smiling" reached number 9 in March 1962 and had hits later that year with "Ain't That Funny?" and "Spanish Harlem."

13. Blackheath and Kidbrooke Girls' School.

14. Shawn Levy, *Ready, Steady, Go* (London: Fourth Estate, 2003), 8

15. Dean Shannon.

16. Later, with Ray, another colleague in Heads, Hands and Feet.

17. Australian noun and verb of the World War I era, meaning "to evade one's own responsibilities and impose on, or prey upon, others" (*Australian National Dictionary Center, Linnaeus Cottage [#96], ANU, ACT 0200*).

18. "If you were a scrappy young musician in London in winter of '62, you might have been able to string together gigs and out food on the table—

maybe—but a roof over your head was another matter. The Jones and Jagger flat in Edith Grove, at the western tip of Chelsea known as World's End. What they got for their money was a hovel of famously fetid squalor and chilly filth. "That revolting fried-up lino pisshole," as [Andrew Loog] Oldham remembered it. And the inhabitants agreed: "It was disgusting," [Keith] Richards recalled, "mould growing on the walls." Nonetheless, he began to crash there so regularly so as to avoid the long commute home that eventually, he his guitar and his fistful of spare clothes became permanent boarders." Levy, 105.

19. Luke Crampton and Dayfydd Rees, *Rock and Pop, Year by Year* (London: Dorling Kindersley, 2003), 117.

20. Jackie Lynton, whom the Jury occasionally backed, describes him as "a funny bloke who was always threatening to leave—he wanted to be the singer, really."

21. "All of Me/I'd Steal" (Piccadilly 7n35064), produced by Les Reed.

22. Graham Vickers, *London's 50 Outstanding Rock Music Landmarks* (London: Omnibus, 2001), 16.

23. Joe Moran, "A chav-free espresso, please," *New Statesman*, September 26, 2005.

24. Leigh, unpaginated.

25. Ibid.

26. Ibid.

27. Tommy Steele's real name.

28. From www.carlolittle.com.

Chapter Four

1. Alan Clayson, *Hamburg: The Cradle of British Rock* (London: Sanctuary, 1998), 27.

2. Roger White, *The Everly Brothers: Walk Right Back* (London: Plexus, 1998), 87.

3. Musicians' argot for skills or technique.

4. This was Bill Wyman.

5. Singles then cost 6/3d., EPs 10/1d. and LPs £1/10/11d..

6. The postwar West German army.

7. Christopher Booker, *The Neophiliacs* (London: Collins, 1969), 190.

8. Fender had made necks out of maple until 1959, when the first necks in rosewood were made.

9. Interview in *Vintage Guitar*, March/April 1999.

10. American soul/R&B singer and an ex–U.S. serviceman. Washington, with the Ram Jam Band, became a major star in the London clubs, notably the Flamingo, in the mid–60s. He is still touring.

11. A British band—no relation.

12. Shawn Levy, *Ready, Steady, Go* (London: Fourth Estate, 2003), 8.

13. Ibid.

14. Formby's lyrics were deemed to have contained too many too obvious double entendres.

15. In 1960, the Fender 4×10" Bassman combo was redesigned as a 2×12" piggyback.

16. The narrow panel Fender Bassman amplifier was manufactured from 1955 to 1960.

Chapter Five

1. "Do You Want to Know a Secret?," "Bad To Me" and "Little Children."

2. *Record Collector*, obituary, June 2006, 27.

3. He was originally named after the legendary American jazz guitarist Tal Farlow. By the end of the year Chris Farlow had some how acquired an "e."

4. Part of the series *Martin Scorsese Present the Blues—A Musical Journey*, 2005.

5. Now O'Neill's.

6. Bernard Levin, *The Pendulum Years: Britain and the Sixties* (London: Jonathan Cape, 1970), 270.

7. Jon Mojo Mills, *Shindig Magazine*, February 2001.

8. *The Guardian*, October 10, 2003.

9. With the arguable exception of "Out Of Time," discussed later in this chapter.

10. Christopher Sandford, *Mick Jagger: Rebel Knight* (London: Omnibus, 2003), 95.

11. With Keith Richard and Andrew Loog Oldham.

12. Interview with Kevin Swift included on *Chris Farlow: The Immediate Anthology* CD.

13. "I joined the Buck Owens Fan Club about 1965. His mother used to run the club and I still have the membership card signed by her. I played at his birthday party up in Bakersfield a few years ago and pulled the card out of my pocket on stage and everybody loved it. He wanted to see it afterwards."

14. Chas Hodges, *The Rock 'n' Roll Years of Chas Before Dave* (Wheathampstead, Hertfordshire, UK: Lennard, 1987), 88.

15. See Chapter 2.

16. In August, with Farlowe at number 1, it cost only 6/- (30p) to see them at the California.

17. Prime Minister Harold Wilson reopened the club in July.

18. Sandford, 95.

19. See Albert's comment, p. XXX.

20. Music business entrepreneur Richard Carl Percival "Rik" Gunnell was born July 23, 1931, and died in Germany, June 3, 2007.

21. The Hollies' cover reached number 2 in February 1964.

22. On the Music for Pleasure label, the LP cost 12/6d., and now commands up to £35 on the Internet.

23. Namely, "Out of Time," "Harper Valley PTA" and "When I'm 64."

24. Quoted on www.platform-end.co.uk.

25. Reissued in February 1993 as *Everything I Do is Wrong* (PILZ 44 8223/2), credited to Albert and Jimmy Page, and also in November 2001 on MagMid /Cadillac. The tracks which feature Albert and Jimmy are "Lovin' Up a Storm," "Boll Weevil Rock," "Livin' Lovin' Wreck," "One Long Kiss," "Down the Line," "Breathless" and "Rave On." Albert thinks its original title was *Burn Up*.

26. *Melody Maker*, February 17, 1968, 10.

27. *Melody Maker*, February 10, 1968.

Chapter Six

1. *The Rough Guide to Country Music*, 164.

2. Ibid., 166.

3. On the LP *Help*, 1965.

4. Ian Macdonald, *Revolution in the Head* (London: Pimlico, 1995), 127.

5. Simon Evans: "Wayne is a very common gypsy name, influenced by country music."

6. *Uncut*, August 2006, 62.

7. James Burton, Jimmy Bryant, Don Rich and Clarence White.

8. Interview with Rob Walker in *Australian Musician*, no. 21, Autumn 2000.

9. Following the success of Deep Purple, Lawrence had latitude and capital to indulge himself—notably his idea of a studio collective.

10. The sole surviving badly scratched acetate of Albert's solo album indicated the following track listing. Side one: "Long Gone," "Too Much of Nothing," "Only Daddy That'll Walk The Line," "Mama Tried," "Rocky Top Tennessee," "Country in Harlem." Side two: "Lay Lady Lay," "Memphis Streets," "Tears of Rage," "The Victim," "Tonight I'll be Staying Here with You," "Milk Float."

11. *Country Fever/Black Claw, Featuring Albert Lee & Chas Hodges*. All tracks produced by Derek Lawrence. Originally recorded at Kingsway Studios, London, between 1968 and 1970. Original mixes at Kingsway and Gold Star, Hollywood. Remix engineer Peter Vince, Abbey Road Studios, May 1991. Reissued in 2003 as *That's All Right Mama: The Country Fever & Black Claw Sessions* on Castle Music (CMQCD 800).

12. Released as Bell BLL 1052.

13. Commonly just called Woodstock.

14. The single appeared as Bell 839.

15. Bell BLL 1089.

16. See Chapter Five.

17. See Chapter Five.

18. Lucky LU 106.

19. "I've Just Seen a Face."

20. Rediffusion International Music (R.I.M ZS50).

21. Lucky 3003.

22. See Chapter 3.

23. Later Gary Glitter.

24. The album was eponymously titled and issued on Verve SVLP6012 in the U.K. and Paramount PAS 5010 in the U.S.A. The UK track listing was: "Please Me, She's Me," "The Days I Most Remember," "Jacqueline," "Now You've Hurt My Feelings" "Light My Fire and Burn My Lamp," "Good Evening, Mr. Jones," "The Fable," "Ride Out on the Morning Train (In the California Dew)," and "Twilight Zone." The U.S. version has two different tracks from the U.K. version: "Dirty Heavy Weather Road" and "Sackfull of Grain" in place of "Jacqueline" and "The Fable." All eleven tracks are available on Rock in Beat Records (RB 0-28), 1999.

25. Issued in January 1996 as Home From Home: The Missing Album on See For Miles (B000001lCR).

26. Track listing: "Bringing It All on My Own Head," "Ain't Gonna Let It Get Me Down," "How Does It Feel to Be Right All the Time?," "Achmed," "Precious Stone," "Friend of a Friend," "Windy & Warm," "Who Turned Off the Dark?," "Can You See Me?," "Home from Home," "Make Me Feel Much Better."

27. Geoff Doherty, *A Promoter's Tale: Rock at the Sharp End* (London: Omnibus, 2002), 81.

28. Interview with *Zigzag* magazine, August 14, 1970.

29. Polydor 56342.

30. Immediate IMLP 024, 1969.

31. British female blues/rock singer. See Chapter Three.

32. Clinton Heylin, *No More Sad Refrains: The Life and Times of Sandy Denny* (London: Helter Skelter, 2000), 117.

33. Ibid., 119.

Chapter Seven

1. Reissued in November 2001 as the two-CD set *Short Stories/Stained Glass* on the Road Goes on Forever label (RGFSGDCD048).

2. Released in March 1972 as Decca 75269 in the United Kingdom and as MCA MKPS 2021 in the United States. The first CD reissue was in 1988 on the See for Miles label, and it was remastered and reissued on CD on November 1, 1991, as *The Green Bullfrog Sessions*, with three unreleased tracks, on Connoisseur (NSP CD 503).

3. *Something* was issued in 1970 on United Artists (UAS. 29100.01). Tracks include "Something," "Spinning Wheel," "The Sea And Sand" and "My Way."

4. *Movements* (Warner Bros. WS 3002/K46054), 1970.

5. Issued in July 1970 on Stateside (SS8054).

6. *The Old And The New Brian Golbey*, LUS 3010.

7. An office and a flat in Edgware Road, where Pete Gavin lived.

8. Interview, August 14, 1970.

9. "Cleanliness is very important—if you go inside most gypsy caravan they are absolutely spotless. There's a Romany word, 'mockadee,' which means 'dirty,' and there's a difference between the inside and the outside of the body. While the outside of the body may be 'mockadee,' what you put inside your mouth must be scrupulously clean, so you'll find they have separate bowls for doing the dishes in, for washing your hands in, for washing your clothes in." Simon Evans, interview.

10. Ray is correct: Listen to side one, track five, on *Mountain Music Jamboree*, Rediffusion International Music (ZS50), 1970.

11. *Exchange and Mart* is a publication of long standing which advertises and facilitates the buying and selling of a huge range of goods—a sort of pre–Internet eBay.

12. The part of a song which links the main verse and chorus to the second half, often called the "middle eight."

13. The other part of the name Elton John refers to Long John Baldry.

14. The songs were rerecorded in Los Angeles for Browne's debut album on Asylum Records, *Jackson Browne*, also known as "Saturate Before Using."

15. Dick Clark Productions produced *American Bandstand*, a weekly teenage music show, during the late 1960s.

16. The lead singer of the Four Seasons, America's major vocal group of the early '60s.

17. Chas Hodges, *The Rock 'n' Roll Years of Chas Before Dave* (Wheathampstead, Hertfordshire, UK: Lennard, 1987), 124.

18. Capitol LP SVBB 680 was a double album in the United States, and Island LP ILPS 9149 in the United Kingdom. The albums were issued with the same covers.

19. Featuring a Heads, Hands and Feet trio (Albert, Chas and Pete) doing a never-recorded number, "A Hard Road" and "Country Boy," on which Albert played his 1960 Telecaster with rosewood fingerboard.

20. A Mini with the roof cut down low. "I bought it when I was with Country Fever. Jed Kelly the drummer had a chopped Mini and when I found one in the Old Kent Road I had to have it."

21. On September 28, 1971, playing "Warming up the Band," now available on *The Old Grey Whistle Test, Volume 2* (BBC DVD 1279). "On OGWT we mimed to a track and I played most of the guitars on the track anyway. Yes, I played a Spanish Dobro."

22. Issued on Purple TPSA 7501.

23. The author is indebted to an e-mail from Charlie James of Little Rock, Arkansas, for these comments.

24. *Melody Maker*, October 23, 1971.

25. *Melody Maker*, November 6, 1971.

26. Albert had bought it from Tony Sheridan, who had used it when playing with the Beatles.

27. Supported by Les Payne and Tamlin, with tickets 13/- (65p) at the door.

28. Later to write "Riverdance" and "The Seville Suite."

29. The U.K. version is on Pye LP NSPL 18376.

30. Issued on Pye (45 7N45114).

31. Released on April 21 on Island ILPS 9185.

32. "Go All the Way," no. 4 in the U.S.A.

33. The piano player on the album, with the pseudonym Rockaday Johnnie, was Elton John.

34. Interview with Chris Welch in *Melody Maker*.

35. *David Elliott*, Atlantic SD-7222.

36. Issued on Atlantic K40465.

37. On "Warming Up the Band."

38. He moved on to join Elkie Brooks and Robert Palmer in Vinegar Joe.

39. Hodges, 125.

Chapter Eight

1. *The London Session*, on Mercury 6672008/Bear Family 1524, released in March 1973.

2. I am indebted to John Pearce of the *New Musical Express*, who was present throughout the sessions.

3. "Sea Cruise," "Early Morning Rain," "Pledging My Love," "Gold Mine in the Sky," "Trouble in Mind," "Bad Moon Rising" and "Don't Put No Headstones on My Grave" were cut on the second day.

4. Nick Tosches, *Country, Living Legends and Dying Metaphors in America's Biggest Music*, revised edition (New York: Scribners, 1985), 222–3.

5. Written during World War II by Stick McGhee, the brother of blues great Brownie McGhee. In the Pacific Northwest, high school students used to call a partially hollowed-out watermelon filled with vodka a "spo-dee-o-dee."

6. John Pearce, *New Musical Express*, February 17, 1973.

7. Tosches, 222–3.

8. Issued on Transatlantic TRA 266, re-released in 2006 on Pier Records (PierCD 503).

9. Reissued in June 2006 on Sunbeam Records (SBRCD5025).

10. Jaki is now living in rural France. Her latest album, by her family band, Court of Miracles, is *Miracle Style*, distributed by Night & Day (ACT03001).

11. *EH in London*, or *The Eddie Harris London Sessions*, issued on Atlantic 1647 in 1974 and re-released on Collectables Jazz Classic, Atlantic Records, 1999.

12. *All Music Guide.*

13. *Music, Music, Music*, issued on Amsterdam 12013 and 12015.

14. A device fitted across all the guitar strings, so as to raise the pitch of each string simultaneously.

15. Jerry Ivan Allison, drummer with the Crickets, always known as "JI."

16. Released in October 1973 on Vertigo 1020. Tracks: "Find Out What's Happening," "Lay Lady Lay Down," "Rock & Roll Man," "I'm Gonna Ruin Your Health," "Rhyme & Time," "Decoy Baker," "Losin' Streak," "Atmore," "The Truth Is Still the Same," "Hitchhike Out to Venus," "Ooh Las Vegas," "Draggin' Chains."

17. *In Style with the Crickets* (Coral CRL 57320/CRL 757320), December 1960; *Bobby Vee Meets the Crickets* (Liberty LRP 3228/LST3228), March 1962; *Something Old, Something New, Somethin' Else!!!* (Liberty LRP 3272/LST 7272), January 1963; *California Sun* (Liberty LRP 3351/LST 7351), February 1964; *A Collection* (Liberty LBY 1258), May 1965; *Rock Reflections* (Sunset SLS 50207), March 1971; *Bubblegum, Bop, Ballad and Boogies* (Phillips 6308149), 1973.

18. One of the original Drifters. He wrote "Move It" for Cliff Richard.

19. Released on Mercury 6310007, only in the U.K., 1974. Tracks: "An American Love Affair," "Lay Lady Lay Down," "Decoy Baker," "He's Got a Way with Women," "Rhyme & Time," "I Got a Thing About You Baby," "You Make It Way Too Hard," "Ain't Protestin'," "Bony Moronie" "Ooh Las Vegas," "Find Out What's Happening," "I Like Your Music" "Now and Then It's Gonna Rain."

20. An engaging singer-songwriter, best known for "Time in a Bottle" and "I'll Have to Say I Love You in A Song."

21. Released on Atlantic (SD1648) in July 1974, reissued in March 2000 on Wounded Bird Records (121029).

22. Jim Newsom, *All Music Guide.*

23. *Sunset Towers*, issued on Ode 77023, 1974; issued in the U.K. on AMLS 2001; re-released in 2000 on Raven (RVCD74) double CD with *Don Everly* (1970). Tracks: "Melody Train," "Jack Daniels, Old No. 7," "Warming Up the Band," "Helpless When You're Gone," "Did It Rain?," "Brand New Rock & Roll Band," "Takin' Shots," "The Way You Remain," "Evelyn Swing," "Southern California."

24. Roger White, *The Everly Brothers: Walk Right Back* (London: Plexus, 1998), 131.

25. *I've Always Been Crazy*, issued on Epic Records and RCA Records (AFL1-2979), September 1978. Tracks: "I've Always Been Crazy" "Don't You Think This Outlaw Bit's Done Got Out of Hand," "Billy" "A Long Time Ago" "As the 'Billy World Turns," "Medley of Buddy Holly Hits" ("Well All Right"/"It's So

Easy"/"Maybe Baby"/"Peggy Sue"), "I Walk the Line," "Tonight the Bottle Let Me Down," Girl I Can Tell (You're Trying to Work It Out)."

26. Bob Carlson.

27. Jim Eaton from Santa Susana, California.

28. The line-up was Joe Cocker, vocals; Albert Lee, guitar; Greg Brown, bass; Mick Weaver, keyboards; Pete Gavin, drums. After a while, Greg Brown was fired, and Andy Denno took his place.

29. In a postcard from the Sunset Marquis on North Alta Loma, Los Angeles.

30. Issued in April 1976 on A&M 3945742; re-released in July 1994.

31. James Chrispell, *All Music Guide*.

32. *New Musical Express*, 1976.

33. The lightning-fast guitarist of Ten Years After, the progressive rock band that was featured playing "Going Home" in the film *Woodstock*.

34. Reissued in March 2004 in the U.K. on Rhino Records 8122735932.

35. Reissued on Wounded Bird Records (WOU 1655), April 2001.

36. Scott Yanow, *All Music Guide*.

37. Issued in May 1976, Anchor 2007.

38. *Chris Farlowe Band—Live*, issued on Polydor 2460259 in November 1975, CD reissue Out of Time CDEC 7. Tracks: "We're Gonna Make It," "Rhyme and Time," "Peace of Mind," "After Midnight," "Only Women Bleed," "Mandy," "Hot Property," "Handbags and Gladrags," "Medley: You Haven't Done Nothin'/It Ain't No Use." CD bonus track: "We Can Work It Out."

39. Issued on Asylum 8122-78912-2, 1976.

40. From "The Road Not Taken" by Robert Frost, published in 1916 in his collection *Mountain Interval*.

Chapter Nine

1. Born Ronald Clyde Crosby in Oneonta, New York, and best known for his song "Mr. Bojangles."

2. See Chapter 8.

3. Issued on Jubilee JGS-8031. Reissued in 1979 on the Emus label in the U.S. (ES-12052); also reissued in the U.K. on the Pye label in 1977, under the title *The Legendary "Gliding Bird" Album*.

4. Issued in June 1975 on Reprise (MS 2213), re-released and remastered in February 2004 on Rhino CD (78108).

5. Peter Doggett, *Are You Ready for the Country?* (London: Penguin, 2000), 410.

6. On Reprise (R2286), re-released and remastered on Rhino CD (78109), March 2004.

7. Doggett, 396.

8. From *Emmylou Harris: From a Deeper Well*, BBC 4, September 3, 2004.

9. Issued in January 1977 on Warner Bros. (7599-27338-2). Remastered and re-released in February 2004 on Rhino/WEA (78110).

10. Emmylou gave Albert a gold copy of the record, which hung on the wall at Kidbrooke Park Road.

11. January 15, 1977.

12. *Zigzag*, February 1977.

13. Both albums were re-released on a Raven CD (RVCD119) on May 8, 2001, under the title *The Ahern Sessions*.

14. Released in 1977 on Reprise (MS 2238), re-released on Wounded Bird Records (3020), 2005.

15. From his 1976 album, *Fearless*. His mother, Mae Boren Axton, was the co-author of Elvis Presley's landmark "Heartbreak Hotel."

16. Albert: "Eric told me that George Harrison heard the album and the standout track for him was my track, 'Evangelina.'"

17. Heroic Records 0002.

18. Released on January 1, 1977 on United Artists (ALA827H) and in the U.K. in 1978 on Chrysalis (CHR 1158).

19. *Joan Armatrading*, issued September 1976 on A&M (AMLH 64588).

20. Sean Mayes, *Joan Armatrading* (Weidenfeld and Nicholson), 73.

21. Telephone conversation with author, October 3, 2005.

22. Issued in the United States on A&M in June 1977 (A&M SP-8414).

23. Mayes, op. cit, 70.

24. Recorded on April 12, 1977, Tim Corcoran directing, Michael Appleton producing.

25. "Feeling Single," "Seeing Double," "I'll Be Your San Antone Rose," "Pancho & Lefty," "Making Believe," "You Never Can Tell," "Tulsa Queen," "Together Again," "Luxury Liner," "Ooh Las Vegas."

26. Bob Howe, writing in *Capital News*, December 1985.

27. Released in April 1977 on Hickory (AH44003).

28. Roger White, *The Everly Brothers: Walk Right Back* (London: Plexus, 1998), 233.

29. Released in January 1978 on Warner Bros. (BSK-3141), re-released on Warner Bros./Rhino (8122-78112) in 2004.

30. Issued as a Warner Bros. single (WBS-8553) in March 1978.

31. Issued on Warner BSK-3228, re-released in October 2002 on Audium Entertainment AUD8164.

32. Doggett, 397.

33. Doggett, ibid.

34. "Albert's solos," says Hank De Vito, "had a beginning, a middle and an end."

35. A term used to describe someone who is half-Romany.

36. Luke Crampton and Dayfydd Rees, *Book of Rock Stars* (Guinness, 1989), 305.

37. *Hiding*, released in 1979 on A&M Records (AMLH 64750). Tracks: "Country Boy," "Billy Tyler," "Are You Wasting My Time?" "Now and Then It's Gonna Rain," "On a Real Good Night," "Setting Me Up," "Ain't Living Long Like This," "Hiding," "Hotel Love," "Come Up and See Me Anytime." Re-released on May 10, 2004, on Raven Records, Australia (RVCD 187). Thom Jurek, in *All Music Guide*: "Why does it take a non–American label to reissue the finest gems from the North American labels that birthed them? Given that both of these records [*Hiding* and *Albert Lee*] appeared on labels now owned by Universal, there is no excuse that they haven't been issued stateside."

38. On Epic FE39410.

39. Doggett, 420.

40. Issued in November 1978 on Warner Bros (BSK3243), re-released in February 2005 on Wounded

Bird 3243. Sadly, she died of a cerebral edema in 1997. Both her albums are available on CD.3SK 3243

41. Released in January 1978 on Capitol (ST11752).

42. Issued on Warner Bros P-10609W.

43. White, 134.

44. Issued in 1979 on Epic/Legacy JE-35544, re-released by Sony in June 2005 (E2K92562). The re-release adds a full album of recordings not included on the original LP and another full CD of his best duets for other albums, both his and other peoples.'

45. Issued on Full Moon/Epic Records (JE35545) in February 1979, re-released in August 1995 on Gadlfy 208.

46. Released on Warner Bros. (BSK-3318) in April 1979, re-released on Warner Bros/Rhino (R2 78112) in 2004.

47. *Melody Maker*, December 16, 1978.

48. Issued on A&M SP4767, re-released in February 2006 on Universal Japan (UICY 93004).

49. Issued in 1981 on EMI EMS1001, re-released in 2005 on EMI Gold 7243-4-77313-2-7.

50. Marc Roberty, *Eric Clapton: The Complete Recording Sessions, 1963–1992* (New York: St. Martin's, 1993), 107.

51. "Lee had been added at the suggestion of Roger Forrester, who felt that a second guitar would bring a fuller sound to such concert staples as 'Badge' and 'Layla.'" Michael Schumacher, *Crossroads: The Life and Music of Eric Clapton* (Little, Brown, 1995), 225.

52. *The Dice Man* was a cult novel in the '70s. The book, written by George Cockcroft under the pen name Luke Rhinehart, tells the story of a psychiatrist who begins making life decisions based on the casting of dice.

Chapter Ten

1. According to Clapton, the "woman-tone" is achieved by rolling the tone control all the way off on either the neck or the bridge pickup of a guitar with humbucking pickups and the volume all the way up. Heavy strings and a bassy-sounding amp at high volume also helps to achieve that wooing, whooshing tone. In fact, a lot of Clapton's "woman tone" was achieved this way (with a wah-wah pedal), with the pedal about three-quarters back from the forward position. (From *Guitar Player* magazine, Gear Guru, March 1993.)

2. From www.sligo-ireland.com/sligobands.htm.

3. Ray Coleman, Coleman, *Survivor* (London: Sidgwick and Jackson, 1985), 193.

4. Issued in November 1978 (RSO 3039), remastered and released on Polydor (31453-1826-2), September 1996.

5. Michael Schumacher, *Crossroads: The Life and Music of Eric Clapton* (London: Little, Brown, 1995), 225.

6. From www.geetarz.org/reviews/clapton/1979-04-20-alabama.htm.

7. Marc Roberty, *Eric Clapton in His Own Words* (London: Omnibus, 1993), 42.

8. Harry Shapiro, *Eric Clapton: Lost In the Blues.* (New York: Da Capo, 1992), 152.

9. Radle died in May 1980, at the age of 37, from the effects of alcohol and narcotics.

10. Schumacher, 228.

11. From www.geetarz.org/reviews/clapton/1979-05-25-augusta.htm.

12. On Swan Song SSK59409, re-released in March 1991 on Atlantic/WEA (ATL 8507).

13. "I took a week off to have a baby [Meghann Theresa Ahern]," born September 9, 1979.

14. Issued on Warner Bros. BSK3422 in April 1980, re-released in 2002 on Warner Bros 8122-78140.2, with two bonus tracks.

15. Composed by Tom James and Jerry Organ, the song was popularized in the early '50s by Lester Flatt and Earl Scruggs and can be found on *Flatt and Scruggs, Country and Western Classics*, Time-Life Records LP (TLCW-04), 1982.

16. Albert also played on Juice Newton's *Take Heart* (Capitol SN16244) and Ricky Skaggs' *Sweet Temptation* (Sugar Hill 3706), both in 1979.

17. Colman took over producing Stevens and took him to #1 in February 1981 with *This Ole House.*

18. On Epic EPC8090.

19. Released for the first time in 2001, on Sincere Sounds (HankCD 001).

20. Hank Wangford, from album sleeve notes.

21. October 8, 1979.

22. Cockney rhyming slang, from "Barnet fair," meaning "hair," from the London borough of Barnet.

23. Schumacher, 228.

24. Ibid.

25. Shapiro, 153.

26. October 27, 1979.

27. On sleeve notes of Polydor CD, 1996.

28. Issued as *Just One Night* in May 1980, (RSO RSDX 2), re-released on Polydor 31453 1827-2 in September 1996.

29. The album includes Albert singing Mark Knopfler's "Setting Me Up."

30. Interview, March/April 1999.

31. Coleman, 270.

32. Schumacher, 230.

33. Marc Roberty, *The Complete Guide to the Music of Eric Clapton* (Omnibus, 1995), 97.

34. Shapiro, 154.

35. Marc Roberty, *The Complete Guide to the Music of Eric Clapton* (Omnibus, 1995), 97.

36. Ibid.

37. Marc Roberty, *Eric Clapton: The Complete Recording Sessions, 1963–1992* (New York: St. Martin's, 1993), 113.

38. There is a bootleg version on MidValley 056/ SB6.

39. Coleman, 233.

40. Coleman, 243.

41. Renowned session player in L.A. who worked with the Grateful Dead and Bonnie Raitt.

42. Issued on Flying Fish 70227.

43. *The Legend of Jesse James* has been re-released twice as a 2-CD set paired with *White Mansions*, first in 1997 on A&M in the U.K. under the title *Confederate Tales*, (A&M 6004) and in 1999 in the U.S. on Mercury Nashville as *White Mansions and The Legend of Jesse James* (314-540 791-2).

44. Brian Hinton, *Country Roads: How Country Came to Nashville* (London: Sanctuary, 2000), 33.

45. Robert K. Oermann, sleeve notes on Mercury-Nashville CD, June 1999.

46. Issued in February 1981 as *Another Ticket* on RSO 2479285. Re-released in September 1996 on Polydor 531-830-2.

47. Marc Roberty, *Eric Clapton: The Complete Recording Sessions, 1963–1992*, 114.

48. See Rodney Crowell's comments in Chapter 9.

49. After Rawicz and Landauer, a popular piano duo in the '40s and '50s.

50. In an article by Rich Kienzle at http://personal.riverusers.com/~debed/tjbs.htm.

51. Issued on Reprise WB 56 880.

52. Warner Bros. Records 23603, remastered and re-released on Eminent Records, May 2000.

53. Issued in 1981 on CBS, FC 37157.

54. Released in April 1982 on Logo, GOL 1035. Re-released by Line in 1990 and Hannibal in July 1993. Bert Jansch believes the album appeared on Kicking Mule in the States.

55. Issued on Warner Bros BSK-3407.

56. Issued on Mercury 6359098, March 1982, re-released on Line CD July 1994.

57. Part of the unreleased album *Turn Up Down*.

58. Released in August 1982 on Polydor POLS 1067, reissued in 2000 on Raven Records RVCD 187.

59. From *Honky Tonk Angel* (MCA /Universal 42223), 1988.

60. *Givin' Herself Away* on Warner Bros. BSK-3636, 1982.

61. Coleman, 167.

62. Schumacher, 244.

63. Coleman, 271.

64. Schumacher, 246.

65. Coleman, 274.

66. Issued in February 1983 on Duck W3773, remastered and reissued on Warner Bros. (9382-47734-2) in 2000.

67. Schumacher, 247.

68. A clip of the show can be seen on YouTube.

69. *Behind the Sun*, produced by Phil Collins.

Chapter Eleven

1. Roger White, *The Everly Brothers: Walk Right Back* (London: Plexus, 1998), 147.

2. Ibid., 148.

3. Ibid, 149.

4. Ibid., 150.

5. Ibid.

6. Richard Williams, *The Times*, 1985.

7. Pete Wingfield: "The Everlys reunion concert—it's been out a million times on CD but has never been out as was, it's always been edited around." Available as a 2-CD set on Castle Music from 2000 (PIEDD 230) and on DVD (BBC/Delilah Films, 82876 50675 9), 2002.

8. Penny Reel, *New Musical Express*, October 8, 1983.

9. White, 152.

10. For *EB84*.

11. Issued in 1985 on Warner Bros., re-released in June 1998 on Warner Bros. in U.S. and WEA International (7599-25205-2).

12. Big Jim Sullivan: "You couldn't bend a normal set of strings. I've got 13s on my jazz guitar and we were using 15s—that's all you could get. Eddie Cochran was using the banjo strings and showed us the way he used them."

13. Issued in May 1980 on Arista AL 9528.

14. On Elektra 60448.

15. Albert reckoned the studios would have cost between £1,000 and £1,200 a day.

16. White, 155.

17. Ibid., 156.

18. On "Love Me Do," "John and Paul's vocal harmony is patterned after the Everly Brothers, minus the refinement" (Tim Riley, *Tell Me Why: A Beatles Commentary* [London: Bodley Head, 1988], 41). On "Please, Please Me," "the main influence was...The Everly Brothers' 1960 No. 1 'Cathy's Clown.' Lennon and McCartney were practiced Everlys impersonators" (Ian Macdonald, *Revolution in the Head* [London: Pimlico, 1995], 44).

19. Issued in the U.S.A. in August 1984 as *EB84* (822431-1M-1) and in September as *The Everly Brothers in Britain* (MERH 44), where it reached #36.

20. It reached #41 in Britain in September (880-213-7 or MER 170).

21. German photographer and film director, 1902–2003.

22. Australian-born pianist, composer, and champion of the saxophone and the concert band, 1882–1961.

23. By Patrick MacDonald, staff critic, August 9, 1984.

24. Michael Goldberg, *Rolling Stone*, March 14, 1985.

25. Issued as *Born Yesterday* in February 1986 on Mercury 826142-1M-1.

26. Jay Cocks, *Time* magazine, March 17, 1986.

27. White, 159.

28. Ibid.

29. Ibid.

30. Issued as *Speechless* in 1986 on MCA Master Series (MCA5693). Tracks: "T-Bird to Vegas," "Bullish Boogie," "Seventeenth Summer," "Salt Creek," "Arkansas Traveler," "Cannonball," "Romany Rye," "Erin."

31. *Bay Area Magazine*, the free music paper in the San Francisco Bay area.

32. Issued in 1987 on Warner Bros. Records 25491.

33. December 2000, 41.

34. July 1987.

35. Issued in February 1987 on MCA Master Series (MCAC-42063). Tracks: "Flowers of Edinburgh," "Don't Let Go," "Midnight Special," "Tiger Rag," "Forty Miles of Bad Road," "Fun Raunch Boogie," "Walkin' After Midnight," "Schön Rosmarin," "Country Gentleman," "Monte Nido," "Oklahoma Stroke."

36. Morris, a motor mechanic, introduced Albert into the mysteries of the vintage Ferrari engine.

37. They are now available on Amazon.com, however.

Chapter Twelve

1. James Baldwin, in "A Talk to Teachers," October 16, 1963, published in *The Price of the Ticket*, 1965.

2. A jazz musician's expression for working on a song note for note until it is perfect.

3. Released in May 1989 as *Some Hearts* (Mercury 832 520-1).

4. Roger White, *The Everly Brothers: Walk Right Back* (London: Plexus, 1998), 160.

5. Ibid.

6. Ibid.

7. Ibid.

8. Ibid., 169.

9. Ibid., 7.

10. Tracks appeared on *Waiting in the Wings* (Line, 1992); originally released in Spain as *Farlowe* (Barsa LP 0025; CD 0025, 1992); also on Freestyle JHD054.

11. MCA 42223.

12. Columbia FC 44384.

13. Epic FE 45027.

14. Issued on Stony Plain Records (Stony Plain 1140), October 1990.

15. Issued by Sony Canada (SCD 2266), 1992.

16. Issued in March 1996 on Avid (MC480), re-released in 2005 on Round Tower Records (RTMCD76).

17. Issued in July 1989 on MCA (MCA 6319). Material from the album is also featured on *The MCA Years: A Retrospective*, issued in 1993 (MCA 10914).

18. In *All Music Guide*.

19. White, 167.

20. The gig with Linda Ronstadt never happened as Andrew Gold and Kenny Edwards were already on guitar. Having signed a contract, Albert was "blown out of the tour, but eventually with the help of lawyers I got paid."

21. Issued as *Turning For Home* in February 1991 on Sony.

22. Issued on Curb Records (CRBD-10630).

23. Issued in 1990 on Reprise (26139).

24. Issued on Giant (4-24499).

25. The show aired in November 1992.

26. In 1988 he was nominated for Best Country & Western Vocal Performance-Duet with Glen Campbell for "The Hand That Rocks the Cradle."

27. Issued in 1991 as *I Am Ready*, on Arista.

28. A celebration of how Irish music has spread its influences across the world.

29. "'The name "Everly" has appeared in Ireland. We never asked our Dad where the songs came from but I guess many of them must have come with the settlers,' says Don." White, 7.

30. Released on PolyGram Records (314512101 2) in April 1992.

31. Released on Philo Records (1144) in 1992.

32. By Trevor Wilks in the *Daily Post*.

33. *Country Music People*, January 1992.

34. Released in on RCA (07863-66117-4).

35. Released in March 1995 on Mill Records.

36. *Advanced Country Guitar* (VHO-0125D), released in May 1993. Also available is *Virtuoso Techniques* (VH0151-D).

37. Albert's old Blackheath friend, who claims to have called their first skiffle group the Dewdrops.

38. Available on Heroic Records (Heroic0002) and from www.albertleeandhogansheroes.com.

39. Released on DVD in May 2001 by Second Sight Films, also in July 2004 by Music Video Distributors.

40. Ron Coleman was a former bass-guitarist with the Everly Brothers and played at the memorable night at the Knott's Berry Farm in 1973.

41. Released in Canada on BMG Music in 1993 and in USA on Arista in May 1995.

42. See Appendix B.

43. Interview with Kenny Ferguson for the Guitar Society.

44. Where Albert took in the Australian Formula 1 Grand Prix with George Harrison.

45. Released in April 1995 on River North label (MC499).

46. Released on Blue Plate (BMP 300-2), re-released 2005 on Aquinnah Records.

47. Released on Elektra 61442.

48. White, 169.

49. Review in *Superpicker* magazine, No. 14, Summer 1993.

50. "A charming guy and a great player": Albert.

51. Released in September 1995 on High Tone Records (HCD8067).

Chapter Thirteen

1. Mark Twain, *Huckleberry Finn*, Chapter 23.

2. Harold (Chuck) Willis (January 31, 1928—April 10, 1958) was an American blues/rock singer and songwriter who topped the charts in 1957 with "C.C. Rider."

3. Bill Wyman with Ray Coleman, *Stone Alone: The Story of a Rock 'n' Roll Band* (London: Viking, 1990), 66.

4. *Struttin' Our Stuff*, released in October 1997 on BMG Classics (74321-51441 2).

5. Issued as *Honky Tonk Reprise* in June 1996 on Rounder Records (3136).

6. Eugene Chadbourne is an American composer, guitarist and banjoist, also known as the inventor of the electric rake. This "musical" instrument is made by attaching a microphone or an electric guitar pickup to an ordinary lawn rake.

7. Released as *Mais Yeah* in August 1999 on PMB Music (PMB 10004].

8. In 1957 Hawkins blended rock 'n' roll with the distinctive blues sound of black Delta players on "Susie Q" while fellow Louisiana guitarist James Burton provided the signature riff and solo.

9. Gypsy swing, or "Django music," has seen a renaissance over the past decade, with a particular concentration in the American Northwest, viz. the DjangoFest held every May in San Francisco.

10. See http://homepage.eircom.net/~albertlee/news.html.

11. On Edsel Records (EDCD547), issued in February 1998.

12. *Anyway the Wind Blows*, on BMG Classics (74321 59523 2).

13. Reviewed in *The Mercury* of southeast London by Peter Cordwell, June 3, 1999.

14. Released on September 7, 1999, on Eagle Records (EDL EAG 237-2).

15. Insley had released his debut album, *Good Country Junk*, in 1997 and went on to release *Tucson* in 2001 and *Supermodel* in 2003.

16. Stephen Foehr, *Waking Up in Nashville* (Sanctuary, 2002), 252.

17. In open tuning the strings are so tuned that a chord is achieved without pressing any of the strings onto the fretboard.

18. Released as *The Brothers: Children of the Fifties* on Beau Town Records BEA 225003.

19. Released in September 2003 on Goodwine Records.

20. Released on PMB Records 10005 in July 2001.

21. See Chapter 12.

22. Released on Heroic Records 0001, available from www.albertleeandhogansheroes.com.

23. Released in October 2003 as *Heartbreak Hill* (SUGCD 3977).

24. Heroic 0003, available from www.albertleeandhogansheroes.com.

Epilogue

1. From the excellent article "Hank Williams and Honky Tonk," by Martin Hawkins, *Record Mirror*, May 1, 1971.

2. At the fourth annual Americana Music Association Honors & Awards in September 2005, Miller received the Album of the Year Award for *Universal United House of Prayer*.

3. *Guitar Player*, May 1981, interview with Steve Fishell and Tom Wheeler.

4. Interview with Jas Obrecht in *Guitar Player*, April 1981.

Bibliography

Books

Aquila, Richard. *That Old Time Rock and Roll: A Chronicle of an Era, 1954–1963*. Chicago: University of Illinois Press, 2000.

Anderson, Terry H. *The Movement and the Sixties*. New York: Oxford University Press, 1995.

Bacon, Tony, ed. *Echo and Twang: Classic Guitar Music of the '50s*. London: Balafon/Backbeat, 1996.

Beattie, Linda. *Sensible Shoes and Big Knickers*. United Kingdom: Authors On Line, 2005.

Bilyeu, Melinda, Hector Cook and Andrew Mon Hughes. *Tales of the Brothers Gibb*. London: Omnibus Press, 2003.

Blake, Andrew. *The Land Without Music: Music, Culture and Society in Twentieth Century Britain*. Manchester, U.K.: University of Manchester Press, 1997.

Blake, Lewis. *Red Alert: South East London, 1939–1945*. Self-published.

Bogdanov, Vladimir, Chris Woodstra and Stephen T. Erlewine. *All Music Guide to the Blues*. London: Backbeat, 2003.

_____. *All-Music Guide to Country Music*. London: Backbeat, 2003.

Booker, Christopher. *The Neophiliacs*. London: Collins, 1969.

Brown, Mick. *American Heartbeat*. London: Michael Joseph, 1993.

Brunning, Bob. *Blues: The British Connection*. Poole, UK: Blandford, 1986.

Carson, Annette. *Jeff Beck: Crazy Fingers*. London: Backbeat, 2001.

Cartwright, Garth. *Princes Amongst Men: Journeys with Gypsy Musicians*. London: Serpent's Tail, 2005.

Cawood, Ian. *Britain in the Twentieth Century*. London: Routledge, 2004.

Chambers, Iain. *Popular Culture: The Metropolitan Experience*. London: Routledge, 1986.

Clarke, Donald. *The Rise and Fall of Popular Music*. London: Viking, 1995.

Clayson, Alan. *Beat Merchants*. London: Blandford, 1995.

_____. *Hamburg: The Cradle of British Rock*. London: Sanctuary, 1998.

Cochran, Bobby, and Susan Van Hecke. *Three Steps To Heaven: The Eddie Cochran Story*. Milwaukee, WI: Hal Leonard, 2003.

Cohen, Stanley. *Folk Devils and Moral Panics*. London: Routledge, 1972.

Coleman, Ray. *Survivor*. London: Sidgwick and Jackson, 1985.

Cornish, C.J. *The Naturalist on the Thames*. Whitefish, MT: Kessinger, 2004.

Crampton, Luke, and Dayfydd Rees. *Book of Rock Stars*. Enfield, Middlesex, UK: Guinness, 1989.

_____. *Rock and Pop, Year by Year*. London: Dorling Kindersley, 2003.

Doggett, Peter. *Are You Ready For The Country?* London: Penguin, 2000.

Doherty, Geoff. *A Promoter's Tale: Rock at the Sharp End*. London: Omnibus, 2002.

Eliot, Marc. *To the Limit: The Untold Story of the Eagles*. New York: Little, Brown, 1998.

Escott, Colin. *The Story of Country Music*. London: BBC Worldwide, 2003.

Evans, Simon. *Stopping Places: A Gypsy History of South London and Kent*. Hatfield, Hertsfordshire, UK: University of Hertfordshire Press, 1999.

Flusty, Steven. *De-Coca-Colonization: Making the Globe from the Inside Out*. London: Routledge, 2003.

Foehr, Stephen. *Waking Up in Nashville*. London: Sanctuary, 2002.

Foster, Mo. *17 Watts? The Birth of British Rock Guitar*. London: Sanctuary, 1997.

Frame, Pete. *The Complete Rock Family Trees*. London: Omnibus, 1979.

Gillett, Charlie. *The Sound of the City*. London: Sphere, 1970.

Green, Archie. *Torching the Fink Books and Other Essays on Popular Culture*. Chapel Hill, NC: University of North Carolina Press, 2001.

Hardy, Phil, and Dave Laing. *The Faber Companion to 20th Century Popular Music*. London: Faber, 1990.

Haslam, Gerald. *Workin' Man Blues: Country Music in California*. Oakland, CA: Heyday, 1999.

Heckstall-Smith, Dick. *Blowin' the Blues: Fifty Years of Playing the British Blues*. Bristol, UK: Clear, 2004.

Heibutzki, Ralph. *Unfinished Business: The Life and Times of Danny Gatton*. London: Backbeat, 2003.

Henderson, David. *'Scuse Me While I Kiss the Sky*. London: Omnibus, 1978, 1981, 1996, 2002.

Heylin, Clinton. *No More Sad Refrains: The Life and Times of Sandy Denny*. London: Helter Skelter, 2000.

Hinman, Doug. *The Kinks: All Day and All of the Night*. London: Backbeat, 2003.

Hinton, Brian. *Country Roads: How Country Came to Nashville*. London: Sanctuary, 2000.

Hodges, Chas. *The Rock 'n' Roll Years of Chas Before Dave*. Wheathampstead, Hertfordshire, UK: Lennard, 1987.

Hoskyns, Barney. *Hotel California*. London: Fourth Estate, 2005.

Jennings, Charles. *Greenwich*. London: Little, Brown, 1999.

Johnston, Richard. *The Bass Player Book*. London: Backbeat, 1999.

Kirby, J.W. *History of the Roan School*. Blackheath, UK: Blackheath, 1929.

Larkin, Colin. *The Virgin Encyclopaedia of Seventies Music*. London: Virgin, 1997.

_____. *All-Time Top 1000 Albums*. London: Virgin, 1998.

Leigh, Spencer, and John Firminger. *Halfway to Paradise: Britpop, 1955–1962*. Folkestone, Kent, UK: Finbarr, 1996.

Levin, Bernard. *The Pendulum Years: Britain and the Sixties*. London: Jonathan Cape, 1970.

Levy, Shawn. *Ready, Steady, Go*. London: Fourth Estate, 2003.

Ludlow, Barbara, and Julian Watson. *The Twentieth Century: Greenwich*. London: Sutton, 1999.

Luttjeboer, Hemme, and Ric Molina. *The Best of Albert Lee*. Miami, FL: CPP/Belwin, 1993.

Macdonald, Ian. *Revolution in the Head*. London: Pimlico, 1995.

Malone, Bill. *Country Music USA: Second Revised Edition*. Austin: University of Texas Press, 1985, 2002. First published American Folklore Society, 1968.

_____. *Don't Get Above Your Raisin': Country Music and the Southern Working Class*. Chicago: University of Illinois Press, 2002.

Marwick, Arthur. *The Explosion of British Society, 1914–62*. London: Pan, 1963.

_____. *The Sixties*. Oxford, UK: Oxford University Press, 1998.

Mayes, Sean. *Joan Armatrading*. London: Weidenfeld and Nicholson, 1990.

McLeary, John Bassett. *The Hippie Dictionary: A Cultural Encyclopaedia of the 1960s and 1970s*. Berkeley, CA: Ten Speed, 2004.

Morrison, Craig. *Go, Cat, Go! Rockabilly Music and Its Makers*. Chicago: University of Illinois Press, 1996.

Nava, Mica, and Alan O'Shea, eds. *Modern Times: Reflections on a Century of British Modernity*. London: Routledge, 1996.

Noyer, Paul, ed. *The Illustrated Encyclopaedia of Music*. London: Flame Tree, 2003.

Olechnowicz, Andrzej. *Working-Class Housing in England Between the Wars: The Becontree Estate*. Oxford, UK: Oxford University Press, 1997.

Porter, Alan J. *Before They Were Beatles*. London: Xlibris, 2003.

Portis, Larry. *Soul Trains*. College Station, TX: Virtual Bookworm, 2002.

Prown, Peter, and H.P. Newquist. *Legends of Rock Guitar: The Essentials of Rock's Greatest Guitarists*. Milwaukee, WI: Hal Leonard, 1997.

Rees, Dafydd, Barry Lazell, and Roger Osborne. *The Complete NME Singles Charts*. London: Box Tree, 1992.

Ricci, Jeanne. *Yoga Escapes: A Yoga Journal Guide to the Best Places to Relax, Reflect and Renew*. San Francisco, CA: Celestial Arts, 2003.

Riley, Tim. *Tell Me Why: A Beatles Commentary*. London: Bodley Head, 1988.

Roberty, Marc. *The Complete Guide to the Music of Eric Clapton*. London: Omnibus, 1995.

_____. *Eric Clapton: The Complete Recording Sessions, 1963–1992*. New York: St. Martin's, 1993.

_____. *Eric Clapton in His Own Words*. London: Omnibus, 1993.

Rogan, Johnny. *The Byrds: Timeless Flight Revisited*. London: Rogan House, 1997.

Rough Guide to Rock. London: Rough Guides, 2003.

Sandford, Christopher. *Mick Jagger: Rebel Knight*. London: Omnibus, 2003.

Scaruffi, Piero. *A History of Rock Music, 1951–2000*. Lincoln, NE: iUniverse, 2003.

Schneer, Jonathan. *The Thames: England's River*. London: Little, Brown, 2005.

Schumacher, Michael. *Crossroads: The Life and Music of Eric Clapton*. London: Little, Brown, 1995.

Shapiro, Harry. *Eric Clapton: Lost in the Blues*. New York: Da Capo, 1992.

Siegel, Kathy Lynn. *Veg Out: A Vegetarian Guide to Southern California*. Layton, UT: Gibbs Smith, 2003.

Soja, Edward W. *Post-metropolis*. London: Blackwell, 2000.

Tada, Joni Eareckson. *Heaven: Your Real Home*. Grand Rapids, MI: Zondervan, 1995.

Tichi, Cecelia. *High Lonesome: The American Culture of Country Music*. Chapel Hill, NC: University of North Carolina Press, 1994.

Tosches, Nick. *Country, Living Legends and Dying Metaphors in America's Biggest Music*, revised edition. New York: Scribners, 1985.

_____. *Hellfire: The Jerry Lee Lewis Story*. New York: Grove, 1982.

Unterberger, Richie. *Music USA: The Rough Guide.* London: Rough Guides, 1999.

_____. *Turn! Turn! Turn!: The 60s Folk-Rock Revolution.* London: Backbeat, 2002.

Vesey, Barbara. *The Hidden Places of East Anglia.* Aldermaston, UK: Travel, 1989.

Vickers, Graham. *London's 50 Outstanding Rock Music Landmarks.* London: Omnibus, 2001.

Welch, Chris. *Cream: The Legendary Sixties Supergroup.* London: Backbeat, 2001.

White, Forrest. *Fender: The Inside Story.* London: Backbeat, 1994.

White, Roger. *The Everly Brothers: Walk Right Back.* London: Plexus, 1998.

Whitford, Eldon, and Dan Erlewine. *Gibson's Fabulous Flat-Top Guitars: An Illustrated History and Guide.* London: Backbeat, 1994.

Wolff, Kurt. *Country Music: The Rough Guide.* London: Rough Guides, 2000.

Wyman, Bill, with Ray Coleman. *Stone Alone: The Story of a Rock 'n' Roll Band.* London: Viking, 1990.

Zimmerman, Keith. *Sing My Way Home: Voices of the New American Roots Rock.* London: Backbeat, 2004.

Magazines

Country Music People
Guitar Player
Q Classic
Record Collector
Shindig Magazine
Superpicker
Uncut
Vintage Guitar
Zigzag
Interviews

Interviews

Allison, Jerry personal, April 6, 2006
Armatrading, Joan telephone, October 3, 2005
Baines, Joan personal, June 14, 2005
Baines, John personal, June 7, 2005
Beecher, John telephone, various, and e-mail, November 11, 2005
Barker, Graham personal, November 2006-August 2007
Baron, Peter personal, September 13, 2005
Barsby, Geoff telephone, January 3, 2006
Bath, Brian personal, July 20, 2005
Bell, Mike personal, August 23, 2006
Bell, Ron personal, September 15, 2005
Berry, Mike personal, November 15, 2005
Birkett, Sam personal, various, September 2005-August 2007

Brooker, Gary personal, December 4, 2005
Brown, Noelle letter, October 5, 2005
Brown, Tony personal, April 4, 2006
Carter, John personal, January 10, 2006
Charman, Ricky personal, May 25, 2006
Clapton, Eric personal, October 10, 2005
Clifton, Mo personal, May 31, 2005
Cole, B.J. personal, April 26, 2005
Collins, Roger e-mails, various, September 2005
Colman, Stuart telephone, November 26, 2006
Colton, Tony personal, April 3, 2006
Conway, Gerry personal, July 1, 2005
Crowell, Rodney e-mail, October 12, 2006
Curtis, Sonny personal, April 6, 2006
De Vito, Hank personal, April 4, 2006
Edwards, Jonathan e-mail, September 21, 2006
Emmons, Buddy personal, April 4, 2006
Evans, Mary personal, September 14, 2005
Evans, Simon personal, May 25, 2005
Everly, Phil telephone, April 2, 2006
Farlowe, Chris personal, January 11, 2006
Fishell, Steve personal, April 4, 2006
Gage, Peter e-mail, November 6, 2005
Grimm, Georg e-mail, May 13, 2006
Hadler, Phil personal, September 27, 2005
Hardin, Andrew e-mail, July 12, 2005
Hargreaves, Sue personal, July 10, 2007
Harris, Bob personal, March 18, 2006
Harris, Emmylou personal, February 6, 2006
Haylock, Johnnie personal, June 13, 2005
Hinsley, Harvey personal, May 4, 2005
Hodges, Chas telephone, May 2, 2005
Hodgson, Brian personal, July 13, 2005
Hogan, Gerry personal, September 8, 2005
Hurst, Mike personal, January 4, 2006
Hutton, Malcolm personal, June 7, 2005
Kemp, Mick e-mail, June 7, 2005
Jenkins, Barrie personal, November 16, 2005
Jones, Clive e-mail, August 21, 2005
Kruger, Jeffrey personal, April 26, 2006
Lee, Abigail personal, June 3, 2006
Lee, Albert personal, e-mails, April 2005-July 2007
Lee, Karen personal June 29, 2007
Lee, Lucy personal, November 26, 2005
Lee, Rebecca personal, September 14, 2005
Lee, Vanessa personal September 27, 2005
Lee, Vikki e-mail, October 6, 2005
Lee, Wayne personal, August 10, 2005
Lovell, Carol personal June 14, 2005
Melville, Robin letter, January 15, 2006
Middleton, Max personal, May 31, 2005
Miller, Buddy e-mail, April 30, 2007
Nelson, Jackie personal, November 28, 2006
Nelson, Keith personal, October 17, 2005
Newman, Tony telephone, April 2, 2006
O'Neill, Mike personal, November 19, 2005
Parton, Dolly letter, March 16, 2006
Roth, Arlen e-mail, July 7, 2007
Russell, Ray personal, March 13, 2006

Scanlon, Terry personal, June 28, 2005
Smith, Ray personal, October 18, 2005
Solley, Pete e-mail, June 17, 2006
Stead, Colin personal, September 26, 2005
Stead, Terry personal, July 20, 2005
Sullivan, "Big Jim" personal, December 12, 2005
Trovato, Steve e-mail, May 3, 2007
Tyson, Sylvia e-mail, June 13, 2007
Tyson, Tom e-mail, July 13, 2007

Waddell, Bruce personal, July 19, 2005
Walker, Les e-mail, December 12, 2005
Walter, Tony telephone, September 2, 2005
Warner, Mike e-mail, August 20, 2006
Waters, Susan personal, July 29, 2005
Winchester, Jesse e-mail, March 7, 2007
Wingfield, Pete personal, October 9, 2005
Wyman, Bill personal, September 17, 2005

Index

Numbers in **bold italics** indicate pages with photographs.